SURVEY OF

American Industry and Careers

Volume 6

Textile and Fabrics Industry—Water Supply Industry

Appendixes

Indexes

The Editors of Salem Press

SALEM PRESS
Pasadena, California   Hackensack, New Jersey

Editorial Director: Christina J. Moose
Project Editor: Rowena Wildin
Manuscript Editors: Stacy Cole, Andy Perry
Acquisitions Manager: Mark Rehn
Administrative Assistant: Paul Tifford, Jr.

Research Supervisor: Jeffry Jensen
Photo Editor: Cynthia Breslin Beres
Design and Layout: James Hutson
Additional Layout: William Zimmerman

Cover photo: ©DreamPictures/Shannon Faulk/Blend Images/CORBIS

Library of Congress Cataloging-in-Publication Data

Survey of American industry and careers / The Editors of Salem Press.
    v.   cm.
    Includes bibliographical references and indexes.
    ISBN 978-1-58765-768-9 (set : alk. paper) — ISBN 978-1-58765-769-6 (vol. 1 : alk. paper) — ISBN 978-1-58765-770-2 (vol. 2 : alk. paper) — ISBN 978-1-58765-771-9 (vol. 3 : alk. paper) — ISBN 978-1-58765-772-6 (vol. 4 : alk. paper) — ISBN 978-1-58765-773-3 (vol. 5 : alk. paper) — ISBN 978-1-58765-774-0 (vol. 6 : alk. paper) 1. Business—Vocational guidance—United States. 2. Industries—United States. 3. Occupations—United States. 4. Vocational guidance—United States. I. Salem Press.
    HF5382.5.U5S87 2012
    331.7020973—dc23
                                                                                    2011019601

First Printing

Contents

Complete List of Contents

VOLUME 4

VOLUME 5

VOLUME 6

List of Tables and Sidebars

SURVEY OF
American Industry and Careers

Textile and Fabrics Industry

INDUSTRY SNAPSHOT

General Industry: Manufacturing
Career Clusters: Agriculture, Food, and Natural Resources; Manufacturing
Subcategory Industries: Animal Production; Carpet Mills; Cotton Farming; Fabric Design; Fabric Finishing and Dyeing; Fiber Research and Development; Fiber, Yarn, and Thread Mills; Flax Farming; Hemp Farming; Industrial Chemistry; Jute Farming; Knitting Mills; Lace Mills; Nonwoven Fabric Mills; Rope Cordage and Twine Mills; Sheep Farming; Spinning Mills; Textile Mills; Woven Fabric Mills
Related Industries: Apparel and Fashion Industry; Farming Industry; Industrial Design Industry
Annual Domestic Revenues: $123.1 billion USD (Datamonitor, 2009)
Annual Global Revenues: $1.14 trillion USD (Datamonitor, 2009)
NAICS Numbers: 11, 31-33, 42, 313, 314

INDUSTRY DEFINITION

Summary

The textile and fabrics industry produces thread, yarn, rope, cordage, twine, and knitted, woven, and unwoven fabrics made from natural and human-made fibers. These products are then used to manufacture apparel and home furnishings, as well as to meet industrial design and engineering needs. From independent craftspeople who produce yarn and fabric in time-honored traditional methods to large-scale factories using cutting-edge technologies, the textile and fabrics industry includes farm production of plant or animal fibers, industrial production of synthetic fibers, design and manufacture of specific types of fabric to meet diverse requirements, and the wholesale marketing and sale of fiber to producers of end-products utilizing textile products.

History of the Industry

The use of fibers for cloth and craft began thousands of years ago, predating writing, agriculture, and perhaps even the use of fire. Early humans learned to twist or braid plant fibers together to produce rope and cordage to secure stone spear-points and arrowheads to wooden shafts, to construct fishing nets and animal traps, and for a variety of other purposes. Animal fibers were also used: Early sheep breeds shed their coats annually, and hunter-gatherers probably learned to collect tufts of wool that could be spun into yarn for garments or simply matted together to produce felt. In warm areas of the planet, early cultures learned to grow plants such as cotton and jute for their fibers. In cooler climates, the flax plant was cultivated for its long stem fibers, which could be spun into linen for thread and fabrics of all types from lace to canvas.

In much of the world, spinning and weaving traditionally were performed by women. Egyptian tomb-paintings from the third millennium B.C.E. depict women and girls using spindles suspended by the thread being spun. In South America, women of the Inca culture spun fibers from the coat of the indigenous alpaca—a relative of the llama—on similar "drop" spindles. Because yarns made of shorter fibers often were too weak to support the weight of a drop spindle, supported spindles were developed in areas where the short fibers of the cotton plant were spun. For thousands of years, all yarns and threads were produced on one of these simple top-like hand spindles.

Making fabric from these yarns or threads required additional processes. Knitting and the related craft of crocheting evolved from skills learned in the manufacture of fishing nets. Both produced stretchy material that easily could be shaped into fitted garments such as hats and socks. While weaving stiff materials could be managed without a loom, weaving flexible thread was only possible with the development of a frame in which one set of parallel threads, the warp, was held taut so that a thread called the weft could be woven over and under the warp threads. Over time, simple frame tapestry looms gave way to movable warp looms in which certain threads in the warp could be lifted and dropped, making it possible to insert a weft with one pass of a shuttle.

Spinning wheels were invented in the middle ages, but until the Industrial Revolution of the eighteenth and nineteenth centuries, textile production was primarily a cottage industry or home-based craft. In the mid-1700's, design advances in both spinning and weaving allowed for more efficient and uniform production of both thread and woven fabric. The change from artisanal cottage industry to factory manufacture was met with resistance from workers who engaged in protests, sabotage, and sometimes violent riots in an attempt to retain control of the means of production. However, hand methods of textile production were not able to keep up with the demand for goods, and over the subsequent centuries, multihead spinning jennies and foot-powered looms gave way to faster and more profitable textile machines run first by water power, then by coal-powered steam engines, and finally by electricity.

Meanwhile, the textile industry was the center of two social developments that would prove to be critical in shaping the future. The first was the extensive use of slave labor in American cotton production during the eighteenth and nineteenth centuries. The impacts of the plantation system were many: It impaired the modernization and industrialization of the American South; it contributed to the success of the brutal slave trade; and it brought the issue of slavery and states' rights to a

Cotton producers include small family farms. (©Natalia Bratslavsky/Dreamstime.com)

head, resulting in the American Civil War. The textile industry also was instrumental in the rise of modern labor unions. Textile workers, who were among the first to work within an industrialized system, also were among the first to establish trade unions, modern guilds, and other social bodies capable of organized protest for better working conditions and higher wages. For example, in the late nineteenth century, many members of the Mule Spinners Guild of New England became early members of the American Federation of Labor (AFL).

To keep up with the demand of the new industrialized factories, fiber producers needed to harvest increasing quantities of cotton, flax, jute, hemp, and sisal. Sheep breeds were systematically improved to produce heavier clips of better-quality wool. New methods of silk production eliminated the time-consuming process of unwinding the silk cocoons by hand, making the manufacture of silk possible on an industrial scale. However, by the end of the nineteenth century, natural fibers alone could not meet market demands. This led to the development of human-made fibers and fabrics. Rayon, a cellulose-based fiber invented by Hilaire de Chardonnet, first was commercially produced by the British textile company Courtaulds Fibers in 1905. Commercial fiberglass first was produced in the 1930's by researchers at the Owens-Corning plant for use as insulation and to reinforce other materials. In 1935, researchers at the DuPont Experimental Station in Wilmington, Delaware, developed nylon, which became vital during World War II, replacing scarce supplies of Asian silk in military parachutes, tents, ropes, and raingear. By the end of the war in 1945, manufactured fibers made up 25 percent of all textiles produced in the United States. While natural fibers—those produced from plants, animals, and naturally occuring minerals—continued to be manufactured after World War II, many other synthetic materials were invented, including acetate, acrylic, latex, and spandex.

Starting in the late 1800's, worldwide textile production migrated from northern areas to the south. By the 1930's, the American South was the center of the domestic textile industry. The shift of

The Contribution of Textile Mills and Textile Product Mills to the U.S. Economy

Value Added	Amount
Gross domestic product	$16.9 billion
Gross domestic product	0.1%
Persons employed	302,000
Total employee compensation	$13.6 billion

Source: U.S. Bureau of Economic Analysis. Data are for 2008.

mills from New England to the South was only the first instance of industry mobility, and it has become common for large-scale textile manufacturers to relocate their mills to any part of the world that will yield the company higher profits.

The Industry Today

Today, new developments in textile fabrication have broadened the use of fibers and textiles to industrial applications in computers, fiber optics, construction, and even the aerospace industry in addition to their more traditional uses in the manufacture of apparel and home furnishings. While the United States still plays a strong role in research and development of new kinds of fibers, new methods of manufacture, and new applications for fibers, most large-scale industrial production of textiles has been moved to factories owned by multinational corporations and located in developing nations. Low labor expense and less rigid health and environmental regulations have made countries such as Ethiopia, Vietnam, Pakistan, India, Mexico, and China more attractive and profitable as locations for large-scale textile production. Some design and finishing operations still are commonly performed in the United States, but hundreds of thousands of jobs in the U.S. textile industry have been lost to foreign workers in recent years.

On a smaller scale, domestic producers have begun to exploit niche markets, developing and marketing traditionally crafted, artisanal yarns and fabrics to cater to the growing domestic market for

Inputs Consumed by Textile Mills and Textile Product Mills

Input	Value
Energy	$1.6 billion
Materials	$33.9 billion
Purchased services	$5.4 billion
Total	$40.9 billion

Source: U.S. Bureau of Economic Analysis. Data are for 2008.

sustainably produced, organic, or "green" fabrics. Concern about water quality, wildlife habitats, and climate change has prompted a number of people to support textile industries that seem kinder to the environment.

In a similar vein, increasing public awareness of the working conditions in the worst of the foreign textile mills has led to the rise of the Clean Clothes Campaign, a consumer activist group dedicated to improving working conditions throughout the world's textile industries. Consumer awareness also has been stimulated by the Buy Local movement; although originally aimed at encouraging consumers to purchase locally grown foods, the idea has spread, and proponents now advocate the use of locally grown products of all kinds, including textiles made from natural and recycled fibers.

Meanwhile, the mainstream textile industry generally is perceived to be controlled by an ogilopolist complex, a small group of producers who together can affect and largely control costs, profits, and trends in the industry as a whole. Using business schema possible only at the most powerful and wealthy levels, including cross-subsidization, business reciprocity, conglomerate mergers, transnational investment, and outsourcing, the largest corporations are able to establish a business environment that is conducive to their continued survival. Large transnational corporations such as DuPont, Celanese, Eastman, and Monsanto that produce synthetic fiber and chemicals, and raw materials for synthetic fiber production, operate profitably within the United States but currently are experiencing stronger growth in sales of chemicals to overseas manufacturing facilities. International trade tends to rise and fall cyclically, however, and some analysts forecast a drop in foreign textile production as the Chinese yuan becomes more highly valued against other world currencies. This situation would make labor and other expenses more costly in American dollars, leading to decreased demand for Chinese products on the American market.

Within the domestic sector, the remnants of the U.S. national textile industry increasingly are threatened by their larger global competitors, who usually can offer greater quantities of product at lower prices. Some domestic firms have responded to these perceived threats by demanding various forms of protectionist regulation, including increased tariffs on goods produced overseas and a reestablishment of higher trade quotas. Debate continues over the efficacy of protected versus free trade as the best stimulus for the fiber and textile industries, as the recent economic downturn has increased anxiety about the future of the industry on all levels.

INDUSTRY MARKET SEGMENTS

The fiber and textile industry is a complex field involving agricultural and chemical production of raw fiber, the processing of fiber into yarn or fabric, and the supportive industries of textile machinery design, industrial and artistic design, and chemical and engineering research. Based on the number of employees, most of these separate but interrelated businesses can further be divided into small, midsize, and large enterprises. It is difficult to entirely divide the industry according to scale, as small producers may conduct business with or provide services to large-scale producers and vice versa. However, in general, work in the textile industry may be carried out by businesses of all sizes. The following sections provide an overview of each of these different segments.

Small Businesses

Many producers of raw materials for the textile industry are small, family-operated farms growing natural fibers such as cotton, wool, and flax. While one or more family members also may engage in off-farm labor, most members of the family live and work on the farm. The work is seasonal, with the heaviest workloads occurring during planting and harvesting or, in the case of wool production, during lambing season and shearing. Small-scale animal producers often are tied to their farms by the necessity of providing daily care for their stock. Virtually no small-scale production of synthetic or human-made fibers is being conducted.

In the processing sector, there are many small producers of textiles. These include individual craftspeople or small shops with a few employees who manufacture yarn and fabric on a relatively small, artisanal scale. There also are individuals and small businesses providing goods and services to the textile trades, including trucking firms, manufacturers and sellers of spinning equipment, looms, and makers of other tools used by the craft fiber industry.

One other small-business segment is that of the independent consultant. This work may involve legal and regulatory services to textile concerns engaged in importation, licensing, permitting, and labor negotiations, or it may involve engineering and industrial services in design, factory layout, setup, and installation.

Potential Annual Earnings Scale. The average income for a small farmer varies from region to region and depends on the kind and quality of fiber produced. Common cotton, for example, does not command as much per pound as long-stapled specialty cotton; even more value can be added by growing the cotton organically. Producers of exotic luxury fibers such as angora and cashmere have the potential for high earnings from a relatively small output of product. As for producers of craft yarn and fabric, much depends on the skill of the producer and the reputation of the company. Many small-scale producers are independent owner-operators who may work only part time. Others may not only work full time themselves but hire additional employees. Therefore, earnings can vary widely depending on the amount and type of product manufactured. The support industries usually attend to the needs of a large number of textile producers and may generate substantial incomes from trucking services, consulting fees, and the sale of equipment to the trade. Incomes can range from only a few thousand dollars a year for the small part-time craftsperson to $250,000 for a family-run farm business.

Clientele Interaction. Producers of fiber sometimes have personal contact with their customers if their fiber or fleece is sold to other small fiber businesses. However, if the agricultural output of a family farm is sufficiently large, its products move into the industrial commodity stream with little personal interaction involved.

In general, small producers of yarn or fabric depend on the loyalty of their customers, and that loyalty is earned by being consistent and on time, by keeping prices competitive and quality high, and by successfully interacting personally with both suppliers and customers. In many cases, the independent craftsperson must perform a number of roles in his or her business; some of these may involve personal contact and close relationships with clientele. Because of the relatively flexible nature of small-scale textile manufacture, opportunities for custom work often are available, but communication is key to the success of such endeavors. For

A woman cooks silk larva, making fine lines of silk. (©Oystein Sando/Dreamstime.com)

those engaged in the support industries as independent businesspeople or as employees of small firms, interpersonal communication is vital to business survival.

Amenities, Atmosphere, and Physical Grounds. Small producers of raw fiber generally are based in rural areas where arable land is available or where livestock is permitted. Acreages, outbuildings, and family accommodations vary widely, from substandard homes on depleted farmland to large, well-appointed homes on well-maintained farms. Specialized equipment pertaining to the type of fiber being grown must be housed somewhere on the farm, and if animal fiber is being produced, housing, fencing, feed storage, and other equipment must be provided for sheep, goats, llamas, or other kinds of livestock.

Small-scale processors and manufacturers sometimes work within their homes, setting up spinning or weaving studios and a home office. Other producers build or buy separate facilities for their textile shops. Shops that operate using traditional wooden spinning wheels and looms may be quiet and picturesque; those utilizing mechanical spinning and weaving equipment may be noisy, oily, and filled with potentially dangerous moving machinery. Textile factories tend to be cluttered and somewhat dusty environments, even on a small scale, and constant efforts must be made to remove debris and waste products from the floors and general premises.

For firms producing textile machinery, some kind of shop or small factory usually is necessary. In the production of wooden spinning and weaving equipment, the premises would house an assortment of saws, lathes, and milling equipment, as well as storage areas for lumber and other materials. For support industries such as equipment sales, trucking, and consultancy services, the business owner provides his or her own vehicle or office, which is not intrinsically different from offices or vehicles engaged in other sectors. Trucking service providers, however, should be prepared to transport material that may be dusty, dirty, or odiferous and to negotiate rural access roads that may be narrow or muddy.

Typical Number of Employees. Many farm producers of fiber hire no outside help at all, relying strictly on family members to perform the tasks required to grow and harvest the crop. Other farms hire one or more full-time employees and as many temporary workers as they need to finish the work on the farm in a timely manner. Full-time employees might perform plowing, tilling, seeding, and other work involving the use of tractors and agricultural equipment. They also might be responsible for the care of the farm operation in the owner's absence. Temporary workers generally are hired during harvest time to assist with simple, repetitive tasks.

Small-scale yarn and fabric producers may work alone or have a small permanent staff ranging from one or two up to half a dozen employees. Some processors adjust their staff seasonally, hiring employees to handle the glut of fiber as it is harvested and then laying them off once the majority of the raw fiber has been spun or woven. Small-scale machine manufacturers generally have fewer than twenty employees, with many operating with only one or two.

Traditional Geographic Locations. Farms producing industrial quantities of commodities such as cotton generally are located where the cost of fertile farmland is the lowest, relegating them to areas some distance from urban centers. Producers of niche crops on small acreages can be found in all areas of the country, even within city limits. Another consideration for the location of fiber-producing farms is the climate. Cotton, for example, requires a long, warm growing season, while other crops such as flax do well in cool, wet areas. Wool production is concentrated in northern areas because sheep with heavy wool coats do not thrive in warm climates.

Many small producers of yarns and fabric tend to cluster in areas where industrial mills once flourished, primarily because of the regional traditions associated with the woolen industry of New England and the cotton mills of the South, but also in part because the closure of many of these large mills has provided a source of used machinery to smaller producers.

Pros of Working for a Small Textile Establishment. Independent fiber producers and small farmers have total control over the business. They are able to determine what products they wish to grow or make and the manner in which business is carried on. Small producers can easily adapt their practices to fill a niche market, providing organic fiber or naturally colored fabric to a small but dedi-

Bolts of fabric in a store. (©Crystal Srock/Dreamstime.com)

cated clientele. Hours and other work schedules can be adjusted to meet the needs of the owner-operators of these firms, and they usually are able to provide flexible work arrangement for the few employees they may hire. An advanced degree or specialized training is not required, although self-education in sales and marketing, accounting, and technical aspects of the industry can prove beneficial.

Cons of Working for a Small Textile Establishment. For most such workers, limited or seasonally determined income means that money can be short during certain times of the year. For owner-operators, investments in equipment and infrastructure can be at risk if the business fails. Small fiber producers rarely can afford to hire additional help, so at times, long hours are required to complete all duties. Finally, the small producer must be competent in a wide array of support ac-

tivities, from accounting to sales and maintenance.

Adding to the challenges of the small textile producer can be the isolation involved in working long hours with little or no companionship. While some individuals enjoy the peace and quiet of working alone or with only a few people, others feel trapped and lonely, adding to the financial and physical stresses of working long hours for an uneven income.

Costs

Payroll and Benefits: If small textile producers hire extra help, they usually do so at hourly wages. Because "micro" businesses like these employ very few, if any, additional staff, benefits often are not mandatory, and health insurance, paid vacations, and sick time may or may not be part of the employment package. Federal regulations expected to come into effect by 2014 may have some impact on the availability of health insurance, however.

Supplies: Family farms require a wide range of supplies, including fuel for tractors and other power equipment, seed, fertilizer, pesticides and herbicides for plant crops, feed, fencing materials, medications and supplements for livestock operations, in addition to the more common office supplies, telephones, computers, and cleaning supplies. Processors must expend a substantial outlay of funds on the raw or intermediate materials to be processed. Additional chemicals for cleaning and dyeing are needed even for producers of natural fibers, while those in the synthetic field must purchase large quantities of necessary chemical components to produce the desired man-made fiber. Cleaning supplies, shipping materials, office supplies, and information and communication costs may also be required.

External Services: Many small producers perform all the steps of manufacture in-house, although some prefer to pay other processors for steps in coloring, carding, or processing fibers. Cotton farms typically send their fiber to a ginning mill to remove seeds before it is baled and delivered to the cotton mill. Legal or financial assistance may be required from time to time, particularly for the preparation of license applications or tax returns. Trucking and storage are services that also may be required from outside parties.

Utilities: Typical utilities for a small textile operation include water and sewer, gas or oil service, electricity, telephone, and Internet. Water for irrigation and livestock needs can be a major factor in arid regions of the country, while water and electricity use can be quite high in processing shops as both are used to clean the fiber and power much of the equipment.

Taxes: All textile businesses are required to pay local, state, and federal income taxes as well as applicable property taxes. If they sell any of their products to end users, they also must collect the appropriate sales taxes. If sales are carried out by mail order or via the Internet, taxes must be collected for each state from which products are ordered, and arrangements must be made with these states to remit the collected revenue, usually on an annual basis, although states vary in their sales tax collection calendar.

Midsize Businesses

While the Small Business Administration regards a manufacturer with fewer than five hundred employees as a midsize business, most midsize textile operations in Europe and the United States have between ten and thirty employees. Midsize textile concerns typically operate regionally or nationally instead of internationally, and they may vary widely as to the efficiency and modernity of their infrastructure systems. Very few agricultural producers have this many workers, but many research and development laboratories working to develop new fibers fall within this category, as do older family-run woolen and cotton mills in the United States and Canada.

Potential Annual Earnings Scale. Wages for employees at midsize textile facilities vary widely by position. The average salary of a textile machine operator for example, is about $24,000 per year, while senior researchers can earn nearly $100,000 per year.

Clientele Interaction. Except for sales and marketing personnel and researchers at academic institutions where they may be expected to teach, clientele interaction is rare. Most workers within this size of operation may interact with their fellow workers but not with the general public or the firm's customer base.

Amenities, Atmosphere, and Physical Grounds. Midsize textile processing plants often are housed in traditional factory buildings in the centers of towns and villages and located at the edges of watercourses, which historically provided the power used to run the mills. Now generally powered by electricity, the mills remain where they had been established, from a sense of tradition as well as for practical reasons such as convenience and proximity to the workforce. Another reason for the continued use of vintage mill buildings has to do with government permitting: In order to build new facilities, environmental permits, impact statements and other local and regional permits would have to be obtained before construction could begin. By using an older facility, the factory is said to be "grandfathered in," and no additional permitting is required unless additions or expansion are planned. These old buildings can be noisy, dusty, and potentially contaminated with heavy metals, asbestos, and other toxic materials. However, their antique charm and waterside situation make them picturesque additions to any town or village.

Research and development facilities, on the other hand, often are located in the science departments of large universities. Usually equipped with the latest scientific apparatus and powerful computing systems, and sharing support staff with the university at large, these laboratories can be pleasant places to work.

Typical Number of Employees. Staff levels tend not to exceed thirty people. However, in the case of research and development laboratories in university settings, a number of temporary student employees and graduate research assistants may be engaged to perform some of the work.

Traditional Geographic Locations. Midsize textile mills may be found all over the world, but in the United States they are most commonly located in small to midsize towns. Some may occupy the center of a small town, while others may be situated at the outskirts of communities, close to rail lines and freeway exchanges.

Pros of Working for a Midsize Textile Establishment. Midsize textile mills offer full-time employment, usually with at least some benefits. Job stability is greater than in a small shop, while the inconvenience of an occasional job turnover can be absorbed by a slightly larger workforce able to cover for the missing worker until a substitute is recruited and trained. The midsize textile firm is able to fill larger orders than small independent shops, while at the same time retaining the ability to produce short runs of custom-ordered goods for the specialty market. Worker morale often is high, as working in a company of this size allows employees to bond with each other and to feel personal pride in the company's product. For those working in research labs, the availability of the most up-to-date equipment, the presence of similarly minded, highly educated coworkers, and the inherent at-

This circular knitting machine bears no resemblance to traditional knitting needles. (©Dreamstime.com)

traction of the work itself make working in fiber research very satisfying.

Cons of Working for a Midsize Textile Establishment. Midsize textile firms often are caught in an economic pinch: Large corporations can outsource labor and undercut prices for similar products, making it very difficult for midsize operations to compete. Some succumb to competitive pressures by borrowing capital in order to expand their operations or to move their facilities overseas. By moving their production offshore, most former employees are no longer needed, and domestic textile jobs are lost. Furthermore, with increased debt burdens, many of these companies fail outright.

For researchers in midsize research and development facilities, the tendency is to become fixated on the work at hand. Some researchers spend almost all their waking hours in the laboratory. There also is a tendency for academic researchers to become isolated from the general community and increasingly out of touch with the concerns of the larger, nonacademic culture.

Costs

Payroll and Benefits: Midsize fiber and textile factories hire most staff at hourly wages. Benefits such as vacation and sick time are offered fairly commonly. For university-based researchers, staff may either be salaried or paid by the hour, depending on rank and job description. Benefits often are liberal.

Supplies: Midsize textile operations require a wide range of items, including common office supplies, telephones, computers, and cleaning supplies. Processors must expend a substantial outlay of funds on the raw or intermediate materials to be processed. Additional chemicals for cleaning and dyeing are needed even for producers of natural fibers, while those in the synthetic field must purchase large quantities of necessary chemical components to produce the desired man-made fiber. Cleaning supplies, shipping materials, office supplies, and information and communication costs also may be required. In the laboratory, special substances, chemicals, computer programs, and other expenses may be necessary.

External Services: Midsize fiber and textile producers may hire other firms to complete steps in coloring, carding, or processing fibers. Legal or financial assistance may be performed internally but also may be hired on an as-needed basis. These businesses also may use accounting services, computer maintenance services, vending machine companies, and trucking and warehouse services.

Utilities: Typical utilities for a midsize textile operation include water and sewer, gas or oil service, telephone, and Internet. Higher voltage electrical hookups often must be installed, and electric and water bills can be a major expenditure. For university-based laboratories engaged in fiber research and development, many utilities are at least partly covered by the university. Additional funding from government and private grants usually covers any remaining utility cost.

Taxes: Midsize commercial fiber mills and processors are required to pay all local, state, and federal income taxes as well as applicable property taxes. Special permits and assessments pertaining to water and air quality also may have to be paid. If the company engages in international import or export of raw material or finished products, customs fees, duties, and tariffs may be levied.

Large Businesses

Large fiber and textile operations generally are corporate in structure, often part of vast multinational conglomerates with immense resources. Oftentimes, the textile component of a large corporation is only a small portion of the business of the entire organization.

Potential Annual Earnings Scale. The earnings of large-scale textile employees vary considerably depending on the position as well as on the geographic location of the workforce. A sizable majority of textile positions throughout the world earn only a fraction of what those in comparable positions in the United States would earn. For example, in 2006, Chinese textile workers earned about 57 cents an hour, or a little more than $100 per month. Meanwhile, positions in international management, import and export, sales and marketing, fiber engineering, and research and development are comparable to similar positions in other industries.

Clientele Interaction. Most workers in large-scale textile concerns do not interact with workers

A fully automated machine weaves denim for jeans. (©Moreno Soppelsa/Dreamstime.com)

in other departments, or on other machines, let alone with the general public.

Amenities, Atmosphere, and Physical Grounds. For the upper echelon of corporate executives, work is carried out in spacious, well-appointed offices in high-rise office towers in urban centers such as New York, Hong Kong, and Tokyo, or in corporate headquarters set on sprawling campuses in smaller towns. Midlevel executives often must travel from plant site to plant site, while lower-level managers and supervisors work in a variety of conditions from crowded dilapidated structures filled with obsolete equipment, to streamlined facilities utilizing the most efficient and modern production equipment available. The scale of the workforce at some of the larger mills makes it possible to provide on-site cafeterias, day care centers and, in some cases, dormitories.

Depending on the plant design, large textile mills can be multistory structures in which the materials are transported from step to step in the pro-

duction process with the aid of gravity. Raw materials enter the factory on the top floor and move down as they near completion, eventually being packed into shipping containers or trucks at the ground level. Other factories use versions of Henry Ford's moving assembly line spread out within a large building with only one level.

Typical Number of Employees. The number of employees at any given textile factory varies based on the size of the facility, the availability of labor, the volume of trade, and other factors. Many large corporations have textile employees numbering in the thousands, but only forty to seventy at any one plant. On the other hand, the largest single factory in Ethiopia, established recently in the city of Alem Gena by Turkish-based AYKA Incorporated, plans to have a workforce approaching ten thousand.

Traditional Geographic Locations. Large textile firms can be found anywhere in the world where there is a large pool of labor, available sources of power to run the machinery, and a transportation system capable of moving raw materials into the facility and finished goods out.

Pros of Working at a Large Textile Establishment. For staff in management, design, sales, marketing, engineering, and other white-collar positions, it can be exciting to see one's ideas carried out on such a vast scale. An individual product idea or technological innovation has a much greater chance of widespread implementation if adopted by companies at this scale. For researchers employed within large textile-based corporations, there is the opportunity to work on cutting-edge technologies in the best laboratories that money can buy. Overall, within these large firms there is ample opportunity for personal career advancement and financial success, although the majority of employees will never reap these rewards. Large fiber manufacturers also encourage worldwide trade, providing steady jobs to classes of people who might otherwise be unemployed.

Cons of Working for a Large Textile Establishment. At this scale, business is more than simply discovering a need and producing a product to meet that need. Global corporate businesses must involve themselves with international politics, trade regulations, environmental concerns, labor and human rights issues, worldwide energy depletion, mergers, conglomerates, international currency values, corporate law, and the stock market. Very few, even those in executive positions, understand all aspects of the company they control. While large corporations act as a positive force by providing employment and affordable textile products to the people of the world, they all too easily can cause a great deal of harm, simply because of the scale of operations and the unforeseen consequences that may follow any action. For example, a case may be made that corporate research into genetically modified organisms in order to produce improved quantities and qualities of fiber may have far-reaching negative consequences for the health and diversity of life on the planet. Finally, workers at the lowest levels sometimes are exploited, forced to endure a combination of long working hours, low wages, and substandard working conditions.

ORGANIZATIONAL STRUCTURE AND JOB ROLES

The organizational structure and distribution of tasks within the textile industry are typically based on the number of employees and the size of the firm. The owner of a small fiber-producing farm typically will handle most of the major tasks involved in the operation because there may be no other full-time employees. Meanwhile, the general manager of a large textile mill may supervise hundreds of workers on the production staff alone. Nevertheless, the tasks themselves remain similar for each segment of the agricultural and industrial divisions within the field.

The following umbrella categories apply to the organizational structure of small, midsize, and large establishments engaged in the manufacture of fiber and textiles.

- Executive Management
- Sales and Marketing
- Design and Product Development
- Production
- Shipping and Storage
- Research and Development
- Information Technology
- Human Resources
- Accounting and Finance
- Maintenance
- Security
- Technical and Legal Services
- Administrative Support

Executive Management

Executive management handles the general direction of the company. These individuals make major decisions, set goals, and implement long-term plans for the business. Because most mills in the United States are incorporated, the very highest executives are corporate presidents and executive vice presidents, who may be engaged in decision making for a number of corporate branches and divisions. Corporate presidents rarely have any involvement in day-to-day operations of shops, factories, or mills. Superintendents or general managers often run the actual production and are responsible for maintaining adequate productivity and quality. They also manage individual teams and departments. Many executive managers have advanced degrees, particularly in engineering, business, or accounting, but in some instances experience or family and business connections can make up for the lack of a degree.

Presidents and other corporate executives earn yearly salaries determined by the corporation's board of trustees. Many of these high-level executives are awarded bonuses of several million dollars or more on an annual basis, ostensibly to encourage exceptional performance. At the company level, supervisors and general managers generally earn the highest salaries of anyone actively engaged in the business.

Executive management occupations may include the following:

- General Manager
- Sales Director
- Chief Financial Officer (CFO)
- Controller
- Floor Supervisor
- Chief of Engineering
- Marketing Director

Sales and Marketing

Sales and marketing personnel work to promote and sell the raw fiber, yarn, or textile products manufactured by the company. While some firms are vertically oriented, producing raw fiber and processing it into yarn or fabric for further manufacture or for direct sale to home crafters, many fiber and textile industries sell their products to other manufacturers. This business-to-business trade requires the development of sales plans, meetings with prospective clients, the writing and presentation of sales pitches, and the delivery of sales contracts to the firm. Sales personnel may work closely with design or engineering staff to develop

PROJECTED EMPLOYMENT FOR SELECTED OCCUPATIONS

Textile Mills

Employment		
2009	Projected 2018	Occupation
6,080	3,600	First-line supervisors/managers of production and operating workers
5,490	3,000	Inspectors, testers, sorters, samplers, and weighers
10,010	6,400	Textile bleaching and dyeing machine operators and tenders
14,050	9,400	Textile knitting and weaving machine setters, operators, and tenders
19,530	13,000	Textile winding, twisting, and drawing out machine setters, operators, and tenders

Source: U.S. Bureau of Labor Statistics, Industries at a Glance, Occupational Employment Statistics and Employment Projections Program.

desirable products and with the accounting or cost analysis team to offer competitive prices to their customers. Sales and marketing personnel often have undergraduate degrees in business management, marketing, or related disciplines. While some in sales work for a small salary augmented by commissions, most textile sales salaries are competitive.

Marketing personnel serve as communications representatives for the business, creating positive publicity for its products and goals. They may engage in the creation of print advertising for trade publications, develop campaigns to build brand-name recognition or interact with the media, trade associations, and other resources to ensure that the firm's interests are met.

Sales and marketing occupations may include the following:

- Corporate Sales Manager
- Sales Director

- Senior Sales Manager
- Salesperson
- Advertising and Graphic Design Staff
- Administrative Assistant

Design and Product Development

Although designers in the fashion and garment industry receive most public attention, design and product development personnel are required at almost every step in the textile industry. Decisions must be made at every step of the process, from deciding what kinds of raw fiber will be included in the product to its ultimate color and finish. Designers and developers work with the sales department to determine the needs of the company's clientele. They work with marketing personnel to provide prototypes and sample product boards to aid in promoting advance sales of new products, and they also provide advice and input about general trends in fashion and design that may impact the direction of product design for the company. They also work with the general manager and the engineering department to help acquire and set up the proper equipment to produce the desired material in salable quantities.

Salaries for textile designers and product developers range from $45,000 to $69,000, depending on experience and performance. An advanced degree in art, industrial design, or a related field is required.

Design and product development occupations may include the following:

- Product Development Director
- Industrial Designer
- Design Engineer

Production

The production staff is central to the work of manufacturing. In the agricultural sector, production pertains to the physical activities necessary to grow and harvest natural fibers. For example, in the cotton industry, the land must be prepared for planting by plowing and tilling us-

---

OCCUPATION PROFILE

Textile Machine Operator

Considerations	Qualifications
Description	Sets up and operates machines producing or processing textiles.
Career cluster	Manufacturing
Interests	Things
Working conditions	Work inside
Minimum education level	On-the-job training; high school diploma or GED; high school diploma/technical training
Physical exertion	Medium work
Physical abilities	Unexceptional/basic fitness
Opportunities for experience	Part-time work
Licensure and certification	Usually not required
Employment outlook	Decline expected
Holland interest score	RCE; RIE

Note: See volume 1, "Publisher's Note," for an explanation of the Holland interest score.

ing heavy equipment. In conventional agriculture, applications of pesticide, herbicide, and fertilizer may be applied either before or after planting the cotton seed, although cotton grown for the organic market is raised without chemical substances in accordance with guidelines established by the National Organic Program of the U.S. Department of Agriculture. The crop is monitored and cared for throughout the growing season to reduce competition from weeds and predation by insects. Late in the season, the cotton bolls are harvested using large machines and packing systems called modules. The modules are stored on the farm until shipment to the ginning mill, where cotton seeds are extracted from the fiber. Jobs producing natural fibers fall into line with general agricultural work, with the addition of the ability to run specialized equipment or to perform specialized activities—shearing sheep, for example.

In the production sector of the human-made fiber industry, the work is industrial, technical, and chemical. High-level chemists and engineers direct the activities of line workers who oversee various automated processes leading to the production of fibers from cellulose, carbon, or petrochemical constituents.

In the strand and fabric sectors, plant managers and supervisors oversee the work of a number of operators who attend carding, spinning, weaving, and fabrication machinery. Other production operations include dyeing and finishing.

Income for agricultural producers varies with the size of the farm and the crop produced, but the average is about $40,000 per year. Chemists working in the field of human-made textile production earn about $50,000 on average, while unskilled United States textile workers earn about $25,000 to $30,000 per year. It should be noted, however, that much large-scale textile production has been moved from the United States to other countries where the salaries are much lower, sometimes only a few thousand dollars per year. Advanced degrees are typical for chemists working in the field of

OCCUPATION SPECIALTIES

Textile Machine Operators

Specialty	Responsibilities
Bleachers	Tend machines that dye or bleach yarn wound on beams, tubes, or spring coils.
Dye reel operators	Tend machines that bleach or dye cloth in rope form and machine-sew pieces together.
Extruder operators	Set up and run machines that extrude and color human-made fibers for textiles.

human-made fibers, but most other positions in production rely on in-house training.

Production occupations may include the following:

- Farm Manager
- Farmhand
- Plant Manager
- Chemist
- Line Worker
- Carder
- Spinner
- Weaver
- Doffer
- Dyer
- Quality Assurance Tester/Inspector

Shipping and Storage

The production of fiber-related products relies on the transport of raw and intermediate materials to processing facilities, and the transport of the finished product to customers. Fluctuations in material on hand at various stages of production necessitate storage or warehousing of goods and supplies. Shipping managers can earn up to $60,000 per year, while forklift operators average about $30,000 per year.

Shipping and storage occupations may include the following:

- Senior Shipping Manager
- Shipping and Receiving Clerk

- Trucking Supervisor
- Truck Driver
- Forklift Operator
- Warehouse Manager

Research and Development

The research and development department engages in experiments in pure and applied science that may result in profitable new products or innovative production techniques at some point in the future. Research workers design experiments, apply for proprietary patents, and conduct tests of new products. They also may assist the engineering staff during retooling or reconfiguration of the plant. Salaries range from about $37,000 for a laboratory technician to more than $100,000 for a project manager.

Research and development occupations may include the following:

- Project Manager
- Systems Analyst
- Laboratory Technician
- Laboratory Supervisor
- Researcher
- Administrative Assistant

Information Technology

Information technology (IT) workers are responsible for the purchase, installation, and maintenance of hardware and software for computer networks within the facility. Specialized knowledge of programs pertaining to computer-assisted automated production devices, testing, accounting, and other specific functions may be required. IT staff members also assist in training other employees in the use of newly acquired computers and computer programs. Top IT management positions earn between $60,000 and $110,000.

IT occupations may include the following:

- Information Technology Manager
- Computer Technician

PROJECTED EMPLOYMENT FOR SELECTED OCCUPATIONS

Textile Product Mills

Employment		
2009	Projected 2018	Occupation
6,030	4,100	First-line supervisors/managers of production and operating workers
3,260	2,300	Inspectors, testers, sorters, samplers, and weighers
33,850	22,200	Sewing machine operators
4,530	3,000	Textile cutting machine setters, operators, and tenders
5,790	3,800	Textile knitting and weaving machine setters, operators, and tenders
7,850	5,100	Textile winding, twisting, and drawing out machine setters, operators, and tenders

Source: U.S. Bureau of Labor Statistics, Industries at a Glance, Occupational Employment Statistics and Employment Projections Program.

- Platform Specialist
- Electrical Engineer
- Network Coordinator

Human Resources

Employees working in human resources assist in hiring, testing, placing, and dismissing personnel within the firm. They create and file salary histories, job performance reviews, and other employment records, and they assist in mandatory training programs and employee relations. Salaries for human resources generalists range from $35,000 to nearly $60,000, while department directors may receive more than $110,000.

Human resources occupations may include the following:

- Human Resources Director
- Human Resources Generalist

- Training Specialist
- Administrative Assistant

Accounting and Finance

Employees in this department are in charge of all financial aspects of the firm from the highest-level decisions to the disbursement of weekly paychecks to employees. Payments to the company are processed and deposited, and outstanding bills are paid. Some employees may work with spreadsheets and accounting programs to determine profitability, tax liability, and other factors, which are used to generate company reports. Chief financial officers (CFOs) may earn from $78,000 to $200,000, while entry-level accounting clerks earn an average of about $30,000 per year.

Accounting and finance occupations may include the following:

- Chief Financial Officer (CFO)
- Controller
- Accounts Receivable Specialist
- Accountant
- Bookkeeper
- Payroll Specialist
- Auditor
- Clerk
- Administrative Assistant

Maintenance

Maintenance staff members are responsible for repair and scheduled maintenance of facilities and specialized textile machinery as well as maintaining and repairing building systems such as air-conditioning, plumbing, and electrical hardware. The maintenance department also is responsible for general janitorial work and trash collection and removal. They also may play an important role in the planning and implementation of structural or mechanical updates, expansions, and other changes to the physical plant. Most employees in this department have vocational education or technical training, and some may hold advanced degrees in engineering or related fields.

Maintenance occupations may include the following:

- Maintenance Supervisor
- Chief Engineer
- Rigger

- Machinist
- Carpenter
- Plumber
- Heating, Ventilation, and Air-Conditioning (HVAC) Specialist
- Custodian/Janitor

Security

While some textile plants operate around the clock, others close overnight, leaving them vulnerable to burglary and unauthorized entry. Security guards conduct periodic inspections of the facilities, monitor surveillance cameras, and generally provide a human presence at the plant to deter illegal entry or activity. Security personnel are expected to have training in public safety and may be required to obtain certification in cardiopulmonary resuscitation (CPR) and other first-aid techniques. Salaries generally start at $25,000 per year for entry-level officers.

Security occupations may include the following:

- Security Officer
- Technical Support Specialist

Technical and Legal Services

These employees may work as full-time employees or consultants on an as-needed basis. Technical service providers may include material testers, calibrators, or mechanical and electrical engineers who perform specialized tasks involving equipment or materials in the plant. Legal services may be required to defend the firm against litigation, to represent the firm in regulatory or licensing procedures, or to write contracts and other legal documents. Advanced and postgraduate degrees are required for these specialized positions. In-house corporate lawyers can expect to earn $79,000 to $140,000 per year, while industrial engineering consultants may earn up to $119,000.

Technical and legal services occupations may include the following:

- Industrial Engineer
- Electrical Engineer
- Materials Engineer
- Corporate Attorney
- Legal Assistant
- Administrative Assistant

Administrative Support

Administrative personnel work in offices in departments throughout the firm, assisting in its overall operations. Administrative staff may answer phones, run errands, type letters and other documents, make photocopies, send faxes, and perform many other tasks. With the advent of voice recorders, the ability to transcribe speech in shorthand is seldom necessary, although the ability to remain calm under pressure will always be in demand. The heart of many departments, administrative support personnel organize schedules, keep track of correspondence, forward phone messages, enter data, file records, and perform innumerable other duties as required.

Administrative personnel benefit from professional training, although many succeed without it. Many are temporary employees, others are full-time permanent employees of their departments, and still others act as private administrative assistants to a single executive or manager.

Administrative support occupations may include the following:

- Administrative Assistant
- Secretary
- Clerk

INDUSTRY OUTLOOK

Overview

Business analysts predict continued declines in employment within the fiber and textile industries because of advances in automated manufacturing processes and because increasing amounts of textiles are being produced in countries where manufacturing is less costly. Both wages and salaries in the textile and textile product manufacturing industries are expected to decline, possibly by as much as 48 percent through 2018, compared with a projected gain of 11 percent for all other industries combined. Despite these figures, some jobs—especially in the engineering and design sectors—will continue to offer competitive salaries.

One significant reason for the projected decline in textile industry jobs over the next decade is the increasing capital investment in technology and a corresponding increase in overall labor productivity. Wider and faster looms, automated robotics, the development of new nonwoven textiles requiring fewer production processes, and the application of computers in almost every aspect of manufacture all add up to greater productivity with a smaller workforce: fewer workers producing more fabric. Companies are opening new, more efficient plants, and eliminating older ones. As this happens, overall demand for operators of obsolete textile machines and material handlers will continue to decline, but demand for skilled operators able to work with the more efficient modern machines will grow.

Another important factor helping to shape the future of the textile industry is the recent relaxation of trade regulations. Because textile manufacturing is so labor-intensive, it is especially sensitive to competition from developing nations in which workers receive lower wages. In 2005, protectionist quotas for textile products were lifted among U.S. trading partners within the World Trade Organization, most significantly China. Almost immediately, Chinese textile imports surged 45 percent, while the European textile industry went into recession. More and more textile products are being imported into the United States from China and other low-wage countries each year. As U.S. firms and multinational corporations continue to outsource their operations, the jobs of machine operators and other low-level production workers within the industry is certain to be negatively impacted.

Employment Advantages

Despite the bleak outlook for employment within the textile industry, engineers, designers, and skilled production workers still should be in demand. In general, the industry will continue to need creative people with good communication skills, and high levels of technological sophistication.

For designers, fiber engineers, and others working within the research sector, future developments seem likely to create demand for skilled scientific and creative personnel. Just on the horizon are scores of innovative new processes and products, including fabrics that can collect solar energy and radiate it as heat or visible light, biosensitive fabrics that can detect the human pulse or toxins in the environment, shimmering fabrics constructed with thermochromic inks that change color in response to externally generated computer programs, and a prototype for a high-rise office building that could be woven from composite carbon fibers.

Collaborative experiments and technical transfer between the fields of electronics, chemistry, engineering, biology, and computers are helping to develop new generations of nonwoven geotextiles to promote plant growth. Other fabrics are being designed incorporating titanium dioxide, which can decompose stains and odors or act as water filtration systems able to strain out bacteria and even viruses. The new field of nanotechnology is being used to redesign fibers at the atomic level, leading to surgical suture fibers that tie themselves into a knot when exposed to a certain temperature, while the "nomads and nanotechnology" research program is trying to develop a self-contained fabric light source capable of providing built-in illumination for refugees and victims of natural disasters who must live in fabric tents.

Annual Earnings

Continuing changes in the world market will exert cost-cutting pressures affecting business dynamics for firms and workers alike. As consumers become more price conscious, producers are finding it increasingly difficult to pass on costs by raising prices. In order to keep costs low, thereby pleasing consumers, companies are likely to increase both foreign production and investment in new, more efficient, less labor-intensive technologies. In attempts to remain competitive, firms will continue to merge or consolidate, driving down the number of firms and the number of jobs within the industry. Some segments of the U.S. textile products sector, like carpets, industrial fabrics, and specialty yarns, already are competitive on a global scale, so free trade will increase market penetration to new customers overseas. Other sectors, such as fabric for apparel, will be negatively affected as apparel manufacturers relocate to other countries, taking their demand for fabrics with them. Textile mills once again are likely to lose jobs as a result.

RELATED RESOURCES FOR FURTHER RESEARCH

AMERICAN ASSOCIATION OF TEXTILE CHEMISTS
AND COLORISTS
P.O. Box 12215
Research Triangle Park, NC 27709
Tel: (919) 549-8141
Fax: (919) 549-8933
http://www.aatcc.org

HANDWEAVERS GUILD OF AMERICA
1255 Buford Hwy., Suite 211
Suwanee, GA 30024
Tel: (678) 730-0010
Fax: (678) 730-0836
http://www.weavespindye.org

INDUSTRIAL FABRICS ASSOCIATION
INTERNATIONAL
1801 County Rd. B West
Roseville, MN 55113-4061
Tel: (800) 225-4324
Fax: (651) 631-9334
http://www.ifai.com

INTERNATIONAL TEXTILE MANUFACTURERS
FEDERATION
Wiedingstrasse 9
CH-8055 Zürich
Switzerland
Tel: 41-44-283-6380
Fax: 41-44-283-6389
http://www.itmf.org/cms

TEXTILE INSTITUTE INTERNATIONAL
St. James's Buildings, 1st Floor
79 Oxford St.
Manchester M1 6FQ
United Kingdom
Tel: 44-161-237-1188
Fax: 44-161-236-1991
http://www.texi.org

ABOUT THE AUTHOR

Helen M. York has worked as a radio host and producer, a musician and classical music reviewer, and a farmer and craftsperson, producing fine handspun yarns from her own flocks of rare-breed sheep at her farm on the coast of Maine. She holds a master of fine arts from the Ohio State University (1980) and is working toward a Ph.D. in American history with a specialization in science and technology at the University of Maine.

FURTHER READING

Aggarwal, Vinod K. *Liberal Protectionism: The International Politics of Organized Textile Trade.* Berkeley: University of California Press, 1985.

Blewett, Mary H. *Constant Turmoil: The Politics of Industrial Life in Nineteenth Century New England.* Amherst: University of Massachusetts Press, 2000.

Clairmonte, Frederick, and John Cavanagh. *The World in Their Web: The Dynamics of Textile Multinationals.* London: Zed Press, 1981.

Colchester, Chloe. *Textiles Today: A Global Survey of Trends and Traditions.* New York: Thames and Hudson, 2007.

Copeland, Melvin Thomas. *The Cotton Manufacturing Industry of the United States.* New York: Augustus M. Kelley, 1917.

Delfino, Susanna, and Michele Gillespie, eds. *Global Perspectives on Industrial Transformation in the American South.* Columbia: University of Missouri Press, 2005.

English, Beth. *A Common Thread: Labor, Politics and Capital Mobility in the Textile Industry.* Athens Ga.: University of Georgia Press, 2006.

Goldenburg, David. *The U.S. Man-Made Fiber Industry: Its Structure and Organization Since 1948.* Westport, Conn.: Praeger, 1992.

McCormack, Richard. "Good Luck Competing Against Chinese Labor Costs—Mfg. Job Growth in China Is Headed Up, Not Down; 109 Million Mfg. Workers in China Dwarfs Number in U.S." *Manufacturing & Technology News* 13, no. 9 (May 2, 2006). Available at http://www.manufacturingnews.com/news/06/0502/art1.html.

Mortimer, John. *Cotton Spinning: The Story of the Spindle.* Manchester, England: Palmer, Howe, 1895.

Munro, John H. *Textiles, Towns and Trade.* Brookfield, Vt.: Varorium, 1994.

Pack, Howard. *Productivity, Technology and Industrial Development: A Case Study in Textiles.* New York: Oxford University Press, 1987.

Rivard, Paul E. *A New Order of Things: How the Textile Industry Transformed New England.* Hanover, N.H.: University Press of New England, 2002.

Ruhm, Herman D. *Marketing Textiles.* New York: Fairchild, 1970.

Toyne, Brian, et al. *The Global Textile Industry.* London: George Allen and Unwin, 1984.

U.S. Bureau of Labor Statistics. *Career Guide to Industries,* 2010-2011 ed. http://www.bls.gov/oco/cg.

U.S. Census Bureau. North American Industry Classification System (NAICS), 2007. http://www.census.gov/cgi-bin/sssd/naics/naicsrch?chart=2007.

Vogel, J. Thomas, and Barbara W. Lowry. *The Textile Industry: An Information Sourcebook.* Phoenix, Ariz.: Oryx Press, 1989.

Yafa, Stephen. *Big Cotton: How a Humble Fiber Created Fortunes, Wrecked Civilizations, and Put America on the Map.* New York: Viking Penguin, 2005.

Theater and Performing Arts Industry

©Katrina Brown/Dreamstime.com

INDUSTRY SNAPSHOT

General Industry: Arts and Entertainment

Career Cluster: Arts, A/V Technology, and Communication

Subcategory Industries: Broadway Musicals; Circuses; Dance Companies; Las Vegas Style Spectacles; Live Performances; Musical Dramas; Opera

Related Industries: Motion Picture and Television Industry; Music Industry

Annual Domestic Revenues: $12.9 billion USD (U.S. Census, 2008)

Annual International Revenues: $39.7 billion USD (U.S. Census /World Bank, 2008)

Annual Global Revenues: $52.6 billion USD (U.S. Census/World Bank, 2008)

NAICS Numbers: 711

INDUSTRY DEFINITION

Summary

The theater and performing arts industry includes organizations that produce or organize live presentations involving performances of actors, musicians, dancers, musical groups, and other entertainers. This industry includes the promotion and production of these events as well as providing the artistic and technical skills necessary for the production of events. The group includes a very wide range of businesses and encompasses nonprofit as well as for-profit entities. The group ranges in size from small businesses, including individual freelance performers, to large organizations such as large opera and theater production companies. Many nonprofit organizations are dependent on significant financial support from government and private-foundation grants. The industry is represented in numerous countries and is most developed in metropolitan cities. In the United States, performing artists are more educated on average than the workforce as a whole.

History of the Industry

The practice of presenting live artistic performances dates back to ancient times. Ancient Greek and Roman cultures included dramatic, tragic, and comedic poetry and theater. During the sixteenth century, *commedia dell'arte*, an improvised comic theater with stock characters, flourished in Western Europe. The roots of current repertoires and performing traditions can be traced to the early seventeenth century, when Williams Shakespeare's plays were written and the first public opera house was opened in 1637 in Venice, Italy. The modern symphony orchestra developed in Germany during the mid-eighteenth century.

Today's large performance organizations, particularly opera companies, originated from the traditions of European royalty. Many modern performing arts organizations were formed during the eighteenth and nineteenth centuries; Italy's famous opera house, La Scala, opened in 1778; the first performing circus in the United States opened in 1793, Broadway musicals began in the early 1800's, the New York Philharmonic was created in 1842, the Boston Symphony Orchestra was created in 1881, and New York's Metropolitan Opera House opened in 1883. In the United States, wealthy patrons started many of the large performing organizations. For example, J. P. Morgan, Andrew Carnegie, and Joseph Pulitzer were important contributors to the New York Philharmonic Orchestra. Numerous artistic leaders and performers were brought from Europe to lead many of the major performing arts organization in the United States.

Many historians identify modern theater's beginnings in 1901 with the founding of the Moscow Art Theatre by Konstantin Stanislavsky. He formulated a revolutionary method of acting and is credited with beginning the modern age of the artistic director in theater.

The modern tradition of ballet dance performance was developed in France by King Louis XIV in the mid-seventeenth century, and in Russia during the mid-eighteenth century. Modern dance traditions departed from ballet in the late nineteenth century. New American theater dance forms such as tap and jazz were developed in the mid-twentieth century.

Major performing arts companies in the United States were aided in the early twentieth century by the creation of tax-exempt status for nonprofit organizations. In the United States, a few large organizations were created in major metropolitan cities on the East Coast in the late nineteenth and early twentieth centuries; attendance of performing arts entertainment in the United States grew rapidly in the post-World War II era. The creation of the National Endowment for the Arts in 1965 also increased public support for the performing arts industry. After World War II, an increasingly educated and wealthy population with more disposable income and leisure time increased the demand for artistic performances in many cities. Numerous regional, permanent nonprofit theater companies, symphony orchestras, and opera companies were subsequently created in other North American cities.

European higher education institutions employed significant numbers of performing artists during the nineteenth and early twentieth centuries. During the mid-twentieth century, American college and university systems developed

Traditional ballet dancers. (©Rumen Baychev/Dreamstime.com)

Japanese Taiko drummers. (©Zepherwind/Dreamstime.com)

another significant segment of the performing arts industry by forming schools specializing in the performing arts.

The Industry Today

The performing arts industry today offers several types of entertainment, including symphony orchestras, theatrical plays and musicals, operas, dance performances, circuses, and large multidiscipline spectacle-style shows. Large metropolitan cities continue to provide the majority of employment opportunities for performing artists. For-profit performing arts organizations generally are focused on popular entertainment, such as musical theater production companies and Las Vegas-style spectacles such as Cirque du Soleil. Nonprofit organizations generally focus on art performances, such as symphony orchestras, opera companies, dance companies (including ballet), and regional theater companies. Performing artists also are often self-employed as freelance performers and teachers in private dance and music studios.

Professional symphony orchestras often provide live weekly concerts in midsize to large cities. Led by a single conductor/music director, they usually feature a large group of local musicians, often paired with a single internationally known virtuoso soloist. While some symphony orchestras offer only classical repertoire, many offer both classical and popular repertoire, usually formatted in separate concert series and marketed to different groups of patrons. To attract new audiences, orchestras are using a growing number of new concert formats, including shorter "rush-hour" concerts and concerts with multimedia presentations.

New York's Broadway is the center of the theater world in America. The highest-profile plays and musicals are produced there; sometimes, Broadway shows spawn touring productions that play in large and midsize cities across the country. Productions of Broadway shows also often have extended runs in large cities; New York, Los Angeles, Las Vegas, Toronto, and Chicago are large enough to support several major shows running simultaneously

High-profile plays and musicals are performed on Broadway in New York. (AP/Wide World Photos)

for months or years. Metropolitan communities also may support regional theater companies. Plays and musicals typically employ numerous performers, including instrumentalists, singers, dancers, conductors, and actors; many stage roles require performers to have high-level performance skills in singing, acting, and dancing. Theaters often employ a technical staff that assists in the production of most performing events. Technical theater positions include lighting designers, carpenters, costume designers, stage managers, and technical directors. Large theater companies that produce works with significant commercial appeal are located in major metropolitan cities such as New York, London, and Chicago. Regional theater companies often produce new plays and challeng-

ing works that do not have the popular appeal necessary for production on Broadway.

Dance companies are led by an artistic director/ choreographer and usually specialize in one tradition—ballet, contemporary, folk, modern, or jazz/ tap. Many of the largest dance performance organizations are ballet companies. Dance companies generally have a home theater for most of their performances, although some tour as well. Many ballet companies have an affiliated school that trains young dancers in the distinctive style used by the company.

Large hotels and casinos in Las Vegas and some other gambling and entertainment centers produce live performances of popular music and theater. Well-known performers in rock and roll, country, and popular music perform concerts for large audiences at these venues. Smaller venues in casinos also host performances by local musicians. Casinos and hotels rely on individual contractors to hire performers.

Military organizations in the United States and some other countries are among the largest employers of performing artists. All branches of the United States Armed Forces maintain high-quality music ensembles for ceremonial, entertainment, and educational purposes.

Many corporations that operate cruise ships employ numerous performers, including musicians, dancers, and actors, for the entertainment of cruise patrons. Performers often are employed for contract periods of three to six months. Churches and other religious groups regularly employ trained musicians as organists, pianists, and directors of choirs and other music ensembles. Dance bands, pop, rock-and-roll, and country bands often are employed in nightclubs. Employment generally is for single or weekly engagements at the discretion of managers and owners.

Public and private primary and secondary schools employ performing artists as teachers. Universities employ numerous performing artists as educators and performers. One of the primary goals of many universities is leadership in the arts for the enrichment of their communities; this requires a significant commitment of resources and creates employment for performing artists in music, dance, and theater.

Cooperation between universities and performing arts companies (principally regional theater companies and orchestras) is common in midsize cities. These cooperative agreements to hire performers reduce labor costs and allow the organizations to attract higher-quality performers and artists than they could independently. Performers also may find employment in related industries such as film and the music industry.

The performing arts industry has different primary sources of economic support in different regions of the world. In Europe and Asia, support comes largely from government subsidies. In the United States, the industry is supported by a blend of public ticket sales, private donors, private foundation grants, and government grants. Many large performing arts organizations seek to create a reliable funding source by creating an endowment.

Performing arts audiences are dominated by highly educated individuals with high income levels.

The performing arts industry continues to face economic challenges. While the economic efficiency of many industries has increased over time, the performing arts industry has been unable to increase productivity substantially. The performing arts industry remains less efficient economically than other industries because its unique live performances are consumed at the point of production. The solution to the fundamental economic problems facing the performing arts industry continues to be philanthropic support and increasing government subsidies. In the United States, much of the government support comes through the National Endowment for the Arts and each state's arts council.

In the early twenty-first century, countries with growing wealth, such as the United Arab Emirates, increased the import of performing arts from Europe and North America. At the same time, the performing arts industry in North America faced significant challenges stemming from the global economic downturn. Many performing arts organizations have had significant budget difficulties resulting from loss of value in endowments, reduced demand, and decreased philanthropic support. For-profit organizations generally have had better financial success in recent years than nonprofit organizations.

INDUSTRY MARKET SEGMENTS

The performing arts industry includes organizations that range in size from very small to large. The industry serves a wide range of audiences as well. The following section provides a detailed analysis of the industry segments.

Small Businesses

Small music ensembles, theater companies, dance ensembles (primarily modern or jazz dance), and some churches typically have only a few employees serving a very small number of patrons. Ticket prices, budgets, and salaries vary, but generally are much lower than those of midsize and large organizations. Some performers act as independent freelance artists or as contractors for other performers, thereby operating as individually owned small businesses.

Potential Annual Earnings Scale. The average earnings for performers in small performing arts organizations vary widely by region. Performers generally do not work year-round, and often are paid on a per-service basis. The average wage in the United States for such a position ranges from $14.10 to $31.65 per hour. In many cases, a union or other collective bargaining agreement does not control compensation for performers; instead, management often sets compensation rates, which may change significantly from year to year. Contractors and freelance performers often set a fee schedule that is negotiated with employers individually.

Clientele Interaction. Small performing arts companies generally cater to audiences with specific artistic interests. As a result, it is important to the success of the company to encourage repeat patronage. Small performing arts companies also often are supported by philanthropic gifts from individuals and grants from private foundations and government agencies. Continued financial support often relies on maintaining strong relationships among performers, artistic staff, management and the donors and/or granting agency staff members. Small companies often seek annual financial support from state arts councils, civic foundations, and individual donors.

Amenities, Atmosphere, and Physical Grounds. Small performing arts companies perform frequently in theaters and other spaces that also are used by others for performances or other purposes. Small dance or theater companies often use a small multipurpose theater in a civic building or school. Many small companies have little or no permanent administrative office space. For small dance and theater companies, the atmosphere of performing spaces usually is designed as a neutral backdrop that does not distract from the artistic presentation.

Small music ensembles often perform in a variety of environments and may use a different space for each performance. Some of the spaces may be theaters or auditoriums, but many are spaces designed for other purposes such as casinos, libraries, nightclubs, churches, and bookstores. Generally, small companies seek performance spaces that suit the particular art, contribute to an intimate environment, are within their budgets, and are more casual than the performance spaces used by larger organizations.

Typical Number of Employees. The number of employees often is determined by the requirements of the specific performance medium. Small music ensembles may have as few as three or four employees. Small theater or dance companies typically are only slightly larger, with five or six employees. Small Christian churches often employ a single choir director and/or organist or pianist to lead a volunteer choir. Many small organizations employ a consistent number of part-time workers. Often, a small number of volunteers serve on a board of directors or as trustees who have duties in fund-raising or other management capacities.

Traditional Geographic Locations. Small performing arts organizations are found in cities of all sizes and in most geographic regions. In small communities, these organizations often are the only performing arts organizations. In larger cities, small performing arts organizations tend to focus on repertory categories that larger organizations generally do not perform. For example, many large metropolitan areas enjoy the presence of a large symphony orchestra, but may also have a small chamber music society that employs only a few part-time performers. These groups typically play music that attracts only a few patrons who attend concerts in small theaters or homes. Small music ensembles may perform only music from a particular historical period, experimental music, modern repertoire, or music designed for particular events, such as wedding receptions. Similarly, small dance companies and small theater companies often focus on modern or experimental repertoire.

Pros of Working for a Small Business. Small companies are able to perform (sometimes exclusively) niche repertoires; they possess greater artistic control for performers, in part because of the absence of large administrative structures and artistic staff direction. Performers often enjoy a close-knit working environment; if there is a small staff, they often are friends or family members of the performers.

Cons of Working for a Small Business. Small companies often have relatively low pay and usually do not pay any benefits to performers. For many small companies, the only full-time employee is the executive director or artistic director. Employment for performers often is part time and can be unpredictable. Sometimes the performers have to take on the business management tasks of the company and can have long periods without employment. Many small nonprofit companies rely on only a few funding sources; the loss of a single grant source or donor can cause serious budget shortfalls.

Costs

Payroll and Benefits: Small companies often pay performers on a per-service basis; employees usually do not receive benefits such as health care, retirement, sick leave, or paid vacation.

Supplies: Supply requirements are specific to the type of performance medium. Musicians usually own the instruments used, as well as sheet music and sound amplification equipment. Theater and dance companies usually require fewer supplies; the performers usually own and supply dance shoes, costumes, and other inexpensive supplies.

External Services: For small organizations, most technical theater requirements are limited to minimal lighting and staging that is supplied by the performance venue or theater. If sound amplification is required and not owned by the performers, the equipment and staff usually are supplied by local companies. Technical theater staff requirements usually are very limited and often supplied by the venue.

Utilities: For small organizations, the absence of permanent administrative offices and performance venues often has the benefit of no ongoing utility costs.

Taxes: Some small nonprofit companies may pay performers through a nonemployee status to avoid paying and managing payroll taxes.

Midsize Businesses

Midsize performing arts companies typically include music ensembles, theater companies, and dance ensembles (often regional ballet companies). Smaller military bands and Broadway shows, off-Broadway shows, and touring productions of plays or musicals often fall in this category as well. Midsize organizations usually have three types of employees: performers, artistic staff, and management staff. Ticket prices, budgets, and salaries vary widely but generally are much higher than those of small organizations.

Potential Annual Earnings Scale. Average earnings for employees in midsize performing arts companies vary by region. Performers generally work a twenty- to forty-six-week season and often are paid on a salary basis per week of employment. Artistic staff and management staff often are employed year-round on salary with benefits. The typical pay range in the United States is between $20,000 and $65,000 per year; artistic and management executives often are compensated at a higher rate. Compensation for performers often is controlled by a multiyear labor contract or other collective bargaining agreement negotiated between management and a national union. The board of directors usually sets compensation for management. Military bands are compensated based on rank; members of smaller organizations generally have a lower rank than members of large organizations.

Clientele Interaction. Midsize performing arts companies generally cater to audiences with specific artistic interests. As a result, repeat patronage of ticket buyers is important for maintaining an audience of sufficient numbers. Midsize companies often market tickets bundled by series, focusing on repertoire interests of clients who purchase tickets for multiple performances at a reduced price. Midsize nonprofit performing arts companies also often are supported by philanthropic gifts from individuals and grants from private foundations and/or government agencies. Continued financial support relies on maintaining relationships among the executive director or development and fundraising staff and the donors or granting agency staff members. Midsize nonprofit companies often seek annual financial support from state arts councils, civic foundations, and individual donors.

Amenities, Atmosphere, and Physical Grounds. Midsize performing arts companies may perform in private or civic theaters that are used by other organizations for performances. Midsize companies also are likely to be the dominant tenant for their performance space. Many use the primary local civic auditorium, which is provided to them by the city at a reduced cost. Midsize companies often have permanent administrative office space and rehearsal spaces. Generally, they will seek performance spaces that suit the particular art form, the size of the organization, the audience size, and their budgets. The performance spaces are more likely to be civic theaters than the specialized private spaces used by larger organizations. Touring productions of Broadway shows usually perform in civic auditoriums. Military bands usually rehearse and perform in dedicated spaces on military bases. Some military bands tour the country, and utilize different performance spaces in each city on the tour.

Typical Number of Employees. The number of employees is determined by the requirements of the specific performance medium. Midsize organizations often have three to ten employees in management; the number of performers varies. For example, a midsize orchestra will employ fifty to seventy performers, while a midsize ballet company will have fifteen to twenty employed performers. For most midsize nonprofit organizations, a volunteer board of directors or trustees assists with duties in fund-raising or other management oversight. Churches often employ two or three full-time employees as artistic management and have numerous part-time performers. Military bands will have one or two artistic directors (officers) who are conductors of the ensemble, several full-time support staff, and twenty to sixty full-time performers.

Traditional Geographic Locations. Midsize performing arts organizations are found in midsize to large cities in many geographic regions. In midsize communities, these organizations usually are the primary performing arts groups. In large metropolitan areas, midsize performing arts organizations target a specific geographic area within the community or a niche repertory. For example, many large metropolitan cities enjoy the presence of a large nationally known symphony orchestra but also may have a midsize orchestra that performs in only one suburb. Touring shows often choose their stops by market size: The midsize companies perform in midsize cities referred to as "secondary markets." Military bands either are in residence at a particular military base or are touring organizations.

Pros of Working for a Midsize Business. Midsize performing arts companies often have greater financial stability compared with smaller companies. The presence of full-time administration allows performers to focus on the artistic work

without the other duties they often have in smaller companies. Performers in midsize companies also may be employed part time or full time as teachers in higher education.

Cons of Working for a Midsize Business. Midsize companies often have lower pay than large companies. Midsize companies can suffer budget shortfalls that result in loss of compensation. In unionized environments, labor disputes can cause stressful working relationships between management and artistic staff or performers. These contract disputes can last for long periods and may result in the cancellation of performances. The financial support for these midsize organizations often is unpredictable, particularly in cities with shrinking economies or struggling industries.

Costs

Payroll and Benefits: Midsize companies often pay performers on a weekly salary basis; all employees including performers usually receive benefits such as health care and retirement, but performers often do not receive sick leave or paid vacation.

Supplies: Supply requirements are specific to the performance medium. Musicians usually own the instruments used in company performances. The company usually supplies large equipment, staging, and sound amplification equipment. Costuming for actors, dancers, and other stage performers typically are supplied by the employer.

External Services: The company, performance venue, or theater supplies most technical theater requirements. If sound amplification is required and not owned by the performers, local companies usually supply the equipment and staff. The company or venue supplies technical theater staff.

Utilities: Midsize performing arts companies usually pay utility costs such as electricity, gas, telephone, and Internet service for office spaces.

Taxes: Many midsize companies are nonprofit and exempt from paying income taxes; they usually pay employees, including performers, in employee status with payroll taxes.

Large Businesses

Large music ensembles, Broadway productions, popular music tours, military bands, theater companies, and dance ensembles (often ballet companies in the largest cities) typically have three types of employees: performers, artistic staff, and management staff. Unlike the small and midsize companies, large companies often have numerous departments within the management staff, including educational programming, fund-raising/development, and production management. Military bands sometimes are considered part of the large business category. Ticket prices, budgets, and salaries vary widely but generally are much higher than those of midsize organizations.

Potential Annual Earnings Scale. The average earnings for performers in large performing arts companies vary by region; performers generally work a forty- to fifty-two-week season. The average range in the United States for such a position is $50,000 to $125,000 per year; compensation for executive managers and executive artistic leadership (artistic directors and music directors, for example) generally is much higher than that of other employees. Compensation for performers sometimes is governed by multiyear labor contracts negotiated by national unions.

Performers in U.S. military bands usually are compensated based on rank. Performers may receive significant additional compensation for recorded performances; sometimes this compensation is included in their employment contract in the form of an electronic media guarantee. Las Vegas-style spectacles employ performers on a full-time salary basis with benefits.

Clientele Interaction. Large performing arts companies generally cater to a wider range of audiences with more varied artistic interests than small companies. Repeat patronage for ticket buyers is important for maintaining an audience of sufficient numbers, but the very large, and often well-educated populations of large cities provide a large audience base. Large companies often market tickets bundled by series, focusing on repertoire interests of clients; clients may purchase tickets for multiple performances at a reduced price. Large performing arts companies also often are supported by philanthropic gifts from individuals and grants from government agencies. Continued financial support often relies on maintaining relationships among artistic staff, management, and the donors and/or granting agency staff members.

Amenities, Atmosphere, and Physical Grounds. Large performing arts companies often rehearse and perform in specially designed theaters constructed specifically for their performances. Large companies often have permanent administrative office spaces and rehearsal spaces in the same facility. Large companies also may tour extensively, often internationally, during which time they use available private and civic performance spaces. Military bands usually rehearse and perform in a dedicated space provided on a military base. Broadway shows rehearse and perform in dedicated theater spaces; their touring counterparts use the large civic theaters found in major metropolitan cities. Most large performing arts organizations present their performances in large spaces for large audiences. For many nonprofit organizations, such as ballet companies, opera companies, and symphony orchestras, the atmosphere and presentation are formal. The large performance halls often prevent the close interaction between performers and audience experienced by small performance groups. Popular music performances often occur in multipurpose stadiums or arenas. Most large organizations require private dressing rooms for star performers, conductors, and soloists. Lounges and communal dressing rooms or "green rooms" are supplied for the comfort of supporting performers and ensemble members.

Typical Number of Employees. The number of employees often is guided by the requirements of the specific performance medium. Large organizations often have dozens of employees in management, including interns. The number of performers varies; for example, a large orchestra will employ 80 to 100 performers, a large ballet company will have 23 to 45 employed performers, and a large military band will have 150 performers. For nonprofit organizations, a volunteer board of directors assists with duties in fund-raising and other management oversight. The number of employees for a Broadway show varies, but these shows often employ a significant number of cast members, orchestra members, technical theater staff, management staff, and production staff. Touring shows may have employees who travel and other temporary employees who are hired in each city of the tour. Large churches often employ several full-time musicians as performers, including organists, choir directors, pianists, and singers.

Traditional Geographic Locations. Large performing arts organizations are found in major metropolitan cities in many geographic regions. In large metropolitan areas, large performing arts organizations serve a specific geographic area and also are viewed as national leaders and innovators in the industry. In the U.S. military, large bands are located at major installations, particularly those in Washington, D.C.

Pros of Working for a Large Business. Large organizations have significantly higher compensation, higher artistic standards, and greater financial stability compared with midsize organizations. Performers often may find additional related employment in education and/or other performance companies from the perceived prestige and reputation for artistic excellence resulting from employment in a large company.

Cons of Working for a Large Business. Large organizations often create significant pressure for extremely high artistic standards. Performers do not have the desired individual artistic control of their performances. There are a relatively small number of employment opportunities in large organizations and significant competition for employment. Budget shortfalls can cause significant loss of income and uncertain employment.

Costs

Payroll and Benefits: Large companies usually pay all employees, including performers, on a salary basis; employees usually receive benefits such as health care, retirement, sick leave, and paid vacation.

Supplies: Supply requirements are specific to the performance medium. Musicians usually own the required musical instruments; the company usually supplies large equipment and sound amplification equipment. Costumes for actors, dancers, and other stage performers often are supplied by the employer.

External Services: The company, performance venue, or theater supplies most technical theater requirements. If sound amplification is required and not owned by the performers, local companies usually supply the equipment and staff. The company or venue supplies technical theater staff.

Utilities: Large performing arts companies pay utility costs for office and performance spaces.

Taxes: Many large companies are nonprofit and exempt from paying income taxes; they usually pay performers in employee status with payroll taxes.

ORGANIZATIONAL STRUCTURE AND JOB ROLES

The organizational structure and distribution of tasks within performing arts companies are based on size and for-profit or nonprofit status. Most organizations have a strong functional division between management of the artistic product and the business management of the organization. A board of directors, artistic director, and executive director are likely to handle most of the major management oversight tasks, while the general manager and/or production manager will delegate tasks to other staff. Nevertheless, the tasks themselves generally remain similar throughout the performing arts industry.

The following umbrella categories apply to the organizational structure of small, midsize, and large performing arts companies:

- Business Management
- Administrative Support
- Development and Fund-Raising
- Stage Management
- Personnel Management
- Artistic Management
- Musicians
- Actors
- Dancers
- Costumers
- Composers and Arrangers
- Las Vegas-Style Spectacle Performers

Business Management

The board directs the global mission of the company, sets goals and implements plans, and may assist in specific management oversight. The board issues contracts with and sets compensation for the management staff, executive director, and artistic director. Many board members are wealthy community leaders and/or business executives with vested interests in the success of performing arts in their community.

Board members of nonprofit performing arts companies generally are volunteers; they often make philanthropic gifts to the organization and solicit gifts from others in the community. The board usually includes specific offices, such as president, that are held for designated terms. The board also may have an executive committee that manages specific and regular oversight of the company. In many cases, the officers and executive committee of the board do the majority of the work.

The executive director oversees the operations of the company. These individuals help oversee major operations, goal setting, and the implementation of plans for the organization. They also manage individual teams and departments. Executive managers usually have college degrees; some have advanced degrees and/or significant performance experience, particularly in the company's specific performing art. Some executive managers also have experience as a general manager.

Executive directors generally earn higher salaries than other staff employees. Their job is to manage the overall functions of the company, address large management issues, manage the budget, ensure that all departments are functioning well, and communicate and plan with the artistic leadership and the board of directors. Executive directors often attend many of the performances to maintain quality control and lines of communication.

General managers handle the overall operations of the company. These individuals help oversee specific aspects of budget, operations, the details of productions (including purchase or rental of equipment), setting tour dates, booking venues, transportation for touring groups, communication with stage managers, and managing production budgets. They also may manage individual teams or departments and may communicate with artistic staff about the specific requirements of productions. Some general managers have academic degrees and/or significant performance experience, particularly in the company's specific performing art. General managers usually are salaried employees.

The director of education manages the educational programs of the company. These individuals help oversee specific aspects of programs that seek to engage young audiences in education. This includes the details of productions such as purchase or rental of equipment, rental of venues, communication with production and general managers, and budget management for educational programs. They may also manage interns, individual teams, or departments and may communicate with artistic staff about the specific requirements of educational programs. Education directors often have academic degrees and/or significant performance experience, particularly in the company's specific performing art. Directors of education usually are salaried employees. Directors of education also often coordinate programs with area public schools. Organizations often give performances for youths, send performers to visit classrooms, and offer performances in the community as part of their educational programming. For ballet companies, the director of education is responsible for the ballet company's school, which teaches the style of the company and has classes for various age groups.

Occupations in this category include the following:

- Member of the Board of Directors or Trustees
- Executive Director
- General Manager
- Production Manager
- Director of Education

Administrative Support

The administrative support staffs handle operational tasks or office work of the company. These individuals carry out specific aspects of operations, including rental and distribution of sheet music, sales of subscriptions and individual tickets, and managing appointments and communication for the general manager and/or executive director. Librarians often have academic degrees and/or performance experience, particularly in the company's specific medium. Many employees in administrative support are compensated on a full-time or part-time hourly basis.

Occupations in the area of administrative support include the following:

- Librarian
- Office Staff
- Ticket Manager
- Box Office Manager

Development and Fund-Raising

Development and fund-raising staff members handle all aspects of fund-raising for the company. These individuals write grant proposals, meet and communicate with donors and potential donors, and report the results to granting agencies. They work with and directly for the board members and the executive director. Some development staff members have academic degrees and/or performance experience, particularly in the company's specific performing art.

Development and fund-raising employees usually are compensated on a salary basis.

Stage Management

Stage management staff members handle all physical and technical duties in the rehearsal and performance spaces. These individuals construct stage plots, move equipment, and communicate with theater staff to ensure proper lighting, temperature control, and safety in the working environment for performers. They work with and directly for the general manager or production manager. Stagehands work for the stage manager, assist performers, and set up equipment including chairs, stands, sets, lighting, and props.

Stage managers usually are compensated on a salary basis while stagehands often are hourly employees. Occupations in the area of stage management include the following:

- Stage Manager
- Stagehand

Personnel Management

Personnel managers handle hiring, payroll, and communication with all regular performers employed by the company. These individuals distribute information to performers about the locations and times of rehearsals and performances to performers. They also coordinate auditions and hire new performers in cooperation with artistic management. They work with and directly for the general manager and artistic director.

Personnel managers for large and midsize organizations usually are compensated on a salary basis. Personnel managers for small organizations often are performers and usually are compensated on an hourly basis.

Artistic Management

Artistic managers oversee the artistic goals and direction of the company. These individuals program and direct specific repertoire, set artistic norms and standards, decide on the hiring of company and guest performers, and manage all other matters affecting the artistic product and production. They work for the board of directors and in cooperation with the executive director.

For orchestras, the music director often is also the primary conductor. The music director selects repertoire, plans concert series, hires musicians including soloists, rehearses the orchestra and conducts performances. For ballet companies, the ballet master often is the main choreographer for the company, selects repertoire, plans performance series, hires dancers including soloists, and rehearses the company. For theater companies, the director selects repertoire, plans performance series, hires actors and directs the rehearsal process.

Artistic managers usually are hired with multiyear contracts and compensated on a salary basis at a much higher rate than other performers. Occupations in the area of artistic management include the following:

- Music Director
- Ballet Master/Choreographer
- Director

Musicians

Performers actively prepare and give performances solo or with a band, orchestra, or other group. Orchestral musicians possess highly developed and specific performance skills as musicians. They work for the conductor and/or music director and in cooperation with the personnel manager. Orchestral musicians often are organized into two or three classes with slightly different responsibilities. Principal players play solos and the most prominent parts and lead their sections of the orchestra; associate principal players may also play some prominent parts; section players have no leadership roles and play less prominent parts. Music theater pit musicians collectively accompany the on-stage ensemble. Instrument requirements and skills are slightly different from those for orchestral performers.

Jazz musicians may be employed by performing arts organizations, but more often they work as independent artists or groups playing in clubs, restaurants, and other venues. These individuals possess highly developed and specific performance skills (particularly improvisation) in a particular repertoire. Instruments commonly found in jazz performances include trumpet, trombone, saxophone, bass, drums, and piano.

Performers' compensation varies widely; as independent performers they usually are hired on a per-service basis, while in larger companies, performers usually are hired with multiyear contracts and compensated on a salary basis.

Occupations for musicians include the following:

- Orchestral Musician
- Opera Orchestra Musician
- Ballet Orchestra Musician
- Theater Pit Musician
- Chamber Musician
- Military Band Musician
- Jazz Musician

Actors

Actors actively prepare and give performances in stage roles. These individuals have highly developed and specific performance skills as actors; some actors also may be dancers and singers and specialize in musical theater roles. Opera performers primarily are singers, although they also must be capable actors. Performers are organized into voice classes by range and type, such as baritone, tenor, alto, and soprano. Actors work for artistic managers and directors.

Compensation varies widely. In small companies, they usually are hired on a per-service basis; in larger companies, performers usually are hired with contracts and compensated on a salary basis. Some music theater performers may also work as actors in other contexts. Occupations for actors include the following:

- Actor
- Music Theater Stage Performer
- Opera Singer

Dancers

Some performers possess highly developed and specific performance skills as dancers. They work for the artistic manager and choreographer and in cooperation with the personnel manager. Performers in ballet companies in particular often are organized into two groups: principal dancers, who have more responsibilities, and company dancers. Training and skills vary widely among the different styles of dance; for example, ballet dancers have distinctly different skills, development, and repertoire than jazz/tap dancers.

Performers' compensation varies widely; in small companies they usually are hired on a per-

---

OCCUPATION SPECIALTIES

Actors

Specialty	Responsibilities
Announcers	Introduce radio, television and stage productions to audiences.
Drama coaches	Evaluate and coach the performance of actors. They coach performers in character interpretation, voice projection and stage technique.
Drama teachers	Instruct individuals and groups in acting and drama techniques. Special emphasis is placed on diction, voice inflection, enunciation, dialects and nonperformance aspects of stage production.
Extras	Perform as nonspeaking members of a cast in dramatic television, movie, or stage productions.
Narrators	Make explanatory comments to accompany action parts of motion pictures.

service basis, while in larger companies performers usually are hired with multiyear contracts and compensated on a salary basis.

Occupations for dancers include the following:

- Ballet Principal Dancer
- Ballet Company Dancer
- Ballet Intern Dancer
- Tap/Jazz Dancer
- Modern Dancer

Costumers

Costumers design and construct the costumes for performances of the company. They work for the artistic manager and in cooperation with the producer, director, or choreographer. Costumers' compensation varies widely; in small companies, they usually are hired on an hourly basis, while in larger companies, they usually are compensated on a salary basis. Occupations for costumers include the following:

- Costume Designer
- Costumer

Composers and Arrangers

Composers or arrangers construct musical works for the performances of the company. They work for the artistic manager and in cooperation with the producer, director, or choreographer. Composers usually are hired on a fee basis. Some organizations, including military bands, hire arrangers on a full-time salary basis.

Composers and arrangers also are highly trained professionals skilled in the construction of music for specific performance needs. Occupations in this area include the following:

- Military Band Arranger/Composer
- Orchestral Arranger/Composer
- Film and Television Arranger/
  Composer

OCCUPATION PROFILE

Dancer/Choreographer

Considerations	Qualifications
Description	Plans and designs a dance sequence as well as performing the dance.
Career cluster	Arts, A/V Technology, and Communications
Interests	Data; people
Working conditions	Work inside; work both inside and outside
Minimum education level	Junior/technical/community college; apprenticeship; bachelor's degree
Physical exertion	Heavy work
Physical abilities	Good to excellent fitness; requires strength and flexibility
Opportunities for experience	Apprenticeship; volunteer work; part-time work
Licensure and certification	Usually not required
Employment outlook	Slower-than-average growth expected
Holland interest score	AER; AES

Note: See volume 1, "Publisher's Note," for an explanation of the Holland interest score.

OCCUPATION SPECIALTIES

Dancers/Choreographers

Specialty	Responsibilities
Acrobatic dancers	Perform a style of dancing characterized by gymnastic feats.
Ballet dancers	Perform a dancing technique based on the turned-out leg, pointed foot, and five fundamental foot and arm positions.
Ballroom dancers	Demonstrate social dancing ranging from the waltz to the latest popular dance.
Dancing instructors	Instruct students in ballet, ballroom, tap, and other forms of dancing.
Tap dancers	Perform a style of dancing that is distinguished by rhythm tapped by the feet in time with the music.

Las Vegas-Style Spectacle Performers

Performers possess highly developed and specific performance skills as actors, dancers, jugglers, or musicians. They work for the artistic managers and in cooperation with the personnel manager. Performers usually are hired with contracts and compensated on a salary basis. Occupations for Las Vegas-style spectacle performers include the following:

- Orchestral Musician
- Jazz Musician
- Music Theater Pit Musician
- Actor
- Tap/Jazz Dancer
- Modern Dancer
- Ballet Dancer
- Circus Performer

INDUSTRY OUTLOOK

Overview

The outlook for this industry shows it to be in decline. Although the near-term outlook for the industry is unstable, the recent history of the industry has shown growth. Between 1970 and 1990, the number of artists doubled in the United States, growing at twice the rate of the overall labor force. This growth reflects the great expansion of theaters, orchestras, and other venues in the industry and collegiate community. In recent years, the number of performing artists as a percentage of the U.S. population has stabilized and the rate of growth of the industry has been the same as the rate of the overall labor force. The stability of this measure suggests that the performing arts labor force has reached a balancing point in the overall U.S. economy.

Performing artists continue to live and work in the largest metropolitan cities, with 20 percent of performing artists living in Los Angeles, New York, Chicago, Washington, D.C., and Boston. Half of all the professional artists in the United States live in thirty metropolitan cities. The Sun Belt cities have the most performers per capita; the western and southern states have seen the largest growth in performing artists recently. One third of performing artists are employed only part of the year, and it is likely that the profession will continue to trend toward seasonal employment. Performing artists are more likely to have college degrees than other members of the labor force; they receive relatively less compensation for their education level and are more likely to be self-employed.

Approximately 400,000 Americans identify the performing arts as their major area of employment, including a growing number of Hispanic people. In the United States from 1990 to 2005, the number of actors grew 16 percent; the number of musicians grew 14 percent; the number of dancers grew 36 percent; the number of producers and directors grew 14 percent; and the number of entertainers and performers (comedians, jugglers, puppeteers) grew 283 percent, with most of the increase taking place in Las Vegas.

The near-term outlook for the performing arts industry is unstable. The performing arts industry is reliant on the ability and willingness of consumers to spend disposable income, the ability of individuals and families to give philanthropic gifts, and the support of government agencies and private foundations. The global economic crisis of 2007-2009 created significant loss of performing arts funding from all of these sources. Most performing arts companies have experienced significant loss of revenues and budget difficulties in recent years. However, global economic recovery and further improvement of the U.S. economy may allow for modest growth in the performing arts industry in the long term. The outlook for international opportunities in the performing arts industry varies widely by region.

The U.S. Bureau of Labor Statistics projects that wage and salary jobs in arts, entertainment, and recreation in general are projected to grow about 15 percent over the 2008-2018 period, compared with 11 percent for all industries combined. Because of an overall global economic downturn and competition from other forms of entertainment, employment in the performing arts is not expected to grow significantly during the same period, 2008-2018.

Employment Advantages

According to the U.S. Bureau of Labor Statistics, the performing arts industry will not grow significantly in the 2010's. Employment in many of the performance sectors of the industry is likely to remain challenging in the near future; the advantages of the industry are likely to be found in the management positions within performing arts organizations. Performers in the United States may seek to increase the stability of their income through multiple sources of employment, often including the combination of performance employment with educational employment in institutions of higher or secondary education.

Opportunities outside the United States are more likely to grow in the near future; performing artists willing to relocate to the large cities of Europe, Asia, or the Middle East may find advantages. Large cities with concentrations of significant wealth, such as Monaco, Dubai, and Singapore for example, are likely to maintain significantly higher levels of funding for the performing arts early in the twenty-first century.

Annual Earnings

On average, the performing arts industry in the United States receives half of its annual income from tickets sales, 40 percent from donations and private grants, and 10 percent from government support. In the near future, domestic performing arts organizations will be negatively affected in all these revenue areas. *The Recession and the Arts*, published in 2009 by the Alliance for Arts, documented the

PROJECTED EMPLOYMENT FOR SELECTED OCCUPATIONS

Performing Arts

Employment		
2008	Projected 2018	Occupation
9,900	11,100	Actors
900	1,100	Artists and related workers
500	600	Fashion designers
200	300	Makeup artists, theatrical and performance
29,100	30,300	Musicians, singers, and related workers
5,100	5,700	Producers and directors

Source: U.S. Bureau of Labor Statistics, Industries at a Glance, Occupational Employment Statistics and Employment Projections Program.

effect of the economic recession on arts organizations throughout New York City. This document reveals that in 2008, 80 percent of arts organizations in New York City were reducing their budgets, and more than half were reducing staff. Of the fifteen largest organizations, 53 percent planned to lay off employees, and 80 percent planned to defer new hires. While this report focuses on the effects of the recession on the performing arts in New York City, many large metropolitan cities in North America experienced similar declines in earnings and budgets during 2009 and 2010.

Some experts believe that the 2007-2009 economic recession taught performing arts companies and executives difficult lessons about budget management, and that, in the long term, the performing arts will also likely be more resilient as a result.

RELATED RESOURCES FOR FURTHER RESEARCH

ACTORS' EQUITY ASSOCIATION
165 W 46th St.
New York, NY 10036
Tel: (212) 869-8530
Fax: (212) 719-9815
http://www.actorsequity.org

AMERICAN FEDERATION OF MUSICIANS
1501 Broadway, Suite 600
New York, NY 10036
Tel: (212) 869-1330
Fax: (212) 764-6134
http://www.afm.org

AMERICANS FOR THE ARTS
1 E 53rd St., 2d Floor
New York, NY 10022
Tel: (212) 223-2787
Fax: (212) 980-4857
http://www.artsusa.org

NATIONAL DANCE EDUCATION ASSOCIATION
8609 2d Ave., Suite 203-B
Silver Springs, MD 20910
Tel: (301) 585-2880

Fax: (301) 585-2888
http://www.ndeo.org

NATIONAL ENDOWMENT FOR THE ARTS
1100 Pennsylvania Ave. NW
Washington, DC 20506-0001
Tel: (202) 682-5400
Fax: (202) 682-5496
http://www.nea.gov

ABOUT THE AUTHOR

David Steffens is professor of percussion and coordinator of graduate studies at Oklahoma City University's Bass School of Music, principal percussionist of the Oklahoma City Philharmonic Orchestra, and a regular performer with Lyric Theater of Oklahoma and the Tulsa Symphony. As a performer, he has extensive experience in symphony orchestras, opera orchestra, Broadway shows, and as a chamber musician. He holds degrees from Central Michigan University, Michigan State University, and the Eastman School of Music at the University of Rochester. He has published previous articles focusing on the music of Edgar Varese, the Broadway show *Blast!*, Art Blakey, Gary Burton, Les Paul, Tupac Shakur, and Chick Webb.

FURTHER READING

Alliance for the Arts. *The Recession and the Arts: The Impact of the Economic Downturn on Nonprofit Cultural Groups in New York City.* New York: Author, 2009. Available at http://www.allianceforarts.org/images/EcImpactSurvey_2009report.pdf

Carson, Nancy. *Raising a Star: The Parent's Guide to Helping Kids Break into Theater, Film, Television, or Music.* New York: St. Martin's Press, 2005.

Gaquin, Deirdre. *Artists in the Workforce: 1990-2005.* Washington, D.C.: National Endowment for the Arts, 2008.

McCarthy, Kevin, et al. *The Performing Arts in a New Era.* Santa Monica, Calif.: Rand, 2001.

O'Neil, Brian. *Acting as a Business: Strategies for Success.* New York: Vintage Books, 2009.

Stein, Tobie, and Jessica Bathurst. *Performing Arts Management: A Handbook of Professional Practices.* New York: Allworth Press, 2008.

U.S. Bureau of Labor Statistics. *Career Guide to Industries*, 2010-2011 ed. http://www.bls.gov/oco/cg.

U.S. Census Bureau. North American Industry Classification System (NAICS), 2007. http://www.census.gov/cgi-bin/sssd/naics/naicsrch?chart=2007.

Vogel, Harold L. *Entertainment Industry Economics: A Guide for Financial Analysis.* New York: Cambridge University Press, 2007.

Webb, Duncan. *Running Theaters: Best Practices for Leaders and Managers.* New York: Allworth Press, 2004.

Themed Entertainment Industry

©Dreamstime.com

INDUSTRY SNAPSHOT

General Industry: Hospitality and Tourism
Career Cluster: Hospitality and Tourism
Subcategory Industries: Amusement and Theme Parks; Amusement Arcades; Themed Resorts and Casinos
Related Industries: Casino Industry; Hotels and Motels Industry; Museums and Cultural Institutions Industry; Restaurant Industry; Travel and Tourism Industry
Annual Domestic Revenues: $12 billion USD (PricewaterhouseCoopers, 2008)
Annual Global Revenues: $18 billion USD (StarParks, 2009)
NAICS Numbers: 72, 713

INDUSTRY DEFINITION

Summary

The themed entertainment industry is part of the third-largest industry in the world—tourism. Its hosts travelers, tourists, and others at concept-based attractions, such as zoos, aquariums, theme parks, museums, and similar venues. The industry also encompasses themed tourism, such as farm tours and ecological preserves. Theme-based entertainment is designed to draw like-minded tourists for short-term visits and stays. The industry is diverse, complex, and composed of a wide range of venues and attractions.

History of the Industry

Many components of the themed entertainment industry have long histories, dating back to antiquity. Rome, during the first century B.C.E. reign of Emperor Pompey, for example, had a number of circuses featuring animals, freak shows, acrobats, death-defying performances, and other attractions. The fall of the Roman Empire in the fifth century C.E. brought a relative disappearance of circuses, although traveling shows of circus performers were still seen around Europe during the Dark Ages that followed Rome's collapse.

More than a millennium later, Philip Astley, a member of the British cavalry, developed an interest in fancy riding and began performing a number of feats while riding a galloping horse. Occasionally, during his performances, clowns would interrupt the show with their own antics. Astley developed and perfected an iconic component of the modern circus: the ring, which he used to help contain the horses he rode. A contemporary and competitor of Astley, John Bill Ricketts, helped bring the act to the United States in the early nineteenth century. At the same time, the tradition of the traveling circus was reborn in America, with exotic animals, clowns, acrobats, stunt riding, and other performances. Over time, the circus retained these sorts of acts and became a profitable industry, traveling all over the country and the world and mounting sizable productions that could be transferred from one large venue to another.

The modern amusement park also has its roots in the ancient civilizations of the Mediterranean region. In fact, the ancient Greeks used such entertainment venues to generate political support. The Roman Empire made similar use of fairs, which combined selling and buying goods with entertainment and religious celebrations at permanent marketplaces. In the fifth century C.E., more fairs appeared in permanent locations in modern-day France and Italy. As was the case with their prede-

cessors, these newer fairs combined religious celebrations with commerce and entertainment.

The first amusement-park rides were introduced in the seventeenth century at pleasure gardens throughout Europe. However, rides such as the first incarnations of the roller coaster and the Ferris wheel did not appear until the late 1800's. (The first vertical roller coaster was introduced in Toledo, Ohio, and the Ferris wheel was unveiled at the Chicago World's Fair in 1893). By the beginning of the twentieth century, driven by the introduction of many new rides, amusement parks exploded into popularity in the United States after the openings of Coney Island and, later, Water Chutes Park in Chicago in the 1870's. By 1910, there were two thousand amusement parks in operation, although the number decreased after the beginning of the Great Depression. In 1952, children's filmmaker Walt Disney opened one of the

A child watches animals at the zoo. (©Ingrid Balabanova/Dreamstime.com)

most storied theme parks in the world, Disneyland Park in Anaheim, California.

Theme-based venues have been built on creating innovative attractions for visitors. Many, such as the former site of Alcatraz Prison in the San Francisco Bay, are designed to educate. Others, such as ethnic restaurants and performing arts venues, pay homage to various cultures and civilizations. Still others, such as film studios in California and Florida or the Guinness brewery in Ireland, focus on industries. In recent years, the industry has given rise to new forms of tourism, such as agritourism and ecotourism, which have helped redevelop the economies of many formerly war-torn and economically depressed countries.

The Industry Today

The themed entertainment industry has evolved into a vast, diverse, and cosmopolitan industry encompassing a broad range of other industries. Theme-based resorts are located throughout the world, and each country utilizes at least one or two sites as tourist attractions celebrating its culture and heritage. As it has throughout history, the theme-based industry seeks to entertain visitors; in many cases, it also seeks to educate, enlighten, and even inspire them.

There are a number of subsectors within the themed entertainment industry. The first of these may be categorized as amusement, gambling, and recreation. This subsector encompasses fairs, amusement parks, arcades, and some gambling facilities. In addition to the venues themselves, the subsector includes the vendors that supply the machinery and equipment in use at those venues. Amusement parks and similar venues vary in size and substance, depending on the target audience and the activity promoted. Some have theatrical themes, featuring characters and live performances, while others are geared toward activities themselves, such as sports and recreational pursuits, or provide rides and concessions to patrons.

Another subsector of the themed entertainment industry is museums and historical sites. This segment is included in the broader themed entertainment grouping because of the growing trend of injecting entertainment value into museums and similar attractions. Many such venues do not simply have stationary displays but feature interactive video displays, IMAX (Image MAXimum)

movie theaters, music and dance performances, historic reenactments, and other attractions that draw larger audiences than do traditional sites. Colonial Williamsburg, a living reconstruction of the colonial capital located in Virginia, is an example of a prominent tourist destination and historical area populated by reenactors and museums. It also features resort amenities such as spas, golfing, and shopping. This themed site reported $18.5 million in ticket revenue in 2008.

Hotels and restaurants are increasingly falling into the themed entertainment arena. Many hotels and resorts are self-contained destinations and have entertainment-oriented motifs—most notably, the casino resorts of Las Vegas, Nevada, and Atlantic City, New Jersey. The designs of these resorts are intended to draw like-minded tourists to the properties and keep them on site, where they may attend live shows, dine, and gamble. Many casinos and resorts are quite large, and they may have horticultural displays, canal cruises, or even safaris.

Natural attractions also fall under the heading of the themed entertainment industry. Zoos have long been staples of this field, drawing crowds daily to view and often physically interact with exotic animals. Aquariums are also popular venues. Like zoos and aquariums, safaris (which have become major contributors to the economies of previously underdeveloped countries in sub-Saharan Africa) also bring tourists into close encounters with wildlife in wide open areas. Safaris exist not just in Africa but also in the United States and other countries. Lastly, agritourism (or agrientertainment), which consists of vacations or outings to farms or ranches, has long been an established sector of the tourism trade in portions of Western Europe, and it is becoming increasingly popular in the United States. For example, according to a report from Rutgers University, agritourism generated an estimated $5.75 million in revenue for New Jersey in 2007, with one-fifth of Jersey farmers offering some form of entertainment. Additionally, Massachusetts has over 250 farm attractions open to the public throughout the state.

In the light of the marketability of themed entertainment, retailers are increasingly developing stores into tourist attractions. Some, such as outdoor retailing magnate L. L. Bean, offer fly-fishing and other outdoor training courses, free outdoor concerts, and other attractions to customers. In

A water park in Orlando, Florida. (©Dreamstime.com)

Minneapolis, Minnesota, the Mall of America features an enormous selection of retail shops—over four hundred stores as of 2010—and popular restaurants, along with a full amusement park, aquarium, miniature golf course, an "eco park," and numerous hotels.

The themed entertainment industry is driven by numerous forms of tourism. Families and vacationers seek not just one attraction but several activities while visiting a venue. Corporate travelers and sponsored functions tend to contribute considerably more to a given venue in terms of overall revenue, as they are often less concerned with bargain hunting than are frugal family travelers. Themed venues seeking to attract business travelers must incorporate conference and business services into their facilities.

The themed entertainment industry employs hundreds of thousands of people. In addition to executives such as corporate managers, the industry employs thousands of servers, cooks, actors, musicians, tour guides, and associated vendors. It is represented in nearly every country, with venues (both private and government-funded) bringing much-needed revenues to economically underdeveloped areas. In 2009, the U.S. amusement park industry generated approximately $12.9 billion in revenues at four hundred parks and attractions throughout the country. Although the United States remains the largest market for amusement parks and theme parks, a growing number of similar venues have been developing in large numbers in Europe and in East Asia. About 335 million visitors descended on American amusement parks, while in Europe 40 million people visited the continent's top-ten theme parks. The themed entertainment industry today is a broad-reaching collection of tourist attractions. Like any other industry, it has suffered through economic hardships, but its countless venues around the world continue to thrive and contribute heavily to regional economies with jobs and taxable revenues.

INDUSTRY MARKET SEGMENTS

In addition to so-called theme parks, many tourist and entertainment industries include components that participate in the themed entertainment industry. For example, some casinos are merely casinos, but many feature themes to differentiate themselves from their competitors, ranging from medieval knights in armor to ancient Egypt to pirates. Hotels, restaurants, and outdoor recreation venues all use themes to increase their brand power or otherwise introduce an element of fun and whimsy into their promotional endeavors. The following sections detail major subsectors of the themed entertainment industry.

Amusement Parks and Recreational Sites

Amusement parks, often also known as "theme parks," are the prototypical themed entertainment venues. Together with recreational sites, the largest are destinations, driving tourism to their locales and sometimes anchoring their local economies. Even small amusement parks contribute to the culture and atmosphere of their communities, and a single large carousel or Ferris wheel may be enough to turn a local pier into a popular destination for weekend and evening entertainment.

Potential Annual Earnings Scale. With the exception of management, employees at amusement parks are generally paid hourly, often at minimum wage. In 2008, amusement park attendants and recreational protective service personnel (such as lifeguards) earned between $8 and $9 per hour, while food service personnel earned an hourly wage between $9 and $10.

Clientele Interaction. Amusement parks and recreational sites are designed for use by large, diverse crowds. Employees at such venues are therefore in constant contact with the public, ensuring their safety while acting as entertainers and service personnel. People who work at amusement parks, carnivals, and recreational areas such as nature and theme parks must be able to work well with large volumes of people.

Amenities, Atmosphere, and Physical Grounds. Amusement parks and recreational sites are typically crowded, especially during vacation periods and weekends. Often, amusement parks and other themed sites offer a large number of attractions in close proximity to one another, such as food stands, stores, and amusement rides. Both types of venue require large amounts of open space, where amusements such as roller coasters, performance stages, and other relevant attractions may be constructed. Such space is also necessary for parking and transportation purposes.

Typical Number of Employees. Some recreational facilities employ only a few attendants full time but increase their workforce during summer months or holiday seasons. Others employ thousands of people, both in the front-lines of consumer interation and behind the scenes. Walt Disney World resort, near Orlando, Florida (considered the most visited resort in the world), employs over sixty-six thousand people, making it the largest single-site employer in the United States.

Traditional Geographic Locations. Amusement parks and recreational sites are usually located in areas frequented by tourists, such as coastal or warm-weather locales, or near popular metropolitan areas. For example, Disney's two main parks—Walt Disney World and Disneyland—are located in the heavily populated and warm-

The Ferris wheel is a common ride at amusement parks. (©Dreamstime.com)

weather areas of Florida and California, respectively. Such locations encourage tourists staying elsewhere to take day trips to the venues. Still others are located near highways, so that passing travelers may stop along their routes.

Pros of Working for an Amusement Park or Recreational Site. The atmosphere of amusement parks and recreational sites is typically festive, enjoyable, and, for the most part, full of friendly guests. In addition, a majority of these sites are outdoors and in open areas, giving workers regular access to fresh air and sunlight. Discounts on park merchandise and complimentary park passes are also typical benefits of amusement park employment.

Cons of Working for an Amusement Park or Recreational Site. With the exception of senior management, amusement park or recreational site workers generally earn low salaries (wages hover around the minimum wage level). Additionally, while the atmosphere is designed to entertain visitors, there are many occasions when guests are unruly or confrontational with one another and the staff. Furthermore, many parks and sites close for part of the year or inclement weather, making employment seasonal and sometimes unpredictable.

Costs

Payroll and Benefits: Senior management and executives in amusement park companies are paid salaries, but many other employees are hourly workers. Benefits vary, but the largest venues typically provide standard benefits to full-time workers at all levels.

Supplies: Amusement parks and recreational sites require a great deal of supplies of a wide variety. Depending on the size and nature of the attraction, such venues will need food and beverage services; heavy equipment and rides; prizes and merchandise; first-aid supplies; office supplies; feed for animals; electrical equipment; computer software and hardware; audiovisual systems and construction materials (for stages, booths, and other staging areas); and maintenance equipment.

External Services: Many rides and attractions at theme parks are built, maintained, and operated by external companies. Security may also be managed by private organizations, and any number of attractions may be operated by separate staff. Although food and beverages are sometimes prepared on-site, they may be brought into parks by external grocers and food and beverage personnel. Finally, many amusement parks contract road-repair crews and construction personnel to keep their facilities in operation.

Utilities: Amusement parks and recreational sites use a great deal of electricity in order to power rides and attractions and for nighttime operations. They also require a great deal of water, not just for restrooms and food and beverage services but for many water rides as well. Additionally, they require a number of separate telephone services and Internet connections for the purposes of both internal operations and guest services (such as emergency phones in parking lots and at help desks).

Taxes: By virtue of their size, amusement parks and similar recreational sites pay a considerable portion of their expenses to cover property taxes. They must also pay regional taxes, which may cover a number of areas, including public safety, health care coverage, and excessive utility usage. In some countries, entertainment taxes are levied on venues that host performers from other areas.

Museums and Historical Sites

Many museums are explicitly marketed as themed entertainment venues. These include small specialty and novelty museums, such as barbed-wire museums or dinosaur exhibits, as well as major cultural establishments. While large museums attempt to draw tourists to travel in order to visit them, smaller novelty sites cater primarily to those already "passing through" the area, and they are often situated at designated highway rest areas alongside restaurants and other services.

Potential Annual Earnings Scale. Curators are typically the highest-paid museum employees. In 2008, the average curator's salary was $48,000 per year. Archivists earned an average of $45,000 per year. At the lower end of the spectrum, tour guides and escorts earned about $22,000 per year.

Clientele Interaction. Museums are generally designed for large crowds. Most employees at these venues are expected to interact regularly with guests during the course of their workdays. The exceptions are maintenance personnel, surveillance

The Alamo in San Antonio, Texas, is an important historical site and museum. (©Sally Scott/Dreamstime.com)

security officers, and after-hours security and custodial staff. Recently, interactive displays have become a more frequent aspect of museum design, lessening employee interaction with visitors.

Amenities, Atmosphere, and Physical Grounds. The atmosphere of a museum or historical site is generally crowded but reserved in terms of guest behavior. Museums vary in size, from very small to multistory properties. Because displays can be very delicate, facilities tend to be very clean and organized, with strict rules for staff and visitors.

Typical Number of Employees. Some museums employ only a handful of full-time personnel, while others require dozens, if not hundreds, of employees to function. For example, the world's largest museum, the Smithsonian Institution in Washington, D.C., employs six thousand people working throughout nineteen museum facilities, nine research centers, and the National Zoo.

Traditional Geographic Locations. Museums and historical sites are found all over the world, although they tend to be located along or near road-

ways and other areas that attract visitors and passers-by. Most are located in heavily populated areas, such as metropolitan and suburban centers, in order to attract the maximum number of visitors.

Pros of Working for a Museum or Historical Site. Employees of museums and historical sites have access to their venues' exhibits and resources. Many of those who work at museums are themselves students of art, history, or the field explored by the museum.

Cons of Working for a Museum or Historical Site. Salaries for museum and historical site employees may be on the lower end of the spectrum. Museums are typically beholden to private donations, grants, and government budget earmarks, and when those monies are not contributed, the museum's personnel are at risk.

Costs

Payroll and Benefits: Large museums' staff are typically salaried, while smaller tourist venues and roadside displays are more likely to pay by the hour. Similarly, while major cultural institutions generally offer full benefits, smaller attractions may offer no benefits at all.

Supplies: Museums and historical sites require some hardware supplies, such as frame hangers, display materials, and other equipment. They also need cleaning supplies and office supplies and equipment, such as stationery and computers, as well as telecommunications equipment, research equipment, and preservation technology.

External Services: Museums and historic sites may use external vendors for cleaning and janitorial services, grounds maintenance (such as lawn care and snow plowing), and security. They may also use external services for Web site maintenance, marketing, advertising, and accounting.

Utilities: Museums and historical sites require basic utilities, such as electricity, water, and sewage. They also need multiple phone lines for Web-based interactive displays, public telephones, and internal office systems.

Taxes: A large percentage of museums and most historical sites are government-operated, -owned, or -subsidized. They are largely exempt from most federal, state, and local property and commercial income taxes. Private museums and sites may and typically do apply for nonprofit, tax-exempt status from the federal government as well.

Hotels and Restaurants

Many hotels and restaurants cultivate a clientele that is at least as interested in an establishment's theme as in its amenities. Such themes involve uniforms or costumes for employees, interior design, and thematically appropriate names for dishes, rooms, and so on. These types of establishments, while sometimes of high quality, often expend

A fife and drum corps at Colonial Williamsburg. (AP/Wide World Photos)

more effort on creating an atmosphere of fun than they do on luxury per se.

Potential Annual Earnings Scale. Hotels' and restaurants' general managers are typically their highest-paid employees, with senior managers just below general managers on the salary scale. According to the U.S. Bureau of Labor Statistics (BLS), the median annual salary for a general or operations manager in 2009 was $110,550. At the lowest end of the salary scale is the service staff, including dishwashers and housekeepers, who typically earn the minimum wage.

Clientele Interaction. The purpose of hotels and restaurants, particularly those within the themed entertainment industry, is to provide a direct service to customers. Client interaction for workers in this subsector is thus constant. Workers in the industry must demonstrate excellent interpersonal skills and the ability to show patience and courtesy to large numbers of diverse guests and customers.

Amenities, Atmosphere, and Physical Grounds. Themed hotels and restaurants are professional, service-oriented facilities designed to manage large groups of people. Their atmosphere is therefore usually high-paced and diverse, as employees must work as a team to handle groups with varying aims, whether it be dining, gambling, or lodging. Employees in this segment tend to work long, demanding hours in their respective positions.

Typical Number of Employees. Some casino hotels employ hundreds if not thousands of employees, while some independent themed restaurants employ fewer than one hundred people.

Traditional Geographic Locations. Themed entertainment hotels and restaurants are found all over the world, in major cities as well as rural areas where real estate is more easily obtained. Typically, however, such properties are located near transportation networks, such as a major highway, an airport, or any area with access to public transportation; such convenience ensures that guests may easily travel to and from the property.

Pros of Working for a Hotel or Restaurant. Themed hotels and restaurants are dynamic working environments, often with exciting, high-profile guests and celebrities on-site. For servers, game-table attendants, and other employees who rely on tips to supplement their regular hourly wages, the potential for higher tips from these clients and guests is greater than may be found at other properties.

Cons of Working for a Hotel or Restaurant. The dynamic in a themed hotel or restaurant is often intense and high-pressure, as guest demands are often greater than in other properties. Also, although the potential for tips at such locations is higher, many employees still do not earn large paychecks unless they work long hours.

Costs

Payroll and Benefits: Hotels and restaurants pay hourly wages or annual salaries, depending on the position. The hourly wage for tipped employees may be at or even below the minimum wage, as they may be expected to earn the bulk of their income from tips. Benefit packages range from generous to nonexistent.

Supplies: The supply needs of a themed hotel or restaurant are numerous and significant. They may include daily food and beverage deliveries, as well as daily linen deliveries. These businesses also require audiovisual and stage equipment for live shows, as well as gaming supplies (such as dice, slot machines, and playing cards) for any gambling facilities. Additionally, they need internal office supplies and hardware in order to handle credit-card payments, conduct sales and marketing activities, and perform other related endeavors.

External Services: Themed hotels and restaurants use a number of external services and vendors. They may contract with linen and laundry services, casino-equipment vendors, and marketing and public relations firms as part of their routine and external operations. Those properties that feature live entertainment generally employ visiting entertainers, although some have permanent "lounge acts." Additionally, hotels and restaurants may outsource any number of their internal operations, including housekeeping, security, maintenance, game attendants, and financial management services.

Utilities: Hotels and restaurants use a great deal of electricity to power not just internal lighting but also casino and other attraction-related machinery and air-circulation systems. They also have water and sewage requirements and use oil or natural gas to heat the building and water. In many cases, hotels and restaurants purchase "green energy" credits to help power their systems, using solar, wind, or hydroelectricity instead of conventional energy.

Taxes: Themed hotels and restaurants are required to pay commercial income and property taxes. Many casinos are required to pay an additional percentage of their profits to state governments. Hotels and restaurants must also pay unemployment insurance taxes and other state and local taxes.

Natural Attractions

Natural attractions include venues for experiencing nature, such as parks and reserves, as well as artificial venues that feature wild animals, such as zoos and, aquariums. As themed entertainment, they range from the sublime to the ridiculous, and, like museums, they vary from major tourist attractions to roadside curiosities that cater only to coincidental passers-by.

Potential Annual Earnings Scale. According to the BLS, the median 2009 annual salary for a zoologist was $60,670, while PayScale.com estimates the average park ranger salary at between $35,197 and $46,549.

Clientele Interaction. The level of client interaction for employees of natural attractions such as zoos and aquariums depends on the position itself. Many veterinary and animal-care professionals working at such venues tend to work with the animals behind closed doors, although some give demonstrations of animal care to the general public. Tour guides and animal handlers (at live animal displays) have a higher degree of public interaction.

Amenities, Atmosphere, and Physical Grounds. Natural attractions, such as zoos, aquariums, and parks, are generally outdoor, open areas (or, in the case of aquariums, large, enclosed structures) designed to handle large flows of visitors. They are designed to provide the appearance of close interaction between people and the animals or vistas found at such sites, while at the same time maintaining public safety and the integrity of the attraction. Employees must be able to handle large crowds of tourists, including many families with young children.

Typical Number of Employees. The number of employees at a natural attraction depends on the size of the attraction and the need for profes-

sional care and oversight. For example, some state parks employ only a handful of individuals, who collect entrance fees and sell bottled water and gifts. Larger zoos and aquariums, by contrast, may have hundreds of employees working on every operational system from animal care and feeding to engineering and waste removal.

Traditional Geographic Locations. Natural attractions are typically found in open areas or in large structures in or near major cities and population centers. Some, such as safaris, are located in remote locations to minimize disruptions to resident animals. Open spaces are also conducive to providing enough space and for the property to expand if necessary.

Pros of Working for a Natural Attraction. Natural attractions such as zoos, aquariums, and national and state parks are often operated by students of the natural sciences or animal lovers, who gain hands-on experience in animal care and environmental protection. The open-air environments of zoos and parks are also beneficial to those who enjoy the outdoors. Marine biologists have an opportunity to work with exotic species from all over the world within a confined environment, yet they may be called upon to travel locally to retrieve or treat a distressed animal in nearby waters.

Cons of Working for a Natural Attraction. Salaries paid by zoos, aquariums, and parks are often lower than those paid in other industry sectors, in part because of the limited financial contributions they may receive from government and private donors. In some cases, the working environment is unpleasant, as employees may be called upon to clean animal waste or tend to unruly visitors.

Costs

Payroll and Benefits: Government employees, such as those at national and state parks, usually earn annual salaries, although part-time employees, such as park docents, may be paid hourly. Government benefits are often more generous than those in the private sector, in part in order to compensate for the fact that salaries are often lower. Employees of private attractions earn annual or hourly wages, depending on the position.

Supplies: The supply needs of a natural attraction are many. Among these supplies are animal and plant feed, medical supplies (for humans and animals alike), and maintenance equipment. Interactive venues such as zoos and aquariums also require computer technology for displays, as well as for internal operations. Most sites also need motor vehicles and other forms of transportation, and sites with wild and caged animals need to prepare and protect against any animal escape.

External Services: Natural attractions may use a number of external vendors, including accountants, Web site consultants, and marketing consultants. Some use independent security teams, food and beverage companies, custodial workers, and uniform vendors. They may also use private companies to handle garbage and animal-waste disposal, as well as visitor shuttle and transportation services.

Utilities: Natural attractions such as zoos, aquariums, and nonenclosed parks utilize a number of utilities. Lighting and heating the enclosures of an aquarium or zoo exhibit, for example, require significant expenditure on electricity, oil, natural gas, or other fuel sources. Additionally, such facilities may require multiple phone lines for both visitors and employees.

Taxes: Most open spaces used for recreation, such as national and state parks, are operated by the federal or state government and are exempt from income and property taxes. Private zoos, aquariums, and similar venues may also be exempt from these taxes, although they must register with the government as nonprofit, 501(c)(3) organizations in order to achieve tax-exempt status.

ORGANIZATIONAL STRUCTURE AND JOB ROLES

The organizational structure of the themed entertainment industry is often specific to each industry subsector. However, there is a wide range of general positions that span the industry, each of which plays an important role in ensuring that visitors receive the highest quality of services and have enjoyable visits.

The following umbrella categories apply to the organizational structure of businesses in the themed entertainment industry:

- Management
- Public Safety
- Guest Services
- Sales and Marketing
- Entertainment
- Maintenance

Management

Managers establish and implement policies, set goals and strategies, assign tasks to subordinate personnel, draft and implement budgets, and review all data and information that is to be issued to the public. In most situations, they also serve as the public face of their venues, making public statements on behalf of the property or attraction to the media, the government, and the public at large. They also raise money to support their venues, particularly in the case of museums, zoos, aquariums, and historical sites, as these venues are often nonprofit and rely on private donations and government appropriations. Managers oversee large groups of diverse employees, ensuring that each function is operating smoothly. The sizes of their workforces vary, from a small handful to hundreds or thousands of employees performing a wide array of tasks.

The management of a themed entertainment attraction generally earns the highest salaries of any individuals directly employed by the attraction. Managers are generally well educated in the operation of their facilities, often having built their careers by working from within the company (in some cases, from the bottom rungs of the workforce). Many are college-educated, and some have advanced degrees such as a master of business administration (M.B.A.) in fields such as accounting, human resources, or hospitality management.

Management occupations may include the following:

- General Manager
- Chief Operating Officer (COO)
- President/Chief Executive Officer (CEO)
- Chief Financial Officer (CFO)
- Curator
- Director

Public Safety

Public safety at themed entertainment complexes and attractions is managed by a collective team of security specialists and professionals. Public safety personnel oversee the security of the entire venue, eject guests for unruly or unlawful behavior, enforce company rules for guest and staff decorum, and safeguard against trespassers during and after business hours. They also manage evacuations and other emergency responses as they arise.

Public safety officers generally have strong backgrounds in law enforcement and security. Many have experience in the military or are former police officers, so they have formal training in security procedures and protocols. They must coordinate with law enforcement agencies when they encounter multijurisdictional situations, such as bomb threats, tracking dangerous individuals, and other security threats. They must also be experienced in dealing with large crowds, able both to redirect crowds during emergencies and to pay careful attention to individuals' behavior amid such crowds.

Public safety salaries are dependent on the size of the property and the nature of the work. For example, a night watchperson at a small museum may earn less than a security guard at a large casino resort as a result of the comparatively lower threat level at the former facility. However, every public security officer and employee is expected to ensure the safety of customers and guests, as well as of the property itself.

Public safety occupations may include the following:

- Security Director
- Security Guard
- Night Watchperson
- Security Specialist
- Park Ranger

Guest Services

Guest services personnel address the needs of customers and visitors. They are part of a diverse series of occupational groups, such as check-in, reservations, special services (including concierge and room service), tour guidance, and customer complaints. As their duties are varied, so too are their backgrounds. Some have college educations in such disciplines as hospitality management, history, and environmental protection and management. Their primary concern is directly interfacing with guests and customers, handling large numbers of visitors, including demanding and unruly guests. Thus, they must have strong diplomatic and interpersonal skills. Most guest services staff are paid on an hourly basis, although some earn yearly salaries. Many also receive tips from customers.

Guest services occupations may include the following:

- Concierge
- Server/Bartender
- Front-Desk Manager
- Reservations Manager
- Maitre d'
- Tour Guide
- Administrative Assistant

Sales and Marketing

Sales and marketing personnel develop strategies for attracting large groups and sponsors to their venues. They create public relations campaigns, assemble attractive visitor packages, and seek to draw large groups in addition to individual visitors. Salespeople try to book large, corporate groups in particular, as such groups tend to pay more to stay in rooms, dine, and participate in other activities.

Sales and marketing professionals are generally well educated and experienced in their respective industries. Most have undergraduate degrees in business, marketing, or similar fields and have spent significant time working within their fields. They must be familiar with all of the most up-to-date technologies relevant to their fields in order to ensure that any sales and marketing campaign reaches the maximum number of potential clients and guests. Many sales and marketing personnel are given base salaries with sales quotas and performance incentives (such as bonuses), while others are offered simple salaries on an hourly or yearly basis.

Sales and marketing occupations may include the following:

- Sales Director
- Sales Manager
- Marketing and Communications Manager

- Marketing Coordinator
- Administrative Assistant
- Intern

Entertainment

Themed entertainment venues and attractions often feature performers and artists who are either contracted within the company or visit the establishment for limited-run shows. These individuals, as well as their stage production crews, assemble and perform a wide range of shows for children and adults. They come from a wide range of backgrounds: Many are formally trained in music, theater, or the arts, while others have no formal training. They are supported by choreographers, sound and lighting technicians, stage construction crews, and artistic designers, among many others.

Entertainment occupations may include the following:

- Dancer
- Musician
- Singer
- Performance Artist
- Comedian
- Stage Manager
- Stagehand
- Choreographer
- Director
- Lighting Technician
- Sound Technician
- Set Designer
- Costumer

Maintenance

Maintenance personnel ensure that the many technological systems of a themed entertainment venue are operational. They replace and repair malfunctioning equipment and ensure that heating and air-conditioning systems are functioning properly. In some cases, they may work with law enforcement and fire departments to locate and isolate public safety threats, such as fires and electrical short circuits, and they help monitor and provide for evacuation routes.

Maintenance personnel come from a wide range of backgrounds applicable to the venue at which they are working. Some have vocational training in such fields as carpentry, plumbing, electrical repair, or HVAC (heating, ventilating, and air-conditioning) operation. Others have formal educations in engineering and handle large-scale repairs and renovations. They may specialize in upgrading on-site systems while causing minimal disruption to guests. The nature of the work performed by maintenance personnel is a major determinant of their salaries. Some are hired on a contract term, while others are paid full time on an hourly or annual basis.

PROJECTED EMPLOYMENT FOR SELECTED OCCUPATIONS

Amusement Parks

Employment		
2008	Projected 2018	Occupation
3,200	3,300	Actors, producers, and directors
30,700	32,200	Amusement and recreation attendants
900	900	Art and design occupations
8,100	7,800	Building and grounds cleaning and maintenance occupations
23,100	24,700	Food and beverage serving workers
800	900	Musicians and singers
15,100	15,800	Retail sales workers
200	300	Tailors, dressmakers, and sewers
200	200	Tour and travel guides

Source: U.S. Bureau of Labor Statistics, Industries at a Glance, Occupational Employment Statistics and Employment Projections Program.

Maintenance occupations may include the following:

- Engineer
- Environmental Services Specialist
- Carpenter
- Electrician
- Plumber
- Apprentice

INDUSTRY OUTLOOK

Overview

The themed entertainment industry is one of the more diverse groups of businesses in the twenty-first century global economy. Although its primary focus is tourism, the industry spans a wide range of attraction types within several other industries, including lodging, amusements, parks and recreation, dining, and historical preservation, among others. This diversity gives the themed entertainment industry staying power in the light of the large volumes of visitors who frequent each establishment during the course of a given year.

However, like other segments of the tourism industry, themed entertainment properties and venues are vulnerable to economic downturns. Tourists may be less inclined to stay at themed resorts, opting instead to vacation locally or to drive shorter distances for recreational diversions. As is the case with many other industries (such as retail), themed entertainment venues may offer special packages or reduced rates and entrance fees in order to attract customers. These special incentives and rates have helped generate business, although industry profits did not spike because of reduced revenues. Between 2004 and 2007, for example, the amusement park industry saw 13 million more visitors, but the revenues generated by that increase were modest: The industry realized an increase of about $1 billion during that four-year period.

Despite the global downturn of 2008-2009, Asian markets are set to expand. Universal Studios, anticipating this potential has expanded to Singapore, while the first Legoland in Asia is set to open in 2012 and Disney is preparing to construct a theme park in Shanghai, China. In addition, while attendance at the top twenty-five theme parks in the world has declined in recent years, according to the Themed Entertainment Association, the ten most visited park destinations in the Asia-Pacific region have seen an increase in attendance.

Overall, the outlook for the themed entertainment industry is strong, especially in the light of the general stability created by the industry's diverse composition. According to the International Association of Amusement Parks and Attractions, the top twenty parks in Europe experienced a growth rate of 1.1 percent in 2008; visits to the top twenty parks in North America remained level from 2007 through 2008 (after growing nearly 4 percent from 2005 to 2007); the top fifteen water parks in the United States showed an attendance increase of 1.8 percent in 2008; and, overall, the total attendance for the top twenty-five global theme parks was 189.6 million in 2008, down only 0.3 percent from the previous year.

The industry is projected to add more jobs, up to about 31 percent more, by 2016, with all position types (from management to attendants and servers) seeing double-digit increases in availability. Wages and salaries, on the other hand, are expected to continue to be on the low end of the payroll spectrum. The volume of the workforce helps keep pay at a low rate, and, despite the influx of revenues from guests, the growing number of employees at such venues will result in increased revenues being distributed among a larger complement of employees. Still, the themed entertainment industry continues to grow and diversify, offering potential employees a wide range of venues and interest areas that meet their personal and professional tastes. Although the industry is subject to economic flux, it is forecast to continue its growth and attractiveness to tourists in every part of the world.

Employment Advantages

The themed entertainment industry is a vast network of venues that stand apart from standard hotels, restaurants, and parks. The industry offers consumers exciting and unique experiences. As a result, those who work in this field are likely to work in an area that is both exciting and stimulating.

Additionally, there is a great deal of opportunity within the industry for employees to experience upward professional mobility. Many of the industry's senior leaders, such as general managers, executive directors, curators, and even venue owners, began their careers as doorpersons, tour guides, or servers. Those at the lower end of the organizational hierarchy may, drawing from their experiences at this level, climb the ladder consistently over the course of their careers.

Adding to the benefits of employment within this industry is the fact that themed entertainment, while already vast and diverse, will likely continue to expand and succeed in the years to come. As parks, resorts, and attractions continue to draw visitors, more job opportunities in more venues will likely become available.

Annual Earnings

Amusement parks in the United States generate about $12 billion annually, while American zoos and similar attractions generate about $9 billion (although many are nonprofit organizations and do not report profits and revenues generated against expenses). Many highly concentrated and competitive niche industries also participate in the industry. The ski resort industry, for example, realized an annual revenue of $200 billion in 2007 from approximately 350 companies at over four hundred locations.

Like other segments of the global economy, the themed entertainment industry is susceptible to recessions and other forms of economic stagnation. Revenue for the Walt Disney Company's Parks and Resorts division in fiscal 2008, for example, decreased an estimated 7 percent, to $10.7 billion, despite attendance trending up (a factor largely attributed to discounted prices). Additionally, in January, 2009, Disney was reported to have offered over six hundred buyouts to theme park and resort managers, and it cut an estimated nineteen hundred jobs the following April, the majority in Orlando. Other parks have declared bankruptcy in response to low attendance and increased debt. These include Six Flags, which owns twenty amusement parks, most in the United States.

Nonetheless, the diversity of the themed entertainment industry, as well as its sheer size, gives it an ability to weather periodic declines in revenues. It is predicted that the industry will continue to grow over the next decade in terms of venue volume, employment, and revenues generated.

RELATED RESOURCES FOR FURTHER RESEARCH

AMERICAN ASSOCIATION OF MUSEUMS
1575 Eye St. NW, Suite 400
Washington, DC 20005
Tel: (202) 289-1818
Fax: (202) 289-6578
http://www.aam-us.org

AMERICAN GAMING ASSOCIATION
1299 Pennsylvania Ave. NW
Washington, DC 20004
Tel: (202) 552-2675
http://www.americangaming.org

INTERNATIONAL ASSOCIATION OF AMUSEMENT
PARKS AND ATTRACTIONS
1448 Duke St.
Alexandria, VA 22314
Tel: (703) 836-4800
Fax: (703) 836-6742
http://www.iaapa.org

INTERNATIONAL HOTEL AND RESTAURANT
ASSOCIATION
41 Ave. General Guisan (Lausanne)
1009 Pully
Switzerland
Tel: 41-21-711-4283
http://www.ih-ra.com

SMITHSONIAN INSTITUTION
P.O. Box 37012
SI Building, Room 153, MRC 010
Washington, DC 20013-7012
Tel: (202) 633-1000
http://www.si.edu

THEMED ENTERTAINMENT ASSOCIATION
175 E Olive Ave., Suite 100
Burbank, CA 91502-0126
Tel: (818) 843-8497
Fax: (818) 843-8477
http://Info@themeit.com

WORLD ASSOCIATION OF ZOOS AND AQUARIUMS
Lindenrain 3
3012 Bern
Switzerland

Tel: 41-31-300-2030
Fax: 41-31-300-2031
http://www.waza.org

ABOUT THE AUTHOR

Michael P. Auerbach has over sixteen years of professional experience in public policy and administration, economic development, and the hospitality industry. He is a 1993 graduate of Wittenberg University and a 1999 graduate of the Boston College Graduate School of Arts and Sciences. He is a veteran of state and federal government, having worked for seven years in the Massachusetts legislature and four years as a federal government contractor.

FURTHER READING

Adams, Judith A. *The American Amusement Park Industry: A History of Technology and Thrills.* Boston: Twayne, 1991.

Clavé, Salvador Anton. *The Global Theme Park Industry.* Cambridge, Mass.: CABI, 2007.

Davis, Susan G. *Spectacular Nature: Corporate Culture and the Sea World Experience.* Berkeley: University of California Press, 1997.

Dickey, Robert. *Dynasty of Dimes: Eccentric Entrepreneur Engineers Empire.* St. Augustine, Fla.: St. Margaret, 2009.

Harris, Richard. *Early Amusement Parks of Orange County.* Charleston, S.C.: Arcadia, 2008.

Indeed.com. "Zookeeper Salaries." http://www.indeed.com/salary/Zoo-Keeper.html.

Kurtti, Jeff. *Walt Disney's Imagineering Legends: And the Genesis of the Disney Theme Park.* New York: Disney Editions, 2008.

Marketdata Enterprises. *The U.S. Amusement and Theme Parks Industry: A Marketing, Operational and Competitive Analysis.* Tampa, Fla.: Author, 1999.

Merryman, John Henry, and Albert Edward Elsen. *Law, Ethics, and the Visual Arts.* 4th ed. New York: Kluwer Law International, 2002.

Telotte, J. P. *The Mouse Machine: Disney and Technology.* Urbana: University of Illinois Press, 2008.

U.S. Bureau of Labor Statistics. *Career Guide to Industries,* 2010-2011 ed. http://www.bls.gov/oco/cg.

U.S. Census Bureau. North American Industry Classification System (NAICS), 2007. http://www.census.gov/cgi-bin/sssd/naics/naicsrch?chart=2007.

U.S. Department of Commerce. International Trade Administration. Office of Trade and Industry Information. Industry Trade Data and Analysis. http://ita.doc.gov/td/industry/otea/OTII/OTII-index.html.

Toys and Games Industry

INDUSTRY SNAPSHOT

General Industry: Manufacturing

Career Cluster: Manufacturing

Subcategory Industries: Action Figures Manufacturing; Children's and Adult Games (Except Coin-Operated) Manufacturing; Children's Vehicles (Except Bicycles and Metal Tricycles) Manufacturing; Craft and Hobby Kits and Sets Manufacturing; Doll and Stuffed Toy Manufacturing; Doll Clothing Manufacturing; Electronic Toys and Games Manufacturing; Kites Manufacturing; Rubber Balls and Marbles Manufacturing; Structural Toy Sets and Science Kits Manufacturing; Toy and Hobby Models Manufacturing; Toy Furniture and Household-type Equipment Manufacturing; Toy Rifles Manufacturing; Toys Manufacturing

Related Industries: Casino Industry; Computer Software Industry; Video, Computer, and Virtual Reality Games Industry

Annual Domestic Revenues: $21.47 billion USD (NPD Group, 2009)

Annual International Revenues: $38.4 billion USD (Data Monitor, 2008)

Annual Global Revenues: $60.8 billion USD (Marketline; Data Monitor, 2008)

NAICS Number: 33993

INDUSTRY DEFINITION

Summary

The toys and games industry manufactures games, toys, and children's vehicles (except bicycles and metal tricycles), including toys and games for adults. Key functions for industry manufacturers include purchasing raw materials, designing prototypes, ramping up production of market-ready products, and marketing those finished products to wholesalers and retailers. The industry has an international presence, with the United States accounting for about one-third of the global market share.

History of the Industry

Archaeologists have found evidence of ancient toys and games in the form of dolls, balls, and activities from five thousand years ago. Early toys were not manufactured on a large scale. Generally, toys and games were created by individuals for specific children or to be sold at fairs or by travelling peddlers.

The early beginnings of the modern toys and games industry emerged in sixteenth century Central Europe as clusters of German villages became specialists in the creation of particular toys. For example, in the mid-1700's, the town of Nuremberg became known for a mass-produced, uniformly designed kitchen playset that was affordable to middle-class families. By the end of the nineteenth century, the Industrial Revolution expanded into the toy industry as toy production moved from handmade creations in homes and small shops to machine-made toys in factories. This movement was assisted by the introduction of new, inexpensive materials such as papier-mâché, rubber, and sheet metal that could be utilized by the new machines.

The United States industrialized the toy business after the Civil War; however, many toys were produced only as sidelines to other products. One early manufacturer, J. & E. Stevens, originally focused on the manufacture of cast-iron hardware and hammers and then added cast-iron mechanical banks in 1870 as a third product line. Toys were marketed to parents, not children, and meant to be educational and durable. Most toys in this era were sold through local general stores or catalogs, such as that of Sears, Roebuck, and Company.

In 1900, Germany led the global toys and games industry, exporting 75 percent of the toys and games it made. One-quarter of Germany's toy exports at this time were to the United States. However, American toy and game manufacturing was in the process of transformation. In the 1880's, Morton Converse made his rocking-horse, wooden-playset, and puzzle factory into the "Nuremberg of America," using modern machinery, a formal planning department, and a trained, specialized workforce. Innovations such as increased mechanization, new materials, and new production methods also allowed U.S. toy and game manufacturers to get toys and games to consumers quickly. Toys began to move from a sideline into a main product line.

Stuffed toys remain popular with children. (©Elena Elisseeva/Dreamstime.com)

As toy and game manufacturing grew, stores focusing on toys and games exclusively also became a presence in the retail market. By 1908, F. A. O. Schwarz, one of the first retail toy stores, expanded into a large toy and game business. In 1875, Macy's created the first department-store toy section. Woolworth's began selling toys purchased directly from Germany at a cheaper price than department stores did. After 1910, toy companies began advertising specific toys in family, women's, children's, and do-it-yourself periodicals. The wholesale value of U.S. toys and games rose from $8.29 million in 1899 to $70.17 million in 1919. During this era, U.S. toy manufacturers founded the Toy Manufacturers of the United States and began a trade journal called *Playthings*.

Board games are played by children and adults. (©Dreamstime.com)

World War I ushered in an environment of patriotism and isolationism that was instrumental in the next major change in American toy manufacturing. During World War I, European imports of toys were halted. In 1939, restrictions were lifted on European imports; however, stiff tariffs were levied on foreign toys. Between tariff-increased prices of European toys and games and U.S. toy and game makers' appeals to purchase American-made goods, buying American toys became a patriotic act. By the time of World War II, 95 percent of toys purchased in the United States were American-made. Although non-U.S. toymakers would recapture some of the market over time, toy and game manufacturing in the United States had become a mature industry.

World War II found toys labeled nonessential manufactured products. Restrictions were placed on the use of metal and rubber. Accordingly, several toy and game businesses directed their factories to produce military equipment and other items needed for the war effort. Although some companies replaced metal and rubber components with wood, the toys and games industry stagnated in the United States.

After weathering the restrictions on manufacturing during World War II, the 1950's brought about significant expansion in the toys and games industry. This expansion stemmed from the perfect storm conditions of a dramatic rise in personal disposable income, increased leisure time, the so-called baby boom, and the introduction of television. More disposable income and increased time to fill left room for toy and game manufacturers to suggest purchasing their entertaining toys and games to make that time fun and productive for children and adults. Television brought about a major revolution in the toys and games industry in the 1960's, as it allowed toy and game manufacturers such as Mattel and Hasbro to market directly to their major consumers: children. Marketers quickly learned effective strategies in promotion, packaging, and product-line expansion to increase children's desire for their products. However, television advertising required more capital than other forms of advertising, making it more difficult for small manufacturers to get the word out about their products. Large toy and game manufacturers with their larger budgets and effective marketing teams pushed many of the small toy and game companies out of the market.

In the late 1980's and early 1990's, many American toy manufacturing operations were moved to China and other overseas locations that offered reduced labor costs and decreased government regulation. However, after a series of Chinese-

Toy cars are often made to closely resemble real cars.
(©Alain Lacroix/Dreamstime.com)

manufactured-toy recalls in 2007 related to lead-based paints on toys, concerns were raised about the safety standards maintained by overseas manufacturing plants. To address safety concerns, the Consumer Product Safety Improvement Act of 2008 (CPSIA) was signed into law. The law increased the budget of the Consumer Product Safety Commission (CPSC), imposed new testing and documentation requirements for manufacturers of toys, clothes, jewelry, shoes, electronics, and other children's products; increased penalties for violating the consumer product safety law; and set new acceptable levels of several substances such as lead.

The CPSIA has affected all sizes of toy and game companies, in that it requires all manufacturers to implement new, and often expensive, testing, tracking, and quality assurance measures. Many small U.S. manufacturers complained of what they saw as unfair inclusion in the stringent CPSIA test-

ing and tracking standards and felt that the law decreased their ability to remain in business. At the same time, many small and midsize toy companies that continued operations saw an upsurge in revenue, as customers focused on purchasing American-made toys and games, often at a premium cost, to avoid the recalls and perceived safety issues of foreign products.

The Industry Today

Today, the international toys and games industry is an integral part of the global economy with revenues of $60.8 billion in 2008. The U.S. industry accounted for about 36.8 percent, or approximately $22.4 billon, of that revenue. The growth of the industry is tied to the size of disposable personal income and the effectiveness of promotional programs at capturing that income.

The size of toy and game manufacturers ranges from independent inventors with one product to smaller companies specializing in a certain toy or game to large international corporations such as Mattel and Hasbro, which produce a wide variety of products. The industry's top fifty companies generate about 75 percent of overall toy and game revenue in the United States. Toys are sold in retailers such as specialist toy stores, department stores (traditional and discount), and supermarkets. The toys and games manufactured continue to fall into categories such as arts and crafts, building and other learning and hobby products, dolls, jigsaw puzzles, board and card games, action figures, die cast models, soft toys, and outdoor and sports-related toys and games. However, the kinds of toys in these categories are constantly changing in response to an influx of new creative ideas, as well as the need to meet customer demand.

The most common distribution method for toys and games begins with the manufacturers, who sell their products to wholesalers or retailers. The wholesalers sell to retailers. Then, retailers sell directly to consumers. Although large retail stores such as Walmart, Target, and Toys"R"Us control a large portion of the toys and games market, specialty toy stores compete by emphasizing convenience, top-notch service, and quality products.

The revenue of companies in the toys and games industry is highly seasonal. Despite attempts to increase year-round toy and game purchases, the year-end holiday time during November and

December continues to be the most important for businesses to generate revenue. Many industry analysts focus on the sales during this timeframe to predict future earning and industry stability. Accordingly, many new toy designs and product lines follow a production and marketing schedule that tries to create excitement prior to the holiday season so that the items will be in high demand by the end of the year. Nearer to the actual holiday season, toy and game manufacturers will adjust prices and market their most popular products extensively.

Toys and games continue to be used in the entertainment and education of adults and children. The toys and games market has developed several niches to address commercial trends. For example, infant and preschool toy sales now generate 15.8 percent of the U.S. toys and games market's total revenues. This toy category grew from parental demands for early stimulation and learning toys to assist infants and toddlers. In order to meet consumer demand for effective toys, developmental and behavioral study results have become standard in the toy development and design process. Following environmentally friendly trends and more parental agitating, the manufacturing market has developed green lines of toys that focus on the use of recycled woods and plastics as the raw material to create standard toys such as trucks and puzzles. The green toy lines have even entered large-market retailers such as Toys"R"Us. In a move to address concerns about purchase of toys during a turbulent economy, other manufacturers have focused on the production of toy and game lines that produce economical toys, costing $10 to $20, in addition to more expensive luxury toy items.

Beyond stand-alone toy lines, toy and game manufacturers have also created character-focused toys and games that take advantage of the popularity of particular images from books, television shows, and films. For example, the Sesame Street character Elmo can be found on products that range from stuffed animals to play sets, puzzles,

Toys that feature Hispanic characters such as Dora the Explorer are increasingly popular as manufacturers vie for the shopping dollars of the fastest growing population in the U.S. (AP/Wide World Photos)

and board games. Likewise, a toy and game company may work with a television production team to create a cartoon or show based on a new toy. Through use of a known character, manufacturers can capture the interest of consumers already familiar with the character. After creation of a successful image or character, toys and games can increase their revenue by licensing that image to other toy and game companies, as well as clothing and shoe companies or party goods stores.

A very important component of the toys and games industry over the past two decades has been adjustment to the changes in technology and consumer demand. The increased use of the Internet and decreased price of electronics has stimulated toy and game manufacturers to think creatively about ways to join traditional toys and games with modern technology. Innovative thinking was particularly important as the growth of the computer games market decreased the sales of traditional toys.

INDUSTRY MARKET SEGMENTS

The toy and game businesses range from small start-up companies specializing in a certain toy or game to giant, multinational corporations such as Mattel and Hasbro, which produce a wide variety of products. The positions of these companies in the industry are dynamic, with small companies being acquired by large companies or midsize sized businesses expanding over time.

The following sections provide a comprehensive breakdown of each of these different segments.

Small Businesses

Small toy and game companies earn average annual revenues of $1.0 million to $3.6 million and have fewer than one hundred employees. This industry segment is an important source of new product ideas. Independent inventors who sell their ideas to toy and game companies are also included in this category. The small toys and games community was given a large boost by the Internet, which provided an increased opportunity for small toy and game companies to sell their items in virtual stores and boutiques on the World Wide Web.

Potential Annual Earnings Scale. The average earnings for employees of small toy and game companies vary widely depending upon the region and position in the company. For example, an independent inventor will often earn 5 to 10 percent standard patent royalty rates for toy inventions. According to the U.S. Bureau of Labor Statistics (BLS), the average annual salary of all employees in the miscellaneous manufacturing category, of which toy and game manufacturers are a component, was $39,590 in 2009. Commercial and industrial designers in this category earned an average of $53,490. The annual salary of a small toy and game company owner is directly dependent upon the business's sales.

Clientele Interaction. Independent inventors and employees of small toy and game companies often have the unique opportunity to interact directly with customers. As there are fewer layers of employees in many small companies, even business owners may work directly with product purchasing adults, parents, and children during transactions. However, in somewhat larger small businesses, employees are increasingly specialized, and direct clientele interaction can be confined to a designated customer service individual or department. Additionally, if a small company's business model is focused on wholesale business with retail chains or larger companies, interaction with the end user is decreased.

Amenities, Atmosphere, and Physical Grounds. Working in a small toy and game business can be dynamic, interesting, and fun. Toy and game companies often have more of a casual work environment than a traditional business. Employers encourage comfort to increase employee creativity. Employees and owners in a smaller company often have a greater range of job responsibilities than the more specialized employees of a larger company. Sole proprietors and/or inventors have an increased amount of flexibility in hours and schedules. However, sole proprietors, small-business owners, and inventors also have increased personal responsibility for the financial performance of the business.

Typical Number of Employees. Although the United States government considers a toy and game company with fewer than five hundred employees to be a small business, the typical number of employees in a small toy and game business is fewer than one hundred. Independent inventors often work on their own, while in other small businesses the number of employees grows based on product demand and company income. Many small companies seasonally increase their number of employees to meet demand of toys and games for the winter holiday season.

Traditional Geographic Locations. Small toy and game companies are found across the United States. Many smaller companies and independent inventors have home-based businesses. Depending on the small company's product, manufacturing may be conducted in overseas factories, primarily in China.

Pros of Working for a Small Business. Small toy and game companies offer opportunities for employees to interact very closely with both company owners and customers. Often each employee may serve many roles and have broader responsibilities than in a larger business. In addition, as there are few employees, an individual employee stands a greater chance of being noticed if he or she is a strong performer. Owners and independent inventors also have increased freedom to make their own decisions, take their own risks, and reap the rewards of their efforts.

Cons of Working for a Small Business. Employees in small businesses can face problems based on the companies' size. For example, a small-business staff and its owners may be required to work more hours during busy times of the year. Small businesses are at increased risk of failure in times of economic downturn. Small companies lack scale advantages and have difficulty achieving widespread distribution because of concentration in the retail market. In addition, small businesses may not be able to offer benefits such as health or life insurance.

Costs

Payroll and Benefits: Small businesses generally hire their staff at hourly wages rather than salaries. Based on their small size, the government does not mandate benefits such as health insurance, vacation time, and sick time for small businesses.

Supplies: The supplies required by a toy and game business vary depending upon the product being sold and whether it is being manufactured on site. For example, a wood toy company would require raw materials such as wood, paint, and screws, as well as the tools to create the items. An independent inventor would require enough raw materials to make a prototype for use in focus groups and to show to buyers. Typical supplies needed by most businesses would include office supplies and information technology (telephones and computers).

External Services: The external services for a small business depend on the product being sold and size of the company. Some small toy and game companies use off-site manufacturing plants. Other small companies require external agents or marketers to sell their products. Still others may use Web hosts for their Web sites to sell their products.

Utilities: Typical utilities for a small business include water and sewage, electricity, gas or oil, telephone, and Internet access.

Taxes: The taxes paid by a small toy and game company depend on the type of business and its location. Some locations require payment of local and state taxes. All locations require payment of federal income taxes. Federal income taxes are based on net income, with sole proprietorships having the lower tax rate, while corporations have the highest. Most companies must collect sales taxes from purchasers. Small businesses with employees must pay an employment tax. Some small toy and game companies that manufacture their own products may also have to pay an excise tax.

Midsize Businesses

Midsize toy and game businesses are usually small businesses that have succeeded in raising a profit and have a larger number of specialized employees. These companies are traditionally more financially stable than small businesses and have annual sales revenue between $100 million and $1 billion.

Potential Annual Earnings Scale. Although potential earnings at a midsize company are usually higher than those of a small or start-up business, the average earnings for individuals involved in midsize toy and game companies vary widely depending upon the region and position in the company. According to the BLS, the average annual salary of all employees in the miscellaneous manufacturing category, of which toy and game manufacturers are a component, was $39,590 in 2009. Commercial and industrial designers in this category earned an average of $53,490. Marketing managers, the occupation that most closely relates to product or brand managers at toy and game companies, earned an average of $106,410.

Clientele Interaction. Midsize toy and game company employees may have the opportunity to directly interact with clientele on a routine basis as they purchase the company's product. However, the larger number of specialized employees at a midsize company means that clientele interaction is often confined to a designated "customer service" individual or department. If the company's business model is focused on wholesale business with retail chains or larger companies, interaction with the end user is decreased.

Amenities, Atmosphere, and Physical Grounds. Working in a midsize toy and game business is often described as dynamic, interesting, and fun. Toy and game companies often have more of a casual work environment than a traditional business atmosphere. Employers encourage comfort to increase employee creativity.

Typical Number of Employees. Midsize toy and game companies typically have one hundred to five hundred employees.

Traditional Geographic Locations. Toy and game companies are found across the United States. Many midsize companies have their products manufactured in overseas factories, primarily in China.

Pros of Working for a Midsize Business. Midsize toy and game companies may allow increased opportunity for employees to specialize in one position or role as compared to a small company. However, midsize companies still offer an increased likelihood for skill-building opportunities related to cross coverage of positions. The company bureaucracy is usually on a small scale so that employees may have the chance to be involved directly in changes in company procedures and products. In addition, midsize businesses are often more financially stable than small businesses and may offer increased job security and benefits.

Cons of Working for a Midsize Business. Midsize businesses still are often unable to offer the long-term financial stability of larger companies. In addition, midsize businesses may not offer benefits such as health insurance, sick time, or vacation leave.

Costs
Payroll and Benefits: Midsize businesses generally have a mix of staff at hourly wages and salaries. Depending on their exact size, the government may not mandate benefits such as health insurance, vacation time, and sick time.

Supplies: The supplies required by a toy and game business vary depending upon raw materials needed to create the product being sold and whether it is being manufactured on site. Typical supplies needed by most businesses would include office supplies and information technology (telephones and computers).

External Services: The external services for a midsize business depend on the product being sold and size of the company. Many midsize toy and game companies utilize off-site manufacturing plants. Other midsize companies require external agents or marketers to sell their products.

Utilities: Typical utilities for a midsize business include water and sewage, electricity, gas or oil, telephone, and Internet access.

Taxes: The taxes paid by a midsize toy and game company depend on the type of business and its location. Some locations require payment of local and state taxes. All locations require payment of federal income taxes. Federal income taxes are based on net income with sole proprietorships having the lower tax rate, while corporations have the highest. Most companies must collect sales taxes from purchasers. All businesses with employees must pay an employment tax. Some toy and game companies that manufacture their products may also have to pay an excise tax.

Large Businesses
Large competitive corporations dominate the toys and games industry. The revenues of U.S. toy and game companies range from $765 million to $5.9 billion annually. The top fifty toy and game companies, which include Mattel and Hasbro, generate about 75 percent of total industry revenues. Many of these large businesses are publically owned companies that produce a wide variety of products and outsource their production to other countries, such as China.

Potential Annual Earnings Scale. The average earnings for an individual involved in large toy and game companies vary widely depending upon the region and position in the company. According to the BLS, the average annual salary of all employees in the miscellaneous manufacturing category, of which toy and game manufacturers are a component, was $39,590 in 2009. Commercial and industrial designers in this category earned an average of $53,490. Marketing managers, the occupation that most closely relates to product or brand managers at toy and game companies, earned an average of $106,410. However, most salaries at large companies are higher than at small or midsize businesses. For example, toy and game designers at large toy and game companies can earn salaries of $150,000 to $200,000.

Clientele Interaction. Most large toy and game company employees generally have little opportunity to interact directly with clientele. The large size of the companies isolates employees from product-purchasing adults, parents, and children, unless those employees work in a development, marketing, or customer service department.

Amenities, Atmosphere, and Physical Grounds. Working in any toy and game business is often described as dynamic, interesting, and fun. However, larger toy and game companies often have a more stable and traditional corporate atmosphere than their smaller counterparts.

Typical Number of Employees. The typical number of employees in a large company often numbers two thousand or more.

Traditional Geographic Locations. Although large toy and game companies are located across the United States, approximately half of them are in California, New York, Pennsylvania, Ohio, Illinois, Florida, Colorado, Michigan, Missouri, and Maryland. Many large corporations also have numerous satellite offices across the United States in addition to their main offices. Almost all manufacturing of the large toy and game companies' products is conducted in overseas factories, primarily in China.

Pros of Working for a Large Business. There are several benefits to working in a large toy and game company. A large company can often offer more job security and higher starting salaries than a smaller business. In addition, larger companies offer health care packages to their employees and their families in addition to other benefits such as paid vacations, paid holidays, retirement benefits, and health insurance. Large companies also tend to operate in a structured manner that links raises and bonuses to the performance of the company. As an employee of a larger corporation, employees have access to more resources and training programs. Many large toy and game companies operate in multiple locations and as such there is also often the option to relocate to another locale and remain employed by the same company.

Cons of Working for a Large Business. The downsides in working for a large toy and game business tend to relate to their size. Large businesses have increased layers of corporate structure that may tend to decrease a particular employee's chance at promotion or being noticed for a job well done. In a large business, each job is much more specialized and there is less opportunity to serve multiple roles or interact with end users or top company executives.

Costs

Payroll and Benefits: The payroll and salary structure of a large toy and game business is complex given its large number of employees and job positions. Personnel directly involved in building the toys will often be paid hourly while others are paid a salary. Benefits such as vacation time and sick time are usually offered to all employees.

Supplies: The supplies required by a toy and game business vary depending upon raw materials needed to create the product being sold and whether it is being manufactured on site. Typical supplies needed by most businesses include office supplies and information technology (telephones and computers).

External Services: The external services for a large business depend on the product being sold and size of the company. The majority of large toy and game companies utilize off-site manufacturing plants.

Utilities: Typical utilities for a large business might include water and sewage, electricity, gas or oil, telephone, and Internet access.

Taxes: The taxes paid by a large toy and game company depend on the type of business and its location. Most locations require payment of local and state taxes. All locations require payment of federal income taxes. Federal income taxes are based on net income with sole proprietorships having the lower tax rate, while corporations have the highest. Most companies must collect sales taxes from purchasers. All businesses with employees must pay an employment tax. Some toy and game companies that manufacture their own products may also have to pay an excise tax.

ORGANIZATIONAL STRUCTURE AND JOB ROLES

The organizational structure and distribution of tasks within a toy and game company depends on the specific business. Traditional toys and games industry jobs range from creative positions such as toy designers and marketers to more traditional roles in accounting, administration, and engineering. The number and type of positions in each company is determined by the size and scope of the business. For example, a very small toy and game business would be that of an independent inventor. A toy and game inventor often begins a company with an idea for a toy or game. The inventor serves as designer, marketer, and financial services employee, all in one individual. Large corporate toy and game businesses have hundreds of employees each of whom specializes in different arenas such as design, production, marketing, and administration. Each of these areas requires employee administrative support personnel and executive supervisors. Often, the actual manufacture of the products in a large corporation is performed at off-site plants with their own organizational structure.

The following umbrella categories apply to the organizational structure of businesses in the toys and games industry:

- Business Management
- Customer Service
- Advertising, Sales, and Marketing
- Facilities and Security
- Technology, Research, Design, and Development
- Production and Operations
- Distribution
- Human Resources
- Information Technology
- Administrative Support
- Legal and Licensing
- Engineering
- Buying and Merchandising

Business Management
Business executives direct the policies and operations of the organizations to meet specific goals and objectives. The executives also supervise and manage the various sectors, departments, and teams to optimize performance and oversee operations. Many executives have advanced degrees in business, accounting, or similar fields; however, experience may substitute for lack of a degree. Business management positions usually command the highest salaries at the company.

Business management occupations may include the following:

- Chief Executive Officer (CEO)
- Chief Operating Officer (COO)
- Chief Financial Officer (CFO)
- General Manager
- President
- Vice President
- Marketing Director
- Sales Director
- Corporate Controller

Customer Service
Customer service personnel directly interact with a company's customers to provide answers to customer questions and resolve customer problems. Interaction with customers can occur in person or via telephone, e-mail, fax, or standard mail. Depending on the position and company, entry-level customer service personnel positions may require a high school diploma or an undergraduate degree.

Customer service occupations may include the following:

- Customer Service Manager
- Customer Service Representative
- Account Manager
- Client Services Representative

Advertising, Sales, and Marketing
Advertising, marketing, public relations, and sales personnel play a crucial role in promoting

their companies' products and name recognition through a variety of internal and external activities. Their responsibilities may include sales, advertising, promotion, pricing, product development, coordinating market research of target audiences, developing marketing strategy for particular toys or lines, and public relations activities. Their positional goal is to incite interest in the company and induce customers to purchase the company's products. Individuals in these positions may attend toy trade shows and other events, and visit retail stores to promote the company and its product lines. Most sales, advertising, and marketing employees have undergraduate degrees in business management, marketing, sales, communications, or related subjects. Many sales employee compensation packages include a component based on performance tied to product sales and new accounts.

Advertising, sales, and marketing occupations may include the following:

- Advertising Manager
- Account Executive
- Account Associate
- Creative Director
- Media Director
- Marketing Manager
- Product Development Manager
- Market Research Manager
- Market Research Analyst
- Promotions Manager
- Public Relations Manager
- Public Relations Specialist
- Sales Manager
- Sales Representative
- Sales Director
- Corporate Sales Manager
- Senior Sales Manager
- Administrative Assistant

Facilities and Security

The responsibilities of employees in the facilities and security sector of toy and game businesses center on protecting the safety of employees, maintaining the physical manufacturing facilities and equipment, and guarding proprietary company information. Positions range from entry-level security guards who protect physical property to skilled computer systems managers who ensure network security. Another frequently seen position in this

category is the occupational health and safety inspectors who design safe work spaces, inspect machines, and test air quality. Salaries and education requirements vary greatly based on the position.

Facilities and security occupations may include the following:

- Occupational Health and Safety Inspector
- Security Officer
- Security Guard
- Night Watchperson
- Administrative Support Manager
- Computer Systems Manager
- Computer Network Security Specialist

Technology, Research, Design, and Development

Positions in the technology, research, design, and development category are focused on development of future products, expansion of product lines, and modification of current items. The individuals and teams in this job category significantly affect the future earnings of the toy and game company as they create new products to capture their customers' attention. Many design and development positions are filled by creative individuals who develop their own products and ideas or build upon specific toy and game requirements provided by the company. Engineers in the research and develop teams also research raw materials, production costs, toy safety and durability, and create electronic and mechanical components. Salaries and education requirements vary greatly based on the position, but usually require a specialized college or graduate degree.

Technology, research, design, and development occupations may include the following:

- Toy/Game Designer
- Inventor
- Research and Development Specialist
- Mechanical Engineer
- Materials Engineer
- Electronics Engineer

Production and Operations

Employees in production and operations have positions focused on the manufacturing of toys and games. Many positions in production and operations in large toy companies have moved to sites overseas following the move of manufacturing plants. Individuals in production focus on the manufacture of products while the operations team attempts to develop and optimize the production process. Supervisory positions in production and operation such as industrial production managers often require a college degree and production operations experience.

Manufacturing jobs are focused on the transformation of raw materials into finished toys and games. Many manufacturing positions in large toy companies moved away from the United States in the late 1980's and early 1990's leading to decreased job availability in this sector. These positions range from entry-level assembler and fabricator positions to manufacturing supervisors. Assembler and fabricator positions usually are hourly and generally require only a high school diploma. More supervisory positions may require college degrees and/or manufacturing experience.

Production and operations occupations may include the following:

- Industrial Production Manager
- Operations Team Leader
- Operations Director
- Operations Manager
- Industrial Production Engineer
- Health and Safety Engineer
- Assembler and Fabricator
- Maintenance and Repair Worker
- Production Machinery Operator
- Production Shift Supervisor

Distribution

When toys and games are manufactured or imported, they often go to large distribution centers

---

OCCUPATION PROFILE

Painting/Coating Machine Operator

Considerations	Qualifications
Description	Uses painting and coating machinery and equipment to apply finishes to machines and to other manufactured products, from toy and games to cars to candy.
Career cluster	Manufacturing
Interests	Things
Working conditions	Work inside
Minimum education level	No high school diploma; on-the-job training; high school diploma or GED; high school diploma/technical training; apprenticeship
Physical exertion	Medium work
Physical abilities	Unexceptional/basic fitness
Opportunities for experience	Part-time work
Licensure and certification	Recommended
Employment outlook	Slower-than-average growth expected
Holland interest score	CRE

Note: See volume 1, "Publisher's Note," for an explanation of the Holland interest score.

OCCUPATION PROFILE

Packer/Packager

Considerations	Qualifications
Description	Sets up and runs machines that package products; sometimes manually packs products.
Career clusters	Manufacturing; Marketing, Sales, and Service; Transportation, Distribution, and Logistics
Interests	Things
Working conditions	Work inside
Minimum education level	On-the-job training; high school diploma or GED; high school diploma/technical training; apprenticeship
Physical exertion	Medium work
Physical abilities	Unexceptional/basic fitness
Opportunities for experience	Apprenticeship; military service; part-time work
Licensure and certification	Usually not required
Employment outlook	Slower-than-average growth expected
Holland interest score	RCS; RES

Note: See volume 1, "Publisher's Note," for an explanation of the Holland interest score.

or warehouses. Workers in these facilities handle incoming and outgoing shipments, coordinate transportation, and track customer orders. They also might work with federal agencies, including U.S. Customs, to ensure that proper importation procedures are followed. Distribution positions range from entry-level loading/unloading positions to higher-level distribution supervisors. Many distributor positions are hourly and do not require a specific educational degree. Some supervisory positions may require college degrees or distribution experience.

Distribution occupations may include the following:

- Warehouse Manager
- Warehouse Supervisor
- Warehouse Worker
- Freight Agent
- Distribution Supervisor
- Distribution Manager
- Distribution Worker
- Loader/Unloader
- Material Logistics Specialist
- Shipping and Receiving Clerk
- Heavy Truck Driver

Human Resources

Human resource positions in toy and game companies focus on the administrative management activities of a business's employees. Responsibilities in this area involve coordinating a range of worker-related processes, including employee recruitment, hiring, training, performance/conduct/behavior management, and compensation. They also may include development of company policies, standards, organizational structure, and processes. The majority of human resources positions are salaried and require undergraduate degrees. The variety and number of human resource

OCCUPATION SPECIALTIES

Packers/Packagers

Specialty	Responsibilities
Hand packagers	Package materials and products manually by cleaning packaging containers, lining and padding crates, obtaining and sorting products, and wrapping protective material around the product.
Machine packagers	Tend the machines that perform one or more packaging functions, such as filling, marking, labeling, banding, tying, packing, or wrapping containers. They feed the product into the packaging machine and unload the packaged product.
Wrappers	Wrap materials and products before packaging them in order to protect them after they have been weighed and counted.

positions in a company depend on the business's size.

Human resources occupations may include the following:

- Human Resources Director
- Human Resources Manager
- Human Resources Assistant
- Recruiting Manager
- Compensation and Benefits Analyst
- Compensation and Benefits Manager
- Human Resources Administrator
- Human Resources Representative
- Benefits Manager
- Talent Manager

Information Technology

Positions in information technology (IT) relate to the study, design, development, implementation, support, and management of computer-based information systems. Individuals in IT use computers to manage information in a secure manner. Specialist positions may focus on networking, Web site development, storage, user support, or many other career paths. IT positions are usually salaried and require at least an undergraduate degree at the entry level.

IT occupations may include the following:

- Chief Information Officer (CIO)
- Network Administrator
- Network Engineer
- Project Manager
- Web Designer
- Systems Administrator
- Help Desk Staff
- Information Technology Support Specialist

Administrative Support

Toy and game companies require a variety of administrative support personnel in each department to operate effectively. Administrative personnel perform day-to-day tasks related to everything from answering telephone calls to detailed financial accounting. Some administrative positions focus on inventory control and shipping of the toys and games to and from producers, distributors, and consumers. Other administrative personnel focus on taking and fulfilling order requests from customers. Still other positions focus on billing, bookkeeping, and accounting. Administrative positions range from entry-level receptionist positions to specialized accountants. Although some positions are hourly and do not require a specific educational degree, other specialized positions may require college or graduate degrees. The variety and number of administrative positions in a company vary greatly depending on the business's size.

Administrative support occupations may include the following:

- Shipping and Receiving Clerk
- Order Clerk
- Financial Clerk
- Bill/Account Collector
- Bookkeeper/Auditor
- Information Clerk
- Receptionist
- Shipping and Receiving Clerk
- Desktop Publisher
- Office Clerk
- Secretary
- Administrative Assistant
- Billing Clerk
- Machine Operator
- Communications Equipment Operator
- Computer Operator
- Credit Authorizer/Checker
- Data Entry Clerk
- Dispatcher
- File Clerk
- Office Manager
- Administrative Support Manager
- Order Clerk
- Payroll and Timekeeping Clerk
- Procurement Clerk
- Production, Planning, and Expediting Clerk
- Stock Clerk/Order Filler

Legal and Licensing

Lawyers and licensing specialists play an important role in the toys and games industry. Lawyers and other legal specialists draft and interpret contracts, advise companies about laws and regulations, and secure copyrights, trademarks, and patents for new products. Licensing specialists have become increasingly important in the industry as the rights to develop products using a familiar image or brand are transferred from one company to another. Most legal and licensing positions are salary based and require a graduate degree.

Legal and licensing occupations may include the following:

- General Counsel
- Attorney/Counsel
- Paralegal
- Licensing Specialist

Engineering

Engineering positions play an important role in the toys and games industry. Engineers can help to improve the design or function of toys, increase toy safety, reduce production costs, and determine the best production methods. They may work closely with research and development teams or they may independently assess toy designs. Engineers also work at the factories that produce toys, including factories abroad. Engineering occupations generally require at least a bachelor's degree in engineering, although those with some other related college degrees may qualify as well. Some more specialized or advanced positions, however, may require a master's or doctorate degree or a certain amount of relevant work experience.

Engineering occupations may include the following:

- Engineering Manager
- Industrial Engineer
- Industrial Engineering Technician
- Materials Engineer
- Materials Engineering Technician

Buying and Merchandising

Toy and game positions in buying and merchandising are important to the industry. Buyers make purchasing decisions for toy, hobby, and game stores and for merchant wholesalers. Buyers may attend trade shows, visit production facilities, negotiate with vendors, and track sales. Merchandisers, many of whom are employed part time or seasonally, set up displays of products within stores and give in-store demonstrations. Most entry-level buying and merchandising positions are hourly and do not require an undergraduate degree. Higher-level positions are often salaried and require a college degree as well as experience.

Buying and merchandising occupations may include the following:

- Buyer
- Merchandiser
- Merchandising Manager

INDUSTRY OUTLOOK

Overview

The U.S. toys and games industry is a large and diverse industry that leads the world in the production of toys and games. The industry's success is a result of high value-added domestic operations, such as product design, engineering and strategic marketing, with substantial overseas production in countries such as China. The toys and games industry depends heavily on the disposable income of its customers and a receding economy often damages the industry's outlook. However, the toys and games industry has weathered the global economic downturn of 2007-2009 well, with U.S. toy sales holding stable in 2009, generating $21.47 billon in retail sales (down only 0.8 percent in 2009 from 2008). These data have resulted in optimism for the future sales in 2010 and beyond. As Anita Frazier of the NPD Group noted in 2009, "While many industries are feeling the effects of the economy, [the revenue from toys and games] shows that toys remain a vital part of total spending on kids." Growth areas with sales increases over 2009 included building sets, crafts, and action figures. According to Data Monitor research data published in September of 2009, the United States toy and game market is forecast to have a value of $23.4 billion by 2013, an increase of 4.3 percent since 2008, which accounts for 36.8 percent of the global toy and game market's value.

The toys and games industry is a dynamic business environment which has usually found increasing market success through innovation. However, at the same time, familiar characters can also provide a stable revenue stream. In 2009, profitable industry attention and increased revenue have been in focused on: lower wholesale toy prices; increased licensing of known television, film, and book characters to increase the success of new toys; large companies purchasing smaller companies in order to diversify holdings; green products; and extending known brands.

Areas of opportunity important to the growth of the toys and games industry include reducing development and production times in order to respond to toy fads; a focus on toys and games directed at 'tweens (children aged nine to twelve); targeting grandparents; exploring the market for premium higher-price toys; producing educa-tional toys for all age groups; focusing on nonviolent toys; and developing more toys that result in active play to reduce childhood obesity.

Employment Advantages

Industry research suggests that in 2013, the U.S. toys and games market will have a value of $23.4 billion, an increase of 4.3 percent since 2008. Continued industry growth suggests that overall average toys and games industry wages and salaries are expected to continue to be at or above the national average, but this projection varies by position. As examples, overall employment for computer systems designers is expected to grow very quickly, by 45 percent between 2008 to 2018, while overall engineering employment is expected to have a more average growth rate of 11 percent during that period, and overall employment of production workers is expected to decrease as advances in manufacturing technology allow fewer workers to produce greater output.

The competitive, fast-paced nature of the toys and games industry can be a significant benefit to individuals seeking entry into this challenging field. Careers can have an element of excitement focused on the constant flow of new ideas and new products needed in an industry sensitive to trends and fashion.

Annual Earnings

The toys and games industry has weathered the global economic downturn of 2007-2009 well, with United States toy sales holding stable in 2009 (down only 0.8 percent in 2009 from 2008). The industry's domestic revenue for 2009 was approximately $21.47 billion. In 2008, the international toy and game market generated total revenues of $38.4 billion.

RELATED RESOURCES FOR FURTHER RESEARCH

AMERICAN SPECIALTY TOY RETAILING
    ASSOCIATION
    432 N. Clark Ave., Suite 401
    Chicago, IL 60654
    Tel: (312) 222-0984
    Fax: (312) 222-0986
    http://www.astratoy.org

INTERNATIONAL COUNCIL OF TOY INDUSTRIES
  80 Camberwell Rd.
  London SE5 0EG
  United Kingdom
  Tel: 44-207-701-7271
  Fax: 44-207-708-2437
  http://www.toy-icti.org

PLAYTHINGS MAGAZINE
  360 Park Ave. South
  New York, NY 10010
  Tel: (646) 746-7419
  http://www.playthings.com

TOY INDUSTRY ASSOCIATION
  1115 Broadway, Suite 400
  New York, NY 10010
  Tel: (212) 675-1141
  Fax: (818) 883-3809
  http://www.toyassociation.org

ABOUT THE AUTHOR

Dawn A. Laney is an author, genetic counselor, and research coordinator in the Atlanta, Georgia, area. She received a bachelor's degree from Trinity College in Hartford, Connecticut, in 1996 and a master's degree in human genetics from Sarah Lawrence College in Bronxville, New York, in 1999. In addition to her main career path in clinical care of lysosomal storage disease patients, she is the developer of a line of baby toys and gifts focused around her children's story *A Late Night Lullaby* (2009).

FURTHER READING

British Library Business and IP Centre. "Toys and Games Industry Guide." June 3, 2009. http://www.bl.uk/reshelp/pdfs/Toy_and_Games_Industry_Guide.pdf

Cross, Gary. *Kids' Stuff: Toys and the Changing World of American Childhood.* Cambridge, Mass.: Harvard University Press, 1997.

Datamonitor. *Global Toys and Games: Industry Profile.* New York: Author, 2009.

_____. *Toys and Games in the United States: Industry Profile.* New York: Author, 2009.

Giacobello, John. *Choosing a Career in the Toy Industry.* New York: Rosen, 2001.

Miller, Richard K. *The 2009 Retail Business Market Research Handbook.* 11th ed. Loganville, Ga.: Richard K. Miller and Associates, 2009.

Parker, Philip M. *The 2006-2011 World Outlook for Accessories, Clothes, Parts, and Playsets for Dolls, Toy Animals, and Action Figures.* San Diego, Calif.: ICON Group, 2005.

Phillips, Sam. "Toys to Fight Their Corner." *License,* January/February, 2010, p. 12.

Scott, Sharon. *Toys and American Culture.* Santa Barbara, Calif.: ABC-CLIO, 2010.

Torpey, Elka Maria. "Toy Jobs: Work in the Business of Play." *Occupational Outlook Quarterly,* Winter, 2008-2009. Available at http://www.bls.gov/opub/ooq/2008/winter/art01.pdf.

U.S. Bureau of Labor Statistics. *Career Guide to Industries,* 2010-2011 ed. http://www.bls.gov/oco/cg.

_____. *Occupational Outlook Handbook,* 2010-2011 ed. http://www.bls.gov/oco.

U.S. Census Bureau. North American Industry Classification System (NAICS), 2007. http://www.census.gov/cgi-bin/sssd/naics/naicsrch?chart=2007.

U.S. Department of Commerce. International Trade Administration. Office of Trade and Industry Information. Industry Trade Data and Analysis. http://ita.doc.gov/td/industry/otea/OTII/OTII-index.html.

The Wall Street Journal. "U.S. Tramples Small Toy Makers," September 19, 2009, p. A14.

Travel and Tourism Industry

INDUSTRY SNAPSHOT

General Industry: Hospitality and Tourism

Career Cluster: Hospitality and Tourism

Subcategory Industries: Convention and Visitor Bureaus; Cruise Lines (to and from Domestic Ports); Cruise Lines (to or from Foreign Ports); Other Travel Arrangement and Reservation Services; Tour Operators; Tourism Bureaus; Travel Agencies

Related Industries: Airline Industry; Hotels and Motels Industry; Passenger Transportation and Transit Industry

Annual Domestic Revenues: $221 billion USD (U.S. Department of Labor, 2007)

Annual International Revenues: $534 billion USD (U.S. Department of Labor, 2007)

Annual Global Revenues: $792 billion USD (Research and Markets, 2009)

NAICS Numbers: 5615, 483112, 483114

INDUSTRY DEFINITION

Summary

Travel and tourism is one of the world's largest industries and one that continues to grow. It serves the needs of those who choose to be, or must be, temporarily away from their homes. The industry includes travel agencies, public and private tourism enterprises, cruise operators, group tour packagers, and packaged vacation providers such as Club Med and Sandals. The travel and tourism industry also meets the special interests of business travelers, ecotravelers, adventure travelers, and senior travelers, to name a few target markets. Travel industry professionals must help their clients select the best products from an ever-expanding menu of available options.

History of the Industry

The first known professional tour operator was Thomas Cook, a Baptist missionary, who in 1841 made all the travel arrangements for a British group traveling from Leicester to Loughborough and back to attend a temperance meeting. By the end of the nineteenth century, Thomas Cook and Son was a successful company escorting travelers around the world. Carlson Wagonlit Travel began in 1872 as Wagon-Lits (from the French term for a sleeping car, *wagon lits*) because the founder, Georges Nagelmackers, added sleeping accommodations to his rail cars. The Ask Mr. Foster company came on the scene in 1888. Other companies followed, but the industry grew slowly.

During the early decades of the twentieth century, the so-called golden age of travel lured the privileged few to travel on the Orient Express and other storied trains. Some chose safaris in colonial Africa, and the European Grand Tour was still considered an essential part of the education of the wealthy. Travel service providers emerged to serve these travelers. Most travelers were still of the armchair variety, enjoying their adventures vicariously through the works of Marco Polo or Mark Twain.

For most Americans, however, such journeys were impossible. Not only were they prohibitively expensive, but also, in the days before air travel, most people lacked the time to leave their daily lives and jobs to board an ocean liner and spend weeks reaching and traveling in Europe. Playgrounds outside North America remained off limits to the average vacationer. While visits to far-flung relatives or a week at Yellowstone were considered travel, such jaunts required no travel agents or other industry professionals. The family gassed up the car, or boarded a train. As recently as 1950, fewer than 10 percent of Americans had passports.

The United States' growing prosperity and the emergence of air travel opened the world to more people, and the travel industry simplified reaching it. Travel agents wrote tickets and made hotel reservations. They bought packaged tours for their clientele. Vacationers going abroad had once satisfied their wanderlust in Western Europe, but Asia, Africa, and Australia now beckoned. Corporate travel expanded to the extent that large companies often had in-house departments to take care of travel arrangements for their increasingly mobile executives and managers.

The cruise segment of the travel industry began as a necessary means of transporting people from one side of the ocean to the other, usually from New York to London. Accommodations varied greatly aboard grand old ships such as the *Queen Mary*. Most passengers sailed second or third class, while those traveling first class had "POSH" stamped on their tickets. POSH stood for "Port Over, Starboard Home," meaning that in addition to receiving upgraded quarters and amenities, they would travel on the sunny side of the ship both ways; the term found its way into the lexicon as a synonym for luxurious. In 1912, four days into its maiden voyage, the *Titanic* hit an iceberg and sank off the coast of Newfoundland. The death toll was 1,517, including many poor emigrants who had booked passage to North American in the less well-appointed sections of the ship. Among the survivors was Denver socialite Molly Brown, whose *Titanic* adventure was chronicled in the musical, *The Unsinkable Molly Brown.*

Cruises feature onboard attractions as well as interesting port cities. (©Don Mace/Dreamstime.com)

As air travel increased, travel by ship decreased as a means of point-to-point travel until the emergence of the cruise industry—which featured attractions aboard ships, as well as those at ports of call. Fueled in part by the long-running television series *The Love Boat*, cruising surged in popularity until, by the late 1990's, millions of vacationers were choosing that form of travel. Cruisers were likely to be repeat customers. Once clients experienced the entertainment, food, spas, casinos, and other amenities of modern cruise ships, they wanted to do so again. Dollar for dollar, cruises represented good value, and the passenger had to unpack only once. More and bigger ships appeared each year, and they began traveling to places such as Alaska, not just the tropics. Operators of river barges began taking people down the Danube and other European rivers, offering yet another type of cruise competing for tourist dollars.

The Durango-Silverton train in Colorado is a journey into the past. (©Richard Semik/Dreamstime.com)

The Industry Today

New interests and greater opportunities have changed the industry. Since the end of the Cold War, new destinations have opened up to tourists. Russia and other countries of the former Soviet Union are now popular European destinations. People are visiting Asian nations such as Thailand, Korea, Vietnam, and Cambodia, countries brought to their attention by U.S. involvement in events happening there.

While travel and tourism soften during economic downturns such as the global recession of 2007-2009, they experience growth with the growth of new middle-class travelers in newly developed nations. In the United States, as in many other countries, tourism is the primary generator of revenue in many communities, where it drives the profits not only of the travel and tourism industry itself but also of the hotels and motels industry, the restaurant industry, the outdoor recreation industry, and many local retail industries. Taken together, these various industries represent one of the largest sectors of the economy in the United States and in many other countries.

Despite the cutbacks in recent years driven by recession, reduced corporate travel, and fear of terrorism, the travel and tourism industry is viable and will remain so. Some demographics, retirees for example, are less affected by downturns in the economy, and they are still traveling in large numbers.

In the twenty-first century, the industry has undergone major changes that are due in large part to Internet companies that allow people to act as their own travel agents. The proliferation of self-help travel sites on the World Wide Web continues. Travelocity, Orbitz, and Hotels.com are but a few of the companies that rendered the old-style travel agent obsolete. They triggered the end of travel agencies with mall or storefront offices that depended on walk-in trade. Travel agents and agencies reinvented themselves to fit the times, offering specialized services to niche markets. Some large companies remain, however, allowing home-based agents to affiliate with larger entities and gain the right to issue airline tickets. Even the online companies engaged in travel arrangements need employ-

A sightseeing bus is one way to see New York City. (AP/Wide World Photos)

ees. Today's savvy travel agent knows everything there is to know about a small and identifiable segment of the travel market, such as honeymoon destinations, river rafting, ecotravel, adventure travel, inn-to-inn walking vacations, archaeological explorations, or deep-sea fishing.

Cruising still draws heavily from the senior population, a market segment that is expected to reach 60 million people by 2015. Many of these people like the idea of unpacking only once, having their shore excursions preplanned, and enjoying a plethora of activities while at sea. Segments of the cruise industry have adapted to meet the more sophisticated demands of special-interest cruisers. Themed cruises are available for singles, the physically challenged, opera buffs, art and history lovers, and murder mystery enthusiasts, to name just a few. Luxury cruises on small vessels where the staff-to-passenger ratio is about one to three appeal to the affluent. "Barefoot cruises" on small vessels, where

passengers participate in sailing the ship and preparing the food, attract a younger, more adventurous clientele. Those with unlimited time can indulge in around-the-world freighter cruises.

Another major industry segment is packaged tours, a broad category that includes everything from industry giants such as Globus and Trauck, which offer escorted coach tours in all the tourism hot spots, to individuals who put together themed walking tours of their hometowns—Al Capone's Chicago, for example. Globus reports that its clientele has become discerning over the years and demands authentic experiences, unique to a given region. For example, a group visiting Moscow may be more interested in dinner with a true Russian ambience, with caviar and vodka, than in the familiar fare offered by the local Hard Rock Cafe. Visitors want to browse in Russian amber shops and look for nesting dolls or Fabergé-style eggs.

Here, too, specialization is gaining in popularity. Tourists enjoy being with a coachload of people who have purchased a travel package based on shared interests, rather than having to work at finding common ground with their fellow-travelers. Singles trips are popular, not to meet possible mates but to avoid expensive "single supplements," surcharges levied by many tours to make up for lost revenues when there is no double occupancy. The more exotic a locale, the more its tourists seek the perceived safety of organized tours. It is one thing for a Westerner to sightsee independently in London but quite another for the same person to do so in Ho Chi Minh City, Vietnam.

Twenty-first century travelers are informed, know what they want, and will continue to patronize those providers able meet those special needs. They are equally loyal to successful providers in related industries, such as airlines, restaurants, hotels, motels, and themed entertainment venues. One example of a fast-growing travel market is ecotravel. Many of today's travelers are choosing to leave smaller carbon footprints. They want accommodations with green practitioners who share their concerns. Hunting safaris are losing favor, while photo safaris are gaining in appeal. Some travelers seek total immersion in a different culture and choose home stays over traditional hotels. Industry professionals must keep abreast of the times and adapt to their clients' wishes.

Medical tourism has also risen to prominence, as Americans without adequate health insurance seek lower-cost treatment in India, Thailand, Mexico, South Africa, and the Caribbean, among other destinations. This market segment is expected to see rapid growth in the years to come. The travel professionals best able to evaluate those offshore clinics and advise traveler-patients seeking medical attention may reap huge rewards.

Financial considerations have also changed the way people vacation. Fluctuating gas prices have caused some recreational vehicle enthusiasts to stick closer to home and explore their own states or geographic regions. This means local tourism promoters now court their neighbors, as well as potential clients across the country. The travel and tourism industry is poised for growth and is continuously evolving as it develops new travel products and new twists on the old. Its success will depend on offering something different, seamless service, and good value for money spent.

INDUSTRY MARKET SEGMENTS

The various segments of the travel and tourism industry comprise small, midsize, and large operations, ranging from independent, self-employed travel agents and one-person local tour companies to the largest cruise companies, which employ thousands of workers. Following is a breakdown by size and by type of company.

Small Businesses

Small businesses within the industry include independent travel agents and other home-based industry professionals, such as entrepreneurs who conduct local tours. The more successful of these carve out niches for themselves, specializing in specific types of travel for a specifically targeted clientele.

Potential Annual Earnings Scale. According to the U.S. Bureau of Labor Statistics (BLS), the combined average annual salary of all employees in the travel arrangement industry was $38,390 in 2009. Tour guides earned an average of $28,230, while travel agents earned an average of $32,170.

Clientele Interaction. The business owner is the person with whom clients interact, so an independent travel agent or tour provider needs both excellent communication skills and excellent people skills. For the agent, that means determining the client's needs, meeting them, and running interference when problems arise.

The local walking tour provider makes arrangements to meet the tour group, provide an informative and entertaining tour, take care of any problems that arise during the tour, and make sure the group members have a good time and feel they have received good value for money spent. In addition, he or she is responsible for the group's safety while on the tour.

Amenities, Atmosphere, and Physical Grounds. Most operators of small businesses in this industry work out of home offices and have no walk-in traffic. Their only requirements are a comfortable place to work, ample space, and sufficient technology.

Typical Number of Employees. Small businesses may have as few as one employee, perhaps with temporary help during peak times. Employees seldom number more than two or three and—other than owners—are usually part time and paid hourly wages.

Traditional Geographic Locations. Local walking tours and similar businesses must be located in places of sufficient interest to attract tourists. It is also helpful if more than one tour can be developed. For example, an architectural tour, a tour of historically significant landmarks, a Christmas tour, and a haunted building tour would make a nice mix. Travel agents working from home may be located anywhere.

Pros of Working for a Small Travel Business. Starting and running a small business can be immensely rewarding, and persons with the right combination of skills and personality traits can be happier and achieve more success than they would working for someone else. An owner-operator has total control over the direction the company and consequently of his or her earnings. An enterprise can be started without advanced education, but an outgoing personality is necessary, along with the ability and the willingness to pay attention to the smallest detail. Since the owner does everything, each day is different, with little time or opportunity for boredom. An employee can earn a little extra money while learning the business. Also, the start-up costs are minimal and primarily consist of obtaining technology, stationery, brochures, business cards, and any required licenses. Advertising is necessary but can be as simple initially as calling on everyone in town who is a potential customer.

Cons of Working for a Small Travel Business. When one is in business for oneself, all time spent not working shows up in the bottom line. Forces over which one has no control can wreak financial havoc. These include catastrophic weather, downturns in the economy, or unexpected illnesses. The business owner is responsible for all phases of the operation and has to perform marketing, accounting, customer service, and all other functions to keep the business running smoothly. Everyone is better at performing some tasks than at others, so the owner has to either gain expertise where lacking or pay someone else to provide those services.

An employee in such a business is limited in earnings, as there is no corporate ladder to climb. What could be seen as either a pro or a con, depending on the point of view, is that many tourism business are seasonal, requiring that profits be made in the peak season. While this creates tremendous pressure to be productive within a limited window, it also gives the owner and the employees the opportunity to pursue other interests during the off-season.

Costs

Payroll and Benefits: Most employees are part time and paid hourly wages. Owners pay themselves out of the business's profits. If there are no profits, they will not be paid. Benefits are usually not offered to part-time staff.

Supplies: Small-business owners require standard home-office supplies and equipment, including computers, telephones, copiers, fax machines, toner and ink cartridges, and paper of various stocks and quality levels for business cards, brochures, flyers, and other marketing hand-outs.

External Services: Gone are the days when every mall had a travel agency. Today's agents are likely to be home-based, doing their work by telephone, fax, and e-mail. One problem this poses for the agent is that airlines sanction only those agencies housed in commercial space to write tickets, and in today's market, renting office space is financially prohibitive for most independent agents. The way around that is for the home-based agent to affiliate him- or herself with one of the large agencies for the privilege of issuing tickets. This is a win-win situation, as the independent agent gets tickets printed by the host agency, and the host agency receives an average of 30 percent of the agent fees.

A person conducting local tours has to make arrangements for admissions to both private and public stops on the tour. Costs vary, but the group rates are usually considerably lower than an individual admission ticket. The arrangements and payments should be made before the tour to simplify the tour itself and give the impression of being totally in control. Otherwise, small-business owners may contract occasional accounting or advertising services.

Utilities: Utility costs are usually minimal, as they are a prorated portion of the owner's residential expenses. An exception would be high-speed Internet service or a dedicated telephone line for business use only.

Taxes: Employers must pay payroll taxes on their employees' earnings and file quarterly reports.

Property taxes, like utilities, can be prorated and the portion deemed business can be deducted as a cost of doing business. Owners must also pay any applicable state and local business taxes and charge taxes on sales when required. Income is generally reported on owners' personal tax returns, in which case, they must also pay self-employment taxes.

Midsize Businesses

Midsize businesses in the travel and tourism industry include travel agencies larger than home-based independent agents and smaller than the larger chains. Local tour operators may become midsize when they go beyond special-interest walking tours and include coach or water tours. Government tourism boards also fit in this category. These are local, state, and federal entities that promote tourism in assigned regions. Chambers of commence and convention and visitor's bureaus likewise promote the merits of their communities to potential visitors.

Potential Annual Earnings Scale. According to the BLS, the combined average annual salary of all employees in the travel arrangement industry was $38,390 in 2009. Tour guides earned an average of $28,230, while travel agents earned an average of $32,170. Sales representatives selling services within the industry earned an average of $50,190, sales supervisors earned an average of $59,590, and sales managers earned an average of $91,470. Captains of deep sea, coastal, and Great Lakes vessels, such as cruise ships, earned an average of $87,750, while those guiding small scenic and sightseeing watercraft earned an average of $44,160.

Clientele Interaction. Clientele interaction is high, as there are few behind-the-scenes jobs in midsize businesses. From the person who sells the package to the person who entertains the tour participants, all must have good people skills and be proactive in solving potential problems. Even those in the lower echelons—for example, the waiters who serve clients on a sightseeing dinner cruise—deal directly with the client, and the impression made reflects favorably or unfavorably on the company.

Amenities, Atmosphere, and Physical Grounds. Clients do not usually visit company offices, but there are other physical grounds to consider. For example, tour coaches must be kept clean, comfortable, and attractive, as must boats from which tourists enjoy shoreline sightseeing, brunch cruises, or sunset dinner cruises. Points of embarkation must have ample, safe parking, and, in the absence of that, the operator should provide valet parking for tourists with rental cars, as well as for locals who are often entertaining business associates or out-of-town visitors.

Typical Number of Employees. These companies usually have fewer than fifty employees, often no more than fifteen or twenty, but this varies from location to location. Employers may also employ part-time or temporary workers in response to seasonal fluctuations.

Traditional Geographic Locations. Travel agencies can be located anywhere and often choose suburban office space over more expensive city offices. Government tourism boards maintain offices in government-owned buildings, usually in areas of their jurisdictions frequented by tourists. Some have branch offices at their borders to greet motorists entering the territory. Chambers of commerce opt for the visibility of offices in the heart of the areas they serve. Coach tours typically embark from midcity, and cruises from the most convenient spots on lakes or rivers. Sometimes, the geographic location is the most appealing part of a cruise, as in the sightseeing boats that ply the river along the Riverwalk in San Antonio, Texas.

Pros of Working for a Midsize Travel Business. Midsize companies offer employees more opportunities and higher financial compensation than do smaller companies. They also provide a good entry into the industry for someone seeking experience for a future career with a large company or learning the ropes before striking out alone. Without the cumbersome layers of management typical of larger firms, employees have greater access to decision makers and thus more opportunity both to offer input and to have that input acted on. Because employees play a vital role in the overall success of a midsize company, the employee gains more visibility and more hands-on experience. There is also some room to rise in the company; the administrative assistant in the chamber of commerce can conceivably become the director.

One of the biggest benefits of working for a midsize travel company is the opportunity for deeply discounted travel, sometimes even free travel. Familiarization, or "fam," trips are given by resorts and other glamorous destinations to those who can steer clients to their properties. These are awarded to those agents with proven track records or to travel writers who can give them favorable media exposure.

Cons of Working for a Midsize Travel Business. The biggest con, from the employee's point of view, in working for a midsize travel company is the limited room for advancement and thus access to higher earnings. Although there are greater opportunities than in small companies, midsize companies are still no match for the industry giants. Because there are fewer employees, some workers may need to perform tasks not in their job descriptions. The tour coach driver may be required to wash the bus and clean its interior. The agent may have to spend time at the reception desk or do routine paperwork. Because of the blurring of responsibilities and the lack of a formal complaint department, any employee may be called upon to smooth things over in the event of misunderstandings and other difficulties.

An NBC page gives a guided tour of the NBC Studios in Burbank, California. (AP/Wide World Photos)

Costs

Payroll and Benefits: Midsize travel companies generally have mostly salaried employees as well as a few who generate sales and are paid on commission. Full-time employees are given sick leave, vacation, and other benefits, while the owner typically decides whether to give benefits to seasonal or part-time workers.

Supplies: Midsize businesses require standard office equipment and supplies. Some need tour vehicles such as coaches or boats, as well as the tools and supplies to maintain, repair, and clean them.

External Services: Midsize companies may contract accounting or legal services. They also require insurance coverage and may choose to rent rather than purchase tour buses or boats.

Utilities: Utilities include telephone, Internet service, electricity, water, gas, and heat.

Taxes: Midsize businesses must pay payroll taxes on employees and submit quarterly statements, as well as paying local, state, federal, and possibly international corporate and property taxes. A subtle form of taxation is any licenses or permits required for the privilege of doing business.

Large Businesses

Large businesses form the bulk of the travel and tourism industry, and they employ most of its workers. The industry giants fit, for the most part, into three categories: cruise ship operators, packaged tour operators, and the companies such as Apple Vacations or Club Med that offer packages at single destinations. The less adventurous of travelers prefer these vacations because they involve less risk; are available at low, all-inclusive group rates; and allow all details to be taken care of by the provider.

Potential Annual Earnings Scale. According to the BLS, the combined average annual salary of all employees in the travel arrangement industry was $38,390 in 2009. Tour guides earned an average of $28,230, while travel agents earned an average of $32,170. Sales representatives selling services within the industry earned an average of $50,190, sales supervisors earned an average of $59,590, and sales managers earned an average of $91,470. Captains of deep sea, coastal, and Great Lakes vessels, such as cruise ships, earned an average of $87,750, while those guiding small scenic and sightseeing watercraft earned an average of $44,160.

Clientele Interaction. As in all facets of the industry, client interaction is high, though the large companies have more opportunities for behind-the-scenes support employees.

Amenities, Atmosphere, and Physical Grounds. Clients of travel companies seek attractive, well-maintained facilities, whether they are on a cruise ship, at a Club Med resort, or on a guided coach tour where more than one property is visited. The physical property must be meticulously maintained, provide sufficient amenities to occupy the guests, and ensure that everything contributes to an atmosphere that is welcoming and conducive to making new friends while enjoying new experiences.

Typical Number of Employees. The largest cruise ships can employ a thousand or more people, and the large companies that run them employ many thousands each. On the other end of the spectrum, an escorted tour through several countries might have a dozen employees at most, including the drivers. This also includes local guides who join the tour for a half day to extoll the virtues of their home cities. These professionals are supported by corporate workforces of marketers, accountants, administrative assistants, and others.

Traditional Geographic Locations. Locations vary, but tour sites usually include large cities with cultural, architectural, and entertainment opportunities. Cruises sail to the tropics, to Alaska, and along many other routes as well. Planned vacation destinations are usually in resort areas, and, while beaches are the most popular, spa, skiing, and golf resorts also compete for vacationers' dollars.

Pros of Working for a Large Travel Business. Large companies offer greater opportunities for professional advancement. The larger companies also employ hundreds, if not thousands, of people, so there is ample opportunity for advancement or geographic change. Motivated employees can start at the bottom of a department and work their way up, or move from department to department to learn the entire business before striking out on their own. These companies also have the potential for higher earnings and better benefits. Only the most motivated of small or midsize company employees reach the higher levels.

Cruise ship employees report to work from their onboard cabins and are constantly traveling to exciting ports of call. While they may have to remain on board performing their duties, they also have ample opportunities to visit favorite locales on their off time. For those afflicted with wanderlust, the greatest plus of working for the larger industry companies remains the opportunity for personal travel. Between "fam" trips and deep professional courtesy discounts, the possibilities are endless.

An intangible but important consideration is the personal satisfaction that comes when a client's trip is all he or she hoped it would be. For some people, travel is a way of life, and they make arrangements through a variety of small-to-large companies depending on the situation. For others, a trip abroad or to Hawaii can represent a lifelong dream, and they are likely to turn to a large company for the perceived lack of risk involved in dealing with major organizations. To have had a part in making someone's dream a reality is heartwarming.

Cons of Working for a Large Travel Business. Employees have little or no say in how large businesses are run. As in any large corporation, they can feel invisible, where in smaller companies everyone's contribution is both needed and highly visible. While traveling for a living is at first glamorous, it also means being away from home for long periods of time, and that can cause difficulties in maintaining family and personal relationships. Another problem for those working aboard a ship, or who live at the vacation resort where they are employed, is the lack of a clear division between work and play. It is harder to change gears at the end of a shift without physically leaving the job site. Burnout occurs.

Costs

Payroll and Benefits: Salary structures vary to accommodate the wide range of positions. At the lower end of the hierarchy, employees are often paid an hourly wage. Higher up the ladder, salaries are annual and sometimes include commissions, bonuses, and tips. With union jobs, compensations and benefits are collectively bargained. One industry-specific benefit is travel. Even those who do not travel as part of their jobs, are usually given opportunities for discounted travel. Other benefits include sick leave, vacation time, and paid insurance.

Supplies: Cruise ships and company-owned hotels require the same supplies as any resort hotel and entertainment complex, including massive amounts of fuel.

External Services: Large companies may contract accounting or legal services. While they typically employ advertising or public relations staffs, they may also contract external firms to plan or help plan major advertising campaigns. They also require significant amounts of insurance coverage, and many subcontract for such service providers as local tour guides or entertainers.

Utilities: Utilities include telephone, Internet service, electricity, water, gas, and heat.

Taxes: Large businesses must pay payroll taxes on employees and submit quarterly statements, as well as paying local, state, federal, and international corporate and property taxes. A subtle form of taxation is any licenses or permits required for the privilege of doing business.

ORGANIZATIONAL STRUCTURE AND JOB ROLES

While travel and tourism include jobs unique to the industry, certain functions, such as accounting, have to be performed in any business to ensure smooth overall operation. The number of people assigned to complete these tasks varies widely. A one-person travel agency requires the owner to wear many hats, with perhaps an assistant, part-time help as needed, or periodic input from professionals that may include auditors or tax preparers. Local, state, or federal tourism bureaus typically operate with staffs of less than twelve. The cruise industry giants and vacation packagers are major corporate entities with all the attendant levels of hierarchy.

The following umbrella job categories apply to the organizational structure of businesses in the travel and tourism industry:

- Business Management
- Sales and Marketing
- Security
- Human Resources
- Information Technology/Multimedia
- Tour Guides and Support
- Primary Shipboard Personnel
- Housekeeping and Maintenance
- Food and Beverage
- Casino and Entertainment
- Recreation and Fitness

Business Management

This category is responsible for the overall direction of the company and can be as simple as a lone proprietor sitting down and devising short-term, midterm, and long-range plans. A midsize operation typically has one person, usually the owner, calling the shots with input from employees with various responsibilities. Large companies are run by boards of directors, a chief executive officer, and other layers of management. Those with decision-making authority plan the company's activities and oversee the execution of their plans.

With the exception of those employees who sell travel products and earn commissions, the top managers are the highest paid. Generally speaking, the larger the company, the more educational credentials and experience are required for positions in this employment category. Degrees helpful here include business management, accounting and finance, sales and marketing, hospitality, and advanced degrees in any of those specialties, such as a master of business administration. Smaller company owners or managers may overlook the lack of formal degrees and choose an applicant with a solid industry track record coupled with enthusiasm and proven ability to achieve goals. The smallest, especially if they have limited budgets, are more likely to train an applicant with no experience, as this person can be had for a lower salary.

Business management occupations may include the following:

- Director
- Chief Executive Officer (CEO)

- President
- Vice President of Marketing
- Vice President of Public Relations
- Sales and Marketing Manager
- Chief Financial Officer (CFO)
- Controller
- Human Resources Manager

Sales and Marketing

This department is the lifeblood of a company and of the whole industry. The travel and tourism industry exists to match clients to their travel needs. Nothing happens until a cruise reservation is made, an escorted tour is booked, or a vacation package is bought. Large companies have marketing departments to analyze the most effective ways to reach their target clients and sales departments to sell products to individual travelers. Sometimes, the client is a corporation that hires an agency to handle all its travel arrangements. In that case, several employees may be responsible for servicing the client.

More often, the product is sold to individuals or small groups of family or friends who want to travel together. The smallest of enterprises, the local walking-tour company, for example, is the simplest. Owners place advertisements in local papers, especially those that will be found in hotels and inns, and they also make sure their advertising brochures are in information racks anywhere a tourist is likely to be. In small agencies or tour companies, the operator handles all aspects, from making itself known to the chosen niche market to closing the sale and handling all the details involved.

Midsize companies have greater divisions of duties, and administrative support staffs take care of details such as maintaining client mailing and e-mail lists and routine customer service. The sales staff is responsible for finding new customers through cold calling, referrals, and often inviting prospects in for presentations on cruises and other travel packages. Large companies operate similarly to midsize companies, but with more layers and a more distinct hierarchy.

The travel agent, whether home-based and independent or a corporate employee, must understand the client's wishes. For example, someone traveling to the charming towns of southeast Alaska can choose between a large cruise ship and the lesser-known Alaska state ferry system, which transports passengers to the ports southeast and south-central Alaska. A major selling point is that ferry passengers can stay at a port for as long as they wish, while traveling the same waters and seeing the same eagles and whales as cruise passengers at considerably lower cost. The travel adviser must determine the client's agenda. If the bells and whistles of the cruise itself are the main source of

---

OCCUPATION SPECIALTIES

Reservation and Ticket Agents

Specialty	Responsibilities
Automobile club travel counselors	Plan trips, map suitable routes, reserve hotel or motel accommodations, calculate mileage, and make bus, train, and plane reservations for members of automobile clubs.
Gate agents	Assist passengers and check flight tickets at the entrance gate or station when passengers are boarding or disembarking. They assist passengers to the correct boarding area, check flight tickets, make boarding announcements, and assist elderly, disabled, or young passengers when they board or depart.
Ticket agents	Sell tickets for transportation agencies such as airlines, bus companies, railroads, and steamship lines.

appeal, the adviser should book a cruise. If experiencing Alaska itself is the objective, the ferry is a better choice.

Government tourism departments do not sell products per se, but they aggressively market the locale's attractions in magazines, in newspapers, and sometimes on television, and they attempt to reach those outside the area who arrange conventions, business meetings, and other events.

Sales and marketing occupations may include the following:

- Marketing Director
- Sales Manager
- Sales Representative
- Administrative Assistant
- Travel Agent
- Advertising Director
- Director of Tourism

Security

Cruise lines and tour operators need to provide security for their clients. They must guard against thieves, con artists, vandals, pirates, and terrorists, among others. This department also intervenes in the event of altercations between passengers and makes sure no illegal activities are carried out onboard ship or within tours. Security responsibilities sometimes include fire prevention and periodic fire drills.

The stakes involved in this industry segment have risen, and the need for highly sophisticated security has increased substantially. Acts of terrorism and piracy are very real threats. Security officers must be highly trained and computer savvy. Those at the top are college educated, and many have additional training or experience with military or law enforcement organizations. Security officers often train other staff members to notice and report suspicious behavior.

Motor coach operators have a responsibility to select safe stops and to make sure their vehicles are secured during passengers' absences. Even local walking-tour guides have to be sure they do not take tourists into high-risk areas. Clients may become separated from tours, despite all precautions, and their safety remains the responsibility of the tour operators.

Security occupations may include the following:

- Chief Security Officer
- Investigator
- Network/Computer Security Specialist
- Plainclothes Operative

Human Resources

Human resources personnel make sure the right people are hired for all positions, manage insurance programs and other benefits, and offer ongoing training and continuing-education opportunities. They ensure that employees are up-to-date on the latest trends and are thus able to anticipate their clients' needs. They also participate in contract negotiations with employees represented by collective bargaining units and respond to employee grievances.

Human resources occupations may include the following:

- Human Resources Director
- Human Resources Manager
- Human Resources Representative
- Employee Training Manager
- Employee Trainer
- Labor Relations Manager

Information Technology/Multimedia

The small-business owner does everything via technology and needs both information technology equipment and the expertise to use it. Midsize companies need the same type of equipment but more of it. Both need to be aware of new products as they are introduced, so they can stay competitive in an increasingly technological world.

Cruise ships run on technology. The captain and crew use navigational technology. Nightclubs onboard need amplifiers, special-effect lighting, and computerized synthesizers. A public address system aids communication. Wide-screen televisions keep passengers entertained and informed. Music adds to the serenity of the spa experience. Word-processing programs and printers produce daily agendas and menus, along with instructional materials detailing fire-drill procedures and the location of lifeboats, for example.

Because technology is only as good as the person using it, the larger companies have to not only be aware of constant advances but also make sure their employees are fully trained.

Information technology and multimedia occupations may include the following:

- Information Technology Director
- Multimedia Technician
- Computer Technician

Tour Guides and Support

Large guided tour companies constitute a substantial segment of the travel industry. Travelers who want an overview of a region rely on the expertise of those conducting the tour. For some, the tour is an end in itself, while others use it as an introduction before traveling to the destination independently. Tour guides must have extensive knowledge of the area visited, including speaking both the country's language and the language of the people being guided. Also needed is knowledge of the history of the area, and ability to weave colorful or humorous anecdotes into the presentation. Strong organizational skills, attention to detail, and strong people skills keep the tour on track and ensure that all participants come away satisfied.

The large companies have support staff, usually at the company's headquarters, who handle the arrangements for hotels, included meals, and included sightseeing venues. These people need intimate knowledge of the cities where overnight stops are scheduled so that chosen hotels are located in areas where guests can walk in safety to dining, shopping, or other entertainment, as well as explore independently.

PROJECTED EMPLOYMENT FOR SELECTED OCCUPATIONS

Scenic and Sightseeing Transportation

Employment		
2009	Projected 2018	Occupation
3,460	3,500	Bus drivers, transit and intercity
3,300	16,400	Captains, mates, and pilots of water vessels
780	1,100	Reservation and transportation ticket agents and travel clerks
1,420	1,900	Sailors and marine oilers
2,520	3,300	Tour guides and escorts

Source: U.S. Bureau of Labor Statistics, Industries at a Glance, Occupational Employment Statistics and Employment Projections Program.

Smaller companies offer tours to local destinations. For example, travelers on a tour that includes France, may on one of their free days in Paris, opt for a local company's tour to Claude Monet's gardens at Giverney. Included in this category are those local city, museum, and other guides who board coaches at predetermined itinerary stops.

Tour guide and support occupations may include the following:

- Company Tour Guide
- Local Tour Guide
- Personal Escort
- Motor Coach Driver
- Support Worker

Primary Shipboard Personnel

Arguably the most important cruise ship employees are the captain and crew. The captain joins passengers for dinner, but most of the crew has little or no client contact. Even with today's high-technology navigational tools, some hands-on effort is required, and these highly trained professionals assist the captain in making sure the passengers enjoy a smooth, safe voyage. They are prepared to deal with unforeseen mechanical difficulties, sudden bad weather, or any other difficulties that could occur. It is also their responsibility to perform the day-to-day maintenance requirements of the ship and handle breakdowns that, though unlikely, can occur.

Primary shipboard occupations may include the following:

- Captain
- Engineer
- Deckhand
- Mate
- Marine Oiler

Housekeeping and Maintenance

These cruise-line positions clean and maintain accommodations and equipment aboard ship. It is estimated that nearly two-thirds of cruise ship passengers are repeaters. Every effort is thus made to ensure they are comfortable and that the vessel sparkles from stem to stern. Cruisers demand cleanliness in their cabins and in the common areas, and although they do not see behind the

scenes, they expect clean food preparation areas as well. Of particular importance is making sure all kitchen surfaces are sanitized to avoid cross-contamination.

It takes a sizeable cleaning and janitorial staff to keep the ship immaculate. Pools must be kept clean and chlorinated. Personal care salons and spas have to be cleaned between services. Dining areas, bars, theaters, and casinos all require frequent attention. Whether the vessel is the *Queen Elizabeth II* or a ferry, the decks have to be swabbed, the bed linens fresh, and the bar glasses free of water spots.

Housekeeping and maintenance occupations may include the following:

- Facility Manager
- Housekeeping Director
- Cleaner
- Custodian/Janitor
- Laundry Worker
- Pool Maintenance Worker
- Dishwasher
- Maintenance Manager
- Electrician
- Painter
- Plumber
- Carpenter
- Heating, Ventilation, and Air-Conditioning (HVAC) Specialist
- General Maintenance and Repair Worker

Food and Beverage

Cruise passengers expect gourmet cuisine, prepared perfectly, and presented creatively. In addition to the formal dinners, and endless buffets, food is available in bars and snack and coffee shops. This requires a large and well-trained staff. In addition to cruise ships, these jobs are a factor in company-owned planned-vacation resorts such as Club Med.

Food and beverage occupations may include the following:

- Chef
- Sous Chef
- Pastry Chef
- Prep Cook
- Food Server
- Bartender

Casino and Entertainment

Casinos continue to be popular with passengers. The staff keeps the casino running smoothly and handles the occasional situation where a patron might become unruly. Most of the casino visitors are recreational, not hard-core gamblers, and are there to have a good time and add to the overall cruise experience.

High-quality entertainment is expected, and the cruise line obliges with nightclub acts, formal shows, and cinema. Entertainers are professionals in their field. Cruise lines also hire lecturers to give talks about areas to be visited or, in the case of a themed cruise, on the subject theme. Sometimes classes are offered, such as on cooking the foods of the region visited.

Casino and entertainment occupations may include the following:

- Manager
- Card Dealer
- Film Projectionist
- Musician
- Night Club Entertainer
- Instructor

Recreation and Fitness

This category includes those onboard people who make sure passengers are aware of their many options and who encourage them to take part in those activities. They have to be good with people and have the ability to draw shy passengers out of their shells. They lead the aerobics classes, act as trainers in the weight room, and provide instruction on the climbing wall. Some cruise lines offer free or reduced sailings to single men in return for their dancing with unescorted ladies. Employees make sure these gentlemen spread themselves around and avoid spending too much time with one individual.

Recreation and fitness occupations may include the following:

- Social Director
- Activity Leader/Instructor
- Personal Trainer
- Spa Manager
- Massage Therapist
- Skin Care Specialist
- Hair Stylist
- Manicurist
- Pedicurist

INDUSTRY OUTLOOK

Overview

The outlook for the travel and tourism industry shows it to be stable in some areas and in decline in others. The industry has been affected by the global recession of 2007-2009, but it is expected to resume growing in the near term. Corporate travel has lessened, as companies have tightened their belts, but not all business travel can be eliminated. A large portion of it is conducted in the pursuit of sales, so the need exists to continue or even increase such travel. In addition, couples are choosing parenthood later and taking more vacations before becoming encumbered with families. That said, family travel represents a sizable chunk of the industry, and families will continue traveling, though they may make budgetary adjustments such as exploring their home states' riches and postponing the trip to Disney World.

The BLS projects that the number of jobs for travel agents in the United States will decline by 1 percent between 2008 and 2018. The job market for travel guides is also expected to remain flat. This compares to an average growth rate across all occupations of 11 percent for this same period, and tour guide jobs, by contrast, are expected to grow at this average 11 percent rate.

The cruise ship segment of the industry has snowballed. In the seven years between 2002 and 2009, approximately forty-seven thousand cruise ship jobs were created. With new and bigger ships coming, it would seem that anyone could find a job in this industry sector. However, most of these jobs are at the low end of the scale, involving cleaning, food preparation, and so on. Turnover is high on cruise lines, as most who work on these ships do not intend to make doing so a permanent career. As a result, there are always openings, as workers go back to school, start a family, or decide to put down roots on land.

It is predicted that growth will continue in other areas of travel and tourism, particularly exotic and luxury travel, as that market is less affected by the economy. Medical tourism will grow as well. Travel for volunteerism and humanitarian purposes has mushroomed in the wake of Hurricane Katrina and the devastating earthquakes in Haiti and South America. People with time and disposable income feel a responsibility to help. While that category of traveler does not spend lavishly, they can help keep the industry afloat until the economic situation turns around.

Another industry threat is the ever-present danger of terrorist attacks. Increased security will help ease fears, but there are some who will not fly unless absolutely necessary. This may be a boon to the cruise industry, as departure ports can be reached by car. People will continue traveling, but they may look for creative solutions to safety and economic issues. The industry, too, must find creative ways to make travel appealing.

Some trips cannot wait for better days. Travel professionals can reach out to those who want to treat children and grandchildren to an extensive multigenerational trip. There is a small window of opportunity when the kids are old enough to appreciate the wonders they will see and still young enough to want to take such a trip. Such trips are often planned around a milestone birthday or wedding anniversary, and that, not the state of the economy, dictates when the trip will be taken.

Employment Advantages

Tourism is one of the largest drivers of revenue in the United States. Thus, opportunities will always exist for those seeking employment in tourism-boosting professions, which remain crucial to the health of regional economies. Published salary ranges can be misleading, as lodging and meals can be part of one's compensation package while traveling. Some industry professionals, tour guides and escorts for example, also receive tips.

Not all advantages are monetary. Entrepreneurs enjoy independence. Some choose to work only part of the year and specialize in locations with peak seasons. There is room for laidback individuals to work extremely hard for shorter periods of time, just as there is room for careerists who wish to work long hours to reap great rewards. Those afflicted with wanderlust—who are the most likely to seek jobs in this industry—can see the world while showing it to their coach or cruise ship passengers. Whether self-employed or an employee of a large agency, an employee in this industry will likely have great opportunities to travel. "Fam" trips are a

mainstay as resorts, hotels, attractions, and even governments invite agents to their destination in the hope those agents will steer clients to the destination.

Annual Earnings

According to the U.S. Department of Labor, the domestic travel and tourism industry earned revenues of $221 billion in 2007. The department predicts modest to average growth in some facets of the industry and substantial growth in others.

As many agents and other travel professionals are self-employed, it is difficult to gauge their earnings. Jobs often pay commissions, not salaries, and some work only part time. Commissioned sales representatives or travel agents earn less during lean years but can make up for it when business is good. This requires strategic planning and preparing in advance for slow periods.

RELATED RESOURCES FOR FURTHER RESEARCH

AMERICAN SOCIETY OF TRAVEL AGENTS
1101 King St., Suite 200
Alexandria, VA 22314
Tel: (800) 275-2782
Fax: (703) 739-0453
http://www.asta.net.org

NATIONAL ASSOCIATION OF CRUISE ORIENTED AGENCIES
7600 Red Rd., Suite 128
Miami, FL 33143
Tel: (305) 663-5626
Fax: (866) 816-7143
http://www.nacoa.com

NATIONAL BUSINESS TRAVEL ASSOCIATION
110 N Royal St., 4th Floor
Alexandria, VA 22314
Tel: (703) 684-0836
http://www.ustoa.com

ABOUT THE AUTHOR

Norma Lewis is the author of four nonfiction books, one an account of the Yukon gold rush for young adults and the other three pictorial histories of the southwestern Michigan area she calls home. She is a prolific writer for magazines and, during the twenty years she has been writing travel articles, has covered destinations, escorted group travel, solo travel, and recreational vehicle camping. She holds a bachelor of science degree in business administration from Aquinas College.

FURTHER READING

Beaverstock, Jonathan V., et al. *International Business Travel in the Global Economy.* Burlington, Vt.: Ashgate, 2010.

Chin, Christine B. N. *Cruising in the Global Economy: Profits, Pleasure, and Work at Sea.* Burlington, Vt.: Ashgate, 2008.

Goeldner, Charles R., and J. R. Brent Ritchie. *Tourism: Principles, Practices, Philosophies.* Hoboken, N.J.: John Wiley & Sons, 2008.

Mancini, Marc. *Cruising: A Guide to the Cruise Line Industry.* 2d ed. Florence, Ky.: Cengage Learning, 2003.

Medlik, S. *Dictionary of Travel, Tourism, and Hospitality.* 3d ed. Oxford Butterworth-Heinemann, 2003.

Mintzer, Rich. *Start Your Own Travel Business.* New York: Entrepreneur Media, 2007.

Smith, Melanie K., and László Puczkó. *Health and Wellness Tourism.* Boston: Elsevier/Butterworth-Heinemann, 2009.

United Nations World Tourism Organization. http://www.unwto.org/facts.

U.S. Bureau of Labor Statistics. *Career Guide to Industries,* 2010-2011 ed. http://www.bls.gov/oco/cg.

U.S. Census Bureau. North American Industry Classification System (NAICS), 2007. http://www.census.gov/cgi-bin/sssd/naics/naicsrch?chart=2007.

U.S. Department of Commerce. International Trade Administration. Office of Trade and Industry Information. Industry Trade Data and Analysis. http://ita.doc.gov/td/industry/otea/OTII/OTII-index.html.

Vogel, Harold L. *Travel Industry Economics: A Guide for Financial Analysis.* Cambridge, England: Cambridge University Press, 2001.

Veterinary Industry

©Dreamstime.com

INDUSTRY SNAPSHOT

General Industry: Health Science
Career Cluster: Health Science
Subcategory Industries: Animal Hospitals; Livestock Inspection and Testing; Livestock Veterinary Services; Pet Veterinary Services; Veterinary Offices; Veterinary Research and Development; Veterinary Testing Laboratories
Related Industries: Animal Care Services; Livestock and Animal Products Industry; Museums and Cultural Institutions Industry; Public Health Services
Annual Domestic Revenues: $20 billion USD (Hoover's, 2009)
NAICS Numbers: 541712, 541940

INDUSTRY DEFINITION

Summary

The veterinary industry is dedicated to protecting the health of nonhuman animals, from wildlife to livestock and companion animals. In addition to veterinarians, the industry includes a variety of semiskilled and skilled support positions, such as veterinary research technicians, animal grooming and maintenance workers, and veterinary assistants. The industry is closely tied to both the medical research industry and the study of animal behavior in general. Many veterinarians contribute to the study of animal biology, behavior, and physiology, as well as other facets of the life sciences.

History of the Industry

Since its inception, veterinary medicine has been closely related to human medicine, and both industries emerged before the advent of written history. Between 3000 and 2500 B.C.E., humans began domesticating animals for food and other animal products. In the process, they began to learn about the ailments that affect livestock and other working animals, and they began to develop treatments to keep their animals healthy. The first animals studied from a veterinary perspective were horses and other livestock, as well as dogs and cats, the most common companion animals. The early study of animal health served a utilitarian purpose, as humans depended on animals for food and labor. Horses were used for transportation and to aid in farm labor, while dogs and cats hunted pests and protected property.

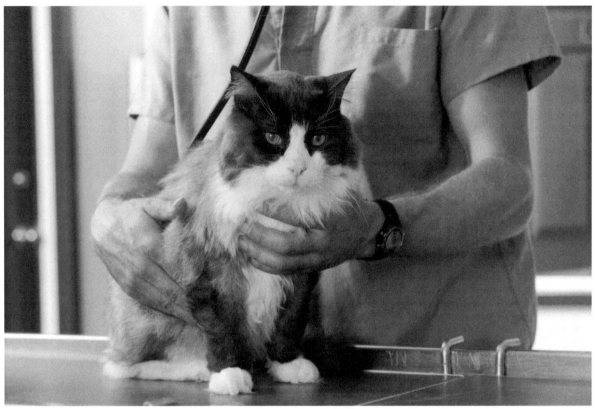

A cat gets a checkup at a small animal hospital. (©Tyler Olson/Dreamstime.com)

Ancient texts indicate that veterinary medicine emerged as a specialty largely in ancient Egypt, where early veterinarians cared for cats and dogs, which were considered sacred animals, as well as a variety of livestock. In ancient India, veterinary medicine was described in manuals written as early as 1800 B.C.E., and it was considered one of the most prestigious fields of study. Records indicate that the first animal hospitals were established in the Indian subcontinent as early as 230 B.C.E. Ancient writings from Greece and Rome also indicate that veterinary studies gained a foothold in those Western societies, from which they spread through Europe.

Modern veterinary science emerged during the European Renaissance, along with major developments in human medicine and the life sciences in general. Researchers and biology enthusiasts in Europe and around the world dissected animals in order to further their studies in human medicine; likewise, medical developments instituted for the benefit of humans filtered into the veterinary field.

Rapid advancements in scientific knowledge and a widespread increase in experimentation on animals led to the systematic development of the veterinary field.

One of the first veterinary schools on record was established in Lyons, France, in 1761. The French government sponsored the establishment of a professional veterinary program out of economic concerns, mostly in an effort to protect and aid the agricultural industry. The development of institutionalized veterinary medicine continued to follow the evolution of the agriculture industry. Veterinary institutions were soon established in many European colonies, including the United States and Canada.

In 1855, the U.S. Department of Agriculture supported the foundation of the Veterinary College of Philadelphia, the first college of veterinary medicine in the United States. In 1879, Iowa State College opened the first public veterinary college, and in 1883, the University of Pennsylvania became the first institution to operate an accredited veterinary program. The American Veterinary Medical Association (AVMA) was established in 1863, and it became the national authority on veterinary practices and education. The AVMA helped popularize veterinary medicine by publishing peer-reviewed journals, by funding its development, and by organizing meetings among professionals in the field.

In the late nineteenth century, funds for veterinary medicine were concentrated on treating maladies that affected work animals and livestock. Veterinarians, however, were also capable of treating companion animals. One of the first major milestones for veterinary medicine in the United States was the discovery of ticks' role in transmitting disease after a major outbreak of Texas fever. Groundbreaking work on ticks and disease transmission helped enhance the relevance of modern veterinary study and led to increased funding for veterinary colleges. Early animal researchers and veterinarians also played an important role in human medicine by studying and investigating a variety of diseases that affect both humans and nonhuman

animals. For example, pioneering work on tuberculosis and a variety of other diseases depended on the work of veterinary specialists.

Following World War I, the U.S. population became increasingly urbanized and the demand for agricultural veterinarians rapidly declined. Many veterinarians began specializing in the treatment of dogs and cats instead. The market for such specialists expanded as cities grew, and the companion animal veterinary industry eventually eclipsed livestock medicine as the largest facet of the veterinary industry. During this same period, the specialty of wildlife veterinary medicine grew, as concern over the health of wild animal populations spread among the populace. The demand for wildlife veterinarians was bolstered during the 1960's by a movement to improve the condition and practices of zoos and other wild animal parks.

The development of the urban veterinary industry resulted in increased specialization. Building on human medical research, veterinarians developed a wide variety of subdisciplines to treat spe-

A dog rests after surgery on his leg. (©Dreamstime.com)

cific types of animals or disorders. By the close of the twentieth century, veterinary medicine constituted a multifaceted and rapidly growing industry serving both commercial and personal interests. While livestock and commercial medicine remained important facets of the field, treatment of companion animals became one of the primary pillars of the industry.

The Industry Today

The veterinary industry remains a robust and rapidly growing field in the early twenty-first century. The growth of the industry is closely linked to the growth of the human population, increasing urbanization worldwide, and the continued popularity and ownership of cats, dogs, and other companion animals. In addition, as disposable income increases in Western countries such as the United States—and as specialty products and industries catering to pet owners, such as pet insurance, develop—the demand for veterinary specialists will continue to increase.

In 2008, according to Hoover's, the U.S. veterinary industry earned more than $20 billion, making it one of the largest segments of the $34 billion domestic pet-care industry. There are no reliable estimates for earnings in the global veterinary industry, but estimates indicate that the global pet industry is also in a state of rapid growth. The Japanese pet industry, for example, accounts for more than $2.2 billion annually, while other countries, such as Australia and the United Kingdom, spend more than $10 billion each on pets and pet health each year.

In the United States, the rapid growth of cat and dog populations has helped fuel the growth of the veterinary industry, even as the demand for agricultural veterinarians has decreased. Veterinary medicine for companion animals has splintered into a number of subfields dedicated to treating specific ailments. In addition to general practitioners, there are veterinarians specializing in dentistry, ophthalmology, cardiology, orthopedics, and a number of other areas.

Veterinary surgery has become one of the major specialties in the field; surgical procedures range from spaying and neutering pets to a variety of specialized procedures. Veterinary oncology is another growing field, driven by the number of pets susceptible to various types of cancer. Veterinary surgeons and oncologists are often employed within animal hospitals or clinics, though some may opt for private practice. Another specialty that is growing rapidly is veterinary orthopedics, largely in the treatment of canines. The large number of dog breeds that suffer from congenital orthopedic disorders has helped veterinary orthopedics become a thriving specialty.

A number of related fields have emerged to supplement traditional veterinary medicine in the twenty-first century. Among these are holistic veterinary medicine, which is a branch of the industry concerned with treating animals using herbs and alternative medical treatments, such as massage, energy therapy, acupuncture, and other types of therapy. Veterinary psychology involves evaluating and treating animals with psychological problems. It is closely related to the study of animal behavior and involves similar methods of evaluation and treatment.

The veterinary industry has also changed in response to the evolving ecological consciousness of the population. Concern over species depletion and extinction has led to greater interest in wildlife veterinary medicine and in helping stop the spread of disease in wild populations. Wildlife veterinarians also play an important role in the medical industry by helping study and evaluate the transmission of disease and the effects of population dynamics on health.

While veterinary practices were once closely tied to utilitarian needs, modern veterinarians serve many clients who desire luxury care for their pets. Some modern vets offer a variety of "comfort services" in addition to basic care, including aromatherapy, alternative medicine, and luxury examination rooms for extra comfort. In addition, the number of veterinarians working in some countries has allowed increased specialization within the profession, where some veterinarians specialize in certain types of animals, such as birds, dogs, cats, horses, or reptiles.

The veterinary industry includes not only veterinarians, technicians, and other workers in animal hospitals and clinics but also pet medication manufacturers and specialists who research and develop new treatments and techniques. Indeed, veterinary research and development has grown into a multibillion-dollar industry, largely buoyed by veterinary pharmaceuticals. The veterinary industry remains tightly tied to the medical industry. Research and development in human medicine and medical technology filters into the veterinary industry and similarly, veterinary research provides essential information used to further the advance of human medicine.

INDUSTRY MARKET SEGMENTS

One method that can be used to analyze the veterinary industry is to examine the division between small, midsize, and large veterinary businesses. According to Hoover's market analysts, the division of wealth within the industry is distributed among a wide variety of companies, from small operations with only a single veterinarian, to veterinary hospitals with dozens of practicing veterinary doctors, to veterinary pharmaceutical companies that may have hundreds of employees.

Small Businesses

Most veterinary practices are small businesses, having twenty or fewer employees and close ties to their immediate communities. The "neighborhood vet" and smaller urban and rural veterinary clinics fall into this category, as do small laboratory, animal testing, and veterinary equipment manufacturing businesses. The average small veterinary business has revenues of less than $1 million per year, although revenues may vary widely, from less than $90,000 to several million dollars.

Potential Annual Earnings Scale. According to the U.S. Bureau of Labor Statistics (BLS), the average annual salary for a veterinarian in 2009 was $90,110.

Clientele Interaction. Most small veterinarian businesses have strong ties to their local communities. In many communities, customers may visit the same veterinarian for the life of their pets and may develop close relationships with their veterinarians. Cultivating relationships with these repeat cus-

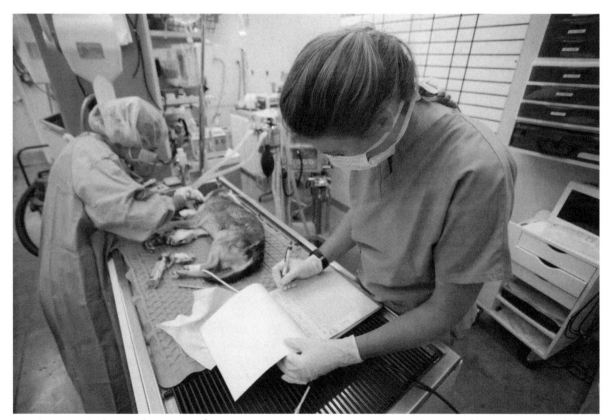

Veterinary surgical procedures range from spaying and neutering pets to setting bones and removing tumors. (©Scott Griessel/Dreamstime.com)

tomers and patients is likely essential to the practice of local veterinarians, as the success or failure of a small practice often depends on the staff's success in building relationships with clients who then become repeat customers.

Small businesses that specialize in the manufacture of veterinary equipment or in animal testing and laboratory work generally survive by filling a specific niche within the industry. A small laboratory might compete by offering types of testing or research not offered by the larger laboratories and testing facilities. These companies depend less on client-patient interaction, but because they typically do not have the marketing or advertising resources of larger companies, they must be able to cultivate a list of repeat clients.

Amenities, Atmosphere, and Physical Grounds. Some veterinary businesses operate within spaces no larger than a midsize one-bedroom apartment, while others occupy one or more large buildings. The layout of a business depends largely on the atmosphere. Urban businesses, for instance, often have to work within smaller spaces than those available in rural and suburban areas.

Space requirements vary widely according to the specifics of the business. For example, a veterinary office specializing in horses and livestock requires a stable or some other accommodating area to separate and examine large animals, while a veterinary office specializing in pet dogs and cats requires a smaller amount of space. Many veterinary offices must also set aside space for quarantining animals and performing surgeries or other procedures. Veterinarian businesses also require different amounts of space depending on the number of clients served in a typical business day. While the smallest veterinary offices may serve no more than ten customers per day, some may see more than fifty clients on a busy day.

Though designs may vary, most veterinary offices must have one or more examination rooms, a waiting room and check-in area for customers, an administrative area for paperwork, and a storage area for supplies. Customers typically see only the waiting area and examination rooms. Waiting areas in most veterinary offices contain seats for customers and may have amenities such as magazines and other reading materials, television, and some amenities for dogs and cats, which represent the most commonly treated clients.

A typical veterinary office has an atmosphere similar to that of a doctor's office, with the addition of animal- and pet-themed decorations. Many veterinary offices hang pictures of animals and clients' pets on their walls, as well as informative posters and signs displaying information about pet health risks such as fleas, ticks, and intestinal parasites. The magazines and other reading materials kept in the waiting room are also typically animal-themed.

Typical Number of Employees. Most small veterinary businesses have twenty or fewer employees. Some businesses, including private veterinary practices, may have as few as five employees, including a veterinarian, one or more technicians and assistants, and one or more office assistants. Veterinary businesses that handle larger numbers of clients or offer many different types of medical procedures require larger staffs. Veterinary supply, animal-testing, and laboratory companies also typically have fewer than twenty employees, though some small laboratories require a large number of support staff, including administrative and laboratory technicians.

Traditional Geographic Locations. Small veterinary businesses can function in virtually any environment with a sufficient population of people with pets or working animals. Smaller veterinary businesses are especially common in larger cities, where space limits the size of the typical business and large populations of pet owners support multiple, neighborhood-style veterinary offices. Small veterinary offices also thrive in smaller rural communities, where they often serve as the only veterinarian for the entire community.

Pros of Working for a Small Veterinary Business. Veterinarians, technicians, and support personnel who work in smaller businesses have the opportunity to build strong, personal relationships with their clients. With a smaller number of clients and a large number of repeat customers, employees of small veterinary offices can get to know their clients and their patients with an intimacy that may be impractical in a larger business. In addition, a small vet's office or animal hospital draws its clients primarily from the immediate area, allowing the veterinarians and other staff to become or feel part of the larger community.

Smaller veterinary businesses require less overhead than do larger businesses, in terms of staffing, supplies, equipment, and real estate costs. Because smaller businesses draw many of their clients from the immediate area, they are not as dependent on advertising and not as closely tied to economic fluctuations. In periods of recession, for instance, when businesses must cut back on advertising and marketing, smaller businesses may weather economic downturns by relying on their repeat and local customer base.

Cons of Working for a Small Veterinary Business. Working in a small veterinary office presents a number of challenges. Because smaller businesses earn less in a typical working day, income potential for the business owner and managers is less than can be earned by working for a larger business. In addition, although there are economic advantages to having a relatively stable customer base of local and repeat clients, small businesses may be vulnerable during prolonged periods of reduced business because they lack the financial resources to maintain their supplies and staff until business rebounds.

Because they often must complete jobs from a number of different categories, employees of small businesses may also find that they have a more demanding workload than those working in similar positions at larger companies. A neighborhood veterinarian, for example, might be asked to treat gerbils, rats, mice, fish, birds, snakes, lizards, dogs, cats, and a variety of other animals, while veterinarians at larger animal hospitals and clinics can specialize in only one type of animal.

Costs

Payroll and Benefits: While most veterinarians work on salary, other staff members are typically paid an hourly wage. Many small veterinary businesses are unable to offer traditional benefits to their employees but may offer alternative benefits, including free treatment for employees' pets or discounts on pet medication and supplies.

Supplies: All veterinary offices require a wide variety of supplies, including medications, equipment, cleaning and sanitation supplies, office supplies, and other items. While larger businesses and chains can reduce supply costs by purchasing in bulk quantities, maintaining sufficient supplies is a significant challenge for many small businesses.

External Services: Most veterinary offices require few external services other than the delivery of supplies. Some hire external vendors to dispose of expired medication and other biohazardous materials or to launder uniforms and medical gowns. Some veterinary businesses also hire outside vendors to handle laboratory tests, including blood, urine, and feces screening.

Utilities: Most veterinary businesses pay for basic utilities, including gas/oil, water, sewage, electricity, telephone, and Internet services.

Taxes: Small businesses are required to pay state, local, and federal taxes, as well as licensing fees applicable to their region. Most veterinary offices also must carry significant insurance to protect staff and customers from both injury and litigation.

Midsize Businesses

Midsize veterinary businesses include animal hospitals and clinics, joint private practices with several staff veterinarians, and many animal-testing and laboratory facilities. These businesses are more generalized than are small businesses, and they must draw clients from outside their immediate community to earn sufficient revenues. Midsize businesses are often part of larger chains that operate branches in various locations.

Potential Annual Earnings Scale. Wages in midsize veterinary businesses tend to be at the higher end of the salary range. Most midsize businesses earn between $1 million and $3 million annually, and the average veterinarian's salary according to the BLS was $90,110 in 2009. Veterinarians in the seventy-fifth income percentile earned $105,190. Most technicians, assistants, and supporting staff members are paid hourly wages.

Clientele Interaction. While the atmosphere of many small veterinary businesses may seem hectic, with each employee struggling to complete tasks in a variety of categories, midsize businesses usually have sufficient staff to institute a more functional division of labor. In some midsize businesses, veterinarians and other staff members are able to dedicate a greater proportion of their time to clientele interaction, despite having to handle large customer volume.

Many midsize veterinary businesses are animal hospitals, which may employ specialists in a variety

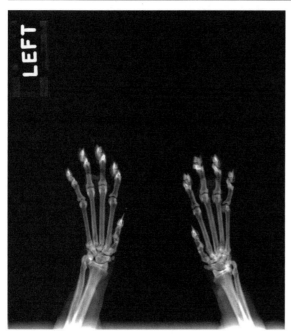

An X ray of a cat's paws. Other diagnostic imaging used for pets includes magnetic resonance imaging, ultrasound, and computed tomography. (©Dwight Smith/Dreamstime.com)

nesses catering to livestock and commercial animals need significantly larger areas than do those catering to domestic cats, dogs, and other pets. Whatever the type of business, most midsize veterinary establishments have one or more waiting areas for clients, several examination and quarantine rooms, and rooms for storage and supplies. Since many midsize veterinary businesses are animal hospitals, they may have examination rooms set aside for certain types of treatments, including X-ray rooms and surgical rooms.

The waiting rooms and client areas of a veterinary office are usually decorated with animal-themed pictures, posters, and other items. Outside of the animal themes, the offices resemble medical waiting rooms, with magazines and other reading materials and, often, televisions for clients who are waiting while their pets are treated.

While a midsize business is often more formal and organized than a small business, most veterinary offices strive to create a friendly and inviting atmosphere in those areas set aside for clients. As midsize businesses often have significant funds for designing their interior spaces, they are more able to offer amenities to their clients, including multiple restrooms, cable or satellite television, wireless Internet access, and comfortable furniture.

Typical Number of Employees. Midsize veterinary practices generally employ between twenty and thirty employees, including veterinarians, technicians, customer service attendants, supply and equipment specialists, cleaning staff, and temporary workers. While a midsize laboratory or testing facility may require between ten and twenty employees, many animal hospitals provide late-night hours and may therefore require a much larger staff, divided among two or more shifts.

Traditional Geographic Locations. Midsize veterinary businesses are often located in areas with significant traffic, such as outside a major metropolitan area or at the intersection of a major highway system. While small veterinary practices specialize in providing community care, midsize veterinary businesses must draw clients from across the surrounding area. Midsize businesses are best situated where they can draw some business from their immediate area while being easily accessible to those traveling from other nearby areas. Locations at the edge of cities or in suburbs are ideal, as businesses can attract clients from all surrounding

of veterinary fields. Staff specialization can lead to greater customer satisfaction, as clients feel that their animals are receiving the most appropriate treatment. In addition, midsize businesses can often afford support personnel who specialize in client interactions, helping customers feel welcome and comfortable.

While midsize businesses have some distinct advantages in providing service, the atmosphere of midsize veterinary offices is often more formal than that of small-business offices. Because midsize businesses depend on drawing customers from outside the immediate community, they do not cultivate the same community-oriented atmosphere that many smaller veterinary offices do. In addition, higher volumes often prevent the relationships between staff and clients from becoming as intimate as they do in smaller businesses.

Amenities, Atmosphere, and Physical Grounds. Midsize businesses require more space than do their smaller counterparts. Whereas smaller veterinary businesses more often need to organize themselves to fit within an existing space, midsize businesses often have the luxury of designing their space to fit their needs. Veterinary busi-

communities that have few or no small veterinary offices serving them.

Pros of Working for a Midsize Veterinary Business. One of the primary benefits of working at a midsize veterinary business is job security. Midsize businesses are often financially stable relative to their smaller counterparts. Because many midsize veterinary businesses offer veterinary specialists, they receive business from clients who cannot receive specialized care at their local veterinary offices. Midsize businesses are also able to compete by offering longer hours and less wait time.

Employees of midsize veterinary businesses are also more likely to enjoy employment benefits than are those working at smaller businesses. This is especially true for employees of veterinary chain businesses, as these businesses often offer group medical and dental plans and other benefits. Even independent midsize veterinary businesses often have a large enough staff and high enough annual revenues to offer health insurance, retirement plans, and other benefits to their employees.

Employees of midsize businesses also benefit from an increased division of labor, which often translates into less hectic workloads and more assistance being available for all employees. While receptionists at small veterinary offices might have to handle tasks ranging from customer service and scheduling to cleaning patient and customer areas, receptionists at midsize businesses might enjoy the assistance of other customer-service specialists, cleaning staff, and other personnel, helping lighten their workload.

Cons of Working for a Midsize Veterinary Business. Some individuals may prefer the atmosphere of small businesses, which provide more personal client interactions and greater diversity of activities, over that of midsize businesses. In addition, some prefer small businesses because of their community-oriented nature, which is often lacking at a larger veterinary firms.

Midsize businesses have higher costs than do small businesses, for both staff and supplies. For this reason, midsize businesses must maintain higher customer volume. Some employees may find that the need to maintain high numbers of customers results in uncomfortable levels of activity during a given shift. Employees at midsize businesses might also find that they work longer hours than do those at smaller businesses, particularly since midsize businesses often offer late shifts and some offer twenty-four-hour emergency services. Veterinarians at midsize hospitals may need to answer calls overnight or visit the hospital at all hours to handle emergencies that require special attention.

Costs

Payroll and Benefits: Midsize veterinary businesses typically pay veterinarians and managers annual salaries, while most other employees earn hourly wages.

Supplies: Midsize veterinary businesses require numerous supplies, from medical equipment and medication to cleaning, sanitary, and paper supplies.

External Services: Many midsize veterinary businesses have in-house laboratory equipment, but others use outside vendors to process some materials and conduct advanced testing. Some may also contract external laundry and disposal services to clean uniforms and dispose of biohazardous materials and expired medication.

Utilities: Midsize businesses are responsible for paying for gas/oil heating, electricity, water, sewerage, telephone, and Internet services.

Taxes: Midsize businesses are responsible for paying all applicable state, federal, and local taxes. Most veterinary businesses also incur significant expenses for insurance, to cover both injury and malpractice. In some states, veterinary offices must pay special licensing fees for animal care and housing.

Large Businesses

There are relatively few large veterinary businesses. Such businesses have more than fifty employees and revenues generally ranging above $5 million annually. Banfield Pet Hospitals, a multinational corporation owned by the Mars Corporation, earns in excess of $180 million annually. According to Hoover's, the fifty largest companies in the United States hold only 10 percent of the nationwide veterinary market. Most of the largest veterinary businesses are part of national or international chains, such as those in the Banfield and VGA Antech companies, which are part of the PetSmart chain of pet and pet-supply retailers.

Potential Annual Earnings Scale. Most employees in the largest veterinary businesses earn salaries commensurate with those in midsize businesses. The average veterinarian's salary according to the BLS was $90,110 in 2009. Veterinarians in the ninetieth income percentile earned $142,910. Because their income level is determined by the overall earnings of the chain rather than an individual branch, general and district managers for chain businesses may earn significantly higher incomes on average. The average salary of a general or operations manager in 2009 was $110,550. Most technicians and veterinary support staff, as well as cleaning staff and other personnel at larger veterinary businesses, are paid hourly wages.

Clientele Interaction. Managers and veterinarians at large businesses tend to interact with clients in a more formal manner than do their counterparts at smaller businesses. Greater overall customer volume translates into the need for a more rigid system of customer service and does not always allow time for personal interaction. Despite these constraints, large veterinary businesses are capable of employing personnel dedicated to customer satisfaction and customer relations.

Many of the larger veterinary businesses operate in conjunction with veterinary universities or veterinary technician programs. As a result, customers of large veterinary businesses often interact with students who are learning the veterinary practice. The presence of student assistants sometimes allows veterinarians and other staff members to dedicate more time to customer interaction.

Amenities, Atmosphere, and Physical Grounds. Large veterinary businesses differ widely in appearance and atmosphere. A veterinary university, for instance, may be a complex operation with numerous examination, laboratory, and medical rooms and several waiting areas capable of handling a large volume of customers. A veterinarian business located within a pet store may occupy only a small section of the larger retail environment, with a significantly different overall atmosphere.

Because they handle large volumes of customers, most large veterinary businesses provide a number of basic amenities, from restrooms and vending machines to television and Internet service for customers. The waiting and lobby areas of large veterinary businesses, like those of midsize and small businesses, tend to resemble those of doctors' offices. Decorations often include posters and postings with information about animal illnesses and office policies. Magazines and reading materials usually include a number of animal-themed publications and materials.

Typical Number of Employees. A single office within a chain of veterinary offices may have only ten or twenty employees, while the company as a whole may employ thousands of people. For example, Banfield Pet Hospitals employs more than five thousand veterinarians, technicians, and support personnel through its offices in the United States, the United Kingdom, and Mexico. In addition, companies such as Banfield provide employment for hundreds of temporary and student workers.

Traditional Geographic Locations. Many of the largest veterinary businesses are part of national or multinational chains, with locations spread across a vast geographic area. Large single-location veterinary businesses include major veterinary colleges and other learning centers. These are generally located in or near major metropolitan areas. Large veterinary businesses must maintain significant customer volume to afford their considerable costs, but most are able to expend a significant amount on advertising and marketing. Veterinarian offices located within pet stores often offer veterinary services to customers purchasing pets, thereby maintaining a consistent level of customers.

Pros of Working for a Large Veterinary Business. Large companies are generally able to offer employment benefits, including insurance and medical care for employees, because they are able to secure group rates for coverage. In addition, large companies have the financial backing to purchase better equipment and supplies for their employees and to hire more support personnel to enhance their operations.

For employees of veterinary learning institutions, working in a student environment can entail access to experimental and emerging veterinary techniques, medications, and equipment. In addition, medical learning institutions can sometimes provide employees with amenities not available through smaller companies, such as parking permits, gym or fitness-center access, and access to a larger university or college campus with its associated resources.

Cons of Working for a Large Veterinary Business. Large veterinary businesses are usually the least community oriented, and many employees may not want to work in a more corporate and less personal environment. Larger businesses are also more complicated in terms of operation, supplies, and staffing, which can be an important factor to some potential employees.

Another con to working in a large veterinary business is that the success of the business is more closely tied to the state of the local economy, as large businesses are dependent on maintaining significant customer flow. Unlike small veterinary businesses, a large veterinary chain must rely on attracting new customers on a regular basis and must therefore invest heavily in advertising and marketing. If the local economy deteriorates, large businesses are the first to suffer, as new customers become less frequent, while small businesses can weather some financial fluctuations by relying on their repeat clientele.

Costs

Payroll and Benefits: Salaries and benefits vary in large veterinary establishments. In veterinary hospital chains, many employees are offered benefits along with full-time employment. Most veterinarians, managers, and executives are paid salaries, while assistants and technicians are often paid hourly wages.

Supplies: Large veterinary businesses require a wide variety of supplies, from medical equipment and medication to cleaning and administrative supplies. Medical learning institutions must also provide a variety of additional supplies, including learning materials, student computer systems, and other equipment. Larger businesses have some advantages in terms of supply costs, as they are generally able to purchase supplies in bulk.

External Services: Large businesses may hire outside companies to deliver supplies, in addition to hiring laundry services to clean staff uniforms. Most veterinary colleges and universities hire external companies to dispose of hazardous materials and medications. Veterinary colleges may also hire external companies to provide food and beverages to their students and staff.

Utilities: Large businesses pay for water, sewage, gas/oil, and electricity, in addition to telephone and Internet access.

Taxes: Large properties must pay all applicable state, federal, and local taxes, in addition to maintaining specialized insurance against both injury and malpractice. Many businesses must also pay annual licensing fees specific to companies that handle animals.

ORGANIZATIONAL STRUCTURE AND JOB ROLES

The organizational structure of a veterinary business depends on both the size of the business and the type of services offered. Some job roles are specific to certain kinds of businesses. For example, some businesses that treat dangerous or large animals must employ handlers specializing in managing these animals, while a veterinarian who primarily handles domestic pets has no need for these specialized employees. While some businesses require an organized hierarchy of executives and managers, smaller businesses may function with a single manager. Likewise, larger businesses often require a more complex organizational structure to accommodate larger numbers of customers.

The following umbrella categories apply to businesses in the veterinary industry:

- Medical Staff
- Executive Management
- Medical Support Staff
- Animal Care
- Nutrition and Food Services
- Maintenance and Sanitation
- Administrative Support
- Laboratory Services
- Advertising and Marketing
- Human Resources
- Alternative Care

Medical Staff

Veterinarians and veterinary specialists are trained in animal medicine. Like human medical staff, veterinarians attend veterinary school for between three and five years. Though a veterinarian may begin practicing immediately after graduating from veterinary school, most graduates choose to complete a year-long residency program to obtain practical experience.

OCCUPATION SPECIALTIES

Veterinarians

Specialty	Responsibilities
Poultry veterinarians	Advise poultry raisers on problems, gather information from owners, and inspect flocks, pens, and housing.
Public health veterinarians	Control and prevent diseases that are transmitted from animals to humans. They inspect livestock and food- and drug-processing plants and provide information to the public.
Veterinary livestock inspectors	Test animals for the presence of disease by performing standard clinical tests and submitting specimens of tissues and other parts for laboratory analysis.
Veterinary meat inspectors	Inspect establishments engaged in slaughtering livestock and processing meat to detect evidence of disease or other conditions.
Veterinary virus-serum inspectors	Inspect establishments that manufacture serums, toxins, and similar products used in the treatment of animals to enforce state or federal standards.

After completing veterinary training at an accredited program, veterinarians may choose to become board certified, meaning that they receive endorsement from the American Veterinary Medical Association (AVMA), an organization that is empowered by the U.S. Department of Education to represent veterinarians and measure quality in the industry. Those veterinarians who seek endorsement from the AVMA must complete an additional three- to four-year residency in one of twenty AVMA-recognized specializations.

Like medical doctors, veterinarians can specialize in various disciplines, including internal medicine, surgery, oncology, dermatology, radiology, anesthesiology, neurology, and cardiology. Specialized veterinarians have more diverse employment options, including working in veterinary learning institutions and animal hospitals. Veterinarians who do not obtain board certification generally work in private practice or for private veterinary clinics. In addition to specializing in a branch of medicine, veterinarians may also specialize in a certain type of animal or a certain type of veterinary environment. For instance, some veterinarians specialize in treating animals in zoological parks, and others specialize in treating commercial animal populations, such as livestock and other working animals.

In a private practice or small veterinary clinic, the veterinarian generally also serves as the executive manager. Other veterinary businesses have separate employees serving as managers and executives. Veterinarians are generally paid a salary, ranging from under $50,000 to well over $150,000 per year in the United States.

Medical occupations may include the following:

- Executive Veterinarian
- Veterinary Associate
- Veterinary Neurologist
- Veterinary Surgeon
- Veterinary Anesthesiologist
- Veterinary Oncologist
- Veterinary Dentist
- Veterinary Nutritionist
- Veterinary Dermatologist
- Veterinary Cardiologist

Executive Management

Executive managers oversee the daily operations of veterinary businesses, from hiring and human resources management to ensuring financial stability. While some veterinary businesses, such as private practices, may not have management roles, others, such as the large Banfield Pet Hospitals operated in conjunction with nationwide pet-supply stores, have dedicated executive managers in addition to veterinarians.

In some veterinary businesses, individuals in management are trained or former veterinarians. In other businesses, managers and executive officers are hired for their expertise in management and may not need to have any veterinary experience. In veterinary learning institutions, for instance, executives and managers are generally separate from the medical department and do not handle veterinary duties in addition to their executive functions.

Executive management occupations may include the following:

- Chief Executive Officer (CEO)
- Chief Operating Officer (COO)
- Chief Financial Officer (CFO)
- General Manager
- Personnel Manager
- Administrative Support Manager
- Assistant Manager
- Human Resources Manager

Medical Support Staff

Veterinary technicians and technologists are trained to assist veterinarians in their practice. There are two levels of training recognized by the AVMA: technicians, who undergo a two-year training program, and technologists, who receive four years of professional training. In 2006, there

---

OCCUPATION PROFILE

Veterinary Assistant/Technician

Considerations	Qualifications
Description	Assists veterinarians in procedures performed on animals and monitors animals in veterinarians' offices.
Career clusters	Agriculture, Food, and Natural Resources; Health Science
Interests	People; things
Working conditions	Work inside
Minimum education level	On-the-job training; high school diploma or GED; high school diploma/technical training; junior/technical/community college
Physical exertion	Medium work
Physical abilities	Unexceptional/basic fitness
Opportunities for experience	Military service; volunteer work; part-time work
Licensure and certification	Required
Employment outlook	Faster-than-average growth expected
Holland interest score	IRE

Note: See volume 1, "Publisher's Note," for an explanation of the Holland interest score.

were 131 accredited training programs in the United States, located in forty-four states.

Veterinary technicians and technologists are the equivalent of nurses. Technicians assist veterinarians in performing medical procedures and can perform some basic examinations and other procedures on their own. Technicians and technologists also assist in handling animals and are often responsible for speaking with customers and discussing care and handling with owners.

Like veterinarians, veterinary technicians and technologists may specialize in certain types of animals. There are technicians and technologists who specialize in livestock and the commercial animal industry, while others are trained to handle wildlife and exotic animals. The vast majority of technicians and technologists work with domestic animals.

Most technicians and technologists are paid hourly wages and may be paid between $10 and $20 per hour. Some technologists and technicians work on salary and may earn between $25,000 and $50,000 per year. As they are trained professionals, many technicians and technologists receive basic benefits, including health and dental insurance, from their employers.

Medical support occupations may include the following:

- Veterinary Technician
- Veterinary Technologist
- Managing Technician/Technologist

Animal Care

Animal care assistants fill a wide variety of roles in the veterinary industry, generally occupying a subordinate role to both veterinarians and veterinary technicians and technologists. Animal care assistants are generally required to have high school degrees or the equivalent, and they must receive on-the-job training in the industry.

Animal care experts may specialize in several different areas, including animal training, grooming, handling, and basic care. Many animal care assistants help veterinarians and other veterinary workers by physically handling animals and assisting with grooming and other procedures that require hands-on care.

Animal care workers are generally paid hourly wages of between $6 and $15 per hour, depending on the type of institution employing them. They generally earn more when employed at an animal hospital or a veterinary clinic than if employed at a private practice. Larger corporations, animal hospitals, and learning institutions are more likely to offer animal care workers some benefits, including medical and dental insurance.

Animal care occupations may include the following:

- Animal Care Attendant
- Groomer
- Animal Trainer

Nutrition and Food Services

Some veterinary businesses provide nutrition and diet services for clients. While veterinarians are generally trained in nutrition and diet, there are also assistant positions for those who handle animal nutrition. In the livestock industry, for example, food preparation and the feeding of animals is often handled by trained technicians who study nutritional requirements.

Nutritionists and food service providers are generally paid hourly and may earn wages ranging from $7 to over $10 per hour. Many veterinary businesses assign food service duties to technicians, technologists, or other animal care workers, rather than hiring staff members specifically for food preparation and maintenance. In larger corporations and veterinary colleges and universities, nutritionists may be offered some benefits along with full-time employment.

Nutrition and food service occupations may include the following:

- Nutritionist
- Nutrition Assistant
- General Assistant

Maintenance and Sanitation

Larger veterinary businesses often hire employees to clean and sanitize their facilities. These workers remove trash and recyclable materials, clean floors and surfaces, and may also dispose of hazardous materials, including expired medications. Some maintenance workers are also called on for other activities, including transportation of supplies and equipment, or repair and upkeep of equipment. Maintenance workers who fix equipment may require special training, which is offered through many colleges, universities, and technical training organizations.

Maintenance workers are generally paid hourly wages, which may depend on the type of business. In some larger corporations and in veterinary learning institutions, maintenance workers may be offered some basic worker benefits, such as health insurance, dental coverage, and retirement plans, or life insurance.

Maintenance and sanitation occupations may include the following:

- Custodian/Janitor
- Housekeeper
- Sanitation Assistant
- Maintenance and Repair Worker

Administrative Support

Many veterinary businesses hire staff to handle administrative functions. Administrative assistants handle clerical and bookkeeping functions and may also be responsible for ordering and maintaining office supplies. Administrative assistants may also be responsible for scheduling appointments and organizing schedules for veterinarians and other professionals.

The specific roles and duties assigned to administrative personnel differ widely depending on the type of business. In a veterinary learning institution, for instance, an administrative assistant might have duties related to student enrollment and degree attainment, while an assistant in a small practice might handle some roles that would be assigned to animal care experts or technicians in larger veterinary businesses.

Training courses for administrative assistants are offered through colleges, universities, community colleges, and technical training institutions. Not all administrative assistants complete specialized training, and some companies offer on-the-job training for those interested in administrative positions. Most administrative assistants are paid hourly wages, ranging between $6 and $10 per hour. Some companies offer benefits, such as health and dental insurance, to administrative personnel.

Administrative support occupations may include the following:

- Administrative Assistant
- Bookkeeper
- Clerk

Laboratory Services

Laboratory work is an essential part of veterinary medicine. Laboratory technicians test animal blood and waste and help screen animals for various types of diseases and parasites. In addition, dedicated laboratories perform experiments that help create new medications and treatments. University, college, and technical training programs are available for those seeking to become laboratory workers and technicians. Many independent laboratories hire chemists and other specialists as assistants.

Some veterinary offices have internal personnel dedicated to performing laboratory procedures and managing laboratory operations. There are also dedicated laboratory businesses that serve more than one veterinary office, providing testing and other services for veterinarians. Independent laboratories often have an administrative structure that may include laboratory managers, researchers, specialists in certain procedures, and animal care providers.

Most laboratory assistants are paid hourly wages, typically between $7 and $10 per hour, while some laboratory managers and executives may earn salaries. In some companies, laboratory assistants may be offered benefits, including health insurance.

Laboratory occupations may include the following:

- Laboratory Manager
- Laboratory Technician
- Laboratory Assistant
- Laboratory Maintenance Assistant

Advertising and Marketing

Advertising and marketing staff create and organize advertising and marketing campaigns for their businesses. While small veterinary clinics might not typically engage in any advertising other than placing print advertisements in local publications, large animal-hospitals and major corporations must create advertising, branding, and marketing strategies to compete in the larger market. Some companies hire outside vendors to handle their marketing and advertising needs, while other companies hire one or more full-time employees to help organize marketing and advertising strategies.

In companies large enough to have marketing and advertising departments, advertising executives and assistants often earn salaries similar to those of lower-level managers. Some advertising and marketing specialists have college degrees in marketing, advertising, or business administration. As they are generally part of the executive staff, many advertising and marketing workers receive benefits, including medical and dental insurance.

Advertising and marketing occupations may include the following:

- Advertising and Marketing Director
- Events Director
- Advertising Executive
- Advertising Assistant
- Marketing Assistant

Human Resources

Human resources staff hire, fire, manage, and train personnel, as well as responding to employee conflicts and grievances and administering benefits and payrolls. Some larger veterinary companies and veterinary learning institutions have dedicated human resources staff, whereas others assign human resources duties to general managers and administrators. Human resources personnel may receive training in various disciplines, including psychology, business administration, or specialized human resources programs. They may be either salaried or hourly depending on the type of business. Hourly wage earners may receive between $7 and $20 per hour, depending on the organization. In some businesses, human resources personnel are offered benefits such as medical and dental insurance.

Human resources occupations may include the following:

- Human Resources Manager
- Human Resources Assistant

Alternative Care

The alternative health industry includes a number of disciplines that are generally outside the realm of a standard veterinary education but that have come to represent a major facet of the veterinary industry. Veterinary psychology, holistic animal health, veterinary chiropractic medicine, and veterinary wellness are all growing disciplines that have gained increasing respect in the early twenty-first century.

Most alternative veterinary health professionals receive their training from specialized institutions that may offer certificate programs or other measures of attainment. Some accredited veterinary learning institutions have begun to offer training in certain alternative health practices. As many alternative health professionals are employed in private practice, salaries for these professionals can be similar to those for veterinary professionals, ranging from $50,000 to over $100,000 annually.

Alternative care occupations may include the following:

- Veterinary Chiropractor
- Veterinary Psychologist
- Holistic Veterinary Specialist
- Holistic Dietician

INDUSTRY OUTLOOK

Overview

While many U.S. industries suffered as a result of the 2007-2009 global financial crisis, the veterinary industry, like other medical services, remained strong. Veterinary services are generally considered essential, rather than elective. In addition, the overall increase in the affluence of the American population and a constantly increasing population of domestic animals have contributed to the continuing growth of the veterinary industry.

In 1995, the Pet Food Institute estimated that there were approximately 144 million pet dogs and cats in the United States. The Pet Food Institute also estimated that the pet population was growing at an annual rate of 1.2 percent for dogs and 1.9 percent for cats. Another estimate, conducted by the American Pet Products Association in 2006, indicated that there were 164 million pets in the United States, slightly fewer than the number projected by the the Pet Food Institute's statistics. According to the AVMA, more than 70 percent of working veterinarians concentrate on domestic animals, and approximately 75 percent work in private practice. According to the BLS, there were approximately sixty-eight thousand veterinarians in the United States in 2006, serving a population of more than 140 million pets (growing at a rate of between 1 and 2 percent each year). Taken together, these statistics indicate that there is ample room for growth within the veterinary industry.

The BLS estimates that the number of jobs for qualified veterinarians will grow by 35 percent between 2006 and 2016, which is much faster than the average rate of 11 percent for all industries combined. Because the domestic cat population is growing at a faster rate than is the domestic dog population, the demand for cat services is expected to be the fastest growing segment of the veterinary industry. For each veterinarian entering the industry, moreover, there is a demand for one or more veterinary technicians. The BLS estimates that the technician and technologist industry will grow by more than 41 percent between 2006 and 2016.

As of 2008, there were only twenty-eight accredited veterinary schools in the United States, leading to considerable competition among prospective students. The situation is similar for those seeking to become veterinary technicians and technologists, as there are too few programs available to serve all the nation's prospective students. In addition, most veterinary technicians and technologists leave their jobs after eight years or fewer, creating more employment opportunities for those wishing to enter the industry.

Another factor affecting the amount of work available for veterinary workers is the number of pet owners who regularly use veterinary services. About six of every ten pet owners use veterinary services, a number that is expected to grow as the general population increases in affluence. Job prospects are expected to increase, both for those seeking to provide high-end veterinary services and for those interested in offering cheaper veterinary options to low-income pet owners. Job prospects remain good in both urban and suburban areas, and there are numerous additional opportunities for those seeking to work in underserved rural areas. The veterinary industry is always evolving with the advent of new therapies, techniques, and technology. In the first decade of the twenty-first century, alternative therapies and specialized veterinary medicine were the two major trends dominating the field.

The modern veterinary field has kept pace with human medicine in terms of procedures, equipment, and research. Many procedures that were once available only to humans—such as advanced cancer treatments, joint-replacement surgery, kidney transplants, and other advanced surgical techniques—are now regularly performed on animals. In addition, veterinary specialists, once relatively rare, are becoming more common. Specialist veterinarians generally work at veterinary hospitals or learning institutions and tend to cater to the more affluent customers who can afford the considerable costs of special procedures. The veterinary oncology and orthopedic surgery subsectors, in particular, have grown considerably. This increase is partly related to inbreeding to create purebred dog strains, which has exacerbated degenerative ailments among dogs. Veterinary specialists have allowed many animals to survive that might have been euthanized in the past.

Another area of growth in the specialized veterinary industry is veterinary dentistry, a field that has grown rapidly in the 1990's and early twenty-first century. Many pet owners purchase preventive dental care for their dogs and cats, preventing tooth decay and tooth loss in elderly animals. The emergence of veterinary dentistry has also led to growth in the technician and technologist fields, as veterinary dentistry often requires specially trained assistants.

In a trend similar to those affecting human medicine, the specialization of veterinary professionals has led to a situation in which trained technologists now routinely handle basic veterinary care, while veterinarians handle more advanced diagnoses and procedures. This situation is analogous to that in human medicine, in which nurse practitioners have begun to take a larger role in primary care, while physicians concentrate on advanced care.

The other major growth area in the veterinary industry is alternative care, which includes veterinary psychology, holistic veterinary care, and other alternative treatments. While alternative care is still a relatively small subsector—and is typically available only in urban environments—the number of practitioners offering alternative care has grown in the twenty-first century, as have the number of alternative treatment options for human patients.

Holistic veterinary care has a number of subfields, including herbal medicine, acupuncture, massage, and relaxation therapy. While basic veterinary care is often considered an essential expenditure, holistic care generally appeals only to affluent pet owners with considerable disposable income. Alternative treatments appeal to those who have found that traditional treatments have been ineffective and also to those who have a strong personal belief in the efficacy of alternative treatment options.

Like holistic care, veterinary psychology is generally considered optional rather than essential, and it appeals only to those who have sufficient disposable income. The field has grown, however, because many animal trainers and animal care experts have begun to offer veterinary psychology as part of their behavioral analyses. Veterinary psychology has therefore thrived because of its association with the more popular and practical animal training industry.

Another area of growth within the veterinary industry is wildlife medicine. Increasing global concern over extinction of species and the threats affecting wild populations of animals has increased the demand for specialists in the fields of veterinary medicine and wildlife health. Veterinarians specializing in exotic animals and wildlife may find work in zoological parks and wildlife parks, as well as through conservation organizations.

As populations of wild animals shrink to vulnerable levels, disease can rapidly spread through a population and bring a species to the brink of extinction. Wildlife veterinarians specializing in infectious diseases have therefore found a strong niche in the industry, and the demand for wildlife specialists is expected to grow as the environmental crisis increases in intensity.

Veterinarians may also be employed by state and federal agencies, and they often play an important role in monitoring and preventing the spread of disease between animal and human populations. As concern over diseases such as avian flu and H1N1 (swine flu) have increased in the early twenty-first century, the demand for veterinarians working in infectious diseases and related specialties continues to grow.

Employment Advantages

The BLS and the AVMA both predict that the veterinary industry will continue its current trend of robust growth and increasing availability of jobs.

Because animal care will remain an essential service, the animal care industry will enjoy greater stability than some consumer and recreation industries. Job losses are less likely among veterinarians, technologists, and technicians, and most veterinary clinics are able to maintain sufficient volume to maintain a full staff, even in times of economic turmoil.

The veterinary industry offers a diverse array of career paths, from executive management and education positions to organic chemistry and advanced medical research. The increasing diversity of veterinary medicine, with a growing list of specializations and subspecializations, allows veterinary graduates to choose from a larger list of potential career options. As veterinary medicine diversifies, new career paths are created within the technician and technologist professions as well.

In addition, the veterinary industry offers unique opportunities to have a direct impact on the environment and ecological health, as well as opportunities to positively affect human culture. Veterinarians, technologists, and technicians are essential to efforts to control loss of species, to promote environmental health, and to slow the processes of ecological decay. Veterinary workers are also essential in the effort to provide sufficient food for the global population and to study, prevent, and cure many different kinds of diseases.

While veterinary medicine and skilled assistant positions require investment in education, the veterinary industry provides a number of positions for semiskilled and unskilled workers. These workers serve as janitorial assistants, animal handlers, and maintenance technicians, among other roles. In addition, veterinary hospitals, clinics, and learning institutions employ a large number of students and young workers for temporary jobs and aid in the training of a large number of individuals hoping to enter the animal care industry as professionals. As animal care is available in a variety of areas, from urban environments to rural communities, the industry also spreads job availability around the globe.

Most veterinary workers are drawn to the industry by a basic love for animals and a desire to aid in their care and well-being. Along with zoological parks, wildlife sanctuaries, and the animal sciences, the veterinary industry allows persons with a love for animals to earn a living engaging with animals on a daily basis. Many who work in veterinary positions are drawn more by their own passion for animals than by the wages and job security afforded by the industry.

Annual Earnings

Hoover's estimated the 2009 total revenues of the veterinary industry at $20 billion. The BLS estimated the median annual income of U.S. veterinarians in 2009 at $80,510, with a range from under $47,670 to more than $142,910. Veterinarians employed by federal agencies earned an average of $84,200 in 2009. Veterinary technicians and technologists earned a median income of $12.88 per hour in 2006, within a range of between $10.00 and $18.00 per hour. While technicians and technologists earn far less on average than veterinarians, the lower cost of training and greater job availability continue to make veterinary medical support an attractive option.

According to the BLS, animal caretakers, trainers, and handlers earned an hourly wage in the range between $7 and $12 in 2006. Though this category earned wages significantly lower than the more specialized facets of the industry, animal care workers require less training: On-the-job training often suffices. Because of the low pay compared to other employment opportunities requiring similar levels of educational attainment and experience, animal-care positions tend to attract a large number of students and young workers.

RELATED RESOURCES FOR FURTHER RESEARCH

AMERICAN ANIMAL HOSPITAL ASSOCIATION
  12575 W Bayaud Ave.
  Lakewood, CO 80228
  Tel: (303) 986-2800
  Fax: (303) 986-1700
  http://www.aahanet.org

AMERICAN ASSOCIATION FOR LABORATORY
  ANIMAL SCIENCE
  9190 Crestwyn Hills Dr.
  Memphis, TN 38125-8538
  Tel: (901) 754-8620
  http://www.aalas.org

AMERICAN SOCIETY FOR THE PREVENTION OF
  CRUELTY TO ANIMALS
  424 E 92d St.
  New York, NY 10128-6804
  Tel: (212) 876-7700
  http://www.aspca.org

AMERICAN VETERINARY MEDICAL ASSOCIATION
  1931 N Meacham Rd., Suite 100
  Schaumburg, IL 60173-4360
  Tel: (800) 248-2862
  Fax: (847) 925-1329
  http://www.avma.org

ANIMAL BEHAVIOR SOCIETY
  402 N Park Ave.
  Bloomington, IN 47408
  http://www.abs.org

ASSOCIATION OF AMERICAN VETERINARY
  MEDICAL COLLEGES
  1101 Vermont Ave. NW, Suite 301
  Washington, DC 20005
  Tel: (202) 371-9195
  Fax: (202) 842-0773
  http://www.aavmc.org

HUMANE SOCIETY OF THE UNITED STATES
  2100 L St. NW
  Washington, DC 20037
  Tel: (202) 452-1100
  http://www.hsus.org

INTERNATIONAL VETERINARY INFORMATION
  SERVICE
  P.O. Box 4371
  Ithaca, NY 14852
  http://www.ivis.org

NATIONAL ASSOCIATION OF VETERINARY
  TECHNICIANS IN AMERICA
  50 S Pickett St., Suite 110
  Alexandria, VA 22304
  Tel: (703) 740-8737
  Fax: (202) 449-8560
  http://www.navta.net

UNITED STATES ANIMAL HEALTH ASSOCIATION
  P.O. Box 8805
  St. Joseph, MO 64508

Tel: (816) 671-1144
Fax: (816) 671-1201
http://www.usaha.org

ABOUT THE AUTHOR

Micah L. Issitt is a freelance writer specializing in animal behavior and ethnology. He has been working with veterinarians and animal care experts since his childhood and has had the opportunity to work closely with wildlife and zoological veterinarians, as well as those in private practices. Issitt has published works in journals and textbooks on industry and the development of the American marketplace.

FURTHER READING

American Veterinary Medical Association. "Market Research Statistics." http://www.avma.org/reference/marketstats/1yremploy.asp.

Aspinall, Victoria. *The Complete Textbook of Veterinary Nursing.* St. Louis, Mo.: Elsevier Health Sciences, 2006.

Dobbs, Katherine. *101 Veterinary Technician Questions Answered.* Lakewood, Colo.: American Animal Hospital Association, 2009.

Fox, Michael W. *Laboratory Animal Husbandry: Ethology, Welfare, and Experimental Variables.* New York: SUNY Press, 1986.

Heinke, Marsha. *Practice Made Perfect: A Guide to Veterinary Practice Management.* Lakewood, Colo.: American Animal Hospital Association, 2009.

Hoover's. "Veterinary Services." http://www.hoovers.com/veterinary-services/ID__110—/free-ind-fr-profile-basic.xhtml.

Hunter, Pamela. *Veterinary Medicine: A Guide to Historical Sources.* Surrey, England: Ashgate, 2004.

Koshgarian, Lindsay, et al. *Veterinary Medicine in New England: State-by-State Industry Characteristics and Economic Impacts.* Boston: UMass Donahue Institute, Economics and Public Policy Research Unit, 2008.

Miller, Louise. *Careers for Animal Lovers and Other Zoological Types.* 3d ed. New York: McGraw-Hill, 2007.

Pratt, Paul W. *Medical, Surgical, and Anesthetic Nursing for Veterinary Technicians.* Goleta, Calif.: American Veterinary Publications, 1994.

Rose, Rebecca. *Career Choices for Veterinary Technicians: Opportunities for Animal Lovers.* Lakewood, Colo.: American Animal Hospital Association, 2009.

Shenk, Ellen. *Careers with Animals: Exploring Occupations Involving Dogs, Horses, Cats, Birds, Wildlife, and Exotics.* Mechanicsburg, Pa.: Stackpole Books, 2005.

Shilcock, Maggie, and Georgina Stutchfield. *Veterinary Practice Management: A Practical Guide.* St. Louis, Mo.: Elsevier Health Sciences, 2003.

Swope, Robert E., and Julie Rigby. *Opportunities in Veterinary Medicine Careers.* New York: McGraw-Hill Professional, 2001.

U.S. Bureau of Labor Statistics. *Career Guide to Industries,* 2010-2011 ed. http://www.bls.gov/oco/cg.

U.S. Census Bureau. North American Industry Classification System (NAICS), 2007. http://www.census.gov/cgi-bin/sssd/naics/naicsrch?chart=2007.

U.S. Department of Commerce. International Trade Administration. Office of Trade and Industry Information. Industry Trade Data and Analysis. http://ita.doc.gov/td/industry/otea/OTII/OTII-index.html.

U.S. Department of Labor. *The Big Book of Jobs.* 2009-2010 ed. New York: McGraw-Hill, 2010.

U.S. National Commission on Veterinary Economic Issues. *Study of the Current and Future Market for Veterinarians and Veterinary Medical Services in the United States.* Schaumburg, Ill.: Author, 2000.

Warren, Dean Marvin. *Small Animal Care and Management.* Florence, Ky.: Cengage Learning, 2002.

Video, Computer, and Virtual Reality Games Industry

©Dreamstime.com

INDUSTRY SNAPSHOT

General Industry: Arts and Entertainment

Career Cluster: Arts, A/V Technology, and Communication

Subcategory Industries: Coin-Operated Games Manufacturing; Computer and Peripheral Equipment Manufacturing; Computer Software Games Publishing; Computer Storage Device Manufacturing; Electronic Computer Manufacturing; Electronic Toys and Games Manufacturing; Input/Output Equipment Manufacturing; Software Publishers; Video Game Machines (Except Coin-Operated) Manufacturing

Related Industries: Computer Hardware and Peripherals Industry; Computer Software Industry; Toys and Games Industry

Annual Domestic Revenues: $10.5 billion USD (Entertainment Software Association, 2009)

Annual International Revenues: $42 billion USD (Entertainment Software Association, 2009, and PricewaterhouseCoopers, 2009)

Annual Global Revenues: $52.5 billion USD (PricewaterhouseCoopers, 2009)

NAICS Numbers: 3341, 339932, 339999, 511210

INDUSTRY DEFINITION

Summary

Dedicated to interactive entertainment, the video, computer, and virtual reality games industry is one of the fastest-growing segments of the entertainment industry. Comprising software, hardware, and peripherals, the electronic game industry provides entertainment experiences ranging from immersive games requiring hundreds of hours of play to casual games popularized by social media and mobile devices. The industry relies on innovative technologies to create entertainment for a global audience ranging in age from toddlers to senior citizens.

History of the Industry

Considerable controversy exists as to what constitutes the first video game. In 1952, Alexander Douglas, a doctoral student at the University of Cambridge, programmed his university's computer to run tic-tac-toe simulations. Some historians attribute the first video game to William Higinbotham, a scientist at Brookhaven National Laboratory. In 1958, Higinbotham prepared for a public open house by programming a table-tennis game to run on a laboratory oscilloscope. His game, *Tennis for Two*, was enthusiastically greeted by the public and was the hit of the open house.

Video game players, once mostly teenage boys and young men, have come to include women and older people. (©Stefano Lunardi/Dreamstime.com)

In 1962, the first game available outside a single institute, *Spacewar!*, was created in a Massachusetts Institute of Technology (MIT) computer laboratory after hours by members of MIT's Tech Model Railroad Club. The object of the game was to shoot down one's opponent's spaceship without falling into the Sun. Other programmers who were familiar with academic computers could potentially modify the gameplay of *Spacewar!*, and many did.

The 1970's saw the birth of consumer video games. Instead of being relegated to military bases or universities, video games became coin-operated and were installed in pinball and arcade parlors, pizzerias, and other recreational areas. Clones of *Spacewar!*, based on the original programming at MIT, began appearing in arcades.

In the late 1970's and early 1980's, home video-game consoles began to appear. Manufacturers such as Atari and Magnavox offered simplified versions of coin-operated arcade games playable in consumers' homes, and game consoles sold well. During 1972, the Magnavox Odyssey sold over 100,000 units. These consoles worked with cartridges containing individual games, enabling users to play many different games by purchasing many different cartridges for the same console.

As the decade progressed, consumers became disenchanted with the quality of cartridge-based games, which were noticeably more primitive than the full-sized coin-operated machines found in arcades. Seeking to earn profits quickly, some companies preyed on consumers eager for the latest games by repackaging old games and selling them as new titles. Other companies' game quality dropped precipitously as coin-operated games continued to advance, and consumers became reluctant to purchase titles from an industry that sought only profit.

During this same time period, personal computers (PCs) began to drop in price and become more affordable for families. Personal computers were popular not only for business applications and word processing but also as hubs of game playing. Infocom's *Zork* series and other text-based games formed a genre known as "interactive fiction" that was popular with young adults. As PCs' processing power increased, games with simple graphics became available.

In 1985, the Nintendo Company released the Nintendo Entertainment System (NES), which was sophisticated enough to rekindle interest in game consoles. The Nintendo games were graphically sophisticated for the time, and they introduced a pair of plumbers (the Mario Brothers) and other iconic characters to the gaming public. These characters would become increasingly important as video gaming evolved, because industry sales would come to be driven in part by franchise characters such as the Mario Brothers who would be featured in many different games.

Sega, too, became involved in the console technology race and introduced Sonic the Hedgehog as a franchise character for its Sega Genesis console. While Sega's games were graphically superior to those of Nintendo, the NES had a more agressive marketing and public relations campaign behind it, and it sold significantly better. In 1999, Sega released the Dreamcast, the first game console with

Internet access, but even that could not save the company.

At the start of the 2010's, Sony's Playstation 3, Microsoft's Xbox 360, and Nintendo's Wii systems are battling for dominance of the console market, and PCs remain strong contenders for video game dominance. The video gaming industry has grown into a multibillion-dollar industry, one that consistently earns greater revenues than the motion picture industry and that appeals to a wide range of demographics.

The Industry Today

As the video game industry has grown, it has realized the need to open new markets. A significant portion of the industry still caters to "hardcore" gamers, or those seeking the most advanced possible hardware and software features and who play games that require hundreds of hours to solve. However, the overall industry seeks to provide a wide range of games to appeal to all ages, genders, and tastes. As the industry seeks to reach all possible markets, casual gamers have become important alongside hardcore gamers. Casual games do not require the powerful hardware needed to run hardcore games, and they generally require very little time commitment. Throughout the world, then, gaming is becoming more popular, more accessible, and more profitable.

The video, computer, and virtual reality games industry—like most industries reliant on technology—is evolving quickly. Although consoles and PCs are currently the dominant platforms, casual gaming (often played in conjunction with social media) is gaining popularity. Thus, the video game industry consists of more than just first-person shooters and sports simulations. It includes solitaire and other simple one-person games, social-media-based games such as *Farmville* that are played on social networking Web sites, and games featuring immersive worlds such as the *Grand Theft Auto* series, as well as educational games designed for young players.

Casual games do not require the same time commitment that hardcore games do. Players can drop in and drop out of casual games without having to

A fitness club in Los Angeles featuring Nintendo's Wii Fit Plus. (AP/Wide World Photos)

remember complex plots, tactical plans, or anything else. Dropping in to play a casual game has no impact on the player's enjoyment because there is no plot to remember. Hardcore games encourage players to spend dozens, if not hundreds, of hours exploring and mastering them. Generally played on consoles or PCs, these games can cost millions of dollars to make, market, and distribute. Hardcore games run the gamut from sports simulations to realist military simulations to fantasy role-playing games (FRPGs).

Another typical type of hardcore game is the massively multiplayer online role playing game (MMORPG). Players of MMORPGs usually pay a monthly subscription fee to access a shared virtual space simultaneously with other gamers from around the world. These are known as "persistent worlds," because events continue to occur in them even when the player is logged out of the game. Other persistent virtual worlds are free to play but have in-game advertising or charge fees for specific, premium features. Historically, these online games have been played mostly on PCs, but console manufacturers are increasingly aware that their players desire virtual gathering spaces and are building virtual worlds based around their consoles.

The social aspect of gaming is growing quickly. Some players not only want to interact with other players (for example, through MMORPGs and virtual worlds), but also encourage their friends on social networks to play with them. Social games (often played while logged into social networking sites, such as Facebook and MySpace) encourage players to get other members of their social networks involved in them. *Farmville*, online *Scrabble*, and other social games provide casual gaming experiences on social networks.

More serious games have grown into a serious business. Also known as educational or vocational games, these interactive games are increasingly used by businesses and other organizations. Employers have recognized the value of using games to train their employees in a virtual world before letting them loose in the real world, with real profits and losses. The U.S. Army, recognizing the power of gaming, has experimented with using military simulation games as recruiting tools.

With the increasing popularity of video games, especially social and casual games, the way consumers access their games is shifting. In the past, consoles and personal computers (PCs) were the dominant gaming platforms, with handheld consoles such as Nintendo's GameBoy and Sony's Playstation Portable as the third most popular platform. This system of game delivery is changing, however, with the evolution of mobile phones. As mobile phones become more sophisticated and better able to support processor- and graphics-intensive games, they are poised to take over as the most popular gaming platform.

As with other parts of the entertainment industry, video games borrow from and mix with many aspects of popular culture. Film, television, toys, and video games seed one another with concepts and licensed properties: popular video games have made the leap to feature films, and television shows have spawned their own video games. Indeed, many projects that begin as films, television programs, video games, or comic books seek to develop complementary projects in the other media to maximize profitability, particularly so-called genre projects. It has become extremely common for a science-fiction film, for example, to have a novelization, a comic book adaptation, Web-based and mobile-phone-based casual gaming tie-ins, and a hardcore console and PC game adaptation or spin-off. Cooperating companies strive to release all such adaptations around the same time, so that each will increase the audience for the others. This entwining of various media is moving toward a convergence of seemingly all entertainment. Hardware manufacturers for PCs, consoles, handhelds, and mobile phones are readying themselves for their products to allow consumers to communicate, play games, play video, and surf the Internet.

Within the video games industry, there are several subindustries. In larger companies, each subindustry may be a subdivision of the same corporation. Game design studios come up with game concepts and details of play (known as game mechanics). The design team creates the conflict, writes the plot, and designs the monsters. Designers create the story that the game publisher will flesh out. Some design teams are subsidiaries of larger game-publishing houses, while others are third-party developers who contract with publishers on a game-by-game basis.

Publishers provide the money and the technical

Tom Taylor, a professional video gamer also known as Tsquared, was signed to a $250,000 contract by Major League Gaming. (AP/Wide World Photos)

expertise to make a game. They employ programmers to write the code necessary to turn designs into software. Artists take these lines of code and create models, textures, and animation, as well as audio tracks, to turn the raw code into a full audiovisual experience. After analyzing the game for bad code and other quality problems, the publisher gives the go-ahead to mass-produce and distribute the game, either on physical media or as a downloadable file online.

INDUSTRY MARKET SEGMENTS

The video game industry ranges in size from hobbyists programming in their spare time to large companies spending millions of dollars on a single game release. The following sections provide a comprehensive breakdown of each of these different segments.

Small Businesses

Small video game businesses typically range from one to ten employees. Many owner-founders began creating video games in their spare time. To break into the video game industry, some small companies act as design studios. They pitch their ideas to video game publishers with a working demo in order to get their game into the hands of consumers. Other small companies provide their games directly to the public on the Web through social networks or as shareware (games freely available for download that require or request fees from players who keep and continue to play them).

Potential Annual Earnings Scale. According to the U.S. Bureau of Labor Statistics (BLS), the average annual salary for a computer hardware engineer in 2009 was $107,410, while the average annual salary for an applications software engineer working for a software publisher was $91,910 and the average annual salary for a computer programmer working for a software publisher was $85,510.

Small businesses vary significantly in earnings, and they may well begin as hobbies for their owners. In social and casual games, businesses may receive micro-payments of $0.10 to $1.00 per customer per month or may receive advertising income rather than player fees. Many such games are unable to earn enough revenues to support their publishers, but others become highly popular and earn for their programmers either direct revenue or a reputation that allows them to gain employment as full-time game developers. At the 2010 Canadian Game Developers Conference, Jason Bailey (chief executive officer, or CEO, of a company brokering virtual currency) claimed that one of his clients grew from zero to one million users in a matter of months. Not coincidentally, he also suggested that all game developers wanting to succeed should move to working on casual or social games. Some game platforms encourage such snowballing popularity. For example, Apple's iTunes Store, which sells games for the iPod, iPhone, and iPad, ranks games by their popularity, so a game that begins to be popular may become increasingly popular as its rank increases.

Clientele Interaction. Client interaction in small video game companies varies. If the company makes its game available directly to the public, any employee with public contact information available should be prepared for direct, regular, and frank feedback. Tech-savvy consumers are often very blunt about desired changes. Willingness to accept feedback can help improve games and assure consumers that companies value user opinions.

If the company is acting as a design studio, generally only the owner makes pitches to outside companies. The owner may pitch the game to publishers, venture capitalists, or loan officers to gain the resources necessary to continue working on the game. There are also communities of independent game designers (such as Indie Fund) who want to foster gaming and help develop new independent gaming companies.

Amenities, Atmosphere, and Physical Grounds. Small businesses are typically run from home offices or small, leased business spaces. There are not many amenities, as much of the business's income will be used to gain further business, to improve marketing or game-play, or to begin production on a new game.

Small video game businesses typically have an atmosphere focused on teamwork and fun. Although there may not be much (if any) pay involved, the participants crave involvement in creating video games. Unfortunately, this attitude may also prove detrimental, as the participants may have other priorities in their lives, and the game may be considered more of a hobby than a business.

Typical Number of Employees. Typically, there are fewer than ten employees of a small gaming business, with each employee taking on multiple roles. Often, the founder also designs and programs the games. Many times, the founder will begin the business as an after-work hobby. Without guaranteed income, the owner will have difficulty hiring employees and may have to rely on friends and family for assistance without any promise of a paycheck.

Traditional Geographic Locations. Small video game businesses must have access to technology and to the Internet. Most small businesses are begun in places where Internet access is available, cheap, and speedy.

Pros of Working for a Small Business. Small businesses have the advantage of being nimble. Instead of spending years on one massive title, a small company can survey the marketplace and focus its efforts precisely. It has the luxury of discovering niches and unusual opportunities that bigger businesses are too unwieldy to explore. Teamwork is also a benefit, as willingness to learn and work multiple roles is expected of all employees.

Cons of Working for a Small Business. Video games are a quickly growing industry, but small businesses are volatile, with many not surviving their first few years. There are also significant start-up costs associated with small businesses specializing in video game development because many require cutting-edge technology. (Because of the life cycle of both games and computer hardware, a game created on an older computer may be obsolete by the time it is released.) Without a steady cash flow or dedicated employees, a small video game company may never fully graduate from a hobby to a business. If owners rely too much on friends and family for assistance, they may also find that their personal relationships suffer if their businesses fail.

Costs

Payroll and Benefits: Top-notch programmers and artists require top-notch salaries, so many owners of small video game businesses work as their own programmers, artists, or both to save on employee salaries. Unless the company has a regular cash flow, the owners will not typically offer benefits.

Supplies: Programming graphically sophisticated games requires top-of-the-line computer equipment that must be upgraded frequently to remain viable. Some small companies also buy or lease software engines from larger companies to provide a shortcut for some programming tasks, which adds to company expenses. Small companies may also need to invest in office payroll or accounting software, as well as printers, toner, and other typical office supplies.

External Services: Small video game companies may contract printing, legal counsel, accounting, Web hosting, and other professional services. Some, particularly shareware companies, may contract art or graphic design services rather than hiring full-time artists.

Utilities: Telephone, electricity, and Internet service are imperative for any company in the games industry. Higher-speed Internet access is desirable but also increases the cost of a small business's utilities. At minimum, a small company should be prepared to pay for a DSL or cable modem and upgrade to a higher-bandwidth line when possible. Water and sewage, gas, and other utilities may be included in the rental of office space, or the company may be responsible for payment.

Taxes: All video game companies are responsible for paying local, state, and federal business taxes, including payroll taxes if there are any employees. Self-employed company owners may report their income on their personal returns, in which case they must also pay self-employment taxes.

Midsize Businesses

In the video game industry, it is difficult to remain a midsize business. Entrepreneurs begin small businesses every day, and large companies grow relatively quickly. Midsize businesses are often on their way to either downsizing to a small business or growing into a large business. Few

midsize businesses in the video game industry are planned to remain midsize.

Potential Annual Earnings Scale. According to the BLS, the average annual salary for a computer hardware engineer in 2009 was $107,410, while the average annual salary for an applications software engineer working for a software publisher was $91,910 and the average annual salary for a computer programmer working for a software publisher was $85,510. Salaries for employees in a midsize video game business generally range from $20,000 to $25,000 for administrative and support staff and from $50,000 to $75,000 for programmers, artists, and management.

Clientele Interaction. Although some midsize companies release games directly to the public via social networks, online gaming, or through mobile applications, many others work as third-party contracted developers for larger game publishers. Like smaller companies that release games directly to the public, midsize companies must be prepared to receive frank, often blunt feedback about their games and their playability. Any employee in the company with public contact information must expect to be contacted by players with suggestions, complaints, and other concerns.

Those employees who do interact with the public must remain calm and civil. Hardcore gamers who are heavily involved in one's game can either be the game's best advocates or its worst critics. Polite, quick responses to criticism will often sway gamers to a more positive outlook. For companies working on a contractual basis with other businesses, owners or CEOs must be prepared to meet with and pitch to loan officers, game publishers, venture capitalists, and other partners who may be putting up money.

Amenities, Atmosphere, and Physical Grounds. Midsize game companies function mostly the same way as other midsize, office-based businesses. Work is typically in an office building, with cubicles as well as other open spaces in which the team can regularly gather to discuss game problems, milestones, and progress. Midsize video game companies often share office space with other companies in downtown areas of larger cities.

Amenities for midsize businesses are generally not extensive and may only include pizza and soda paid for by management when working late. In larger, shared office buildings, there are usually coffee shops, small restaurants, and other cafés within walking distance.

Typical Number of Employees. Midsize businesses generally employ ten to seventy-five people, with many remaining in the range of twenty to thirty employees until the company has a strong cash flow and can sustain a larger workforce on a long-term basis.

Traditional Geographic Locations. Midsize video game companies are often found in the same areas that larger companies are found. These businesses thrive in larger, technologically forward cities with strong creative cultures. The Pacific Northwest; Austin, Texas; and other coastal metropolises are inviting environments for growing video game companies.

Pros of Working for a Midsize Business. Midsize businesses are generally grown from successful small businesses. With a modest history of success, companies learn what does and does not work. This lends midsize businesses more stability than most small businesses, as well as a more significant cash flow. Midsize companies may also be successful enough to pick and choose their projects, only working on games that interest them. Midsize video game companies are often still small enough that employees are not forced to work only in specific roles but instead may work on a variety of tasks that stretch their skills and build their resumes.

Many midsize companies also have the good fortune to be small enough that every employee works toward a common goal. While larger companies may have too many employees to be personal and small companies' employees may work too hard to constitute a strong team, midsize companies are often just big enough that employees are not overwhelmed by their projects but small enough that everyone is working on the same game, toward the same goal.

Cons of Working for a Midsize Business. As midsize businesses are often contractual partners with larger companies, they may not have as much flexibility as either smaller or larger companies in developing their own game titles. If a large game publisher asks a midsize game design company to assist on a project, the smaller company may have to compromise its creativity and vision in order to fulfill the contract. Midsize companies do not have the same monetary resources that large companies

have, so their equipment may be older than that of larger companies. They are also not as nimble as smaller companies and may take too long to change course, if that is what the market dictates.

Costs

Payroll and Benefits: Midsize video game companies dedicate most of their money to employee payroll and benefits. While not required to by law, most midsize companies provide vacation, sick days, and health benefits to their employees.

Supplies: Midsize video game companies rely on technology to provide their income and should purchase the most powerful computers available. If working with large companies, midsize businesses may have to invest in proprietary engines and other expensive gaming software just to stay at the minimally acceptable levels of graphics rendering and playability. Additionally, midsize businesses require typical office supplies, such as printers, paper, telephones, and other office goods.

External Services: Midsize companies may contract payroll, accounting, and other office services in order to keep their administrative overhead expenses low. Additionally, midsize companies should have relationships with good entertainment or intellectual property lawyers to ensure their interests are represented in contracts with game publishers and other companies.

Utilities: Telephones, electricity, and Internet are necessary for any video game company, including midsize companies. If a company leases space in an office building, there may be shared costs for water, sewage, heating, and other building services provided by the building owner.

Taxes: All video game companies are responsible for paying local, state, and federal business taxes.

Large Businesses

Large video game companies are often multinational corporations and are sometimes subsidiaries of parent entertainment companies. Large companies may be design studios or game publishers. Many large publishers establish contracts with third-party designers for game titles, while other corporations keep in-house design staff. In-house designers typically have more money available and greater creative flexibility with their games than do third-party developers.

Potential Annual Earnings Scale. According to the BLS, the average annual salary for a computer hardware engineer in 2009 was $107,410, while the average annual salary for an applications software engineer working for a software publisher was $91,910 and the average annual salary for a computer programmer working for a software publisher was $85,510.

Employees directly involved in game design (including art and audio) earn starting salaries around $40,000 to $50,000 per year, and programmers start higher. Many companies offer bonuses based on a game title's success. Upper management generally earns over $100,000 per year and will also receive additional compensation based on the company's performance. Support staff often earn less than game team members. Employees responsible for grounds maintenance, amenities, and other support functions generally earn from $20,000 to $35,000 per year.

Clientele Interaction. Typically, there is no direct clientele interaction for most large corporate jobs. Customer service representatives (CSRs) and marketers are the exception. CSRs may interact with gamers online, in-game, or via telephone to assist them with problems or concerns. Marketers may attend industry conferences, gaming conventions, or other entertainment expos in order to promote the company and its games, as well as giving interviews and crafting press releases. Sales and distribution managers meet and negotiate with wholesalers and retailers but generally do not speak directly to consumers.

Amenities, Atmosphere, and Physical Grounds. Large video game companies are sprawling campuses with plenty of amenities for their employees. Free snacks, gym facilities, and playrooms are common amenities to keep programmers, designers, and artists happy. Some companies also provide child care on-site. During crunch times, the company may provide meals, errand running, and sleeping accommodations.

Typical Number of Employees. Large game companies employ anywhere from seventy-five to thousands of employees. Most are organized into smaller teams focused around specific aspects of individual game titles, such as programming, au-

dio, or specific game areas. Large companies may be working on multiple game titles and deadlines at the same time, with team members working on the same title sharing cubicle space.

Traditional Geographic Locations. Large businesses need to have a fresh supply of talent, so most are located in tech-savvy metropolitan areas. Many large businesses have a presence in California's Silicon Valley. Other hotbeds of video game activity for large companies include Austin, the Pacific Northwest, the Washington, D.C., area and Southern California. Internationally, Canada, Japan, and Korea have maturing game industries. With the low cost of doing business, India, China, and Vietnam are also desirable areas for video game companies. As more game companies tailor games to different geographical locations, teams specializing in localizing games to different countries will become more widespread, as will game teams themselves.

Pros of Working for a Large Business. Although the video games industry remains volatile, many large video game companies have diversified sufficiently to avoid the danger of overnight financial ruin. Many large companies also have multiple locations, some abroad. Possibilities for transfer exist, and employees may find themselves on localization teams for countries they wish to visit. Large businesses offer more amenities and benefits than smaller corporations, as well as stock options and significant monetary bonuses for completed games.

Large companies also offer the opportunity to work on different types of games within the same corporation. An industry leader such as Electronic Arts publishes titles in several different genres annually, with more always in development. When one game ends, a successful employee may be transferred to a different game to learn new skills or promoted to new responsibilities. Large companies also tend to promote from within, so the more time one spends with a large company, the more likely an employee is to rise through the ranks.

Cons of Working for a Large Business. In large game companies, employees fill specialized roles. This can lead to frustrating layers of bureaucracy and middle-management, as well as rigid sets of job tasks. Additionally, crunch times can last for months on poorly planned and executed projects, greatly increasing employee stress. Large businesses are sometimes also part of larger entertainment companies, which can dismiss otherwise good ideas if they do not fit within the corporate brand. Large companies also rely more on contract labor—employees contracted to work for the company for a specific game title. Independent contractors are often not entitled to the same benefits and protections that regular employees are, and they may not have a job after their titles ship.

Costs

Payroll and Benefits: Payroll and benefits are the biggest expenses for large companies. Top programmers, designers, and artists are always in demand, and to retain top talent companies must pay competitive salaries and benefits. If a company is profitable, its design and publishing teams are generally granted bonuses, as well as company stock (if the company is publicly traded).

Supplies: For their design, programming, and artistic teams, large video game companies must have cutting-edge computers and other technology to create multimillion-dollar games. In addition to appropriate technology, computer programs requiring strong processor technology are necessary. If these programs are not proprietary (in-house) programs, companies use top-of-the-line creative software, often spending tens of thousands of dollars per team member in software licensing costs alone.

Large video game companies also have the same supply needs as smaller companies. Typical office supplies, such a printing supplies, copiers, and other office machinery, are necessary. Additionally, if the groundskeepers and cleaning crews are not contracted, cleaning supplies, gardening tools, and other supplies are necessary.

External Services: If they are not included on the executive management team, a cadre of top-notch lawyers should be on retainer for large companies. In addition to any labor disputes that may arise, video game companies have the signature problem of protecting their intellectual property. A lawyer specializing in intellectual property and entertainment law should be available, especially to consider and review any licensing or other agreements with entertainment or other companies. In addition, large companies may contract programmers, artists, designers, voice actors, musicians, and other content creators for specific projects, rather than hiring them as permanent full-time employees.

Utilities: Large companies must pay for water, sewage, electricity, gas, telephone, and high-speed Internet service. Some companies also purchase carbon offsets to help mitigate the amount of greenhouse gases they release by doing business.

Taxes: All video game companies are responsible for paying local, state, and federal business taxes.

ORGANIZATIONAL STRUCTURE AND JOB ROLES

Video game industry employees are responsible for the entire gaming experience, from the initial concept through marketing and publishing to retail sales. The main three branches of the industry are game design, game production, and retail. The design team is responsible for the initial concepts, story, and visuals. Publishing breathes life into the creations, making the game real, playable, and fun. Marketing and public relations staff, the quality assurance (QA) testers, and sales associates all support and facilitate the success of video game companies. In smaller companies, an individual may fill many roles, while larger companies assign each task to a different employee.

The following umbrella categories apply to the organizational structure of businesses in the video, computer, and virtual reality games industry.

- Management
- Administration and Human Resources
- Marketing and Public Relations
- Retail Stores
- Customer Service
- Amenities and Facilities
- Security
- Game Design
- Production
- Animation/Art
- Audio
- Programming

- Quality Assurance
- Sales and Distribution
- Professional Gamers

Management

Upper management roles are typically filled by veterans who have at least five years of experience in the video games industry. In smaller companies, upper management roles are filled by just a few people taking on multiple tasks. These executives acquire funding, work with other companies, and broker licensing deals. Many executive managers have worked their way up from the bottom of the gaming industry, acquiring a detailed understanding of what the industry entails. Increasingly, the industry is filling upper management roles with employees who have specialized business training. Management in the video games industry is well compensated, with average salaries ranging from $70,000 to $130,000, plus cash bonuses.

Management occupations may include the following:

- Chief Executive Officer (CEO)
- Business Development Director
- Chief Financial Officer (CFO)
- Chief Information Officer (CIO)
- Chief Operating Officer (COO)
- Chief Technology Officer (CTO)
- Creative Director
- Product Development Director
- Technical Director

Administration and Human Resources

Administrative positions handle much of the day-to-business operations of a company. Secretaries, payroll clerks, receptionists, and other office occupations are necessary to keep the business end of the operation running smoothly. Within the administrative roles, executive secretaries and assistants are usually paid the most. Most training is short term and on the job. Expertise with office software applications and business correspondence is crucial. Salaries range from $25,000 to $50,000 (or more, in the case of executive assistants). Human resources (HR) positions are more specialized and focus on staff retention, training, and benefits. Many human resources jobs require at least a bachelor's degree, with some specific training regarding labor laws. Accordingly, human

resources personnel earn more than other administrative personnel, from $35,000 to $60,000 per year.

Administration and HR occupations may include the following:

- Secretary
- Administrative Assistant
- Executive Assistant
- Receptionist
- Payroll Clerk
- Benefits Specialist
- Recruitment Specialist
- Human Resources Assistant

Marketing and Public Relations

Marketing is one of the video game industry's most difficult tasks. While marketing and good public relations can get a game noticed, an industry research group has found that many casual gamers prefer to learn about games by word of mouth from their social circle. Marketing for hardcore gamers also requires a deft touch, as many passionate gamers resist any sort of organized spin. Viral marketing for both casual and hardcore games has proven to be successful.

As the public face of a company, a successful marketer requires a very specific set of skills. A strong candidate for a marketing or public relations team must have exceptional communication skills (both oral and in writing) and an ability to connect with mainstream news outlets and everyday gamers alike. Many marketing managers have at least a bachelor's degree, and many also have advanced degrees. Salaries for marketing personnel can range from $50,000 for a public relations specialist to $110,000 for a marketing manager.

Marketing and public relations occupations may include the following:

- Marketing Director
- Public Relations Manager
- Brand Manager
- Communications Specialist
- Public Relations Specialist

Retail Stores

Sales jobs in the video games industry are often of the retail store variety. With experience, one can advance to managerial positions. According to

Video Games Careers, these jobs are unlikely to prepare one for work in the larger video games industry.

Retail stores provide short-term, on-the-job training. Retail clerks often earn minimum wage at the beginning of their employment and work their way up to earning approximately $25,000 per year. Retail managers earn more, often up to $40,000 annually. Many retail establishments are decreasing their physical locations and increasing their online operations.

Retail occupations may include the following:

- Electronic Game Store Sales Clerk
- Electronic Game Store Manager
- Retailer

Customer Service

For online games, especially for MMORPGs, excellent customer service is imperative. Paying players expect customer service representatives to be available twenty-four hours a day to provide them with quick answers and to remain cheerful while doing so. As representatives of their companies, customer service representatives must remain fair, civil, and watchful for players abusing the game or other players. Many companies have all in-house staff, but others use offshore customer service representatives, and still others use volunteers to help police their games. Customer service representatives usually earn between $12 and $15 per hour; supervisors earn between $22 and $30 per hour. There is considerable time investment in learning the ins and outs of a given MMORPG, and companies must ensure that customer service representatives are not there just to abuse their administrative privileges.

Customer service occupations may include the following:

- Customer Service Manager
- Customer Service Representative
- Volunteer

Amenities and Facilities

Large companies generally have large campuses, filled with amenities for hard-working programmers and artists. Cafeterias, gyms, and arcades or game rooms are all benefits that larger companies provide in order to keep their employees happy. Groundskeepers work to keep campuses green and well groomed, and janitors ensure that buildings remain clean and well stocked with supplies. In larger companies, game rooms, gyms, and cafeterias are available for staff members during their workdays. Cooks, cashiers, and personal trainers all may be involved in ensuring that employees are fed and feeling their best. Salaries range from minimum wage for janitorial staff and groundskeepers to about $40,000 for supervisors of these positions.

Amenities and facilities occupations may include the following:

- Custodian/Janitor
- Groundskeeper
- Chef
- Personal Trainer

Security

With the expensive technology, intellectual property, and trade secrets on the grounds of many video game companies, security is of paramount importance. Trained security guards protect a company's physical grounds, its surrounding site, and the intellectual property contained on its servers. They ensure no unauthorized persons approach sensitive materials. This is a growing field but is not lucrative. After a short duration of on-the-job training, most security guards earn $20,000 to $30,000 annually.

Security occupations may include the following:

- Security Guard
- Security Officer
- Network Security Specialist

Game Design

Game design is one of the most important parts of the game industry. Designers provide the initial concepts for games, and their vision brings those games to fruition. Designers provide story structures, concepts for the look of characters and items that players will encounter, dialogue, and paths through each level. They are generally paid to use their imaginations. Ultimately, designers receive the kudos (or the blame) for the enjoyability of their games.

Competition for design positions is tough. Many employees on design teams began their careers in the QA department. Design employees usually have at least a bachelor's degree, and the majority have spent at least three years in the industry. The starting salary for a new designer is around $45,000, but with industry experience designers can earn over $85,000 per year.

Game design occupations may include the following:

- Design Director
- Lead Designer
- Level Designer
- Interface Designer
- Associate Designer
- Game Writer
- Quest Developer
- World Designer

Production

Producers have the delicate task of communicating between design teams and game publishers. They report on progress toward game milestones, report whether or not games are on budget and on schedule, and assess whether projects are worth continuing when obstacles crop up. As liaisons, producers must not only continually promote their games to publishing companies but also advocate for publishers' requests to design teams and maintain as much harmony as possible among all parties.

Producers are most often industry veterans. Nearly 50 percent have worked in the industry for over six years. Salaries range from around $42,000 for an unseasoned producer (or assistant producer) to over $95,000 for an executive producer. The great majority of producers have at least some college, and most of them have earned bachelor's degrees.

Production occupations may include the following:

- Executive Producer
- Producer
- Associate Producer
- Assistant Producer

Animation/Art

The art department is tasked with creating the look of a game. Whether the game takes place within a postapocalyptic wasteland of muted tans

and browns or against a hyper-saturated rainbow of colors for a dancing game, the art department must convey the feel of a game visually. Artists must have a strong facility with technology to create electronic reproductions of concept art. Modelers and animators must be familiar with anatomy and physiology in order to ensure an item's movement is appropriate and realistic. Many artists have bachelor's degrees in fine or applied arts. The average salary for an entry-level artist is $45,000, and artists with at least five years of experience in the industry can earn nearly $100,000 per year.

Animation and art occupations may include the following:

- Two-Dimensional Artist
- Three-Dimensional Artist
- Animator
- Concept Artist
- Environment Artist
- Modeler
- Technical Artist
- Texture Artist

Audio

Video game companies' audio departments are responsible for immersing players into their games' virtual worlds. The success of sound effects, musical scores, and character voices all depends on excellent audio teams. Some actors specialize in video game voiceover work and are listed as cast members for dozens of game titles. Many positions in the audio category are independent contractor positions, and some workers may work on several projects at once.

Audio workers usually have bachelor's degrees and some technical experience when entering the video games industry. The entry-level salary is between $40,000 and $50,000 per year, and veterans of the industry can earn more than $85,000 annually.

Audio occupations may include the following:

- Audio Director
- Audio Technician
- Composer
- Sound Designer
- Sound Producer
- Sound Mixer/Editor
- Voiceover Artist

Programming

Programmers write the code that constitutes the core of a video game. Without code, there would be no game. Programmers create the designers' world, allowing artists and audio employees to bring it to life. As code writers, programmers have the most detailed control of the game. Their commands dictate how the world will work and how decisions will play out.

Programmers, in accordance with their status, generally have the highest salaries in the video game industry (outside of upper management). A new programmer, with less than three years' experience in the industry, can earn around $55,000 per year; veterans can nearly double that at $109,000 annually. While a college degree is not strictly necessary for a programming job, familiarity with programming languages is.

Programming occupations may include the following:

- Artificial Intelligence Programmer
- Audio Programmer
- Engine Programmer
- Graphics Programmer
- Interface Programmer
- Lead Programmer
- Networking Programmer
- Physics Programmer
- Quality Assurance Programmer
- Tools Programmer

Quality Assurance

Although quality assurance jobs are seen as the lowest rung of the ladder for this industry, many successful video game veterans began their careers as quality assurance testers. Testers search for problems in programming by repeatedly trying to break games. A quality assurance lead tester takes the list of bugs compiled by testers and communicates those problems to the programmers, allowing them to fix bugs before the game is released to the public. Quality assurance is an often thankless but necessary part of the industry.

Turnover rates are high for quality assurance testers, as many move to other positions in the games industry and others find they do not like working in games. Quality assurance departments pay some of the lowest wages in the industry, averaging $24,000 to start. With experience, a quality assurance lead tester can earn over $65,000 per year, but many find they want to move to another department when possible.

QA occupations may include the following:

- Compatibility Tester
- Quality Assurance Leader
- Lead Tester
- Playability Tester
- Quality Assurance Technician
- Tester

Sales and Distribution

Once a game is complete and ready to be shipped, sales and distribution staff ensure that it will be allocated shelf space at retail outlets. Many game publishers must pay for such shelf space, as well as for advertising space in retailers' advertising flyers. For the sales and distribution team, it is crucial to develop and maintain good relationships with retailers in order to ensure their games receive the best placement possible.

Most sales personnel have at least a bachelor's degree, and many managers have masters in business administration. The average sales clerk's starting salary is around $25,000 per year, and managers can earn up to $110,000. These salaries vary wildly, as many sales positions are based on commission.

Sales and distribution occupations may include the following:

- Sales and Distribution Manager
- Sales and Distribution Representative
- Sales Clerk
- Distribution Director

Professional Gamers

Professional gamers earn their livings by playing in video game tournaments. Most professional players do not earn the bulk of their living through tournaments themselves; instead, the lion's share of their income comes through paid endorsements. Landing one of these lucrative positions requires many hours of unpaid practice per day. Entering tournaments and networking with fellow gamers and companies who sponsor gaming teams may provide a foot in the door for those seeking professional game-playing jobs.

INDUSTRY OUTLOOK

Overview

The outlook for this industry shows it to be on the rise. While buying and playing video games has continued to be popular, the rate of growth in both industry jobs and revenue slowed during the recession of 2007-2009. Nevertheless, the jobs forecast for the video games industry is cautiously optimistic, with steady growth predicted.

The BLS projects that, between 2008 and 2018, the information industry will grow by approximately 4 percent, adding 118,000 jobs. Software publishers make up the lion's share of this growth. In particular, the software publishing job market is forecast to grow by 30 percent, adding nearly 80,000 jobs. Not surprisingly, many of the fastest-growing segments of the software publishing industry are software programmers and system administrators.

Although both revenue and employment are predicted to increase through the next decade, recent studies have shown the current video game industry to be less robust than was originally thought. The Electronic Software Association's 2010 annual report on the state of the industry confirmed a decline in domestic computer and video game sales from a high of $11.7 billion in 2008 to $10.5 billion in 2009. In light of the global recession, this decline was not unexpected, and analysts believe revenue will increase as consumers regain financial confidence. In the United States, domestic jobs for the information industry also declined from 2008 to 2009.

The video game market is undergoing an evolution from focusing on so-called AAA or event PC and console games (the equivalent of film blockbusters or best-selling novels) to producing a greater quantity of smaller, casual games that offer greater returns on investment. Larger games are still made, but in the unstable consumer market fewer companies and venture capitalists are willing to risk millions of dollars on investments that might not pay off.

Additionally, many companies are attempting to save money by changing their distribution channels. Instead of selling games on optical discs in cases on store shelves, producers are considering offering digital downloads and other nonphysical distribution channels as a way to cut costs. Game industry experts also recognize that the flourishing used-game market means that game companies are only in the supply chain for the first step of the market, the initial sale.

Wanting to protect their profits, many video game companies are exploring the future of games with an online or streaming model. Video game companies could bypass consoles and the need for high-performing, top-of-the-line PCs for gaming by offering games primarily as Web applications playable in most browsers. While this type of shift could be good news for video game companies themselves, retail sales of consoles, PCs, and used games could crash.

The outlook is sunnier for the global market. Globally, developing countries are focusing on science, technology, engineering, and math vocations. Cities in China's Guangdong and Shandong provinces are working with the U.S. vocational training company Kaplan to develop video game career programs for their cities. As a country, China is also becoming a stronger consumer of video games, leading to a larger local video game industry.

Mobile gaming is also growing at an exponential rate. Gartner Research predicts that global consumers will spend over $11.4 billion in mobile gaming applications by 2014. Although demand for video games has increased, some salaries may decrease as some video game jobs can easily be outsourced to countries with lower pay rates.

Employment Advantages

The video game industry is a strong field for anyone who loves video games or programming. The growing industry means that there will be additional jobs at middle and larger companies, while do-it-yourself types may want to consider opening their own casual gaming enterprises. The video game industry allows an individual to be part of bringing a creative effort to the marketplace. Although it is highly unlikely that one can be paid exclusively to play games, it is likely that a part of one's job will be play-testing games.

Detail-oriented individuals with a penchant for detective work may also find fulfilling work in the game industry. Replicating and hunting down programming errors can be a full-time job, and the more experience one has in the industry, the more likely one is to move up the ladder. Working in the video game industry also allows one to work with high-end technology. The massive computing power needed for gaming allows industry personnel to work with the latest technology.

Annual Earnings

In concert with other entertainment and media trends, global revenue for the video game industry is predicted to grow at a compound annual rate of 10.6 percent in the period from 2009 to 2014, reaching $86.8 billion, according to PricewaterhouseCoopers. Although the United States witnessed a decline in video game sales from 2008 to 2009, consumer spending is expected to increase as the recession abates.

The domestic job market for video game companies in the United States is a mixed bag. While game companies continue to hire, some industry veterans have expressed dismay that the companies hire for specific projects and then let their senior staffs go before the next game, allowing for decreased salaries. Some programmers have found more success in relocating to other parts of the country, or even internationally. Domestic job opportunities are likely to decrease, because of increased competition from developing countries such as India, China, and Vietnam. These developing countries are providing more technology training to their citizens, allowing large companies to outsource programming positions to countries with cheaper labor.

RELATED RESOURCES FOR FURTHER RESEARCH

ENTERTAINMENT AND LEISURE SOFTWARE
    ASSOCIATION
    111/113 High St.
    Evesham, Worcestershire WR11 4XP
    United Kingdom
    Tel: 44-20-7534-0580
    http://www.elspa.com

ENTERTAINMENT SOFTWARE ASSOCIATION
    575 7th St. NW, Suite 300
    Washington, DC 20004
    Tel: (202) 223-2400
    Fax: (202) 223-2401
    http://www.theesa.com

INTERNATIONAL GAME DEVELOPERS
    ASSOCIATION
    19 Mantua Rd.
    Mt. Royal, NJ 08061
    Tel: (856) 423-2990
    Fax: (856) 423-3420
    http://www.igda.org

MAJOR LEAGUE GAMING
    420 Lexington Ave., #2820
    New York, NY 10170
    Tel: (213) 370-1444
    http://www.mlgpro.com

SOFTWARE AND INFORMATION INDUSTRY
    ASSOCIATION
    1090 Vermont Ave. NW, 6th Floor
    Washington, DC 20005-4095
    Tel: (202) 289-7442
    Fax: (202) 289-7097
    http://www.siia.net

ABOUT THE AUTHOR

Chaunacey Dunklee is senior reference librarian at Fullerton Public Library in Fullerton, California. She received a master's degree in library and information science from San Jose State University and a bachelor's degree in English from the University of California, Davis. She is currently a member of the American Library Association's Outstanding Reference Sources Committee. Dunklee began an outreach program at Fullerton Public Library, using video games to encourage teens to visit their local libraries. Additionally, Chaunacey is an avid gamer and enjoys reading about the future of gaming and libraries.

FURTHER READING

Boyd, S. Gregory, and Brian Green. *Business and Legal Primer for Game Development.* Boston: Charles River Media, 2007.

Chaplin, Heather, and Aaron Ruby. *Smartbomb: The Quest for Art, Entertainment, and Big Bucks in the Videogame Revolution.* Chapel Hill, N.C.: Algonquin Books of Chapel Hill, 2005.

"Computer and Video Game Designers." *Encyclopedia of Careers and Vocational Guidance.* 13th ed. Vol. 2. New York: Ferguson, 2005.

Edery, David, and Ethan Mollick. *Changing the Game: How Video Games Are Transforming the Future of Business.* Upper Saddle River, N.J.: FT Press, 2009.

Ewing, Richard Daniel. "China's Online Video Game Wars." *China Business Review,* July, 2007, 45-49.

Glenn, Lawrence M., and F. Martin Nikirk. "How Career and Technical Education Can Jumpstart a New Industry." *Techniques,* October, 2009, 26-29.

Hodgson, David S. J., Bryan Stratton, and Alice Rush. *Video Game Careers.* Rev. ed. Roseville, Calif.: Prima Games, 2008.

McAllister, Ken. *Game Work: Language, Power, and Computer Game Culture.* Tuscaloosa: University of Alabama Press, 2004.

Novak, Jeannie. *Game Development Essentials: An Introduction.* Clifton Park, N.Y.: Thomson/ Learning, 2005.

Rutter, Jason, and Jo Bryce. *Understanding Digital Games.* Thousand Oaks, Calif.: SAGE, 2006.

Sheffield, Brandon, and Jeffrey Fleming. "Ninth Annual Game Developer Salary Survey." *Game Developer,* April, 2010, 7-13.

Taylor, T. Allan, and James Robert Parrish. *Careers in the Internet, Video Games, and Multimedia.* New York: Ferguson, 2007.

U.S. Bureau of Labor Statistics. *Career Guide to Industries,* 2010-2011 ed. http://www.bls.gov/oco/cg.

_____. "Computer Software Engineers and Computer Programmers." In *Occupational Outlook Handbook,* 2010-2011 ed. http://www.bls.gov/oco/ocos303.htm.

U.S. Census Bureau. North American Industry Classification System (NAICS), 2007. http://www.census.gov/cgi-bin/sssd/naics/naicsrch?chart=2007.

U.S. Department of Commerce. International Trade Administration. Office of Trade and Industry Information. Industry Trade Data and Analysis. http://ita.doc.gov/td/industry/otea/OTII/OTII-index.html.

©Mikael Damkier/Dreamstime.com

Warehousing and Storage Industry

INDUSTRY SNAPSHOT

General Industry: Transportation, Distribution, and Logistics

Career Cluster: Transportation, Distribution, and Logistics

Subcategory Industries: Farm Product Storage; General Merchandise Warehousing and Storage; Hazardous Materials Warehousing; Mini Warehouses and Self-Store Storage Facilities; Moving and Storage; Refrigerated Warehousing and Storage

Related Industries: Rental and Leasing Services; Retail Trade and Service Industry

Annual Domestic Revenues: $985 million (U.S. Census Bureau, Statistical Abstract)

Annual International Revenues: $21 billion USD (Fedstats, 2007)

Annual Global Revenues: $21.985 billion USD (U.S. Census Bureau, Statistical Abstract and Fedstats, 2007)

NAICS Numbers: 49, 4931, 531130

as retail stores. One segment of the industry is connected to the moving industry and typically provides short-term (thirty- to ninety-day) storage for household and other goods as required by families or companies in the process of relocating. The company must provide fireproof and waterproof storage space and ensure that the site is protected from theft and vandalism. Warehousing companies may provide their corporate clients with ancillary services such as packaging, pricing, light assembly, and sometimes delivery. Known as third-party logistics providers, they act as the middleman between the manufacturer and the end user.

INDUSTRY DEFINITION

Summary

The warehousing and storage industry provides storage for goods such as food, general merchandise, furs, automobiles, archival materials, documents, petroleum, books, and many other products awaiting distribution to consumer outlets such

History of the Industry

The possessions of nomadic hunter-gatherers were limited to whatever goods they could readily transport, but as many of the world's peoples adopted settled lifestyles, they began to accumulate numerous items, beyond their immediate needs. As the volume of accumulated goods increased and people began to trade or sell excess items, they began to develop specialized storage facilities. With the advent of mass production, the need for such facilities increased. As businesses grew in size and the number of consumer products increased, the warehousing and storage industry developed to meet the storage needs of businesses and individuals.

Granaries were among the first storage facilities to appear in Europe. They provided a means of preserving grains for later use. As the Europeans became major world suppliers of a diverse number of products and commodities, storage systems became more sophisticated to better serve the increasing demand.

By 1891, the American Warehouseman's Association had been organized in an attempt to lessen the railroads' total control over freight depots. The Hepburn Act of 1906 gave teeth to the Interstate Commerce Commission and significantly helped the budding industry.

In 1898, entrepreneur Max Epstein founded the GATX Corporation, which became an industry leader, in response to the Pittsburgh, Pennsylvania-based Duquesne Brewery's pressing need for the cold storage of beer. Commercial cold storage was developed primarily to preserve food, but in later decades, pharmaceutical and chemical companies found a climate-controlled environment beneficial for the storage of their products and gradually emerged as the largest users. Early cold storage was accomplished by carefully packing goods on ice, but later warehouses used refrigeration. Occasionally, naturally cool structures, such as repurposed mines, are used for cold storage. The Michigan Natural Storage Company, in Wyoming, Michigan, was originally a gypsum mine. Since 1957, it has provided naturally cooled underground storage for everything from business records to burgers for fast-food providers.

The post-World War II economic boom created a growing need for third-party logistics storage professionals. Ever-increasing demands for consumer goods resulted in specialization in the industry. Companies began providing storage for a single product line—appliances, for example—and served multiple manufacturers such as Maytag,

Wine is stored by specialty storage companies. (©Dreamstime.com)

Frigidaire, and Westinghouse, allowing them to ship their products to a warehousing company that in turn would ship appliances as needed to retailers within the region served.

The industry became more complicated and more regulated as it grew. Government regulatory agencies such as the Occupational Safety and Health Administration (OSHA) and the Food and Drug Administration (FDA) developed guidelines to ensure the safety of both industry employees and the end users of stored products. Regulations were created to govern the warehousing and storage of potentially dangerous products such as petroleum, radioactive materials, and flammable materials. Food storage required numerous safety standards, primarily to guard against spoilage. Food imports meant additional regulations, some of which were designed to guard against foodborne diseases, such as bovine spongiform encephalopathy (mad cow disease), which affected the European beef industry in 2001. All these regulations helped the warehousing and storage industry, as the added complications meant more and more manufacturers and importers decided to hire commercial warehousing companies to handle these matters.

At the simplest level, this industry is easy to enter. Anyone with a barn or even vacant land can offer recreational or other vehicle storage as long as they meet local zoning and land-use requirements. For the farmer or landowner, storage is an additional source of income. Some businesses offer storage as a part of their services. For example, furriers offer climate-controlled summer storage for customers' coats. In the mid-twentieth century, dry cleaners often stored their clients' winter garments, keeping their woolens safe from moths.

The 1970's saw the proliferation of self-storage facilities, which have become the fastest growing segment of the warehousing and storage industry. Self-storage units allow renters to store and retrieve items as they please. They are used by small-business owners, people who are in the process of moving, and people who have too many possessions to store in their own living space. One of the largest of the self-storage companies, the Public Storage Company, opened its first facility in 1972 and has experienced phenomenal growth, with more than two thousand facilities in the United States and Europe.

The Industry Today

In the United States, about seven thousand companies are active in the industry, although nearly half of the earnings are generated by only the top fifty companies. This indicates that the industry as a whole is not labor-intensive and that the smaller companies, which are the vast majority, usually operate with five or fewer employees.

The industry has been hit hard by the 2007-2009 recession. One of the hardest hit segments consists of the storage businesses affiliated with moving companies. Corporate moves provide a substantial portion of the profits for companies such as Allied Van Lines, United Van Lines, and Mayflower Transit. When corporate America tightened its belt, the industry suffered. Other companies, such as third-party logistics providers of warehousing, also felt the impact. Large companies in this area include the industry giants Exel, GATX, Tibbett and Britten, and Kenco. Other affected companies, such as the New England regional heavyweight Dean Warehousing, provide warehousing and storage for manufacturers and importers, among other clients, then deliver those goods to end buyers. After the start of the recession, the need for warehousing lessened, and companies have had to come up with creative ways to deal with increased unused capacity.

Although the moving industry is slowly rebounding, the need for storage has lessened. Companies relocating employees

The Warehousing and Storage Industry's Contribution to the U.S. Economy

Value Added	Amount
Gross domestic product	$40.7 billion
Gross domestic product	0.3%
Persons employed	1.208 million
Total employee compensation	$32.0 billion

Source: U.S. Bureau of Economic Analysis. Data are for 2008.

are not as likely to hire a moving company for the packing, moving, and short-term storage of household goods. Instead, they often offer a moving allowance, and the transferring employee can either hire a mover or rent a moving truck. Companies whose business included the storage of household goods are now providing space to commercial clients who need short-term solutions, for example, retail customers who are building a new facility.

As the economy becomes increasingly global, some aspects of the market are expanding. Flash freezing of fish, for example, means halibut caught in Alaska or salmon caught in Norway can be immediately frozen, then stored before being shipped to consumers all over the world. Goods manufactured in emerging world markets such as China and India arrive at warehouses daily to await distribution to retail outlets. GATX operates in Europe and the United States, and continues to provide both warehousing and transportation for a mix of international clients. Warehousing companies have tended to operate out of mammoth centralized facilities, but in the 2000's, many companies began to favor decentralization, operating smaller regional facilities. Factors affecting this trend include extreme weather (Hurricane Katrina, for example), labor issues in some areas, and the threat of terrorism. Regional facilities reduce vulnerability as goods are placed in multiple facilities. Document storage is another example of a growing market segment, as companies, particularly those dealing with sensitive data, seek safe repositories for their archives.

The special warehouse and storage industry is a group of companies serving firms that wish to store products that require extra attention or care, such as petroleum products, data, wine, and liquor. Storage of these products often entails complying with various regulations and the facilities used can be subject to inspection by regulatory agencies.

An emerging subcategory of the warehousing and storage industry is matchmaking companies that pair corporations with short-term needs and storage professionals with underutilized capacity. Among customers availing themselves of the service are retail operations that are building new facilities.

Another subcategory is miniature warehouses, similar to self-storage units, that are single rooms, compartments, lockers, containers, or outdoor

Inputs Consumed by the Warehousing and Storage Industry

Input	Value
Energy	$2.1 billion
Materials	$2.0 billion
Purchased services	$13.8 billion
Total	$17.9 billion

Source: U.S. Bureau of Economic Analysis. Data are for 2008.

spaces. An example is a meat locker, where customers store their butchered farm animals or animals slain while hunting. Although miniature warehouses are popular, self-storage units still dominate the small-user market. They are cost-effective and allow users to move items in and out of the unit at will. Commercial storage remains a better option when access to goods is not an issue. As people age, sell their homes, and downsize their living quarters, they often find that they would like to keep certain items but that they do not have space for them. Alternatively, they may wish to make more living space by storing seasonal items such as outdoor fitness gear, patio furnishings, and holiday decor, and other items such as memorabilia that are not needed in everyday life. For these items, they often turn to storage companies.

The self-storage end of the market can sometimes gain in a slow economy. Young people are often the newest hires and the first to be fired in economic downturns. In the 2007-2009 recession, many adult children were forced to give up their apartments or sell their homes and move in with their parents temporarily. When this happens, they need a place to store their furnishings. People can choose either rental units at the company's warehouse or pod units. Warehouse self-storage units require that customers move their belongings in and out of the unit, but pods are delivered to the customer's home. Pods are convenient for the storage of household goods during a renovation project, for example, or as collection units for those staging flea markets or other one-time sales events.

A worker compares the order number to that on the package. (©Endostock/Dreamstime.com)

The industry is poised for moderate growth, although as in all industries, some areas of the business will experience more growth than others. There is always a need for those people who can successfully deal with the increasing regulatory issues and provide a safe, clean storage environment for their clientele. Fewer jobs are predicted in the labor end of the business, especially in the larger storage facilities, partly because of advances in automation that reduce the need for manpower. That said, there will always be job openings, as these jobs experience high turnover. Workers enhance their skills and move on to other jobs, often in other industries. Some workers take these jobs while completing their education or while searching for other employment following job layoffs.

Self-storage facility owners with a strong entrepreneurial spirit can earn a better than average living by branching out and buying more than one fa-

cility. They can also add revenue by offering recreational vehicle, boat, and automotive storage both outside and in climate-controlled indoor spaces.

INDUSTRY MARKET SEGMENTS

Small Businesses

The small warehousing and storage industry business can be a local independent business owner, a franchisee, or a small branch office of a larger company. The storage portion of a moving and storage company franchise fits in this category, as does any independent provider. U-Store-It, Public Storage, and other large self-storage companies where owners or managers run a single company location make up a large portion of the small business segment. The small-business owner or manager draws customers through local advertising, including newspapers and yellow pages, and increasingly through Web sites. The self-storage provider faces tough competition, so impeccable service is mandatory.

Potential Annual Earnings Scale. This industry does not produce wealth for many, although owners or franchisees can earn a comfortable living. Self-storage facilities may provide on-site living quarters for the owner or manager. Employees of smaller companies can include office personnel, delivery truck drivers, and order pickers, although in the smallest of companies, the owner or manager does all or most of the work. The owner can earn $50,000 or more annually, a manager somewhat less. Support personnel can earn an hourly wage of $12 to $15 per hour or be salaried at about $18,000 to $25,000 annually, depending on responsibilities and experience. The lowest-level jobs could be at minimum wage but are usually paid $12 to $13 on average.

Clientele Interaction. In any small company, clientele interaction is high. All employees have customer contact and must be prepared to be proactive and service the customer's needs effectively.

Amenities, Atmosphere, and Physical Grounds. A small warehousing and storage company will typically be located on main roads, often in light industrial areas. A self-storage company will be on commercially zoned properties close to residential areas, to provide easy access for their major customer base. Wherever the location, a storage company will be clean, with storage areas that are fireproof, waterproof, climate-controlled (if necessary), and protected from rodents and other pests. Security is also a major part of operations, and a small business will provide electronic security systems, whereas a larger company may also hire security personnel. Electronic security fences are often found on the grounds. The office, though not plush, will be clean and comfortable and equipped with all the requisite technology. Warehouse areas have to be arranged in an orderly manner to quickly access products for delivery.

Typical Number of Employees. The staff is usually made up of from two to five people. This includes the owner, franchisee, or manager, an office manager, and warehouse personnel. Some employees may be part time. In a self-storage operation, a husband-wife team may cover all the chores and live in an on-site apartment.

Traditional Geographic Locations. Because there is a universal need for these businesses, they are found everywhere, from the largest cities to the smallest towns. Anywhere that people live, there is some need for warehousing and storage services. They tend to locate in light industrial complexes, commercial areas, and along the highways leading into town. Visibility is not an issue, as they do not depend on walk-in customers.

Pros of Working for a Small Warehousing and Storage Business. Organized, motivated self-starters do well in this and other small businesses. The owner or franchisee has control over the business and has complete responsibility for its success or failure. Whether that is a curse or a blessing depends entirely on the personality of the individual, as the job can be the cause of great stress. Some thrive in the small-business owner arena, while others are overwhelmed by it. A major cause of stress is the fact that the business can be adversely affected by a weak economy or other issues over which the owner has no control.

Employees can use the job to learn the business and gain experience. Employee positions are, for the most part, routine jobs not career positions, so personal factors are often the motivation for filling such a position. Many employees take these jobs knowing they will work a year or two and then move on to something else. They may be students, looking to work around their class schedules.

Cons of Working for a Small Warehousing and Storage Business. The owner or manager works long hours and is required to be there during all open hours. He or she has to handle all problems that arise, and there is no one to go to for help.

Employees in this business have little or no chance for advancement and receive relatively low compensation. This can be viewed as a trade-off for working in a low-stress, noncompetitive working atmosphere.

Costs

Payroll and Benefits: Employees may be paid salaries or an hourly wage. Benefits may include a profit-sharing or a savings plan, health insurance, paid vacation, and sick leave. At the

A worker drives a pallet truck in a large warehouse. (©Dreamstime.com)

owner's discretion, part-time employees may receive prorated benefits.

Supplies: Supplies are one of the smaller budgetary items, limited to routine office supplies, computer, printer, and copier toners and inks, restroom supplies, cleaning supplies, and breakroom supplies. There are no supply items unique to the industry.

External Services: Especially in a small business, it is usually cost-effective to contract out some of the needed services. Security is a key issue, and often the owner subscribes to a security service, which can include restricted entry, security cameras, and motion sensors. Other contracted services can include accounting and bookkeeping, legal, insurance, landscaping and lawn care, janitorial, snow removal, and the handling of routine or emergency maintenance issues. These businesses will also contract a pest-control service in all storage areas.

Utilities: Small businesses in this industry use the basic utilities of any similarly sized enterprise: electricity, gas, water, heat and air-conditioning, along with telephone and electronic hookups.

Taxes: The owner pays social security taxes on employees as well as the usual federal, state, and local income taxes. These are paid quarterly and based on projected earnings. There may also be local business or property taxes, and the owner pays his or her personal income and property taxes as required by the locality.

Midsize Businesses

The midsize business can be a single business, a franchise, or a local branch of a larger business. The owner or president, the franchisee, or the local branch manager runs the business on a day-to-day basis. Some large companies use managing a branch operation as a training ground before promoting an employee to greater responsibilities in its corporate headquarters, but in most cases, the job is a permanent assignment and not a stepping stone to future promotions.

Potential Annual Earnings Scale. A midsize warehousing and storage business offers the opportunity for somewhat higher earnings than the smaller company for both the owner/manager and the employee. Employees may earn between $25,000 to $35,000, depending on experience and responsibilities. Part-time clerical help is generally paid $15 to $20 per hour, and some of the lower-echelon jobs may pay minimum wage. A few of the jobs, such as drivers, may be unionized and paid accordingly.

Clientele Interaction. Jobs in these companies require medium to high clientele interaction. Although many of the jobs require direct public contact, there will always be some behind-the-scenes opportunities. Because this is a service rather than a tangible-product industry, good customer service skills are an added plus for those who want to succeed in the business. The ability to proactively handle small problems before they become major issues can greatly increase an employee's value to the company. Good communication skills are always an asset.

Amenities, Atmosphere, and Physical Grounds. The building and grounds in all warehousing and storage companies must always project cleanliness and attention to detail. Security is a major customer concern, so there will be visible reminders, such as evidence of sprinkling systems and security monitoring devices, to assure customers that they can safely store their goods. Employees work in clean, comfortable surroundings and have all the necessary technological equipment, often including surveillance cameras. Companies providing storage for hazardous materials are required to meet all regulatory requirements, and the facility will be regularly inspected to ensure compliance.

Typical Number of Employees. These companies usually employ from five to twenty-five employees for each location, although some employees may be part time. Jobs include management, bookkeeping, and administrative support. Other jobs specific to the industry are delivery-truck drivers, order pickers, inventory clerks, pricers, labelers, packagers, assemblers, and forklift operators. The larger companies in this category may employ security guards, although often security is a contracted service.

Traditional Geographic Locations. Like their smaller counterparts, midsize companies are found everywhere, from the largest cities to the smallest towns. Anywhere that people live, there is some need for warehousing and storage services. Midsize companies tend to locate in light industrial complexes, commercial areas, and along the highways leading into town. As they do not depend on walk-in customers, visibility is not an issue. Customers do not seek this service until the need arises, and then factors such as convenience of location can influence their decisions.

Pros of Working for a Midsize Warehousing and Storage Business. Employees have a greater opportunity to advance within a midsize company than a small one. For example, a clerical worker can be promoted to office manager, or an order picker can become a warehouse supervisor. As in all industries, the midsize business is a good arena in which to gain experience before joining a larger enterprise or going into business for oneself.

There are more types of jobs available as midsize enterprises employ larger staffs, but as this is not a labor-intensive work environment, there are fewer jobs in this industry per business than in many others.

Cons of Working for a Midsize Warehousing and Storage Business. Owners or managers tend to work long hours, often fifty to sixty per week. Although warehousing and storage is slightly less sensitive to downward turns in the economy, business can stagnate, causing stress to the person charged with the responsibility for profit.

Jobs are more structured than in a smaller business, making it more difficult to gain knowledge of the business as a whole, but midsize companies still offer greater flexibility than their larger counterparts. Salaries tend to be lower than in larger companies but slightly higher than in the smallest ones.

Costs

Payroll and Benefits: Payroll and employee benefits can be one of the largest budgetary items in a midsize business. Most of the workforce is on salary or receives an hourly wage. Benefits can include health insurance, paid vacation, and sick leave, and sometimes employer-matched savings or investment plans for all full-time employees. Part-time employees may receive prorated benefits, at the discretion of the owner. Union members' wages and benefits periodically undergo bargaining, and the midsize or smaller owner has little, if any, input in the bargaining process.

Supplies: Supplies represent only a small portion of the overall costs of doing business. Storage and warehousing businesses need the usual office supplies, including ink and toner for electronic equipment. They also need to stock rou-

tine cleaning and maintenance supplies (even when those services are provided by external sources), as well as restroom and breakroom supplies. There are no supplies peculiar to the industry.

External Services: Purchased services can include legal, advertising, janitorial, insurance, snow removal, trash pickup, security, and pest control, with security being the most important and the most expensive. Customers demand that their goods be protected from weather, fire, theft, and spoilage. Though the owner carries insurance to cover such losses, damages to stored items can do irreparable harm to a company's reputation and result in lost business.

Utilities: Costs for utilities are the same as for any midsize operation: telephone, Internet, and electronic hookups, electricity, water, gas, and heat. Companies specializing in warehousing items that must be stored in a climate-controlled environment will incur significantly higher electricity or gas costs.

Taxes: Owners must pay social security and payroll taxes on employees and submit quarterly statements. In addition to their personal federal, state, and local income taxes, they must file and pay business income taxes. Some localities will also require business licenses or permits.

Large Businesses

The industry giants include moving companies that offer storage, such as the Atlas Van Lines, United Van Lines, and Mayflower Transit, and the industry leaders in third-party logistics warehousing and storage, such as GATX, Dean Warehouse, and DHL. The other segment is made up of the major self-storage companies: Public Storage and U-Store-It. These companies have name recognition and a large national, regional, or even international presence in the business.

Potential Annual Earnings Scale. Annual earnings vary widely, depending on the type of position within the industry. Compensation for management at the corporate level is competitive with that for management in other industries. Annual salaries for management at national or regional headquarters can reach $75,000, with additional pay in the form of performance bonuses. Jobs at local facilities pay slightly more than the same jobs in small or midsize companies. An experienced fork-

Inventory specialists ensure smooth flow from the receipt of stock to its placement on the loading dock. (©Endostock/Dreamstime.com)

lift driver can expect to earn between $25,000 and $31,000 per year. However, many jobs in this industry are considered unskilled, and compensation is in the range of $9 to $16 per hour. Some positions are part time, with reduced, if any, benefits.

Clientele Interaction. Clientele interaction ranges from high to none, with those in sales, customer service, and other sales support positions having the highest customer contact. Other employees, such as warehouse personnel or accounting, may have limited or no interaction with customers. As in all industries, those who regularly interact with customers need good people skills, along with an above-average ability to communicate, both orally and in writing. Large companies are able to provide ample opportunities for those who prefer working behind the scenes.

Amenities, Atmosphere, and Physical Grounds. Corporate headquarters provide comfortable working conditions and cutting-edge technology. Any building that includes storage or warehouse space will have visible security to reassure

potential customers. That security means protection from weather, fire, pests, theft, and vandalism. Loss of a client's property can irreparably damage a company's reputation. Facilities offering refrigerated storage will be equipped with all the necessary electronic devices to monitor temperatures and alert personnel at the first sign of a malfunction. Those storing hazardous materials have strict standards to maintain and are overseen by OSHA and other agencies.

Typical Number of Employees. This industry does not require large numbers of employees. The corporate offices need the same marketing, accounting, administrative, and other departments needed for any smooth-running operation, but the actual warehouses, storage lockers, and other facilities typically require only a small workforce, irrespective of the size of the company as a whole.

Traditional Geographic Locations. Large companies are typically headquartered in metropolitan areas, but most also have facilities in smaller towns. Larger warehousing companies that service certain industries tend to locate close to their customer base for ease of delivery. The services provided by this industry are needed virtually everywhere, so these companies are located near their customers, near the end users, or both. Wherever there are products to be stored, there will be warehouses to store them.

Pros of Working for a Large Warehousing and Storage Company. As in any industry, large companies attract those who want the opportunity for upward mobility and those who value the name recognition a large company provides. An ambitious employee can work his or her way up through the ranks. The larger companies are more likely to provide company-paid continuing education opportunities that enable employees to climb the corporate ladder. However, this applies more to the headquarters—national or regional—than the field locations, where advancement opportunities are few. There is also prestige in working for an industry leader, where salaries are higher and benefits tend to be more generous. The franchisee benefits from the name recognition of a larger company, along with corporate training, advertising, and marketing. Any franchisee is, however, assessed fees for those benefits. With large companies, employees who want or need to make a geographic move for personal reasons may be able to transfer to a branch in the chosen location.

Cons of Working for a Large Warehousing and Storage Company. Employees seeking to advance may find it hard to distinguish themselves from other workers, especially if they work far from headquarters and the attention of top management. In addition, this industry offers fewer employment opportunities, and the competition can be stiff. Outside the main offices, the positions are mostly warehouse workers, truckers, order pickers, forklift operators, and a small office staff. The hours are long, and much of the work is physically demanding. In companies of all sizes in this industry, injuries are common. They include falls, strained muscles, back injuries, and forklift and other equipment accidents.

Costs

Payroll and Benefits: Larger companies can offer not only the typical benefits but also employer-paid educational benefits and profit sharing or other retirement savings plans. By offering better benefits and higher salaries, they can attract more job applicants, but this means the competition is greater for the jobs available. As in any large company, payroll and benefits are typically the largest budgetary items.

Supplies: These companies use the same supplies as smaller ones but in larger numbers. Included are office supplies, printer and copier ink and toner cartridges, routine maintenance supplies, restroom products, and breakroom supplies. There are no supply items used only by this industry.

External Services: Services commonly provided by an outside source include legal services, auditing, janitorial work, landscaping, snow removal, trash removal, security, pest control, and cafeteria management. However, many of the larger companies have personnel or departments to provide some of these services. Insurance is a major expense for the large company, as the customers' goods and the facilities themselves must be protected.

Utilities: Large companies use electricity, gas, water, telephone, Internet, and electronic hookup services. In the largest companies, corporate headquarters is sometimes responsible for contracting these services for all satellite facilities as well as the home office.

Taxes: These companies pay social security, unemployment, and any other federal, state, or local taxes levied on their employees, along with quarterly federal, state, and local income taxes. They also pay taxes to every state and municipality in which they do business, along with fees for any relevant licenses or permits. The largest companies often have a whole department charged with the responsibility of handling this chore for the entire company.

ORGANIZATIONAL STRUCTURE AND JOB ROLES

Every company, irrespective of the industry, has certain tasks that must be performed to ensure that the business runs smoothly, holds its own against the competition, and complies with all government and industry regulations. Those tasks remain the same whether the company is a single proprietorship, a partnership of two individuals, or a corporation employing thousands. Objectives must be established, employees managed, goods or services marketed, accounting records maintained, payrolls calculated, and taxes paid. In a small warehouse and storage operation, the manager or franchisee will handle all or most of the responsibilities, acting as chief executive officer, sales manager, accountant, janitor, and coffee brewer. Midsize companies have employees charged with various, often overlapping duties. In these companies, some flexibility exists because job descriptions are not as rigid as in larger corporate entities. Large companies have whole departments devoted to a single function, such as sales support, billing, accounts payable, or maintenance. In these companies, job descriptions tend to be precise and detailed, which is sometimes frustrating for the employee who enjoys a variety of tasks and new challenges. No company can operate without people with the skills to perform their assigned duties, but obviously, the larger the company, the more diverse job opportunities it can provide. That said, this particular industry does not require the large staffs that are often the norm, as the warehouses run on minimum manpower, and the jobs in these warehouses are often unskilled and low paying, and may even be part time.

The following umbrella categories apply to the organizational structure of businesses in the warehousing and storage industry:

- Business Management
- Customer Services
- Sales and Marketing
- Facilities and Security
- Technology
- Administrative and Clerical Support
- Industry-Specific Jobs

Business Management

Management determines the direction a company will take, identifies its mission, and makes the necessary decisions to support that mission. The larger the company, the more layers of management. The structure of management in warehousing and storage companies can be as simple as a single owner or as complicated as a board of directors to which a chief executive office or president must answer. The chief executive officer oversees the vice presidents, who oversee the department managers in their area of specialization. A vice president of finance would be responsible for the accounting and payroll departments, for example. Those aspiring to top management positions should have a graduate degree in their chosen area of specialization, such as an M.B.A. or master of finance degree, to gain entry to the industry giants.

However, in this industry, more than two-thirds of all businesses have fewer than ten employees, so the need for multiple levels of management is considerably less than in other industries. The owner of a small business will do well with a general business education based on his or her individual needs. The small-business owner needs basic economics, accounting, business planning, communications, and management course work targeted for small businesses. For additional help, the owner or manager of a small business can turn to volunteer organizations such as the Service Corps of Retired Executives (SCORE), whose members have been mentoring and advising entrepreneurs since 1964. Help is also available through programs sponsored by trade organizations and local chambers of commerce.

Occupations in business management include the following:

- Director
- Chief Executive Officer (CEO)
- President
- Vice President
- Sales and Marketing Manager
- Chief Financial Officer (CFO)
- Controller
- Human Resources Manager
- Office Manager

Customer Services

Customer services are the lifeblood of any company and can determine its success or failure. These are the jobs that support the sales and marketing departments or, in small businesses in this industry, serve the customer in respect to accepting payments, handling complaints, arranging for deliveries to end users, and performing related duties. Workers in this field need strong people skills and should be able to effectively handle all problems that arise and be proactive in preventing them. Excellent communications skills, both oral and written, are required, and workers must be detail-oriented and able to multitask. Jobs in customer service require better than average people skills. At least an associate's degree and preferably a bachelor's degree is advisable but not always required. It is sometimes possible to gain an entry-level position, then work one's way up through on-the-job training or company-sponsored continuing educational benefits. A customer service manager in this industry is typically paid $38,000 to $48,000 per year, and customer service representatives begin at between $19,000 and $26,000. In smaller companies, customer service is just one more responsibility of the owner, but it is one of the most important if the business is to flourish.

Occupations within the customer services department include the following:

- Customer Service Manager
- Customer Service Representative
- Expediter

Sales and Marketing

Sales and marketing are essential to any industry and involve multiple layers of employees, from the corporate marketing director to branch sales managers to sales representatives. No company can survive without bringing its product or service to the attention of those who can purchase it.

Advertising is part of sales and marketing, although the warehousing and storage industry, for the most part, does not need the sophisticated advertising campaigns that manufacturers of consumer goods do. Large self-storage companies, such as Public Storage, have national advertising campaigns, but for the most part, advertising in this industry is business-to-business rather than directed at consumers. Keep in mind that many companies hire an advertising agency in lieu of an in-house advertising department.

In the smallest of companies, particularly those in the self-storage segment, the owner may rely primarily on telephone directories, classified advertisements in newspapers, and a Web site to sell his or her service. Potential clients for storage units typically do not seek providers until the need arises. Therefore, something as simple as location can be the deciding factor. Billboards can sometimes be used effectively, providing subliminal brand recognition before the need occurs. Buying

low-cost advertisements in high school yearbooks, community theater programs, and similar local publications is yet another way to place the name of the business in front of the public without damage to the budget. People often prefer to do business with companies or individuals who are perceived as being tied to the community. Another cost-effective way to advertise a self-storage facility is through inclusion in local coupon mailers. Franchisees benefit from the advertising done by the national or international headquarters but must pay periodic assessments for that advantage.

Entry-level positions require a bachelor's degree, and those aspiring to management should also consider obtaining an M.B.A. or another postgraduate degree. Smaller company owners and managers are less in need of formal education, as the most effective way to spread their message is to be attuned to what's happening in the community and what works for other small-business owners.

Occupations within the sales and marketing department include the following:

- Marketing Director
- Sales Manager
- Advertising Manager
- Advertising Creative Personnel

Facilities and Security

In the warehousing and storage industry, facilities and security are extremely important. As in any industry, the buildings that house the company have to be maintained, but in this industry, maintenance is crucial because the facility itself is the product being sold. Warehouses must always be kept up in a manner that makes clients feel that their property will be kept safe from fire, weather, pestilence, theft, and vandalism.

In corporate headquarters, a facility manager oversees the various departments, including maintenance, janitorial, security, landscaping, and even the employee cafeteria, if it exists. The mail room also falls under the facilities umbrella. If maintenance services are purchased externally, the facilities manager is still required to oversee the provider's activities. The corporate department may also dictate the security measures to be taken at satellite buildings. Those measures can include security guards, alarms, surveillance cameras, and motion sensors at points of entry. In smaller companies, some facility and security services may be provided by outside firms, but someone in the company must purchase those services and make sure they are performed satisfactorily. A dual major, engineering and management, is useful for a management position, and workers such as electricians need to be licensed in their respective trades.

Facilities managers earn, on average, $60,000 to $80,000 per year, while department heads under them earn less. Maintenance employees such as carpenters and electricians earn the prevailing rate in their geographic location or the union wage if they are union members. When work is performed by an external provider, that company determines the pay scale.

Specialty warehouses have separate concerns that fall under the responsibility of the facility manager. These can include anything from temperature control for refrigerated storage to regulatory compliance for hazardous materials handling and storage.

Occupations within the facilities and security department include the following:

- Facility Manager
- Housekeeping Staff
- Custodian/Janitor
- Maintenance Manager
- Skilled Tradesman
- Chief Security Officer
- Regulatory Compliance Specialist
- Mail Room Supervisor
- Mail Clerk

Technology

This industry does not provide many technology positions. Computers must be maintained and periodically updated. Databases are used to track inventory and monitor receipts and shipments of customer goods. Most companies also have electronically controlled security systems. Positions in warehousing and storage technology require at least a bachelor's degree and a commitment to ongoing education to keep up with technological advances.

Occupations within the technology departments include the following:

- Computer Systems Manager
- Information Services Manager
- Computer Technician
- Computer Operator

Administrative and Clerical Support

The administrative and clerical positions in this industry are similar to those at many other industries. Employees in this area support the day-to-day functions of a smooth-running enterprise so that management is free to concentrate on the bigger picture. Employees include the administrative assistant who works for a single executive and serves as that person's trusted aide, as well as the payroll clerk who may be part of a larger department. In small companies, the manager and the support staff are often one and the same. A high school education is enough for most entry-level positions but at least an associate's degree is a plus. Those seeking upward mobility should have a bachelor's degree. Most jobs also require computer literacy and familiarity with the most popular word processing and other software programs relevant to the job. In companies with continuing education benefits and a policy of promoting from within, jobs in this area can be stepping stones to greater responsibilities.

Occupations within the administrative and clerical departments include the following:

- Administrative Assistant
- Accounting Clerk
- Data Entry Clerk
- Warehouse Clerk

Industry-Specific Jobs

This industry is not labor-intensive and provides fewer jobs than many other industries beyond those provided by any large company's staffing needs. There are, however, jobs specific to the industry, and these, for the most part, are in the materials handling and management areas. Most are also jobs as opposed to careers.

Warehouse designers strive for ease of stocking and retrieval and for maximal space usage. A warehouse designer might develop a new building concept but most likely will be called upon to create a floor plan that will best utilize an existing structure. When goods appear on the receiving dock, they are packed in cartons, barrels, drums, or other containers. The receiving paperwork is completed, and the goods are placed on pallets or racks, often with the help of a forklift or other materials-moving machinery. The location of all items is stored in a database for easy retrieval. When end users order deliveries, the items must be taken from storage and loaded for shipment. This requires forklift drivers, order pickers, dispatchers, and expediters, although the smaller the operation, the more job functions will overlap. After being prepared for shipment, the order is placed on the loading dock to await transport.

Larger operations rely on inventory specialists and others to ensure smooth flow from the receipt of stock to its placement on the loading dock. Many companies offer ancillary services that include pricing, packaging, breaking down bulk items, order entry, order fulfillment, and even light assembly of goods. These services require additional personnel. Every additional service increases revenue, and the companies that can effectively meet the most client needs have a substantial competitive edge.

For the most part, these jobs are unskilled and thus low paying. They are expected to decline in number because of automation. Although the total number of jobs may be reduced, opportunities will always exist as the turnover rate in this area is high. The reasons for the turnover are varied. People move on to higher-paying jobs both inside and outside the industry, and the work can become too physically demanding. Most jobs require no education beyond high school and are quickly learned through on-the-job training. Good physical condition and the ability to lift heavy packages are primary requirements.

Occupations specific to the warehousing and storage industry include the following:

- Warehouse Manager
- Order Picker
- Dispatcher
- Expediter

OCCUPATION PROFILE

Forklift Operator

Considerations	Qualifications
Description	Drives a forklift and uses it to lift and move objects; may also do some maintenance.
Career cluster	Manufacturing
Interests	Things
Working conditions	Work inside; work both inside and outside
Minimum education level	No high school diploma; on-the-job training; high school diploma or GED; high school diploma/technical training; apprenticeship
Physical exertion	Light work; medium work
Physical abilities	Unexceptional/basic fitness
Opportunities for experience	Military service; part-time work
Licensure and certification	Usually not required
Employment outlook	Decline expected
Holland interest score	RCE

Note: See volume 1, "Publisher's Note," for an explanation of the Holland interest score.

- Forklift Operator
- Inventory Specialist
- Pricer
- Packager
- Clerk

INDUSTRY OUTLOOK

Overview

The outlook for this industry shows it to be on the rise, although growth is slightly slower than for the average industry. The U.S. Department of Labor estimates that some segments will remain stable, while others will grow as much as 12 percent between 2011 and 2018.

In 2008, the Bureau of Labor Statistics reported that there were 15,200 facilities storing general merchandise and refrigerated goods. This does not count the self-storage segment of the industry, which is expected to see the largest growth. The self-service sector had more than 50,000 facilities

in the United States alone in 2010. These facilities are owned by more than 30,000 companies and are likely to continue to multiply as they perform a useful service for many people. It is estimated that 10 percent of American households have items in a self-storage unit, the average size of which is comparable to a one-car garage. However, the self-storage end of the industry provides the fewest jobs. Eventually, the market for self-storage units could become saturated, but until that time, it will experience continued growth. The rebound in the moving industry is likely to increase the need for the short-term storage of household goods, although that market has been eroded by the proliferation of self-storage facilities.

Larger commercial warehousing and storage companies will see gains based on the growing dependence on goods produced offshore. These third-party logistics providers provide a convenience to manufacturers as well as to retailers. They will continue to gain customers as companies increasingly decide not to warehouse their own products. Stricter and more numerous safety regulations have made shipping of certain products complex enough that some suppliers prefer to use professional shippers to avoid problems and legal repercussions. Petroleum products, chemicals, pharmaceuticals, and food products all are highly regulated, and those storing such products need to be knowledgeable in their safe handling. Foods that once were available only during season or in their areas of origin can be flash frozen or otherwise preserved to be enjoyed all year long and all over the world. These foods require special attention throughout the storage process to protect the end consumer.

The trend toward decentralization has made the industry more efficient. The average regional facility operates with six distribution centers, all of which can be tailored to meet the needs of loca.l customers, and most of

PROJECTED EMPLOYMENT FOR SELECTED OCCUPATIONS

Warehousing and Storage

Employment		Occupation
2009	Projected 2018	
83,480	97,700	Industrial truck and tractor operators
148,100	160,600	Laborers and freight, stock, and material movers, hand
33,490	39,000	Shipping, receiving, and traffic clerks
53,550	66,200	Stock clerks and order fillers
6,690	6,500	Transportation, storage, and distribution managers

Source: U.S. Bureau of Labor Statistics, Industries at a Glance, Occupational Employment Statistics and Employment Projections Program.

those centers can move products within twenty-four hours of receiving the order. Just in time is another strategy developed to increase efficiency and reduce long-term storage of unneeded product. Continued corporate downsizing and outsourcing make third-party logistics providers a cost-effective way to handle warehousing and storage needs, thus allowing the corporation to concentrate on its core area of business.

Vacancy rates are expected to decline in the period from 2011 to 2018, leading to greater profitability. Also, new structures are being built anywhere from 25 percent to 40 percent larger than in the 2000's, a sign of industry confidence.

Special warehousing (that not counted elsewhere) is another category expected to see rapid growth. These facilities usually provide bulk storage for petroleum, oil, and gasoline. In the United States, they tend to be found near the oil refineries in Oklahoma and Texas. Another area of special warehousing is the storage of records and data, including microfilm, X rays, computer disks and drives, videotapes, and blueprints. These items must be stored in a climate-controlled environment and protected from damage, theft, and corporate espionage.

Employment Advantages

The industry is poised for growth, and although there are fewer opportunities than in many other industries, the career side of the business will continue to provide opportunities to earn a good living. There is always an advantage to working in an industry that provides a service that will be in demand in the future. The industry will always provide the type of positions that are required in every industry, such as managers, accountants, and administrative assistants. In addition, unskilled workers will always be needed as this area sees higher than average turnover. Workers who take these jobs can earn a modest living and expect to be able to choose from among many companies needing their services.

Self-storage and mini warehousing remains a good opportunity for entrepreneurs willing to work hard for what could be a distant payoff. However, the danger exists that the market will become saturated, and not all companies will survive.

Annual Earnings

The warehousing and storage industry is predicted to rise in overall revenues about 5.9 percent from 2011 through 2018, resulting in domestic growth of approximately $755 million. As with most industries, some categories will experience significantly higher (or lower) growth rates. Wages earned by the majority of employees will remain stable at an average hourly rate of $12 to $13 per hour. Owners, management, and other salaried skilled workers will receive the benefit of the lion's share of the industry's growth, although many workers performing unskilled labor may see increases in hourly wages to reflect increases in the cost of living.

The industry itself is confident about growth. Following a stagnant 2009, *Modern Materials Handling* magazine reported a 12 percent increase in equipment orders in 2010, a trend that is expected to continue into 2011. This means the industry is preparing for growth. An Armstrong Consulting report in the magazine also predicted that third-party logistics warehousing would top $50 billion in 2010 and 2011.

RELATED RESOURCES FOR FURTHER RESEARCH

Dangerous Goods Advisory Council
1100 H St. NW, Suite 740
Washington, DC 20005
Tel: (202) 289-4550
Fax: (202) 289-4074
http://www.dgac.org

International Association of Refrigerated Warehouses
1500 King St., Suite 201
Alexandria, VA 22314-2730
Tel: (703) 373-4300
Fax: (703) 373-4301
http://www.iarw.org

Material Handling Industry of America
8720 Red Oak Blvd., Suite 201
Charlotte, NC 28217-3992
Tel: (704) 676-1190
Fax: (704) 676-1199
http://www.mhia.org

MODERN MATERIALS HANDLING
Peerless Media
P.O. Box 1496
Framingham, MA 01701
Tel: (800) 315-1578
Fax: (508) 663-1599
http://www.mmh.com

SUPPLY CHAIN MANAGEMENT REVIEW
Peerless Media
P.O. Box 1496
Framingham, MA 01701
Tel: (800) 315-1578
Fax: (508) 663-1599
http://www.scmr.com

WAREHOUSING EDUCATION AND RESEARCH
COUNCIL
1100 Jorie Blvd., Suite 170
Oak Brook, IL 60523-4413
Tel: (630) 990-0001
Fax: (630) 990-0256
http://www.werc.org

ABOUT THE AUTHOR

Norma Lewis is the author of four nonfiction books, one an account of the Yukon gold rush for young adults and the other three pictorial histories of the southwestern Michigan area. She is a prolific writer for magazines, and during the twenty years she has been writing travel articles, she has covered destinations, group and solo travel, and recreational vehicle camping. She holds a bachelor of science degree in business administration from Aquinas College.

FURTHER READING

Bourlakis, Paul W., and W. H. Weigtman, eds. *Food Supply Chain Management.* Hoboken, N.J.: John D. Wiley and Sons, 2004.

Center for Chemical Process Safety. *Guidelines for Safe Warehousing of Chemicals.* Hoboken, N.J.: John D. Wiley and Sons, 2008.

Martin, James William. *Lean Six Sigma for Supply Chain Management: The Ten-Step Solution Process.* New York: McGraw-Hill, 2006.

Morris, Peter, and Jeffrey K. Pinto, eds. *The Wiley Guide to Project Technology Management, Supply Chain, and Procurement.* Hoboken, N.J.: John D. Wiley and Sons, 2007.

Ryan, Mary Meghan, ed. *Handbook of U.S. Labor Statistics: Employment, Earnings, Prices, Productivity, and Other Labor Data.* 13th ed. Lanham, Md.: Bernam Press, 2010.

Toigo, Jon William. *The Holy Grail of Data Storage Management.* New York: Prentice Hall, 1999.

U.S. Bureau of Labor Statistics. *Career Guide to Industries,* 2010-2011 ed. http://www.bls.gov/oco/cg.

_____. *Occupational Outlook Handbook,* 2010-2011 ed. http://www.bls.gov/oco.

U.S. Census Bureau. North American Industry Classification System (NAICS), 2007. http://www.census.gov/cgi-bin/sssd/naics/naicsrch?chart=2007.

U.S. Department of Commerce. International Trade Administration. Office of Trade and Industry Information. Industry Trade Data and Analysis. http://ita.doc.gov/td/industry/otea/OTII/OTII-index.html.

Waste Management Industry

©Dreamstime.com

INDUSTRY SNAPSHOT

General Industry: Transportation, Distribution, and Logistics

Career Clusters: Government and Public Administration Occupations; Transportation, Distribution, and Logistics

Subcategory Industries: Hazardous Waste Collection; Recycling; Septic Tank and Related Services; Sewer Cleaning; Solid Waste Collection; Waste Treatment and Disposal

Related Industries: Business Services; Civil Services: Public Safety; Local Public Administration; Public Health Services

Annual Domestic Revenues: $75 billion USD (Hoover's, 2009)

Annual Global Revenues: $375 billion USD (300 billion euros; Veolia Environmental Services, 2009)

NAICS Numbers: 56299, 5621-5622

INDUSTRY DEFINITION

Summary

Waste management is the collection, hauling, treatment, and disposal or recycling of the waste produced by human activity. There are different kinds of waste, including solid waste and hazardous waste. Waste management has become increasingly complex as the human population has increased and its industries and technologies have evolved. The primary goal of waste management is to protect the public and the environment from the potentially harmful effects of waste.

History of the Industry

Historically, there have been three basic methods of managing waste: recycling, dumping, and burning. Recycling and reuse were the earliest recognized forms of waste management: They have always existed in some form, mostly involving gathering damaged or previously used materials. There is evidence that a recycling system for bronze scrap metal was in operation in Europe nearly four thousand years ago and that composting was carried out in China around the same time.

The first recorded landfill site, or dumping site, dates back to 3000 B.C.E. at Knossos, on Crete, during the Minoan civilization. There, waste was placed in large pits and covered with earth at various levels. More than twenty-five hundred years ago, government officials in Athens, Greece, opened a municipal landfill site and established a decree that waste was to be transported at least 1 mile beyond the city gates. Even though landfills were used throughout history, archaeological digs have revealed only small amounts of ash, broken tools, and pottery. Archaeologists have therefore theorized that everything that could be salvaged by ancient civilizations was repaired and used again.

For many ancient civilizations, waste was manageable largely because populations were not heavily concentrated or remained nomadic in nature. As the human population increased and became more sedentary, shifting into urban areas, waste disposal became more difficult and complicated, and the consequences of failure became more severe. For centuries, unregulated waste was a primary source of disease; water supplies, in particular, became infected with untreated waste. In the early 1800's, cholera, which is transmitted to humans through contaminated drinking water, caused millions of deaths after it spread from the contaminated water and filthy living conditions of Calcutta, India. This cholera pandemic spread from India to Southeast and Central Asia, the Middle East, and finally Russia. Great Britain's first

cholera epidemic began shortly thereafter, in 1831. Seventeen years later, in 1848, the Public Health Act was enacted in Britain as a first effort to manage waste. However, major cities such as London were not included in the legislation, and problems with waste continued.

The management of animal waste also became an issue, as many diseases were the result of untreated waste from livestock. Pigs, for example, were often given raw garbage as feed—an early method of municipal waste disposal. However, pigs were found to be the source of diseases such as trichinosis, a parasitic disease passed along to humans who consume undercooked pork. To prevent the transmission of such diseases, Britain developed a waste management system in the early twentieth century that consisted of burning waste. The ash was then disposed of in the ground, where it helped improve the soil.

In the 1930's, commercial plastic, which is manufactured from petroleum, was introduced and used as packaging. While plastics helped reduce food waste, they were nonbiodegradable, but initially the environmental impact of their use was

This labeled bin encourages people to recycle. (©Dreamstime.com)

largely overlooked. During the years following World War II, waste was largely buried as opposed to being burned. The burial of waste was the most convenient and cost-effective method to manage waste, and landfills were created throughout the United States. However, little thought was given to the environmental impact or consequences of landfills, including the effect of buried garbage upon groundwater. Eventually, it was determined that garbage in landfills could contribute to water pollution and the release of methane gas. (Landfills release "landfill gas," which is roughly 50 percent methane and 50 percent carbon dioxide.) As a result of these dangers, strict regulations were initiated during the 1970's to codify and enforce the proper management of chemical and hazardous waste.

The Industry Today

The contemporary waste management industry seeks to reduce waste, not just to dispose of it. Waste generation has slowed considerably as a result of increased recycling and reduced consumption of disposable materials, such as paper. Local municipalities are focusing on increasing recycling and reducing the amount of waste that is dumped in landfills. In fact, a term now being used is "zero waste," a design principle that involves abolishing landfills and dramatically reducing the need to incinerate waste; in short, waste itself is to be eliminated.

Zero waste also involves a reduction in consumption and an increase in recycling—everything a consumer buys can be recycled or reused and can be made from products that have themselves been recycled or reused. In New Zealand, for example, an estimated 45 percent of local governments, as early as 2002, had introduced zero waste programs or policies, with the overall goal of achieving zero waste by 2015 (or coming as close to zero waste as possible). Such policy changes are dramatically increasing the amount of waste that is recycled. For instance, just six years after enacting policy changes to increase recycling and reduce waste, Canberra, Australia, was recycling an estimated 59 percent of its waste, while Edmonton, Canada, was recycling 70 percent of its waste.

The Waste Management Industry's Contribution to the U.S. Economy

Value Added	Amount
Gross domestic product	$40.8 billion
Gross domestic product	0.3%
Persons employed	360,000
Total employee compensation	$21.5 billion

Source: U.S. Bureau of Economic Analysis. Data are for 2008.

Some cities are enacting waste prevention strategies that are geared to reducing the amount of waste created. Such cities include Edinburgh, Scotland, which received £83 million (nearly $136 million in January, 2010, dollars) from the Strategic Waste Fund to develop a waste prevention strategy. Edinburgh's Waste Prevention Strategy is designed to reflect the principles of the waste hierarchy, aiming to reduce waste at every level of the production-consumption chain. The strategy aims to create a culture change among residents, ultimately decreasing the amount of waste sent to landfills.

Organic waste, which generally makes up 30 percent of a typical household's waste stream, has become a key focus of waste management. Organic waste—any waste from something that was once living—includes food scraps, leaves, grass, and agricultural residues, as well as materials that would naturally decay or decompose, such as wood waste, manure, or biosolids. Biosolids are treated sewage sludge generated at wastewater treatment facilities; they consist of the solid and semisolid materials from household sewage.

The waste management industry in the United States is fragmented and highly concentrated. There are approximately twenty thousand companies in the U.S. waste management industry, but the eight leading companies are responsible for one-half of the industry's total annual revenue. Household waste from both single-family and multifamily residences makes up the largest percentage of solid waste, while 35 to 45 percent comes from commercial businesses, schools, and institu-

Inputs Consumed by the Waste Management Industry

Input	Value
Energy	$1.0 billion
Materials	$8.7 billion
Purchased services	$28.2 billion
Total	$37.9 billion

Source: U.S. Bureau of Economic Analysis. Data are for 2008.

tions. Improvements in the U.S. waste management industry—and the global industry as a whole—are largely dependent upon the enhanced use of technology. More advanced processes are being used to map out routes, as well as to treat and dispose of waste. In addition, large companies are forming joint ventures and buying subsidiaries to produce waste-to-energy production facilities.

The waste management industry has several major subsectors and components. The waste combustors subsector comprises two types of operations: waste-to-energy facilities and incinerators that do not recover energy. Waste-to-energy facilities not only burn garbage but also recover heat energy from the incineration process and sell it to producers of electricity or steam. Typical waste-to-energy facilities generate about 2,750 megawatts of electricity, enough to meet the power needs of nearly 2.3 million homes. Traditional incinerators simply burn garbage and allow the heat to escape to the atmosphere. In many cases, incineration facilities also separate recyclable materials, which are either processed through another division of the company or sold.

Through the incineration process, the volume of municipal solid waste is reduced by about 90 percent, while its weight is reduced by about 75 percent. As of 2007, there were 87 waste-to-energy plants operating in the United States, down from 102 in 2000. Of these plants, 40 were located in the Northeast, 23 in the South, 16 in the Midwest, and 8 in the West. Both local governments and private companies are engaged in the waste combustor in-

dustry. The market is split about fifty-fifty between private companies and local governments that own and operate their own waste combustors.

The recycling industry processes household and industrial waste for reuse. Materials that can be recycled include paper, glass, and certain metals and plastics. Recycling slows the depletion of nonrenewable resources and helps prevent pollution. Businesses may specialize in recycling one or more types of material. While the recycling industry includes both public and private entities, private recycling is by far the larger sector. It supports about ten times the number of employees that are supported by the public sector.

The U.S. recycling industry is growing as a result of increasing regulations, and all U.S. states encourage or require local recycling programs. The recycling industry also provides environmental benefits. For example, recycling aluminum scrap saves 95 percent of the energy that would have been needed to make the same amount of new aluminum. Recycling paper saves about 64 percent of the energy that would have been needed to make an equivalent amount from raw materials. However, the 2007-2009 recession forced many local communities to cut back on their recycling programs. The industry was also affected by a drop in the price of commodities following the 2007-2009 global financial crisis.

Glass containers are 100 percent recyclable, making them an extremely environmentally friendly product. Glass recycling is conducted in approximately twenty-five states and employs more than thirty thousand people at approximately sixty-five glass recycling plants. A typical glass processing facility can handle 20 tons of color-sorted glass per hour, and glass bottles and jars can go from a recycling bin back to the retail shelf in as few as thirty days. Glass recycling can serve specialized markets, such as cathode-ray tubes for televisions and computer monitors or window plate and container glass. Some businesses specialize in one or more such markets.

Aluminum is also highly recyclable, and the recovery and recycling of aluminum has become its own industry. While aluminum recycling has been a common practice for more than one hundred years, it remained a low-profile activity until 1968, when recycling of aluminum beverage cans became common practice. (As of 2010, 100 percent of all beverage cans were made from aluminum.) While beverage cans are the most well known example of recycled aluminum, they typically amount to less than 30 percent of the tonnage of aluminum consumer products that are recycled. Other sources of recycled aluminum include appliances, automobiles, windows, and doors, As of 2009, there were more than ten thousand aluminum recycling centers in the United States.

The continued growth of the aluminum recycling industry is due primarily to the fact that it has become cheaper, faster, and more energy efficient to recycle aluminum. As the demand for aluminum increases, aluminum recyclers are expanding their businesses or advancing them by becoming more specialized to meet customers' unique product specifications and market needs. For example, recycled aluminum can be made into cans, pie pans, house siding, lawn furniture, and small appliances. The greatest consumer of aluminum is the automobile industry, which uses almost 6 billion pounds.

Mine waste consists of the by-products of extracting and processing mineral resources. Mine waste from extractive operations is one of the largest and most important waste streams in the European Union, and managing it is vital to preventing or minimizing water or ground pollution. Some mine wastes are inert and are therefore not likely to represent significant pollution threats. Others, however, may contain large amounts of dangerous substances, particularly those generated by metal mining, such as heavy metals. The extraction and subsequent mineral processing of metals and metal compounds tend to make them chemically more available, which can result in the generation of acid or alkaline drainage.

Mine waste management also entails the management of tailings, or the materials left after separating the valuable part from the worthless part of a metal. This separation is a hazardous process that often involves residual processing chemicals and increased levels of metals. In many instances, tailings are stored in large ponds that are retained by

Trash bags stacked at the curb, awaiting removal. (©Dreamstime.com)

dams. If such a dam were to collapse, the resulting release of its tailings could have a serious impact on human health and safety, as well as on the environment. Other possible negative effects of mine waste include the physical footprints of waste disposal facilities, resulting in the loss of land productivity, effects on ecosystems, and dust and erosion.

Hazardous waste poses a serious threat to public health and the environment and cannot be disposed of without treatment or some type of processing. Hazardous wastes may be flammable, toxic, explosive, carcinogenic, or corrosive, and they can be found in several different forms, such as liquids, solids, or gases. Hazardous household wastes include used paint, oils, fuels, automotive products, and fluorescent lightbulbs. Industrial hazardous wastes can be treated or processed through a number of means, including recycling, neutralization, conversion to cement, incineration, and waste-to-energy production.

Hazardous waste management is a fairly new field that began in the second half of the twentieth century. As the field evolved, many companies realized the need for rigorous scientific investigation to solve their environmental problems. Governmental agencies began to issue and enforce stricter waste management regulations that, in turn, required the hazardous waste management industry to seek chemists who could provide the scientific knowledge necessary to comply with the stricter laws. The market for chemists in the hazardous waste management field has been growing ever since, and it will likely continue to grow as environmental protection and concerns continue to rise.

Nuclear waste management involves the cleanup of nuclear and radioactive waste. Nuclear waste refers to the radioactive by-products of nuclear energy and weapons production. The cleanup or management of nuclear waste often takes decades. The U.S. Department of Energy (DOE) spends billions of dollars annually cleaning up nuclear waste from projects that date back as far as the 1940's.

Household waste from both single-family and multifamily residences makes up the largest percentage of solid waste. (©Dreamstime.com)

Birds scavenge at a landfill. (©Dreamstime.com)

Some of these DOE projects take forty years or longer to complete. Nuclear power is the only energy industry that takes full responsibility for all its wastes, as is reflected in the costs of the industry's end product.

Organic waste is typically biodegradable; it is generated from plants or animals and is broken down by other living organisms, such as worms, fungi, and bacteria. Organic waste is generated by households, businesses, municipalities, and industries. Household waste largely consists of food waste such as potato peelings, spoiled fruits and vegetables, and grass and garden trimmings. Restaurants generate waste similar to that of households, only in larger quantities. Industrial waste includes waste generated from food-processing factories and agricultural farms. Composting involves the managed decay of organic waste into humus, a form that can provide nutrients to soil.

Nonfunctional, outdated, or unwanted electronics equipment must be managed separately from other waste. From cameras to computers to broken televisions, the electronics waste management industry continues to grow in correlation to the growth in the technology industry. The industry is also affected by toxic materials and the appropriate handling and disposal issues at the electronics equipment end-of-life.

The scrap metals recycling industry in the United States is largely driven by demand from the auto, steel, and construction industries. Most companies in the scrap metal recycling industry are small and specialize in one type of material. Large companies have a competitive advantage because of economies of scale derived from the ability to purchase equipment and transportation vehicles in bulk. The industry is capital-intensive, meaning it requires large investments in the purchase and maintenance of equipment, as well as in labor.

Landfills can be started with raw land, or they can be purchased as ready-to-go landfills with all the proper permitting in place. Permitting can be a lengthy process, taking several years. Landfill and disposal operations generate billions of dollars in

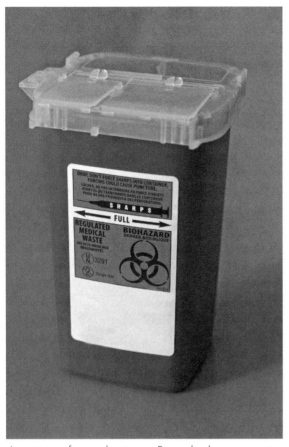

A container for used syringes. Biomedical waste requires special handling. (©Susanne Neal/Dreamstime.com)

ample, many of the landfills in Florida are publicly owned, because many of the state's municipalities have grown rapidly. The landfill industry in Florida is highly competitive.

Private landfill companies often have the flexibility to offer lower prices in competitive markets, particularly where there are several landfills within a reasonable transportation distance of the same market. They also rely on contracts with municipalities to collect residential waste. Ohio, for example, is a highly competitive environment, where private ownership of landfills has proved to be cost-beneficial for landfill owners.

More than 1 million tons of medical or clinical waste is generated each year by hospitals, veterinary clinics, and medical centers in the United States. While the majority of medical waste is harmless, about 15 percent of medical waste poses a potential hazard. Federal and state laws govern the disposal of medical waste, mandating specific methods for packaging or sterilizing the waste so it does not negatively affect people, animals, or the environment. (The Medical Waste Tracking Act of 1988 was enacted following a few highly publicized incidents of medical waste washing up on beaches along the East Coast.) While the Environmental Protection Agency (EPA) provides basic regulations, most requirements for the treatment and disposal of medical waste are dictated by the states.

INDUSTRY MARKET SEGMENTS

Each of the many subsectors of the waste management industry is divided into small, midsize, and large businesses. Some such businesses specialize in only one component of waste management. Others are more comprehensive in their approach to waste, offering multiple services and processing multiple types of waste to maximize their effectiveness and profits.

Small Businesses

Generally speaking, small waste management businesses earn between $1 million and $7 million annually. They typically specialize in one area of waste management, providing one specific service. For example, environmental waste disposal is a growing industry that is particularly suited to small

revenue annually. The latest technology is used in the design and management of landfills to address restrictions and regulations, as well as the increased need for efficiency in managing landfill space that is due to the declining number of landfills. In 1989, there were roughly 7,500 landfills in the United States; in 2000, that number had dropped by more than 50 percent, to 3,091. The competitiveness and consolidation of the waste management industry have caused some landfill operators to purchase waste collection companies to guarantee steady waste streams.

The landfill industry is ever changing—many communities are evaluating and implementing privatization, while others are switching back to public ownership. Cost-effectiveness for private landfills varies from state to state. Certain areas of the United States lean toward public ownership, while other areas prefer private ownership. For exbusinesses. Governmental standards for waste disposal, specifically environmental waste disposal, continue to become stricter. On a federal level, the process begins with the EPA. In addition, numerous permits are required by various environmental organizations and agencies and other types of waste management oversight organizations at the state and local level. As a result of these various regulatory bodies and processes, the environmental waste disposal industry is difficult to enter and highly competitive. Small businesses might also employ an environmental waste engineer to help develop economically advantageous disposal solutions.

Small businesses may also specialize in waste and environmental consulting. Consultants in solid waste management may have varied specialties and skills and may include engineers, geologists, scientists, and chemists. Solid waste consultants and firms help engineer landfills and manage greenhouse gases. They assess and remediate soil and groundwater from service stations that may have contaminated the ground. They also perform due diligence work, determining the assets and liabilities of a company. Solid waste and environmental consultants are also needed in legal proceedings to provide expert witness and litigation support services.

Recycling consultants and firms analyze the amount of trash and recyclables a company, resident, or city generates and provide workable solutions to reduce the waste stream. They identify the types of materials that are in the waste stream and assess their recyclability. Often, a municipality may hire a recycling consultant to help increase its recycling content by determining ways to increase the amount of trash that is recycled.

Medical waste management is a highly regulated industry. Some regulations vary from state to state, while other regulations are federally mandated. In addition, the U.S. Department of Transportation (DOT) requires that all employees transporting hazardous waste, including medical waste, must undergo regular training.

Meanwhile, the composting industry is, for the most part, in its infancy in the United States. As an industry, it is largely focused on decreasing the amount of waste that is sent to landfills. Composting allows for dual revenue streams: Businesses are paid to remove organic waste, and they are paid

again by consumers and retailers purchasing compost. For example, the food scraps of residents and businesses in San Francisco are brought to a composting facility that is paid to take the organic refuse. Once that matter has become compost, it is sold to vineyards. The composting business must deal with odors of decomposing foods and organic matter. This often requires a closed facility or a facility that is removed from residential communities. Some composting facilities are public-private partnerships. It is estimated that up to 30 percent of residential and commercial waste is compostable.

A rapidly growing waste management sector with opportunities for small businesses is animal manure management research. This burgeoning industry develops new or improved technologies for managing animal manures based on economically and environmentally sound approaches. It researches such techniques as combining manure with other materials, including litter, water, and bedding. Animal manure management research is intended to find ways to reduce the negative impact of animal manure on the environment, particularly the impact of factory farming. It also serves to improve the economics of animal production by creating value-added products derived from animal manure and maximizing manure management technologies. Funding is available exclusively to small animal manure management research businesses through the U.S. Department of Agriculture's Small Business Innovation Research (SBIR) program.

Potential Annual Earnings Scale. According to the BLS, the mean annual salary of all workers in the waste management field in 2009 was $46,170. Managers earned an average of $101,690, while liquid waste treatment plant operators earned $50,290 and trash and recycling collectors earned $37,290, on average.

Clientele Interaction. Small waste management businesses, depending on the nature of their specialized services, must deal with clients on the municipal and federal level. They may serve corporations, hospitals, and medical facilities.

Amenities, Atmosphere, and Physical Grounds. Waste management facilities operate within a highly regulated environment. Requirements often include odor and dust management and control. Amenities and atmosphere vary between the executive level and the rest of the workforce, such as those engaged in the actual collection and handling of waste.

Typical Number of Employees. Small waste management businesses may employ anywhere from one person to five hundred people.

Traditional Geographic Locations. Waste management facilities are located throughout the United States, typically a good distance from residential communities.

Pros of Working for a Small Waste Management Business. Small waste management businesses often have more creative control and flexibility. Competitive pricing and access to newly emerging markets are other benefits of small businesses. In addition, because they generally offer specialized services, small businesses serve local markets, establishing ties to their communities.

Cons of Working for a Small Waste Management Business. Small waste management businesses must be aware of and adhere to the various permitting procedures and strict environmental regulations that exist on both the national and local levels. They are more vulnerable to fluctuations in the market than are larger businesses, which usually have greater cash reserves, especially since start-up costs in the industry can be high. Because companies often offer specialized services, competition can also be intense among businesses with the same specialty.

Costs

Payroll and Benefits: Small waste management businesses generally hire a large portion of their staff at hourly wages. Health benefits, including vision and dental, are usually offered.

Supplies: Waste management businesses require large hauling equipment, sorting equipment, and other specialized equipment, as well as standard office equipment and supplies. Those with significant research divisions require all manner of scientific equipment as well.

External Services: Some businesses that focus on on-site disposal or recycling of waste may contract debris hauling and other transportation services. They may also hire external vendors to manage and control dust and odor at their facilities, as well as to provide security, maintenance, accounting, or marketing services.

Utilities: Waste management businesses must pay for standard utilities, such as electricity, gas, water, sewage, telephone service, and Internet access.

Taxes: Small businesses are required to pay local, state, and federal income taxes, as well as applicable property taxes. Other incurred costs include special permits and licenses.

Midsize Businesses

Generally speaking, midsize waste management businesses earn between $7 million and $15 million per year. They typically perform more than one process in a service area. For example, a hazardous waste company may collect hazardous waste, incinerate it, and sell the resulting energy on the open market. Specific services may include waste-to-energy conversion and remediation.

Waste-to-energy conversion has become an important and growing market, as more garbage is being shipped to developing countries from developed nations with insufficient landfill space. (Often, these developing countries lack the technologies to process waste efficiently.) For example, researchers are investigating ways to convert wastewater into ethanol and use it as an automobile fuel. They are also developing technologies to extract hydrogen from waste materials, such as vegetable oil or the glycerol by-product of biodiesel production. In the future, hydrogen-based fuel could be used for large-scale power production, and hydrogen cells could power laptop computers and other electronics.

The remediation services industry is primarily involved in the cleanup and removal of dangerous contamination. It remediates contaminated mine sites, buildings, soil, and groundwater. The industry also treats wastewater and removes hazardous materials such as asbestos and lead paint. When soil has been damaged, remediation services help revegetate the land by rebuilding the soil and then replanting. The growing need for remediation services is also allowing small companies to enter the field with sophisticated technology.

Potential Annual Earnings Scale. According to the BLS, the mean annual salary of all workers in the waste management field in 2009 was $46,170. Managers earned an average of $101,690, while liquid waste treatment plant operators earned $50,290 and trash and recycling collectors earned $37,290, on average.

Clientele Interaction. Midsize waste management businesses, depending on the nature of their specialized services, must deal with clients on the municipal and federal level. They may serve corporations, hospitals, and medical facilities.

Amenities, Atmosphere, and Physical Grounds. Waste management facilities operate within a highly regulated environment. Requirements often include odor and dust management and control. Amenities and atmosphere vary between the executive level and the rest of the workforce, such as those engaged in the actual collection and handling of waste.

Typical Number of Employees. Midsize waste management businesses generally employ between five hundred and one thousand people.

Traditional Geographic Locations. Waste management facilities are located throughout the United States, typically a good distance from residential communities.

Pros of Working for a Midsize Waste Management Business. Midsize waste management businesses are usually more financially stable, with greater cash reserves, than are small businesses. They are able to achieve greater economies of scale and more competitive pricing than are small businesses, while still being large enough to diversify somewhat, covering more than one specialty or segment of the waste management process. At the same time, they may be more nimble and flexible than large businesses.

Cons of Working for a Midsize Waste Management Business. Midsize waste management businesses must be aware of and adhere to the various permit and strict environmental regulations, both on the national and local level. They are more likely than small businesses to operate in multiple jurisdictions, requiring multiple sets of permits and overseen by multiple regulatory structures. However, they may lack the resources to dedicate as many legal and oversight personnel to ensuring compliance as can large businesses. Similarly, while they may have significant financial resources, they will still be less likely to weather economic downturns than are larger firms.

Costs

Payroll and Benefits: Midsize waste management businesses generally hire a portion of their staff at hourly wages, but they have more salaried administrative and management employees than do small businesses. Health benefits, including vision and dental, are usually offered.

Supplies: Waste management businesses require large hauling equipment, sorting equipment, and other specialized equipment, as well as standard office equipment and supplies. Those with significant research divisions require all manner of scientific equipment as well.

External Services: Businesses that focus on on-site disposal or recycling of waste may contract debris hauling and other transportation services. They may also hire external vendors to manage and control dust and odor at their facilities, as well as to provide security, maintenance, accounting, or marketing services.

Utilities: Waste management businesses must pay for standard utilities, such as electricity, gas, water, sewage, telephone service, and Internet access.

Taxes: Midsize businesses are required to pay local, state, and federal income taxes, as well as applicable property taxes. Other incurred costs include special permits and licenses.

Large Businesses

Generally speaking large waste management businesses earn $10 million or more annually. They typically collect, dispose of, and treat many types of waste in various locations. They do not specialize in only one waste management service; rather, they vertically integrate operations into the five primary services: recycling, remediation, waste collection, treatment, and disposal. Large waste management companies usually operate in more than one state, serving millions of customers through hundreds if not thousands of service contracts. The waste management industry is highly concentrated, and the eight largest firms accounted for approximately 50 percent of the industry's total revenue in 2009. In order to serve the market, large companies privately operate transfer stations, recycling facilities, landfills, hauling facilities, and waste-to-energy facilities nationwide.

According to Hoover's, recycling accounts for about 10 percent of the waste management industry's revenue, while waste collection accounts for about 55 percent. Treatment and disposal account for about 20 percent, and remediation and cleaning of ground contamination, lead paint, and asbestos account for about 15 percent. Efficient operations and labor are the primary profitability drivers of large waste management companies.

In the early twenty-first century, the industry's operations have been complicated by growing environmental awareness and concerns. Stricter regulations have been implemented, requiring the use of clay liners in landfills, monitoring devices to detect leakage of garbage, and containment technologies to capture dangerous methane gas. In particular, the need to use green technology and to lower carbon dioxide emissions are two major concerns for large waste management businesses. The industry can help reduce greenhouse gases and reduce emissions in its fleet of vehicles by 50 percent if it converts its hauling vehicles from diesel fuel to clean-burning natural gas. Additionally, joint ventures have become a growing market for large waste management companies, which partner with communities, governments, industries, and environmental groups to redevelop closed landfills and convert them into recreational facilities, such as campgrounds, athletic fields, and golf courses.

Potential Annual Earnings Scale. According to the BLS, the mean annual salary of all workers in the waste management field in 2009 was $46,170. Managers earned an average of $101,690, while liquid waste treatment plant operators earned $50,290 and trash and recycling collectors earned $37,290, on average.

Clientele Interaction. Large waste management businesses, depending on the nature of their specialized services, must deal with clients on the municipal and federal level. They may serve corporations, hospitals, and medical facilities.

Amenities, Atmosphere, and Physical Grounds. Waste management facilities operate within a highly regulated environment. Requirements often include odor and dust management and control. Amenities and atmosphere vary between the executive level and the rest of the workforce, such as those engaged in the actual collection and handling of waste.

Typical Number of Employees. Large waste management businesses generally employ more than one thousand people.

Traditional Geographic Locations. Waste management facilities are located throughout the United States. Their plants are typically a good distance from residential communities. In addition to

such plants, large corporations coordinate their operations from headquarters located in major cities and other business centers.

Pros of Working for a Large Waste Management Corporation. Large waste management businesses have sufficient resources in multiple locations to realize economies of scale, price their services competitively, and vertically integrate those services. They are able to devote substantial resources to compliance—a significant and ever-changing aspect of the industry—as well as to the crucial area of research and development. In addition to their cash reserves, the fact that these corporations operate nationally or internationally increases their financial stability, as their success is not tied to any one state or regional economy.

Cons of Working for a Large Waste Management Corporation. Large waste management businesses face a dizzying array of local, state, national, and international regulations, permitting procedures, and oversight agencies. Like any large corporations, they can be extremely impersonal places to work, and their internal bureaucracies may rival those of the various government entities and agencies with which they must deal.

Costs

Payroll and Benefits: Large waste management businesses generally hire a portion of their staff at hourly wages, but they also have many salaried positions. Because they are national companies, they generally offer competitive health benefits, including vision and dental. Their employees may be members of collective bargaining units that renegotiate their contracts on a regular basis.

Supplies: Large organizations have significant capital expenditures related to equipment for hauling, sorting, and storage. They also have significant costs related to real estate, facilities, and, most especially, fuel. Because they handle a broad cross section of services, specialized equipment may be necessary. Like any business, office equipment and supplies are also required.

External Services: Large, vertically integrated corporations are likely to handle all services directly related to waste management internally. They may contract subsidiary services such as groundskeeping, security, or cafeteria service.

While they often have dedicated public relations and marketing staffs, large corporations nonetheless often contract external public relations firms to create or advise on major advertising campaigns.

Utilities: Waste management businesses must pay for standard utilities, such as electricity, gas, water, sewage, telephone service, and Internet access. For large corporations, these costs may be substantial.

Taxes: All businesses are required to pay local, state, and federal income taxes, as well as applicable property taxes. Other incurred costs include special permits and licenses.

ORGANIZATIONAL STRUCTURE AND JOB ROLES

The waste management industry comprises both governmental agencies and private businesses. In either type of organization, waste pickup and disposal activities need to be both conducted and managed. Government entities, such as cities, often maintain departments that handle waste management in addition to other services, whereas private businesses may be dedicated solely to waste management.

The difference between jobs in governmental agencies versus jobs in the private sector is primarily in the business management area. In a governmental agency, jobs such as accounting, human resources, marketing, and public relations are performed by other portions of the agency or government, rather than within the waste management department. Other differences include the job role of the director or primary manager of a government's waste management department versus a private waste management company. Additionally, governmental agencies have public works directors rather than chief executive officers (CEOs).

The following umbrella categories apply to the organizational structure of businesses in the waste management industry:

- Executive Management
- Administrative Support
- Sales and Marketing
- Technology, Research, and Development
- Operations
- Human Resources

Executive Management

Business or executive management staff establish and achieve the goals of an organization. They create the vision or direction of the business, manage employees who can implement that vision, and oversee finances. In addition to strategy and finances, managers often serve in a business development capacity, coordinating and establishing relationships with suppliers, partners, and clients. Many executive managers have advanced degrees in business management, accounting, or similar fields. They are usually the highest-paid employees of their agency or business.

Executive management occupations may include the following:

- Chief Executive Officer (CEO)
- Chief Financial Officer (CFO)
- Chief Operating Officer (COO)
- Legal Counsel
- Regional Manager
- Business Manager
- Office Manager
- Route Manager
- Accountant
- Procurement Manager
- Public Works Director
- Waste Management Director
- Recycling Manager
- Landfill Manager

Administrative Support

Administrative support staff facilitate all aspects of a company's day-to-day operations. They are usually in-house employees, but their duties can also be outsourced to other companies. They prepare and update internal reports, collecting and verifying all relevant data; schedule appointments and meetings; arrange domestic and international travel; and serve as liaisons or contacts within or outside their organizations regarding issues related to purchasing, personnel, facilities, and operations.

Administrative occupations may include the following:

- Secretary
- Executive Assistant

OCCUPATION PROFILE

Hazardous Waste Manager

Considerations	*Qualifications*
Description	Conducts studies on hazardous waste problems and provides solutions for the treatment and containment of waste.
Career clusters	Agriculture, Food, and Natural Resources; Government and Public Administration; Manufacturing; Transportation, Distribution, and Logistics
Interests	Data; things
Working conditions	Work inside
Minimum education level	Junior/technical/community college; bachelor's degree
Physical exertion	Light work
Physical abilities	Unexceptional/basic fitness
Opportunities for experience	Military service; part-time work
Licensure and certification	Recommended
Employment outlook	Average growth expected
Holland interest score	IRE

Note: See volume 1, "Publisher's Note," for an explanation of the Holland interest score.

- Administrative Assistant
- Recycling Coordinator
- Accounts Payable Clerk
- Accounts Receivable Clerk
- Waste Reduction and Recycling Coordinator

Sales and Marketing

Sales and marketing staff generate revenue growth by securing new accounts and retaining existing accounts. They develop and implement strategies for customer retention and utilize negotiation skills to preserve existing business. They also secure contract agreements from previously non-contracted customers. Sales and marketing employees seek to establish and maintain a high level of customer satisfaction for all account holders, and they work with retention managers to resolve customer issues as quickly as possible.

Sales and marketing occupations may include the following:

- Strategic Accounts Manager
- Account Manager
- Sales Manager
- Sales Coordinator
- Inside Sales Account Manager
- Senior Associate
- Inside Commercial Representative
- Business Development Director

Technology, Research, and Development

Waste management jobs in technology, research, and development often require a high level of technical expertise in designing, developing, coding, testing, and debugging computer software, as well as installing significant enhancements to existing software. Technology, research, and development staff also engage in quality-control tests and analyses to evaluate the ability of software packages to fulfill end-user requirements and comply with established standards. They may use established procedures to administer or assist in the implementation of environmental protection programs. Monitoring and investigating compliance also falls within this staff's purview.

Technology, research, and development occupations may include the following:

- Development Analyst
- Waste Management Specialist
- Facility Engineer
- Instructional Designer
- Trainer
- Senior Engineer
- Solutions Architect
- Environmental Engineer
- Environmental Compliance Specialist

Operations

Operations staff gather and dispose of waste and recycling materials from homes and businesses. Their duties may include heavy lifting and handling disposal containers such as garbage cans and recycling bins, as well as operating hydraulic lift trucks to pick up and empty dumpsters. Most operations jobs require little training or experience; wages are hourly and at the lower end of the scale.

The work environment for this type of job tends to be repetitive and physically demanding. Some jobs may expose workers to hazardous materials, fumes, chemicals, or dangerous equipment. Workers who handle toxic chemicals or substances receive specialized training. Many of the training requirements, particularly for jobs that are potentially dangerous, are standardized through the U.S. Occupational Safety and Health Administration (OSHA). Training is typically provided by the employer.

Operations occupations may include the following:

- Refuse and Recyclable Material Collector
- Hazardous Materials Removal Worker
- Equipment Operator

OCCUPATION PROFILE

Refuse Collector

Considerations	Qualifications
Description	Picks up and collects refuse on an assigned route.
Career clusters	Agriculture, Food, and Natural Resources; Human Services
Interests	Things
Working conditions	Work outside
Minimum education level	No high school diploma
Physical exertion	Heavy work
Physical abilities	Unexceptional/basic fitness; may be required to lift heavy objects
Opportunities for experience	Part-time work
Licensure and certification	Usually not required
Employment outlook	Slower-than-average growth expected
Holland interest score	RES

Note: See volume 1, "Publisher's Note," for an explanation of the Holland interest score.

- Mechanic
- Commercial Driver
- Residential Driver
- Equipment Operator
- Sorter
- Technician
- Welder

Human Resources

A human resources department recruits, hires, fires, and serves the employees of an organization. It administers benefits and payroll and conducts salary analysis, as well as ensuring that all labor laws are complied with. Human resources staff typically post job announcements, interview potential candidates, and ensure that all necessary hiring forms and documentation are completed. Additionally, if workers are injured on the job, the human resources staff completes their worker's compensation claims. Typically, corporate policies and procedures are established through the human resources department.

If a company or public entity works with union employees, the human resources department is charged with ensuring that the organization complies with negotiated contracts. Additionally, when contract negotiations are under way, the human resources department plays a significant role in informing decision makers of the financial and management implications of proposed contract elements.

Human resources occupations may include the following:

- Human Resources Director
- Human Resources Manager
- Senior Recruiter
- Human Resources Coordinator
- Human Resources Generalist

INDUSTRY OUTLOOK

Overview

The waste management industry appears to be on the rise in the early twenty-first century, as stricter regulations require improved disposal techniques, increased recycling, and more awareness of waste prevention procedures. Many states in the United States continue to set and enact stricter recycling goals and restrictions; municipalities are establishing recycling and reuse goals in combination with laws that restrict or ban certain types of products. For example, San Francisco has banned retail plastic bags. While recycling, reuse programs, and waste-to-energy processes are on the rise, more work needs to be done to reduce landfills and the pollution caused by waste.

While municipalities have traditionally been responsible for waste collection and disposal, privatization has become a growing trend in the waste management industry. Many municipalities contract their work out to private companies, and eight of the largest waste management companies in the United States produce more than 50 percent of the industry's revenue.

There are a number of employment areas and opportunities in the waste management industry. For example, the BLS has projected environmental science jobs within the industry to increase by 25 percent between 2006 and 2016, a rate that is much faster than the average of 11 percent for all occupations in all industries. Similarly, sales managers are expected to increase at an average rate of 12 percent during the same period, with intense domestic and global competition spurring job growth for sales personnel. Employment in material-moving occupations is projected to have little or no change, possibly declining by 1 percent between 2006 and 2016. The anticipated slight decrease is due to automated equipment and processes that minimize the need for manual sorting and moving of waste. Job growth will be strongest in the private sector, which is advantageous to the waste management industry since the majority of waste management revenue is produced by private firms.

Recycling is the fastest-growing market segment in the hazardous waste remediation market. Its rate of growth was 19 percent in 2006, and that rate is projected by BCC Research to increase to 27 percent by 2011. Hazardous waste remediation technologies were worth about $10.7 billion in 2005, and they are anticipated to grow to $16.6 billion by 2011.

Employment Advantages

The waste management industry is discovering new ways to prevent, reduce, and manage waste, as stricter regulations are being set by municipalities and governments. Students who are conservation-minded and environmentally concerned may enjoy careers in the waste management industry. Furthermore, students who are creative and enjoy researching and implementing new techniques and technologies might excel in the waste management industry's innovative branches, particularly as new processes are being developed and enhanced. For example, waste-to-energy processes are increasingly important in both the public and private sectors as the need to reduce waste and the need to increase energy efficiency converge. In addition, recycling technology continues to be enhanced to reduce the amount of waste that is dumped in landfills.

Annual Earnings

The waste management industry is heavily influenced by the overall levels of consumer spending and economic activity. Growth is anticipated in the recycling and waste-to-energy market, as increased legislative policies are enacted to address public and environmental concerns. In 2007, the United States generated approximately 254 million tons of garbage; of this amount, 63.3 million tons were recovered for recycling according to *Waste Age*. Hoover's estimates the total annual revenue of the U.S. waste management industry at about $75 billion. By way of comparison, according to *Waste News*, the European Union's industry has annual revenues of about 100 billion euros, or $125 billion.

PROJECTED EMPLOYMENT FOR SELECTED OCCUPATIONS

Waste Management and Remediation Services

Employment		
2009	Projected 2018	Occupation
32,520	38,600	Hazardous materials removal workers
19,740	20,400	Laborers and freight, stock, and material movers, hand
70,950	92,500	Refuse and recyclable material collectors
12,640	15,700	Septic tank servicers and sewer pipe cleaners
44,800	57,600	Truck drivers, heavy and tractor-trailer

Source: U.S. Bureau of Labor Statistics, Industries at a Glance, Occupational Employment Statistics and Employment Projections Program.

RELATED RESOURCES FOR FURTHER RESEARCH

AIR AND WASTE MANAGEMENT ASSOCIATION
1 Gateway Center, 3d Floor
420 Fort Duquesne Blvd.
Pittsburgh, PA 15222-1435
Tel: (800) 270-3444
Fax: (412) 232-3450
http://www.awma.org

AMERICAN COUNCIL ON RENEWABLE ENERGY
1600 K St. NW, Suite 700
Washington, DC 20006
Tel: (202) 393-0001
Fax: (202) 393-0606
http://www.acore.org

ASSOCIATION OF COMPOST PRODUCERS
7860 Alida St.
La Mesa, CA 91942
Tel: (619) 303-3694
Fax: (619) 589-9905
http://www.healthysoil.org

ENERGY RECOVERY COUNCIL
1730 Rhode Island Ave. NW, Suite 700
Washington, DC 20036
Tel: (202) 467-6240
http://www.energyrecoverycouncil.org

INTERNATIONAL SOLID WASTE ASSOCIATION
Auerspergstrasse 15, Top 41
1080 Vienna
Austria
Tel: 43-1-253-6001
http://www.iswa.org

NATIONAL RECYCLING COALITION
805 15th St. NW, Suite 425
Washington, DC 20005
Tel: (202) 789-1430
Fax: (202) 789-1431
http://www.nrc-recycle.org

NATIONAL SOLID WASTE MANAGEMENT
ASSOCIATION
4301 Connecticut Ave. NW, Suite 300
Washington, DC 20008
Tel: (202) 244-4700
Fax: (202) 966-4824
http://www.environmentalistseveryday.org

SOLID WASTE ASSOCIATION OF NORTH AMERICA
1100 Wayne Ave., Suite 700
Silver Spring, MD 20910
Tel: (800) 467-9262
Fax: (301) 589-7068
http://www.swana.org

ABOUT THE AUTHOR

Suzanne Mulvehill is an elected official overseeing and guiding the waste management services provided by the city of Lake Worth, Florida. She is working to establish a waste prevention program, a downtown business recycling program, and a backyard composting program in her city. Mulvehill is also the author of two books, *Employee to Entrepreneur: A Mind, Body, and Spirit Transition* (2007), and *Empowerment for Entrepreneurs: A Ninety-Day Guide* (2008) and the founder of Emotional Endurance Training Programs. She has taught at universities and business organizations throughout the United States and Europe. Mulvehill has a master's degree in business administration and a bachelor's degree in social work from Florida Atlantic University.

FURTHER READING

BCC Research. "Global Markets for Hazardous Waste Remediation Technologies." MarketResearch.com, April 1, 2006. http://www.marketresearch.com/product/display.asp?productid=1300222&SID=31904368-463897374-440422766&partnerid=811788012&kw=global%09waste%09revenues.

Dijkgraaf, E., and R. H. J. M. Gradus. *The Waste Market: Institutional Developments in Europe.* Dordrecht: Springer, 2008.

Hoover's. "Industry Overview: Waste Management." http://www.hoovers.com/waste-management/—ID__99—/free-ind-fr-profile-basic.xhtml.

Institute for Career Research. *Careers in the Waste Management Industry.* Chicago: Author, 2007.

Key Note Publications. *Recycling and Waste Management.* Hampton, Middlesex, England: Author, 2009.

Miller, Debra A. *Garbage and Recycling.* Detroit: Lucent Books, 2010.

Renner, Michael, et al. *Green Jobs: Working for People and the Environment.* Washington, D.C.: Worldwatch Institute, 2008.

Stuart, Tristram. *Waste: Uncovering the Global Food Scandal.* New York: W. W. Norton, 2009.

U.S. Bureau of Labor Statistics. *Career Guide to Industries,* 2010-2011 ed. http://www.bls.gov/oco/cg.

U.S. Census Bureau. North American Industry Classification System (NAICS), 2007. http://www.census.gov/cgi-bin/sssd/naics/naicsrch?chart=2007.

U.S. Department of Commerce. International Trade Administration. Office of Trade and Industry Information. Industry Trade Data and Analysis. http://ita.doc.gov/td/industry/otea/OTII/OTII-index.html.

U.S. Government Accountability Office. "Nuclear Waste: DOE's Environmental Management Initiatives Report Is Incomplete." June 2, 2009. http://www.gao.gov/new.items/d09697r.pdf.

Watches and Jewelry Industry

©Mark Hryciw/Dreamstime.com

INDUSTRY SNAPSHOT

General Industry: Manufacturing
Career Cluster: Manufacturing
Subcategory Industries: Jewelers Material and Lapidary Work Manufacturing; Jewelry (Except Costume) Manufacturing; Watch, Clock, and Part Manufacturing; Watch Jewels Manufacturing; Watch Repair Shops; Watches and Parts (Except Crystals) Manufacturing
Related Industries: Apparel and Fashion Industry; Metals Manufacturing Industry; Mining Industry
Annual Domestic Revenues: $60 billion USD (Idexonline.com, 2008)
Annual International Revenues: $75 to $80 billion USD (Idexonline.com, 2008)
Annual Global Revenues: $135 to $140 billion USD (Idexonline.com, 2008)
NAICS Numbers: 334518, 339911, 339913, 811490

INDUSTRY DEFINITION

Summary

The watches and jewelry industry designs, manufactures, distributes, markets, and sells goods, including precious and semiprecious gems with or without settings, watches, and plated silverware. Previously owned vintage and estate jewelry, particularly high-value items, is also sold in some stores. Repair services are often provided. The current American jewelry industry comprises several segments: bridal/engagement jewelry (mainly diamonds), fine (classic) jewelry, costume (fashion) jewelry, watches, unmounted precious stones, and precious metals, including silver flatware. Of these, the first category accounts for the largest share of sales, between 30 and 35 percent. Classic or fine jewelry is defined as that made of precious metals and precious or semiprecious gemstones. Costume or fashion jewelry is less expensively made from such materials as baser metals (including copper, brass, aluminum, iron, and zinc), glass, plastic, wood, leather, bone, shells, and nonprecious or synthetic stones.

History of the Industry

Clock making in America goes back to seventeenth century New England. Eventually, the so-called American system was developed and led to the mass production of floor-standing and shelf clocks in the very early nineteenth century. Until World War I, nearly all American watches were

Bridal and engagement jewelry accounts for 30 to 35 percent of jewelry sales. (©Dreamstime.com)

pocket watches of the type that first began production in the early nineteenth century. By the mid-1800's, they were being manufactured in volume using a system of interchangeable parts.

Among the manufacturing pioneers was the Waltham Watch Company, formed in 1850, which was to dominate the industry for at least twenty years. Along with the taste for pocket watches came the desire for expensive accessories such as fobs and chains to be placed in vests' watch pockets. Owning and displaying such watches was the nineteenth century equivalent of flashing a Rolex, Patek-Philippe, Omega, or other modern upmarket brand.

By the 1890's, the once-luxury item was being mass-produced, and the so-called dollar watch had been introduced. Jeweled parts were replaced by inexpensive standardized metal parts produced by punch presses. At the opposite end of the spectrum were watches used by railroad employees that had to be extremely accurate. Manufacturing techniques became more sophisticated. American-made wristwatches became very popular during World War I, when they were distributed to the American fighting forces.

Previously, Swiss firms had been almost the exclusive manufacturers of wristwatches, at first marketing them primarily to women. In fact, for a con-

siderable time wearing such watches was considered effeminate. During the Great Depression of the 1930's, manufacturing of watches by American companies declined, partially as a result of overexpansion and the purchase of expensive equipment. The great majority of watch manufacturing reverted to Europe, which maintained primacy until the rise of later industrial powerhouses such as Japan and China.

The American watch industry has continued to decline since the 1980's. The manufacture of parts has largely moved abroad, escalated by the popularity, since 1969, of quartz watches that are produced mainly in Asia. Battery-powered electric and electronic watches were introduced in the 1950's, and the first digital watch, the Pulsar, was introduced in the 1970's. The Tourneau chain, founded about 1900, claims to be the largest contemporary retail purveyor of fine watches.

The fascination with gemstones dates back to ancient times. Some were thought to possess magic powers and the ability to endow those who wore them with special attributes. For example, a ruby supposedly meant nobility and a blue sapphire symbolized wisdom. They were used as talismans and amulets and were even thought to predict the future. Several religions, including Christianity, Judaism, and Hinduism, used them as part of some of their religious practices. It is believed that the ancient Egyptians first combined gemstones and metals to produce jewelry. Such great Renaissance artists as Benvenuto Cellini fashioned timelessly beautiful vessels from precious stones and precious metals, and enameling was perfected about that time.

In the United States, the progenitors of the first jewelers were colonial watchmakers, silversmiths, and coppersmiths. They probably fashioned rings or other pieces of metal jewelry as an occasional sideline. The first business that might be regarded as a jewelry store is believed to have opened about the beginning of the nineteenth century. New York City has been the center of the American jewelry industry since the 1890's. By the early twentieth century, machines had been invented that enabled the mass production of costume jewelry. This allowed a much greater number of people to own jewelry in addition to their wedding rings.

In the late nineteenth century, the De Beers syndicate based in South Africa gained control of most of the world's diamond production, and as of 2010, it controls about 80 percent of the supply. However, its sales declined more than 50 percent during the recession of 2007-2009, and there may even be a glut of diamonds on the market. De Beers also has attempted to gain a large part of the synthetic gemstones market. Through its numerous interlocking companies and the diamond exchanges located throughout the world (Antwerp, Belgium, being the largest), the diamonds eventually make their way to retail sources. Other exchanges are found in New York, Israel, Amsterdam, and other major European cities. Historically, Orthodox Jews have played a large role in the wholesale and retail diamond markets.

The Industry Today

The retail watches and jewelry industry remains highly competitive and fragmented, with less than one-quarter of the revenue being generated by the top ten retailers and one-half the revenue generated by the top fifty chain stores. At the end of 2007, independent stores accounted for 21 percent of sales, discount chains 8 percent, Internet auction sites 11 percent, Internet sales sites 6 percent, shopping networks 11 percent, national chains 15 percent, department stores 13 percent, and other venues 15 percent. About 75 percent of all jewelry businesses had their own Web sites.

Most small jewelry businesses gross less than $2.5 million annually. In fine jewelry, there continues to be strong demand for semiprecious stones, but diamond jewelry accounts for 55 percent of sales, especially in wedding-related items. The sale of fine jewelry to men now composes about 10 percent of the market. Classic jewelry has been considered almost recession-proof, but the sale of cos-

There are more than 130 varieties of gemstones, of which about 50 are customarily sold by retail jewelers. (©Stuart Corlett/Dreamstime.com)

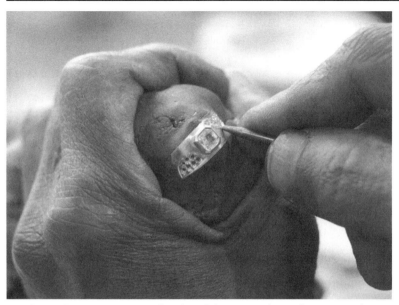

Bench jewelers use a variety of tools to fabricate and manufacture jewelry, set stones, and repair individual pieces. (©Sean Nel/Dreamstime.com)

tume or fashion jewelry has been affected by economic conditions. The holiday period around Christmas continues to be the prime sales time, followed by Valentine's Day and Mother's Day.

At least 90 percent of the fine jewelry sold contained some kind of gemstone. There are said to be more than 130 varieties of gemstones, of which about 50 are customarily sold by retail jewelers. Synthetic gemstones, manufactured by such companies as De Beers, Gemesis, and Apollo, are claiming an increasing share of the market and are offered for sale by some retailers. A majority of jewelry purchasers indicate a willingness to purchase synthetic stones, which usually are much less expensive than naturally grown ones.

Online sales by the industry have risen from approximately 4.7 percent of the market in 2004, with $1.7 billion in sales, to 6.6 percent of the market in 2009, with $2.7 billion in sales. It had taken six years, from 1996 to 2002, for online sales to reach $1 billion. However, the quality of the merchandise sold online does not always match its advertising, and buyers must be cautious when purchasing jewelry unseen or based on photographs published on the Web. This is one of the reasons buyers still want to purchase from stores they know and trust, even though their prices may be higher than those found online.

The sale of costume jewelry increased more than 50 percent annually between 2003 and 2008. This trend may continue with the growing popularity of "bling," or hip-hop jewelry, a term for the flashy jewelry worn on every part of the body (not excluding teeth and toes) associated with hip-hop culture. This trend has brought jewelry to the attention of a relatively new demographic, the very young. To capitalize on the youth market, less expensive watches are now sold in fashion clothing stores. The United States has always been the prime market for the importation of costume jewelry and since 1985 has accounted for more than 50 percent of all such imports. Asian countries are the major exporters.

About 54 percent of all jewelers and precious stone and metal workers are self-employed. Some workers hold credentials as bench jewelers from Jewelers of America, which requires them to pass written and practical examinations. More than forty-two thousand jobs were held, until recently, by jewelers in specialty shops, department stores, and discount stores. Most were in large urban centers, a substantial number being in California, Texas, New York, Pennsylvania, Illinois, and New Jersey. The major centers of jewelry manufacture in the United States are in Rhode Island, New York, and California.

Up to the time of the 2007-2009 economic recession, there were estimated to be more than thirteen thousand wholesale watch and jewelry establishments. The majority of them were small, employing five or fewer persons. The companies, found mainly in Texas, California, and New York, were generating $14 billion in annual sales. The number of positions in all aspects of the industry may be declining, particularly since a majority of the industry's product is imported into the United States, a trend that further limits American employment opportunities. The reduction or elimination of tariffs on nearly all categories of gemstones, with only a small tariff on finished jewelry, has continued to ease the way for imports. Tariffs on imported costume jewelry have traditionally been higher but have also been reduced. For some countries, North American Free Trade Agreement (NAFTA) member Mexico being one, they have been completely eliminated. By the end of the twentieth century, imports accounted for 50 percent of fine jewelry.

Prior to the recession of 2007-2009, the largest retailers of jewelry and watches were Walmart, Finlay Fine Jewelry, Fred Meyer Jewelers, Ben Bridge, Blue Nile, the Zale Corporation, Tiffany's, and Sterling Jewelers, the American arm of Britain's Signet Jewelers. Before the economic downturn, sales in all but discount stores had been increasing, with 50 percent of sales going to specialty jewelry stores. Zales (and its associated stores under other names) has been the largest specialty jeweler, with some two thousand outlets in the United States. The next highest, with some fourteen hundred stores, is Sterling. The top four jewelry retailers accounted for only about 11 percent of sales in 2008. This is a much lower percentage than in some other industries, where the top four may command 50 percent of all sales.

The reason large retailers have not driven small retailers out of the market is that price seems to be of lesser importance to fine-jewelry buyers. This attitude lessens the advantage that large companies, with their greater sales volumes, have over small companies. Among discounters, Walmart has come to the fore because profit margins on each sale can be as high as 50 percent, thus enabling the chain to reduce prices and still make a good profit. The fluctuating prices of platinum, silver, and gold are always one determinant of such profit margins. In 2009, the price of gold exceeded $1,000 per ounce, marking an increase of more than 250 percent since 2001.

Trends in watch purchases include both men and women buying larger and more unusually shaped watches. Colored watches and those with gemstones are also becoming trendy. Men are increasingly purchasing diamond watches. Industry leaders in the watch business are Timex, Seiko, Movado, and Bulova. About 80 percent of the watch repairers in the United States are self-employed, and most are members of the American Watchmakers-Clockmakers Institute, the national trade organization. They may have their own stores or be affiliated with local jewelry businesses.

INDUSTRY MARKET SEGMENTS

The watch and jewelry industry comprises one-person businesses specializing in watch repair or custom jewelry design, as well as massive corporations that hold large percentages of the precious gem markets.

Small Businesses

Small jewelry and watch stores generally have no more than three employees, one of whom is the owner, who may or may not be a bench jeweler. Repairs are usually done on the premises, as are appraisals; in other words, these businesses are often

Costume jewelry is popular among young people. (©Axel Drosta/Dreamstime.com)

all-in-one operations. Small stores may be located in most neighborhoods of urban areas and the suburbs, as well as in malls.

Potential Annual Earnings Scale. The location, number of people employed, and the profitability of the business all factor into earnings. According to the U.S. Bureau of Labor Statistics (BLS), the average annual salary of jewelers and precious stone and metal workers in 2009 was $34,890. The average annual salary of watch repairers was $40,810.

Clientele Interaction. Since small businesses have very few employees, much of a store's clientele may know the sales staff personally and have built up trust with them over the years. In family-owned stores, customers may believe they will receive personalized service that compensates for the somewhat higher prices. Stores may strive to occupy a certain niche by carrying items made by a particular jewelry designer whose work other stores do not carry. They may also carry a selection of gemstones that are not ordinarily featured in many stores.

Return business is likely to be high. Word of mouth from satisfied customers is very important since extensive advertising may not be economically feasible. Approaches to customers are likely be individualized rather than rote. Since turnover of stock is very important in a small jewelry business, it is most important that store owners know their clientele. Knowledge of the customer base is vital for maintaining profits. The presence of appraisal and repair services on the premises may also be a selling point, preventing items from having to be sent to a central location as chain stores may do.

Amenities, Atmosphere, and Physical Grounds. Small businesses, especially repair shops, might be housed in storefronts, sometimes little more than "holes in the wall." Freestanding jewelry stores are usually entered via barred doors controlled by buzzers, and thus the stores may give the impression of being fortresslike. To overcome that impression, jewelry stores strive to be well lit and welcoming to passersby despite the need for tight security. Lighting design is itself an art because "cold" light is better for showcasing diamonds, whereas "warm" light is superior in highlighting gold pieces. Attractive, uncluttered window displays are important in fostering drop-in trade, even when window space is limited and the windows are barred.

Although interior space may be limited, sufficient room for the free flow of potential customers must be provided. Small stores tend to display more of the merchandise they have on hand. If the store is narrow and long, most of the merchandise will be placed toward the front because some browsers may not make it all the way to the rear of the store. Repair facilities are often placed at the rear, so customers coming in for that reason will also see the items placed at that location, often watches, less expensive jewelry, and silverware.

Typical Number of Employees. The average owner-run small jewelry store will have one to three employees, sometimes family members, and an additional person or two may be hired during holiday and traditional gift-giving seasons.

Traditional Geographic Locations. Most small jewelry businesses are located in larger cities and towns, but smaller towns may have one or more stores. Sometimes, they may be located in less prosperous socioeconomic areas because rents are less onerous or because they have built a longtime, loyal customer base. They are often located in malls and in areas with heavy tourism.

Pros of Working for a Small Business. A loyal customer base may be able to sustain a small specialized business through bad economic times. There is satisfaction in working with longtime customers who know employees and come to respect their advice and judgment. Jewelry is something most people know little about, so they depend upon the advice of a jeweler. Since the business will probably be owned by an on-premises person, the policies and procedures will remain relatively stable.

Cons of Working for a Small Business. In a small jewelry business, one or two people may have to accomplish the entire range of services offered. Because good hand-eye coordination and manual dexterity are required, a continuous heavy workload may affect job performance. The physical demands of working on tiny mechanisms, such as the works of a watch, in an uncomfortable position may cause fatigue. Safety can become an issue, especially when sharp tools, jewelers' torches, and certain chemicals are in use.

The financial investment needed to open a jewelry store is considerable, so small retailers are in a difficult place economically when the prices of precious metals and gemstones rise. If they raise their prices too much, they are in danger of losing clients to discount chains; if they do not raise prices, their profit margins may be too small to sustain them in business.

The owner and employees may have to work weekends and evenings. During the busy holiday seasons they may be required to work at times that are not personally convenient for them. They may not be able to take lengthy vacations unless the store is closed or temporary help is hired.

Costs

Payroll and Benefits: Employees of small businesses may not have many benefits, and they may not earn commissions based on sales. Because of the necessities of staffing, vacations are likely to be no more than two weeks per year. Such other benefits as sick leave, maternity/paternity leave, and so on will be at the owner's discretion and are relatively rare in small businesses.

External Services: Small stores handle all aspects of the business in-house, including payroll, displays, and advertising.

Utilities: Since a well-lit and temperature-controlled store is vital to business, it is important that air-conditioning be installed. There is little leeway in controlling lighting expenses because of security and sales concerns.

Taxes: Small businesses must pay local, state, and federal corporate and property taxes, as well as collecting and paying applicable sales taxes. Owners of small businesses may report their income on their personal returns, in which case they must also pay self-employment taxes.

Midsize Businesses

Midsize jewelry and watch businesses are increasingly located in malls and as freestanding stores in more economically advantaged neighborhoods. They tend to carry more midprice items than small businesses and may have a larger range of products in each store. If they are part of a chain, they may or may not have such positions in each location as bench jewelers, appraisers, and so on.

Potential Annual Earnings Scale. According to the BLS, the average annual salary of jewelers and precious stone and metal workers in 2009 was $34,890. The average annual salary of watch repairers was $40,810. In a midsize business, there may be a range of salaries depending on the skill requirements of the positions. Many midsize businesses employ only managers and salespeople in their stores and centralize specialized work in other locations. Some people may work on commission that is dependent on sales volume. Most sales employees will probably not exceed the average wage unless they can earn commissions.

Clientele Interaction. A rate of about 35 percent return business is customary for midsize stores. Among the inducements for return business are that they may be able to offer easier credit terms than small stores and that their location in malls may be more convenient for shoppers. Stores may be open longer periods because of the mall's extended hours, especially at prime sales times. Sales staff are typically well dressed and well groomed and are knowledgeable about the stock. This is very important because staff turnover may be higher in such stores. Approaches to potential buyers should be customized to each person, even if the person is unknown to the salespeople.

Amenities, Atmosphere, and Physical Grounds. Most midsize businesses are pleasant places in which to work and shop and are usually located in more upscale areas, including malls. They are well lit and have displays that are easy to navigate. It is often difficult to control the lighting in a mall-located store or at a department-store counter because the light of the surrounding areas will be dominant. The necessary presence of security should not decrease the pleasurable experience of browsing and shopping. Stores that mainly do repair work generally have minimal facilities because displays of merchandise are not their primary function.

Typical Number of Employees. Three to six employees are standard in a midsize business, and there may be added seasonal help hired in busy sales seasons such as the Christmas holidays.

Traditional Geographic Locations. Midsize businesses are generally found in freestanding locations in larger cities and town and in malls. They tend not to be located in poorer socioeconomic areas.

Pros of Working for a Midsize Business. There are economic positives and negatives in a midsize business. During short-term downward cycles, midsize businesses may be able to weather economic doldrums better than small retailers because they can raise their prices on some items without jeopardizing their business viability. They are usually owned by people with experience in the jewelry industry and hence are less likely than large outlets to base decisions solely on the bottom line. Various tasks can be distributed among several employees, although sales will likely still be their major function. The ability to take time off may be easier than it is in small businesses.

Cons of Working for a Midsize Business. In the sustained recession that began in December, 2007, it is the midsize chains that are downsizing. If they do not have considerable customer loyalty, such firms can sometimes not achieve enough economy of scale to compensate for the higher costs of store operations and materials. Employees need to be on their feet for periods of time and they may work in uncomfortable positions when performing repairs. Sales goals may be set by management that place stress on some employees.

Costs

Payroll and Benefits: Staff members are usually compensated by the hour, and unless they hold specialized jobs, the average wage will probably not exceed the industry norm. Payroll might be done at corporate headquarters rather than by each store manager. Benefits may exceed those that a small business can offer but the exigencies of staffing may preclude long vacations and other benefits, such as maternity/paternity leave.

External Services: Midsize businesses that are part of a chain may centralize such processes as advertising, displays, and payroll rather than performing them in each individual store.

Utilities: Lighting and temperature may be under the control of mall management, and contractual arrangements will determine how much the individual store must pay for them. In freestanding stores, an acceptable level of lighting and temperature control must be maintained for sales and security reasons.

Taxes: Midsize businesses must pay local, state, and federal corporate and property taxes, as well as collecting and paying applicable sales taxes.

Large Businesses

Large jewelry and watch businesses tend to belong to chains and are generally located in more gentrified urban areas as freestanding stores or in malls. They may only have salespeople and managers in individual stores; other activities such as appraisals and gemology are done in centralized locations.

Potential Annual Earnings Scale. According to the BLS, the average annual salary of jewelers and precious stone and metal workers in 2009 was $34,890. The average annual salary of watch repairers was $40,810. Higher salaries may be earned in large-scale businesses, but this is not always the case. Salaries depend on the skill level of the employee and will be hourly for salespeople and per annum for management. Businesses may motivate employees by paying them commissions on each piece sold and there may even be selling "contests" in which the winning employee will get a bonus. However, statistics show that because of competition mall-based stores earn less profits per store than freestanding ones, so wages in such stores may be lower than in freestanding chain stores.

Clientele Interaction. To overcome the presence of tight security, including armed guards at some locations, a store's personnel should be well groomed, relaxed, and welcoming. This is especially important because they may not personally know their potential customers. They should have good knowledge of their stock and be able to converse knowledgeably about it. This is important to overcome the possible high staff turnover in such businesses. Large businesses can generally take advantage of more sophisticated marketing research tools like trend reports, market demand forecasts, and comparative analyses to draw in customers. Their advertising is probably more ubiquitous and professionally produced as well. They may periodically offer specials or discounts that smaller stores cannot match.

Amenities, Atmosphere, and Physical Grounds. Window displays are usually lavish, well lit, and contain a few tastefully arrayed items. Unless a store is freestanding, its lighting will be determined by the surrounding areas in a mall or department store. Large businesses have some advantage over small ones by being able to offer greater selection. The displays are oftentimes professionally designed. Generally, larger stores display less of the merchandise they have on hand, but those pieces displayed are usually the higher-priced items. Because of their economic clout, chain stores negotiate the more desirable locations in a mall, and sometimes a mall will even provide incentives for prestigious stores to locate there. If a business deals primarily in repairs, its facilities will be more modest.

Typical Number of Employees. Five to nine employees are the norm for large stores, and temporary help is usually added during busier holiday seasons.

Traditional Geographic Locations. Large businesses are usually located in malls in the larger cities, but some are in freestanding locations or department stores. The jewelry counters in department stores are generally leased by large chains such as Finlay Fine Jewelry, which has operated outlets in stores such as Bloomingdale's, Macy's, Bon Ton, and Lord & Taylor. The kiosks and carts that are found in malls are also usually operated by large jewelry chains. Major jewelry chains are almost never found in poorer socioeconomic areas unless they are also general merchandisers such as Walmart.

Pros of Working for a Large Business. A large business allows some possibility of advancement to a supervisory capacity such as manager or head or master jeweler. Skilled employees may sometimes gain higher pay even if advancement opportunities are limited. They also get the benefits that obtain within their company. Because some operations like payroll, advertising, and displays are centralized within corporate or regional headquarters, the manager can devote more time to supervision of employees and ways to increase sales. Credit terms may be more generous, potentially increasing sales.

Cons of Working for a Large Business. Many of the large jewelry chains are run by executives who have little or no experience in the industry but instead are professional retailers or even money managers. For instance, the large retailer Zales is partly owned by several hedge funds. When new chief executives assume charge of a company, there may be substantial policy changes that affect each store and create employee instability. Since the bottom line may be the driving force behind the operations of such retailers, the closing of stores and cutbacks in staffing will likely occur during economic downturns.

Higher per hour pay is not always guaranteed in a large business, particularly in malls where profit margins per store may be less. Sales goals may be set that create stress in employees, and retention of employees may be less certain than in smaller businesses. If employment is in a factory environment where jobs like polishing, electroplating, and lacquer spraying occur, workers may be exposed to fumes from chemicals and solvents. Despite safety measures there may be unpleasant odors. Workers who perform bench work may be sitting in uncomfortable positions, and others may be standing for long periods of time in assembly lines. The work, especially at lower skill levels, may be repetitious.

Costs

Payroll and Benefits: Pay scales may vary greatly in a large business depending on the range of specializations found in each location. If skilled employees such as appraisers, display designers, repairers, and gemologists are located in the store, salaries for those workers will be higher. If such tasks are centralized at some other location and there are mainly salespeople in a store, the average wage of $13 to $14 per hour will probably apply. Managers will be paid at accordingly higher rates. Turnover may be higher at such locations; thus, fewer people may advance to higher wages over time.

External Services: Many activities within a large store are likely to be centralized at an off-premises location. These may include payroll, display design, and advertising. Within the store software packages will probably be used for inventory control, employee scheduling, and even for evaluating customer satisfaction.

Utilities: Within malls control of temperature and lighting will be largely under the control of mall management, and costs of such utilities will likely be part of a lease arrangement. In freestanding locations acceptable levels of lighting and temperature control must be maintained for sales and security purposes.

Taxes: Large companies must pay all applicable local, state, federal, and international taxes, including tariffs and import/export fees as appropriate. They must also pay property taxes and collect and pay sales taxes in relevant jurisdictions.

ORGANIZATIONAL STRUCTURE AND JOB ROLES

Although there are several very large jewelry store chains, approximately 40 percent of all those in the retail trade are self-employed, mostly in small, neighborhood businesses or operating a store or kiosk within a shopping mall. There is also a large but declining wholesale component to the industry. Among the different specialized jobs within the jewelry and watch industry are manufacturing, designing, repairing, sales, appraising, gem cutting, polishing, setting and engraving, and gemology. In small businesses, one person may accomplish several of these tasks, while large firms may have the wherewithal to employ different people to perform each of them.

The following umbrella categories apply to the organizational structure of businesses in the watches and jewelry industry:

- Business Management
- Customer Service
- Sales and Marketing
- Security
- Technology, Research, Design, and Development
- Production and Operations
- Distribution, Imports, and Exports

Business Management

Jewelry business owners and managers recruit, hire, train, and supervise employees. They may order the store's merchandise and do appraisals and repairing of merchandise and participate in advertising and marketing their wares. They need to know how best to utilize the increasingly available management computer software packages that are available from numerous companies. Among the features of most software packages are the automation of point-of-sales, inventory control, purchasing, repair, accounting, and reporting.

Managers supervise inventory and are responsible for loss prevention, the optimum presentation of merchandise in displays, and coaching employees in setting the tone for excellent customer service. In many chain stores, some processes such as advertising, marketing, ordering, payroll, and dis-

plays are centrally handled by corporate headquarters. Some large chains employ people specifically to design store displays, which are then generally uniform in each location.

Business management occupations may include the following:

- Chief Executive Officer (CEO)
- Chief Financial Officer (CFO)
- Vice President of Franchising
- Vice President of Business Development
- Business Owner
- Store Manager
- Bench Jeweler

Customer Service

Besides selling watches, jewelry, and accessories such as watch bands, retail stores and kiosks usually do repair work. This may involve increasing or reducing the size of settings, resetting stones, fixing broken settings, and replacing watch batteries. Retail jewelers may sometimes do appraisals, but large concerns may employ specialized appraisers located off-premises who determine and document the value of jewelry. The sales staff should themselves wear tasteful jewelry and watches. Experienced salespeople will intuitively judge how to deal with each potential customer, rather than treat them all the same. For instance, one large chain instructs its salespeople never to ask "May I help you?" because the answer is usually "I am just looking." Instead, they are encouraged to engage browsers in individualized, customer-centered conversation.

Customer service occupations may include the following:

- Repairer
- Appraiser
- Salesperson
- Engraver

Sales and Marketing

Among the venues used to sell jewelry and watches are trade and craft shows and art fairs. Often, these events feature both local and international vendors, who display their wares to other vendors and the public. They sometimes enable purchasers to buy at a discounted price. Advertising is done both in traditional media, such as televi-

OCCUPATION PROFILE

Jeweler and Watch Repairer

Considerations	Qualifications
Description	Repairs jewelry and watches.
Career cluster	Manufacturing
Interests	Data; things
Working conditions	Work inside
Minimum education level	On-the-job training; high school diploma or GED; high school diploma/technical training; apprenticeship
Physical exertion	Light work
Physical abilities	Unexceptional/basic fitness
Opportunities for experience	Apprenticeship; part-time work
Licensure and certification	Recommended
Employment outlook	Slower-than-average growth expected
Holland interest score	REC; REI

Note: See volume 1, "Publisher's Note," for an explanation of the Holland interest score.

sion and newspapers, and using sophisticated on-line technologies.

Sales and marketing occupations may include the following:

- Vice President of Sales and Marketing
- Marketing Director
- Sales Manager
- Sales Representative
- Market Research Analyst
- Public Relations Manager

Security

Smaller businesses usually have a locked front door that employees can open remotely. The employees basically operate on their instinct to determine whether each person seeking admission can be trusted. Windows are often barred. In most malls, jewelry stores generally are physically open to anyone walking by to encourage customers, possibly on the theory that escaping with stolen goods would be more difficult in such a venue. Larger businesses may well have one or more security guards, sometimes armed, on their staffs. All businesses have security systems of varying complexity, at the very least a burglar alarm. Sophisticated security systems are often not visible.

The industry's Jewelers' Security Alliance (JSA) raises awareness among its members and law enforcement authorities about security problems and how to deal with them forcefully. The first ten years of the twenty-first century have seen a sharp decrease in thefts and violent crimes against jewelry businesses in-store, off-premises, and at airports, formerly a frequent venue for theft. Among the reasons for the decline are that fewer salespeople go out on the road and that the number of jewelry outlets has declined. Nevertheless, in 2009, the industry still suffered an estimated $100 million in losses to criminal activity.

Occupations within this category include the following:

- Security Manager
- Security Guard
- Security Alarm/Systems Specialist

Technology, Research, Design, and Development

For many years, computer-aided design (CAD) and computer-aided manufacturing (CAM) have been used to assist in jewelry design and in the manufacturing of molds and models. With the use of CAD, designs can be produced in virtual reality and modified as often as needed until the finished design is decided upon. CAM then produces the mold in wax or another medium. Lasers have been employed in various phases of the industry, including silversmithing, stone cutting, engraving of settings (glyptography), and metal welding for jewelry settings.

Artificial or imitation gemstones have been developed, including those made from glass. Cubic zirconias (also called djevalite) are considered to be among the best diamond simulations to date. They have even been known to fool unwary buyers and are not to be confused with zircons, which are natural stones. Another imitation gemstone is moissanite, a silicon carbide named after Henri Moissan, the French scientist who created it in the laboratory. There are also brand names such as Fabulite (also known as Wellington Diamond), GGG (Galliant), and YAG (Yttrium Aluminum Garnet). These types of stones differ from real gemstones both physically and chemically. The presence of such stones on the market, where naïve buyers might be fooled, is one reason electronic diamond testers have proved useful.

Synthetic gemstones, first synthesized about 1970, are not the same as artificial or imitation stones because they are actual gemstones, but they are produced in laboratories rather than having been formed naturally in the earth. They have been utilized for industrial, scientific, and technological purposes, as well as for fashion. The two major methods used to form these stones are the flux fusion method and the hydrothermal method. Within those broad categories are growth from melt, growth from solution, high temperature or pressure processes, ceramic processes, and skull melting processes.

Synthetic gemstones can be made with fewer imperfections and more vivid color than natural stones, but, because of the methods used in manufacturing them, they may be more brittle and thus breakable. Another category of nonnatural stones is the composite gem, which is midway between the other two. Composite stones are formed by combining different materials together, usually in double or triple layers, to create the appearance of a natural stone. Many buyers of precious gemstones still desire to own stones that were formed deep in the earth millions of years ago by nature.

Technology, research, design, and development occupations may include the following:

- Designer
- Mold and Model Maker
- Geologist/Gemologist
- Materials Engineer

Production and Operations

Jewelers and watchmakers use a variety of highly specialized tools in the various phases of manufacture. During each step, an extremely high degree of skill is required, and any mistakes, especially while working with precious and semiprecious stones, may result in totally destroying their value. The production of jewelry requires several steps, including manufacturing the setting into which a gem will be inserted. This requires shaping the setting according to a previously completed design and soldering together individual parts if required. The latter operation is performed by assemblers.

Although machines mass-produce certain types of jewelry, the necessary models and tools usually are made by a skilled jeweler. The more expensive a piece of jewelry is, the more likely it was not mass produced. The cutting of the gem into its final form, which is the most delicate, difficult, and exacting step in jewelry manufacture, will usually be done at the wholesale level by people who have received long years of training. After securing the stones in their settings, the final steps usually involve polishing and, if desired, engraving the setting. Precious stones can be enhanced by such processes as oiling, which reduces the appearance of flaws, heating, lasers, and radiation.

Among the more skilled, specialized careers in the watch and jewelry industry are bench jewelers, appraisers, horologists, gemologists, repairers, cutters, silversmiths, and jewelry designers. Precision, skill, thorough training, and attention to even the tiniest details are required in all these jobs.

Bench jewelers might be called the backbone of the industry. They utilize a variety of tools such as jewelers' lathes, saws, drills, files, and soldering irons to fabricate and manufacture jewelry, set stones, and repair individual pieces. Some have received bench certification, which may have taken a year or two to earn at a technical school from Jewelers of America, a trade organization. There are four levels of certification: bench jeweler technician, bench jeweler, senior bench jeweler, and master bench jeweler. The jewelers most often encountered in smaller retail stores are probably bench jewelers, but not every retail outlet has one. If they also manage the business they should possess organizational, business, and sales skills.

Appraisers may also be bench jewelers in smaller venues, but they may do appraisals only. They determine the value of a piece by various means, including consulting reference books, the Internet, and previous auction results. They then write a report certifying their findings. They may be employed by large jewelry chains, insurance companies, appraisal companies, or auction houses, or they may be self-employed. Their greatest resource is their own knowledge and experience gained over the years. In a large chain they most probably will work in a corporate facility rather than a retail store.

Horologists, so-called because horology is the study of timepieces, act as clock and watchmakers and repairers. Because inexpensive watches are sometimes just discarded rather than repaired, horologists tend to work on more expensive items. Some timepieces have few moving parts and only a battery replacement is required. Expensive ones have mechanical movements, often with jewels, and still need manual winding. If replacement parts are unavailable horologists may make the parts themselves. The assembly/disassembly, repair, and cleaning of minuscule gears and springs is exacting work requiring mechanical skill, good hand-eye coordination, and patience. Certification by the American Watchmakers-Clockmakers Institute and other bodies is offered by some technical schools and sometimes takes up to two years to obtain.

Gemologists are among the most highly trained personnel in the industry. They study the quality and characteristics of precious and semiprecious stones, grade them according to industry standards, and make reports of their findings. They may work for large retail or wholesale jewelry companies, mining companies, insurance companies, laboratories (including the Gemological Institute of America and the American Gemological Laboratories) or even work as self-employed appraisers. People consulting gemologists for private appraisals may expect to pay up to $200 an hour for their services. Certification for gemologists is available through the Gemological Institute of America, and degrees are offered by colleges and fashion institutes.

Repairers work on both watches and jewelry. With jewelry, they may perform such tasks as altering ring, bracelet, and necklace sizes, resetting stones, restringing beads or jewelry, repairing clasps and hinges, mending breaks in metal pieces, and even refashioning jewelry into new pieces. Watch repairers may do simple tasks like replacing dead batteries or complex ones like mending or replacing the works of watches. Because repairers often work with very expensive articles, this can be a very exacting job. Good hand-eye coordination is vital. In large chains, repairers may work in a central corporate facility rather than a retail shop.

Cutters may specialize in one type of gem, such as diamonds, or perform cutting on various types of gems. Different skills are required for cutting heavy stones like agate than are needed for diamonds. Other gemstones require yet other cutting skills. The cutter must study the "inner life" of a rough gem under a jeweler's loupe (a magnifying device), sometimes for weeks or even months, before attempting a final cut. Many cutting centers are now located in developing countries, such as Thailand, Brazil, China, and India.

At one time, cleaving was the preferred method of producing a finished stone, but any miscalculation with a metal-bladed wedge and mallet could result in a fabulous stone being utterly ruined. In modern times, a diamond saw is generally used. As buyers' tastes evolve in such matters as gem shape, cutters need to keep abreast of the latest trends. Cutters have much to do with the so-called Four Cs of gemstones: carat weight, clarity, cut, and color.

Silversmiths practice an art that goes back to colonial days in America and perhaps earlier in Europe. Silversmiths design, manufacture, decorate, and repair silver and gold articles and sometimes work with other metals such as copper and brass.

They may also perform appraisals on such articles. Excellent mechanical skills are required for using such tools as hammers, anvils, saws, shears, blocks, and torches. They cut the metals into the desired shapes and assemble pieces by means such as soldering and riveting. Laser-beam welding is a newer technology that has been widely adopted.

Jewelry designers sometimes have bachelor's or master's degrees with a specialization in design. They should be creative, have fashion sense and artistic ability, and possess basic math skills. Designers first draw their designs on paper or on wax, and with the aid of computer programs (CAD/CAM) the designs are then transferred to models in metal or stone. Computers may run the machines that produce the finished model. The designers may conceive lines of jewelry for one company's exclusive use or do individual pieces. In more recent years a group of designers has emerged who refer to themselves as jewelry *artists*. They usually design pieces on speculation and sell them to boutiques, galleries, and in craft and trade shows. Some have opened their own specialty shops. Under American law such designs can be patented or even copyrighted.

Other specialties, which run the gamut from highly skilled to relatively unskilled, include buyers, polishers, engravers, mold casters and modelers, solderers, lacquer sprayers, gemstone setters, restorers of pearls and other jewelry, press operators, electroplaters, assembly line workers, and toolmakers.

Production and operations occupations may include the following:

- Appraiser
- Assembler
- Bench Jeweler
- Cutter
- Engraver

OCCUPATION PROFILE

Tool and Die Maker

Considerations	Qualifications
Description	Analyzes specifications and places materials in order to make and repair dies, cutting tools, jigs, fixtures, and machinists' hand tools.
Career cluster	Manufacturing
Interests	Data; things
Working conditions	Work inside
Minimum education level	On-the-job training; high school diploma or GED; high school diploma/technical training; apprenticeship
Physical exertion	Medium work
Physical abilities	Unexceptional/basic fitness
Opportunities for experience	Internship; apprenticeship
Licensure and certification	Usually not required
Employment outlook	Decline expected
Holland interest score	RIE

Note: See volume 1, "Publisher's Note," for an explanation of the Holland interest score.

- Gemologist
- Grader
- Horologist
- Jewelry Designer
- Metalworker
- Mold and Model Maker
- Polisher
- Repairer
- Silversmith
- Stone Setter

Distribution, Imports, and Exports

The watches and jewelry industry has had a large wholesale component. Wholesalers sometimes buy from the mining companies themselves, from local sources near the mines, or from importers. The leading exporters of precious metal jewelry to the United States have been Italy, India, Hong Kong, Thailand, and Israel. The leading exporters of costume jewelry to the United States have been China, South Korea, Taiwan, Hong Kong, and Thailand. Wholesalers may sell directly to retail jewelers, or specialized buyers may purchase gems, jewelry, and watches from wholesalers and resell them to retailers. In recent years, as more retailers buy directly from designers and manufacturers, the size of the wholesale segment has diminished considerably.

Important markets for American-made precious metal jewelry have been Canada, Mexico, Switzerland, and Japan. Major costume jewelry markets include Japan, Canada, South Korea, the United Kingdom, and Switzerland. The import value of watches into the United States was about $4 billion by the middle of the first decade of the twenty-first century. Almost 55 percent of this amount went to Switzerland. China, with its low labor costs, is also becoming an increasingly major player in the watch export market. Various trade agreements, including NAFTA and the General Agreement on Tariffs and Trade (GATT), have reduced or eliminated the tariffs on these goods.

Distribution, imports, and exports occupations may include the following:

- Warehouse Manager
- Shipping and Receiving Clerk
- Truck Driver
- Importer/Exporter
- International Buyer

Overview

The outlook for the watches and jewelry industry shows it to be on the decline. The industry is particularly prone to national and worldwide economic cycles. When economic growth is on an upswing, increased sales are the norm. The rise of two-income families, the generally better economic status of working women, the growing interest by teenagers in costume jewelry, and the increasing fashion interest of men have contributed to the growth of industry sales. However, because higher-end jewelry and expensive watches are considered discretionary items, future economic downturns may continue to take their toll on the industry.

The U.S. Department of Labor predicts that employment in the industry will decline through 2014. The number of jewelry firms declined from more than 27,000 in 1998 to about 22,600 in 2008. Another factor affecting profitability is that jewelry stores have to carry large amounts of inventory, more than almost any other type of retail industry. Some experts expect continuing consolidation of retail outlets in the second decade of the twenty-first century.

The exponential increase in the use of cell phones and other electronic devices that tell the time has led to a decline in the purchase of inexpensive watches among younger consumers, although luxury brands such as Rolex may remain as status symbols with older and more affluent consumers. In keeping with this trend, the importation of plastic watches, such as the-once popular Swatch, has declined. In general, younger buyers are not as interested in wearing watches as status symbols, so marketing them as fun accessories may be a new sales approach. By the same token, repair work on existing items may increase, because new watches are not being purchased.

Even before the worldwide economic crisis began, a decline in the number of industry positions was predicted because of increasing automation, particularly in lower-skilled jobs such as assembly and polishing. The closing of retail stores was hastened by the rise of alternate venues for the sale of jewelry and watches. These include television channels such as QVC, Shop NBC, the Home

Shopping Network (HSN), and Jewelry Television (JTV), which is devoted exclusively to jewelry sales. Another method of purchasing is the online private sale, operated by companies such as Gilt Groupe and Portero.

Discount stores, Internet e-commerce sites (including Amazon.com, Walmart.com, and Shopzilla.com), and mail order or catalog houses will continue to affect brick-and-mortar retail stores, particularly in smaller cities and towns. These nontraditional outlets require fewer employees. Consolidation of retail chains is expected to continue, and increased closure of smaller retail stores is likely in the coming years. Wholesalers are gradually becoming less important, as businesses buy directly from manufacturers or designers.

In spite of this somewhat dire outlook, the forecast by the U.S. Department of Labor is that employment in the industry will grow, but at a slower rate than the average for all occupations. All occupations combined are projected to increase by 11 percent between 2008 and 2018, but the jewelry and watch industry may add positions at a rate of 5 percent during the same period. Projected employment by 2018 is predicted to be approximately fifty-five thousand jobs.

Among Asian countries, China, Japan, and India will continue to increase their demand for jewelry, and China will increase its jewelry production capacity. In Europe, Italy and the United Kingdom should continue to be the leading consumers, and Italy should continue to be one of the largest jewelry manufacturers in the world. Platinum jewelry is expected to increase its market share vis-a-vis gold jewelry.

Employment Advantages

Individuals with artistic talent or an interest in fashion, or those who enjoy working with customers and advising them on purchases, should consider a career in this industry. For those with ability in one or more of the industry's interesting specializations, the opportunities for fulfilling careers and advancement are present, including management positions or even eventual ownership of a business. The present-day decline is likely to be a temporary one because the industry has always rebounded from downturns once better economic times have returned.

One advantage of employment in the watches and jewelry industry is that a higher education degree is not essential for many positions. Some jobs within the trade, such as gemology and jewelry design, require training at a vocational or technical school, but on-the-job-training is frequently sufficient for many others. In the past, certain skills were passed down from father to son, but this form of apprenticeship can work just as well between master jeweler and novice.

Although in difficult economic times positions may be harder to obtain, there is a general dearth of well-trained people, particularly to replace skilled retirees, so employment prospects for such workers are usually good in better economic climates. Employees may earn commissions in addition to their salaries if they prove to be effective salespeople. Working in a jewelry store carries a certain amount of prestige and even glamor, and the ambience is generally very congenial.

Annual Earnings

In 2007, the industry's domestic sales amounted to some $64.8 billion, and about one-half of U.S. consumers had purchased jewelry or watches. By the end of 2008, a year into the recession, sales had declined from the previous year to about $60 billion. Some large chains such as Zales, which sells midprice merchandise, seemed to be in poor financial straits, and some of Zales's stores were closed or consolidated. Before the 2009 holiday season, its sales had declined by almost 19 percent. This experience was probably replicated to some degree by other major chains as well. Two large chains that had been in the top five, Friedman and Whitehall, were completely liquidated. The U.S. Department of Labor estimates a continuing slow decline in jewelry and watch sales for the next few years.

An estimated eight hundred retail jewelry businesses closed permanently in 2008. Some 80 percent of such businesses reported that their earnings were either flat or down, and 65 percent of those with a decline reported a downturn of at least 10 percent. Sales in the prime November-to-December holiday period, the time of year when specialty shops may do up to 90 percent of their business, were said to be the worst since the 1950's. Adding to the uncertainty was the high price of gold and other precious metals, as well as tighter lending policies by financial institutions.

However, by the end of 2009, sales for fine jewelry and watches had begun rising again, fueled primarily by affluent purchasers with annual incomes exceeding $100,000. More than 55 percent of retail outlets reported that their incomes were up over the previous year. Most of this gain was in smaller retail stores and local chains, which outperformed large national chains. Some industry analysts believe that small jewelry chain stores and local businesses would profit from continuing problems among the large chains and that only the behemoth chain Kay Jewelers might survive the consolidations as a large national retailer.

RELATED RESOURCES FOR FURTHER RESEARCH

ACCREDITED GEMOLOGISTS ASSOCIATION
3315 Juanita St.
San Diego, CA 92105
Tel: (619) 501-5444
http://www.accreditedgemologists.org

ACCREDITING COMMISSION OF CAREER SCHOOLS AND COLLEGES
2101 Wilson Blvd., Suite 302
Arlington, VA 22201
Tel: (703) 247-4212
http://www.accsc.org

AMERICAN GEM SOCIETY
8881 W Sahara Ave.
Las Vegas, NV 89117
Tel: (702) 225-6500
http://www.americangemsociety.org

AMERICAN JEWELRY DESIGN COUNCIL
760 Market St., Suite 900
San Francisco, CA 94102
http://www.ajdc.org

AMERICAN WATCH ASSOCIATION
1201 Pennsylvania Ave. NW
Washington, DC 20044
Tel: (703) 759-3377
Fax: (703) 759-1639
http://www.americanwatchassociation.com

AMERICAN WATCHMAKERS-CLOCKMAKERS INSTITUTE
701 Enterprise Dr.
Harrison, OH 45030
Tel: (866) 367-2924
http://www.awci.com

GEMOLOGICAL INSTITUTE OF AMERICA
5345 Armada Dr.
Carlsbad, CA 92008
Tel: (800) 421-7250
http://www.gia.edu

JEWELERS OF AMERICA
52 Vanderbilt Ave., 19th Floor
New York, NY 10017
Tel: (800) 223-0673
http://www.jewelers.org

JEWELERS' SECURITY ALLIANCE
6 E 45th St.
New York, NY 10017
Tel: (800) 537-0067
http://www.jewelerssecurity.org

JEWELERS VIGILANCE COMMITTEE
25 W 45th St., Suite 1406
New York, NY 10036
Tel: (212) 997-2002
http://www.jvclegal.org

JEWELRY CAREER FAIR
http://www.careerfair.gia.org

MANUFACTURING JEWELERS AND SUPPLIERS OF AMERICA
45 Royal Little Dr.
Providence, RI 02904
Tel: (800) 444-6572
http://www.mjsa.polygon.net

ABOUT THE AUTHOR

Roy Liebman is an emeritus librarian (professor) of the California State University, Los Angeles, where he held several management positions during a thirty-five-year career. He is a 1958 graduate of Brooklyn College, a 1961 graduate of Pratt Institute (M.L.S.), and a 1978 graduate of the California State University, Los Angeles (M.A.). He is the author of five reference books, as well as numerous periodical articles, reference book essays, and more than two hundred book reviews covering a wide range of subjects. He also wrote the script for a produced television documentary and has appeared as an interview subject in two other documentaries. Formerly also holding positions at the California Institute of Technology and the Brooklyn and New York Public Libraries, among others, he is currently serving part time as a reference librarian at the Los Angeles Public Library.

FURTHER READING

Barnes Reports. *U.S. Jewelry and Silverware Manufacturing Industry Report.* Woolwich, Maine: Author, 2010.

Blakemore, Kenneth. *Management for the Retail Jeweler: A Companion Volume to the Retail Jeweler's Guide.* London: Iliffe Books, 1973.

Cipriani, Curzio, and Alessandro Borelli. *Simon and Schuster's Guide to Gems and Precious Stones.* New York: Simon and Schuster, 1986.

Glasmeier, Amy. *Manufacturing Time: Global Competition in the Watch Industry, 1795-2000.* New York: Guilford Press, 2000.

Griffiths, Jane. *Jewelry, Watches, and Fashion Accessories: 2000 Market Report.* Hampton, England: Key Note, 2000.

Harrold, Michael C. *American Watchmaking: A Technical History of the American Watch Industry, 1850-1930.* np: Author, 1981.

IBISWorld. *U.S. Industry Report: Jewelry Stores, 2010.* http://www.ibisworld.com/industry/default.aspx?indid=1075.

Institute for Career Research. *Careers in the Jewelry Industry: Design, Manufacturing, Retailing.* Chicago: Institute for Career Research, 2003.

Jewelers of America. *Careers in the Jewelry Industry: Your Guide to a Bright and Shining Future.* New York: Jewelers of America, n.d.

Morton Research Corporation. *The Jewelry Industry: An Economic, Marketing, and Business Manual of the U.S. Precious Metal Jewelry Industry.* Boca Raton, Fla.: Morton Research Company, 1997.

O'Donoghue, Michael. *Synthetic, Imitation, and Treated Gemstones.* London: Robert Hale, 2008.

Parker, Philip M. *The 2007-2012 Outlook for Jewelry Stores in the United States.* San Diego, Calif.: ICON Group, 2006.

Unity Marketing Group. *Jewelry and Watch Report, 2007.* http://www.unitymarketingonline.com/cms_jewelry/jewelry/jewelry_2007.php.

U.S. Bureau of Labor Statistics. *Career Guide to Industries, 2010-2011* ed. http://www.bls.gov/oco/cg.

_____. "Jewelers and Precious Stone and Metal Workers." In *Occupational Outlook Handbook,* 2010-2011 ed. http://www.bls.gov/oco/ocos222.htm.

U.S. Census Bureau. North American Industry Classification System (NAICS), 2007. http://www.census.gov/cgi-bin/sssd/naics/naicsrch?chart=2007.

_____. *2002 Economic Census: Manufacturing Industry Series. Watch, Clock and Parts Manufacturing.* U.S. Department of Commerce, Economics and Statistics Administration, 2004.

U.S. Department of Commerce. International Trade Administration. Office of Trade and Industry Information. Industry Trade Data and Analysis. http://ita.doc.gov/td/industry/otea/OTII/OTII-index.html.

_____. *The U.S. Jewelry Industry: Federal Interagency Report on U.S. Jewelry Competitiveness Issues.* Washington, D.C.: Author, 1997.

U.S. International Trade Commission. *A Competitive Assessment of the U.S. Jewelry Industry, Phase I: Costume Jewelry: Report to the Commission.* Washington, D.C.: Author, 1986.

U.S. Small Business Administration. *Starting and Managing a Small Retail Jewelry Store.* Washington, D.C.: Author, 1971.

Water Supply Industry

©Michael Irwin/Dreamstime.com

INDUSTRY SNAPSHOT

General Industry: Natural Resources
Career Cluster: Agriculture, Food, and Natural Resources
Subcategory Industries: Canal Irrigation; Irrigation System Operation; Water Distribution (Except Irrigation); Water Distribution for Irrigation; Water Filtration Plant Operation; Water Supply Systems; Water Treatment Plants
Related Industries: Beverage and Tobacco Industry; Civil Services: Planning; Electrical Power Industry; Environmental Engineering and Consultation Services; Farming Industry; Local Public Administration; Natural Resources Management; Waste Management Industry
Annual Domestic Revenues: $55.065 billion USD in 2009 (IBISWorld Industry Report, 2010; includes both water supply and irrigation systems)
NAICS Number: 22131

INDUSTRY DEFINITION

Summary

The water supply industry secures, treats, and distributes fresh water for human consumption and use, as well as for crop irrigation. The overriding function of a water treatment plant is to make sure that all incoming raw water is processed so that the finished product meets all of the regulatory standards for a water supply that is safe to drink. In turn, this means that plant and system operators need to have the training, skills, and tools to run all of the various forms of equipment in the plant, safely control all of the numerous processes that are required under state and federal regulations, and monitor all aspects of the treatment process.

History of the Industry

The earliest known water supply system was a development by the Minoan civilization on the Greek island of Crete in the Mediterranean Sea some five thousand years ago. Aqueducts were used to bring water from nearby streams into the palace and city of Knossus until a huge earthquake, about 1450 B.C.E., destroyed the region. The next major development in water supply technology occurred about 1000 B.C.E., when underground tunnels (called qanats) were used in the Middle East, particularly in what is now Iran, and in North Africa.

One of the renowned engineering triumphs of the Roman Empire, albeit one accomplished with slave labor, was the construction of elevated stone

The Owens River, one of the sources of water in Southern California. (©Eugene Everett/Dreamstime.com)

aqueducts beginning about 312 B.C.E. By 300 B.C.E., fourteen major aqueducts were in service, transporting about 151 million liters (40 million gallons) per day to Rome. Similar systems were also constructed at that time in other parts of Europe that were occupied by the Romans, such as the rest of Italy, France, the Netherlands, England, and Spain. One such aqueduct in Segovia, Spain, that was built in the first century by the Romans is still in use today. The Romans also built a system of pipelines in London to convey water from the Thames River and adjacent springs to the people in the city.

The Middle Ages in Europe were noted for filth, disease, and minimal attempts to have personal and public sanitation. Some people bathed only once or twice a year. As cities developed in Europe, North America, and other areas of the world, the easiest way to obtain water was to pipe it in from nearby surface sources or local wells. For example, Paris at the beginning of the sixteenth century had an estimated population of about 300,000 to 400,000 people, who were dependent on water from the Seine River and private wells.

The continued growth in urbanization and the vast array of waste materials that were dumped into the same river systems that were being used for drinking water invariably resulted in the easy spread of waterborne diseases. For example, the cholera epidemic of 1848-1849 caused the deaths of over fifty-three thousand people in London alone. Fortunately, the enterprising physician John Snow of London traced the impure water to one community water pump at Broad Street in Soho in 1854 that was getting its water from a highly polluted portion of the lower Thames River. His solution was simple: He removed the pump's handle, forcing residents of the area to get their water from other sources.

Bethlehem, Pennsylvania, in 1754 built a municipal water plant, reputedly the first such plant in history. Philadelphia followed in 1801, constructing a pumping plant on the Schuylkill River above the point where it flows into the Delaware River. A treatment plant was built in 1804 in Paisley, Scotland, to serve filtered water to the city. Paris in 1806 built a plant on the Seine River that was designed to treat the water by allowing it to trickle slowly through sand filters. Richmond, Virginia, in 1834 became the first U.S. city to adopt the slow-sand filter system. Poughkeepsie, New York, was far enough upstream on the Hudson River to use fresh water to build its first treatment plant in 1870. Chlorination was first used in 1908 in Jersey City, New Jersey, as a viable means of disinfecting the raw water obtained from surface streams. The immediate result was a sharp reduction in the city's typhoid rate, and the technique soon spread to other water purveyors.

The Industry Today

The supply sources for many contemporary large water treatment systems have remained the same. For example, Philadelphia; New Orleans; Washington, D.C.; and Chicago still get their water from the Delaware and Schuylkill Rivers, the Mississippi River, the Potomac River, and Lake Michigan, respectively. For those coastal metropolitan areas that border the salty waters of the ocean, large reservoirs in inland watersheds have had to be constructed. A prime example is New York City, which has seven reservoirs in the Croton, Catskill, and Delaware watersheds that collectively serve 9 million people with an average daily consumption of 4.54 million cubic meters (1.2 billion gallons). Another example is central Massachusetts's Quabbin Reservoir system, which supplies the Boston metropolitan area.

With an average annual precipitation rate of only 381 millimeters (15 inches), Los Angeles during the early twentieth century was quickly exhausting its limited local water supplies. A project was begun in 1907 to import water from the Owens Valley in east-central California, some 375 kilometers (200 miles) distant. The scheme was met with steep resistance from the valley's residents, who destroyed the aqueduct with dynamite. Nonetheless, Los Angeles was able to se-

cure stable access to Owens Valley water, but the city continued to grow, requiring even greater water supplies. Accordingly, the Colorado River Aqueduct Project was started in 1928 and included thirteen Southern California cities, which together established a metropolitan water district. The present-day Metropolitan Water District of Southern California consists of twenty-six water districts and cities that supply drinking water to 18 million people, with an average delivery of 7 million cubic meters (1.8 billion gallons) per day.

The bulk of treated water is used to flush toilets (47 percent) and take a shower or bath (37 percent); only about 5 percent is used for drinking. Nevertheless, since all such water is supplied through the same pipes, it must all meet the standards for drinking, cooking, and washing. New standards for low-flush toilets were introduced in the early 1990's and should help reduce overall water consumption.

Although there are variations in treatment technologies, most plants start with tried and tested pretreatment processes. The first step in pretreatment usually consists of screens that block large items that are floating in the raw intake water, such as debris, dead animals, and fish. This is followed by the diversion of raw water to large tanks, or holding basins, where suspended sediments, such as silt

The aqueduct passes through the Mojave Desert on its way to Southern California. (©Darren Bradley/Dreamstime.com)

and clay particles, can settle out. This step is particularly important if the water source contains large quantities of suspended materials. The next step, called flocculation and coagulation, occurs when chemicals such as alum and soda ash are added to the water to encourage the suspension of fine particles. This coagulation process results in the formation of floc, which with time becomes heavy enough to sink to the bottom of the large tanks as sludge. The flocculation and coagulation procedure can remove 90 to 99 percent of the viruses in the water. It does not kill the viruses, but they become part of the floc that settles out and is removed later in the process.

Filtration is next employed by allowing the water to pass through sand and gravel layers that provide more opportunity for the water to be cleansed of finer particles. These filters over time can become clogged with sediments that have to be removed by backwashing or flushing, a process that results in a waste product that must be diverted to a sewer system for further treatment.

The final stages in the drinking-water treatment process generally include fluoridation and disinfection. Sodium fluoride is one of the commonly added compounds and is recommended for the maintenance of healthy teeth. About half of the U.S. population uses water that is fluoridated at an optimum level of concentration. Chlorine gas is also mixed with the water to kill any remaining bacteria and some viruses. Some people contend that chlorinated water has an unpleasant odor and taste, although the use of activated carbon in the treatment process can increase the palatability of the finished water. Residual amounts of chlorine remain in the treated water as it flows through a maze of pipes to reach individual users, so some level of disinfection travels with the flow and further protects consumers.

Given the complaints of some people about chlorine odor and taste in their water, some utilities use ozone gas and ultraviolet radiation systems as disinfectants. Ozone is both a very effective disinfectant and a strong oxidant of odor and taste compounds. However, ozone not only has a higher price than chlorine but also is unable to travel with treated water and continue to disinfect it in a water system's pipes as chlorine can. Ultraviolet light is particularly effective in killing practically all microbiological organisms that may be in treated water, as the light energy is absorbed in the deoxyribonucleic acid (DNA) of these microbes, thereby eliminating reproduction at the cellular level. Ultraviolet treatment is both costly and slow, however, but it can be very useful in selected situations.

The U.S. water treatment industry has become increasingly privatized in the late twentieth and early twenty-first centuries. Some of the private companies acquiring water treatment systems are domestic and have been around for many years, but many of the larger companies are foreign. In both cases, the companies are well financed and eager to acquire existing firms and facilities. Given the increasing complexity and cost of running a water treatment plant with a variety of state and federal guidelines and regulations that have to be followed, this trend toward privatization is an interesting development in the industry. Although the private share of the total water treatment market is only about 9 percent, economic circumstances and the growth of the trend toward privatization suggest that this number will increase.

The bulk of treated water is used to flush toilets (47 percent) and take a shower or bath (37 percent); only about 5 percent is used for drinking. (©Crystal Craig/Dreamstime.com)

Pipes and valves inside a water treatment plant. (©Dreamstime.com)

A major division of the national U.S. water supply infrastructure is the community water system (CWS), which is defined by the U.S. Environmental Protection Agency (EPA) as a facility that delivers water to at least fifteen service connections that are used by year-round residents or twenty-five residents that are year-round users. CWSs vary from privately owned places, such as a very small mobile home park, to very large publicly owned systems, such as New York City. There are approximately 167,000 public water systems in the United States, serving about 278 million people. The more than 53,000 CWSs serve about 260 million people. Many nontransient water systems (about 20,000) and transient noncommunity water systems (about 93,000) serve a combined population of about 18 million people. CWSs serve about 94 percent of the total amount of water systems.

Even with the development of more technical and complicated equipment, water treatment operators will always be faced with the increasingly stringent state and federal regulations that the product must meet. To put it another way, there are always new chemicals that get into the rivers and groundwater that could cause harm to the unwary consumer. Thus, both the technology and the regulations driving the delivery of water to consumers and crops are likely to continue increasing over time. Studies by the American Water Works Association (AWWA) indicate that substantial changes are coming to the industry based on new technologies, such as information systems, advances in treatment processes, desalination, and telemetry. The water supply industry must respond to each such change.

INDUSTRY MARKET SEGMENTS

Data about the water treatment industry are variable in scope. Some information is reasonably available, while many other aspects of the business, particularly detailed data on expenses and the types of personnel needed in the industry, are generally not available. The EPA has been conducting detailed CWS surveys since 1976. The survey made in 2000 was released in 2002 and listed five size-based categories of CWS. This number of categories represented a reduction from earlier surveys undertaken between 1976 and 1985, which listed eight such categories. The American Water Works Association, the premier professional organization of the U.S. drinking water industry, conducted salary surveys between 2007 and 2009 for selected technical and administrative positions. Wage information is available only for the entire industry, however, and not for individual market segments. In addition, all annual income estimates include both water and liquid waste plant treatment plant and system operators. This mixing of the water and wastewater treatment plant data probably reflects the relatively small number of workers employed by these industries.

Very Small Systems

Very small water supply systems serve up to five hundred customers.

Potential Annual Earnings Scale. The median annual income of industry employees in May, 2008, was $38,430. The middle 50 percent of workers earned between $30,040 and $48,640. The bottom 10 percent earned less than $23,710, and the top 10 percent earned more than $59,860.

Clientele Interaction. Since very few people work in these very small treatment plants, there is very little interaction between personnel working for this level of the industry and clients, who range from other workers to the public.

Amenities, Atmosphere, and Physical Grounds. Plant operators have to work both indoors and outdoors, and they can be exposed to noise from a variety of machines and pumps. Workers have to be aware of safety issues that include gases that may be dangerous, walkways that may be slippery, and equipment that may not function properly. These potential safety issues can result in above-average injury rates on the job. Very small plants tend to have only limited amenities. Many water treatment plants are off-limits to visitors for reasons of security, especially after the terrorist attacks of September 11, 2001.

Typical Number of Employees. According to the EPA's CWS Survey, in 2000 there were 57,608 workers in 29,119 very small plants, for an average of 2 workers per plant.

Traditional Geographic Locations. Water treatment plants are generally located in close proximity to rivers, lakes or reservoirs, or well fields. The smallest ones are generally in extremely rural areas.

Pros of Working for a Very Small Treatment Plant. Workers may have the advantage of handling a greater number of different jobs than would be the case in a larger plant, adding to their breadth of experience. Very small plants have little or no chain of command and considerably less bureaucracy to deal with than larger plants. (There is still some bureaucracy, because the plants are answerable to governmental regulatory entities.)

Cons of Working for a Very Small Treatment Plant. Employees at very small plants may be on their own for extended periods of time. Those who seek guidance and clear direction may prefer positions with greater supervision and less breadth of responsibility.

Costs

Payroll and Benefits: Employees of even very small facilities are salaried and generally receive health benefits, vacations, and sick time.

Supplies: Water supply facilities require tools to maintain their equipment; chemicals and other substances used to treat water; and standard office equipment and supplies.

External Services: Water supply facilities may contract private consulting firms to provide technical assistance in matters beyond the expertise of facility employees or outside contractors to assist in maintenance and repairs.

Utilities: Typical utilities such as water, sewer, electricity, and telephone are needed at the plant.

Taxes: Private, for-profit water treatment plants must pay local, state, and federal income and property taxes. Nonprofit and government entities may be exempt from some or all of these taxes. All plants must pay payroll taxes.

Small Systems

Small water supply systems serve between 501 and 3,300 customers.

Potential Annual Earnings Scale. The median annual income of industry employees in May, 2008, was $38,430. The middle 50 percent of workers earned between $30,040 and $48,640. The bottom 10 percent earned less than $23,710, and the top 10 percent earned more than $59,860.

Clientele Interaction. Since there are very few people working in these small treatment plants, there is very little interaction between personnel working for this level of the industry and clients, who range from other workers to the public.

Amenities, Atmosphere, and Physical Grounds. Plant operators have to work both indoors and outdoors, and they can be exposed to noise from a variety of machines and pumps. Workers have to be aware of safety issues that include gases that may be dangerous, walkways that may be slippery, and equipment that may not function properly. These potential safety issues can result in above-average injury rates on the job. Small plants tend to have only limited amenities. Many water treatment plants are off-limits to visitors for reasons of security, especially after the terrorist attacks of September 11, 2001.

Typical Number of Employees. According to the EPA's CWS Survey, in 2000 there were 40,649 workers in 14,017 small water treatment plants, for an average of about 3 workers per plant.

Traditional Geographic Locations. Water treatment plants generally are located in close proximity to rivers, lakes or reservoirs, or well fields. They are usually located in rural areas.

Pros of Working for a Small Treatment Plant. Workers may have the advantage of handling a greater number of different jobs than would be the case in a larger plant, adding to their breadth of experience. Small plants have little or no chain of command and considerably less bureaucracy to deal with than larger plants. (There is still some bureaucracy, because the plants are answerable to governmental regulatory entities.)

Cons of Working for a Small Treatment Plant. Employees at small plants may be on their own for extended periods of time. Those who seek guidance and clear direction may prefer positions with greater supervision and less breadth of responsibility.

Costs

Payroll and Benefits: Employees of even small facilities are salaried and generally receive health benefits, vacations, and sick time.

Supplies: Water supply facilities require tools to maintain their equipment; chemicals and other substances used to treat water; and standard office equipment and supplies.

External Services: Water supply facilities may contract private consulting firms to provide technical assistance in matters beyond the expertise of facility employees or outside contractors to assist in maintenance and repairs.

Utilities: Typical utilities such as water, sewer, electricity, and telephone are needed at the plant.

Taxes: Private, for-profit water treatment plants must pay local, state, and federal income and property taxes. Nonprofit and government entities may be exempt from some or all of these taxes. All plants must pay payroll taxes.

Midsize Systems

Midsize water supply systems serve between 3,301 and 10,000 customers.

Potential Annual Earnings Scale. The median annual income of industry employees in May, 2008, was $38,430. The middle 50 percent of workers earned between $30,040 and $48,640. The bottom 10 percent earned less than $23,710, and the top 10 percent earned more than $59,860. Between 2007 and 2008, the average salaries of plant operators and utility executives in plants serving fewer than ten thousand customers were $38,168 and $67,993, respectively.

Clientele Interaction. At midsize facilities, a modest level of interaction occurs between plant workers and clients, who range from other workers to the public.

Amenities, Atmosphere, and Physical Grounds. Plant operators have to work both indoors and outdoors, and they can be exposed to noise from a variety of machines and pumps. Workers have to be aware of safety issues that include gases that may be dangerous, walkways that may be slippery, and equipment that may not function properly. These potential safety issues can result in above-average injury rates on the job. Midsize plants tend to have only limited amenities. Many water treatment plants are off-limits to visitors for reasons of security, especially after the terrorist attacks of September 11, 2001.

Typical Number of Employees. According to the EPA's CWS Survey, in 2000 there were 32,333 workers in 5,052 midsize water treatment plants, for an average of 6.4 workers per plant.

Traditional Geographic Locations. Water treatment plants are generally located in close proximity to rivers, lakes or reservoirs, or well fields. Midsize plants serve rural and suburban populations.

Pros of Working for a Midsize Treatment Plant. Midsize plants not only have larger staffs at work at any given time, allowing greater distribution of responsibilities, but also have larger total workforces, allowing different employees to work different shifts. While each employee's breadth of required expertise is likely to be less at a midsize plant than at a small plant, each employee's depth of required expertise may be greater, as midsize plants are more likely to require more complex machinery and control systems.

Cons of Working for a Midsize Treatment Plant. Even at midsize plants, employees may be on their own for extended periods of time. Demand peaks for water and the necessity of repairing damage resulting from accidents, storms, and cold weather may necessitate overtime work in the evenings and on the weekends. In addition, the water industry hires very few part-time workers.

Costs

Payroll and Benefits: Full-time personnel generally receive salaries, health benefits, vacations, and sick time.

Supplies: Water supply facilities require tools to maintain their equipment; chemicals and other substances used to treat water; and standard office equipment and supplies.

External Services: Water supply facilities may contract private consulting firms to provide technical assistance in matters beyond the expertise of facility employees or outside contractors to assist in maintenance and repairs.

Utilities: Typical utilities such as water, sewer, electricity, and telephone are needed at the plant.

Taxes: Private, for-profit water treatment plants must pay local, state, and federal income and property taxes. Nonprofit and government entities may be exempt from some or all of these taxes. All plants must pay payroll taxes.

Large Systems

Large water supply systems serve between 10,001 and 100,000 customers.

Potential Annual Earnings Scale. The median annual income of industry employees in May, 2008, was $38,430. The middle 50 percent of workers earned between $30,040 and $48,640. The bot-

tom 10 percent earned less than $23,710, and the top 10 percent earned more than $59,860. Between 2007 and 2008, the average salaries of plant operators, utility engineers, and utility executives in plants serving between 10,000 and 100,000 customers were $42,174, $64,349, and $98,529, respectively.

Clientele Interaction. Employees of large water treatment plants enjoy greater interaction with their clients than those of smaller plants.

Amenities, Atmosphere, and Physical Grounds. Plant operators have to work both indoors and outdoors, and they can be exposed to noise from a variety of machines and pumps. Workers have to be aware of safety issues that include gases that may be dangerous, walkways that may be slippery, and equipment that may not function properly. These potential safety issues can result in above-average injury rates on the job. The size difference between a large plant and a midsize plant is much greater than the size difference between a midsize plant and a small plant. As a result, large plants are likely to have significantly greater amenities than smaller plants. They are also more likely to be formally secure facilities, requiring keycard access and badges to be worn by all employees at all times.

Typical Number of Employees. According to the EPA's CWS Survey, in 2000 there were 81,247 workers in 3,484 large water treatment plants, for an average of more than 23 workers per plant.

Traditional Geographic Locations. Water treatment plants generally are located in close proximity to a river, lake or reservoir, or well field. However, large and very large treatment facilities may be located some distance away from their water sources. For example, the water for the major metropolitan areas of Phoenix and Tucson, Arizona, has to be pumped uphill from the Colorado River at Lake Havasu on the Arizona-California border, traveling a distance of 540 kilometers (336 miles) and experiencing an elevation increase of 875 meters (2,870 feet).

Pros of Working for a Large Treatment Plant. Large facilities require not only greater numbers of workers but also workers with more specialized skills than are required at smaller facilities. Workers are likely to work on rotating days and shifts, although the number needed varies from place to place. Work skills tend to be more varied as

Aerial view of a water treatment plant. (©Dreamstime.com)

treatment processes, machinery, chemical additions, and more observations of a variety of dials and controls are required. Larger treatment plants are more likely to offer formal training programs than smaller plants. They also encourage further professional development among their employees through such means as the online continuing education classes offered by the AWWA.

Cons of Working for a Large Treatment Plant. Workers at large plants need to be available twenty-four hours a day, every day. Although water demand generally decreases during the evening hours, raw intake water must still be treated during those hours. Large plants serve populations that are not only vast but also complexly distributed, and they are affected by variations in weather and other factors beyond employees' control. For example, rainstorms can increase the turbidity of rivers and necessitate extra alum inputs to raw water prior to other treatment steps. Plant employees must constantly be ready to make quick decisions in response to changing circumstances.

Costs

Payroll and Benefits: Workers at large plants work full shifts. Salaries generally vary based on the variety of speciality skills needed for the different operations. As with the other plants, all personnel are entitled to health benefits, vacations, and sick time.

Supplies: Water supply facilities require tools to maintain their equipment; chemicals and other substances used to treat water; and standard office equipment and supplies.

External Services: Water supply facilities may contract private consulting firms to provide technical assistance in matters beyond the expertise of facility employees or outside contractors to assist in maintenance and repairs. Such external vendors are less likely to be needed at larger plants with greater staffs and resources.

Utilities: Typical utilities such as water, sewer, electricity, and telephone are required.

Taxes: Private, for-profit water treatment plants must pay local, state, and federal income and property taxes. Nonprofit and government entities may be exempt from some or all of these taxes. All plants must pay payroll taxes.

Very Large Systems

Very large water supply systems serve more than 100,000 customers.

Potential Annual Earnings Scale. The median annual income of industry employees in May, 2008, was $38,430. The middle 50 percent of workers earned between $30,040 and $48,640. The bottom 10 percent earned less than $23,710, and the top 10 percent earned more than $59,860. Between 2007 and 2008, at plants serving a population greater than 100,000, water treatment plant operators, water utility engineers, and top utility executives averaged $47,638, $69,505, and $139,611, respectively. A 2009 AWWA survey indicated that the median annual salaries for customer service managers and top executives at water treatment plants serving from 100,000 to 250,000 people were $76,563 and $140,110, respectively; for plants serving from 250,001 to 500,000 people, they were $89,826 and $145,489, respectively; for plants servings from 500,001 to 1,000,000 people, they were $83,059 and $160,655, respectively; and for more than 1 million people, they were $97,009 and $246,580, respectively.

Clientele Interaction. Plants serving more than 100,000 customers have a much greater number of clients than small plants, so employees are more likely to interact with them. Generally speaking, however, only dedicated customer-service employees interact with members of the public.

Amenities, Atmosphere, and Physical Grounds. Plant operators have to work both indoors and outdoors, and they can be exposed to noise from a variety of machines and pumps. Workers have to be aware of safety issues that include gases that may be dangerous, walkways that may be slippery, and equipment that may not function properly. These potential safety issues can result in above-average injury rates on the job. The largest plants generally have the greatest amenities, such as dedicated break rooms for employees. They also tend to employ the greatest level of security, requiring keycard access and badges to be worn by all employees at all times.

Typical Number of Employees. According to the EPA's CWS Survey, in 2000 there were 87,269 workers in 514 water treatment plants, for an average of 170 workers per plant.

Traditional Geographic Locations. Water treatment plants generally are located in close proximity to rivers, lakes or reservoirs, or well fields. In some cases, metropolitan facilities may receive their water from hundreds of miles away.

Pros of Working for a Very Large Treatment Plant. Very large facilities need not only more workers than smaller facilities but also workers that have more specialized skills. Employees at large plants often must be available on rotating days and shifts, although the number required varies from place to place. Work skills are also more varied, as treatment processes, machinery, chemical additions, and more observation of a variety of dials and controls are required. Larger treatment plants are more likely to offer formal training programs than smaller plants. They also encourage further professional development among their employees through such means as the online continuing education classes offered by the AWWA.

Cons of Working for a Very Large Treatment Plant. Workers at very large plants need to be available twenty-four hours a day, every day. Although water demand generally decreases during the evening hours, raw intake water must still be treated during those hours. Large plants serve populations that are not only vast but also complexly distributed, and they are affected by variations in weather and other factors beyond employees' control. For example, rainstorms can increase the turbidity of rivers and necessitate extra alum inputs to raw water prior to other treatment steps. Plant employees must constantly be ready to make quick decisions in response to changing circumstances, including the release of pollutants into the water supply.

Costs

Payroll and Benefits: Workers at very large plants work full shifts. Salaries generally vary based on the variety of speciality skills needed for the different operations. As with the other plants, all personnel are entitled to health benefits, vacations, and sick time.

Supplies: Water supply facilities require tools to maintain their equipment; chemicals and other substances used to treat water; and standard office equipment and supplies.

External Services: Water supply facilities may contract private consulting firms to provide technical assistance in matters beyond the expertise of facility employees or outside contractors to assist in maintenance and repairs. Such external vendors are less likely to be needed at larger plants with greater staffs and resources.

Utilities: Typical utilities such as water, sewer, electricity, and telephone are needed.

Taxes: Private, for-profit water treatment plants must pay local, state, and federal income and property taxes. Nonprofit and government entities may be exempt from some or all of these taxes. All plants must pay payroll taxes.

ORGANIZATIONAL STRUCTURE AND JOB ROLES

The organizational structure and distribution of jobs within a water treatment plant are usually based on the size of the facility and the population served. All water plants must conform to EPA standards and regulations. Although about 91 percent of plants are public, many of the larger systems are private and sometimes operate in a different organizational framework. Interestingly, the standards for bottled water are governed by the Food and Drug Administration (FDA). Although these standards are broadly similar to EPA standards, there are some differences. For example, the number of samples per time period that must be tested are more stringent for tap water monitored by the EPA than for bottled water monitored by the FDA.

All treatment plant and system operators have to be certified within their respective states. The particular requirements and standards vary considerably from state to state, but many specify four levels of certification. Some states may honor licenses from other states, but they are not required to do so and operators may have to pass new sets of exams if they move among states.

The number of levels of certification is generally based on the types of treatment processes used in a particular plant, as well as the plant's size. For example, operators at plants that serve small populations may need only level-one certification. A worker who has a level-one certification is permitted to operate such a plant without any other su-

pervision. Workers in small plants in some states can go up the certification ladder by taking additional tests on their technical knowledge, while other states stipulate that experience in a larger plant is required for advancement. Thus, those workers who want to advance their careers may have to move to larger plants to do so.

As treatment plants get larger and include many more complicated types of equipment, machines, and computers, their employees need to acquire additional skills. Workers in the largest plants who have attained higher levels of certification can become shift supervisors. They may then be in charge of large teams of other workers. In addition, some of the more experienced workers who have higher degrees of certification have the option of getting jobs as technicians in drinking-water-control state agencies. Such technicians monitor and offer technical assistance to plant personnel in their states.

Workers for most positions in water treatment plants are required to have a high school diploma or some form of equivalent degree. Those workers that have an associate's degree or have taken a one-year certificate program in water quality technology receive very useful training for future employment. Workers who are interested in becoming plant operators should have some mechanical aptitude in conjunction with basic courses in math, chemistry, and biology. Computer skills are very desirable, as computers are increasingly used to monitor plant equipment, test performance, and analyze workflow.

The following umbrella categories apply to the organizational structure of businesses in the water supply industry:

- Business Management
- Customer Service
- Facilities and Security
- Technology, Research, Design, and Development
- Human Resources

Business Management

There are substantial variations in water treatment plant management formats. For example, private facilities are often organized differently than public facilities. At public facilities, management personnel may not even have offices in treatment plants but rather work in municipal buildings located elsewhere. Private facilities, likewise, may take their direction from executives operating from corporate headquarters far distant from the facilities themselves. Indeed, the senior executive managers of some large, privately owned systems may be located in foreign countries. On-site treatment plant personnel must include technically qualified engineers, chemists, and skilled operators, particularly if the plant is large.

Business management occupations may include the following:

- Administrator
- Plant Director/Manager
- President/Chief Executive Officer (CEO)
- Vice President of Water Supply Operations

Customer Service

Customer problems with such items as billing, requests for new water meters, and general questions are usually directed to personnel in a separate location or building in the municipal or corporate office. Questions or concerns that involve the operations of a treatment plant directly, such as water taste, chemical additives, or high turbidity levels in raw water usually come from personnel in the state or federal government and are addressed directly to the appropriate on-site specialist.

Customer service occupations may include the following:

- Bookkeeper
- Customer Service Manager
- Customer Service Representative
- Meter Reader
- Administrative Assistant
- Clerk

Facilities and Security

Public visits to treatment plants since the terrorist attacks on the World Trade Center and the Pentagon on September 11, 2001, have been substantially diminished. One needs permission to get into most plants, and the general rule is not to encourage outsiders to visit. Plant personnel must enforce these rules, ensuring that only authorized personnel have access to their facilities. Large plants must also worry about cybernetic access, in addition to physical security, as the computers that con-

trol their operations may be vulnerable to attack.

Facilities and security occupations may include the following:

- Building Inspector
- Maintenance Supervisor
- Maintenance and Repair Worker
- Security Supervisor
- Security Guard
- Computer Security Specialist

Technology, Research, Design, and Development

Government and private entities research new and better ways to deliver high-quality water to consumers and crops efficiently and effectively. States and the EPA generally introduce new techniques as the science of water treatment advances. The fields of engineering, chemistry, and laboratory methodology invariably change as new research is approved and then mandated by regulatory authorities. For example, one problem receiving a great deal of attention in the early twenty-first century is the level of prescription pharmaceuticals in the water supply. Such pharmaceuticals enter wastewater, both after passing through the human digestive system and after being disposed of in toilets directly. Water treatment plants thus far have not developed comprehensive techniques for removing such drugs from the water supply, so trace amounts remain.

In addition to drugs, raw water coming into a treatment plant may contain bacteria, viruses, lead, mercury, and industrial acids. Techniques exist to handle or at least abate these contaminants. It is more difficult, however, to remove or neutralize synthetic organic compounds, such as water-soluble materials (cleaning compounds and insecticides) and insoluble materials (petroleum residues and plastics). These substances, if not properly addressed in the treatment process, can result in a mix of ailments that include kidney disorders and birth defects. Endocrine-disrupting compounds and pharmaceutical and personal care products, known collectively as PPCPs, are also present in wastewater, as they are easily excreted by humans and livestock (such as those animals that have been given food additives). PPCPs that have already been detected in drinking water sources include sex steroids, beta-blockers, painkillers, and

OCCUPATION PROFILE

Water and Wastewater Engineer

Considerations	Qualifications
Description	Specializes in all areas of the water cycle, from designing systems that provide fresh water to determining how to dispose of wastewater and sewage to preventing damage related to floods.
Career clusters	Agriculture, Food, and Natural Resources; Architecture and Construction; Manufacturing; Science, Technology, Engineering, and Math
Interests	Data; things
Working conditions	Work both inside and outside
Minimum education level	Bachelor's degree; master's degree; doctoral degree
Physical exertion	Light work
Physical abilities	Unexceptional/basic fitness
Opportunities for experience	Internship
Licensure and certification	Required
Employment outlook	Faster-than-average growth expected

Note: See volume 1, "Publisher's Note," for an explanation of the Holland interest score.

antibiotics. Most of these PPCPs eventually get into wastewater treatment plants, where they can be only partially removed by existing technology. The remaining PPCPs eventually wind up in surface streams or travel directly from septic systems into the groundwater. In the future, drinking water regulations may include PPCPs, and new treatment procedures will become required.

Technology, research, design, and development occupations may include the following:

- Chemist
- Food Scientist
- Food Technologist
- Microbiologist
- Biologist
- Science Technician
- Industrial Engineer
- Chemical Engineer
- Mechanical Engineer
- Electrical Engineer
- Engineering Technician
- Software Engineer
- Computer Hardware Engineer

Human Resources

Water treatment plants require skilled personnel to operate the equipment, be in control of all processes, and keep tabs on all the equipment that is necessary to make the finished water safe enough to drink. The number of people and the specific mix of specific skills involved in water treatment are related to the size and type of the plant. For example, one operator in a small plant can be assigned all of the responsibility for proper maintenance for all of the systems. This person would most probably work during the day and be available by phone during the nights and weekends. For midsize and large plants, where monitoring of all of the equipment is required constantly, personnel generally work in three eight-hour shifts. Very large plants need more specialized personnel to handle issues that may develop, and weekend and holiday time may be required. Overtime work is also a possibility, especially during an emergency related to plant malfunctions, such as chemical leaks, problems with automated equipment and computers, or storm-induced floods that may block access to or damage the plant.

Human resources occupations may include the following:

- Human Resources Director
- Human Resources Manager
- Human Resources Generalist
- Benefits Specialist
- Payroll Clerk
- Administrative Assistant

INDUSTRY OUTLOOK

Overview

The outlook for this industry shows it to be on the rise. According to the U.S. Bureau of Labor Statistics, the number of jobs for water treatment plant personnel and system operators is projected to grow by 20 percent between 2008 and 2018, significantly faster than the 11 percent growth rate for all occupations combined. In addition, the AWWA has indicated that the water industry will go through a substantial loss of workers resulting from voluntary retirements during the same period. Accordingly, thousands of existing positions will need to be filled, in addition to the new positions that will be created, in the fields of plant management, engineering, and science-related positions. Consequently, qualified individuals should be able to find opportunities based on their mix of skills and experience. The projected growth in jobs is based

OCCUPATION PROFILE

Water Treatment Plant Operator

Considerations	Qualifications
Description	Controls water treatment equipment that cleans water so there will be a continuous supply that is safe for humans and corporations to use.
Career cluster	Agriculture, Food, and Natural Resources
Interests	Data; things
Working conditions	Work both inside and outside
Minimum education level	On-the-job training; high school diploma or GED; high school diploma/technical training; apprenticeship
Physical exertion	Medium work
Physical abilities	Unexceptional/basic fitness
Opportunities for experience	Apprenticeship; military service; part-time work
Licensure and certification	Required
Employment outlook	Faster-than-average growth expected
Holland interest score	RCE; REI

Note: See volume 1, "Publisher's Note," for an explanation of the Holland interest score.

PROJECTED EMPLOYMENT FOR SELECTED OCCUPATIONS

Water Transportation

Employment		
2009	Projected 2018	Occupation
12,180	13,000	Captains, mates, and pilots of water vessels
1,310	1,200	General and operations managers
1,010	1,100	Laborers and freight, stock, and material movers, hand
14,510	15,900	Sailors and marine oilers
6,130	6,600	Ship engineers

Source: U.S. Bureau of Labor Statistics, Industries at a Glance, Occupational Employment Statistics and Employment Projections Program.

in part on the continued need for potable water, as well as the growth rate of the U.S. population and the urbanization of that population. All these factors drive demand for new and expanded water treatment facilities and for the labor necessary to operate them.

The largest employers of treatment plant and system operators are local governments. However, jobs are expected to be more plentiful in privately owned plants than in publicly owned plants. An increase in federal certification requirements will encourage the private sector increasingly to specialize in the more complex aspects governing water treatment plant operation and management.

Another factor for job growth is the ongoing nature of regulatory changes in the water industry, based on continually revised and upgraded water quality standards. Changes in standards are expected to result in the need to have additional workers at each facility, as the complexity of procedures required in the treatment process will increase. On-the-job training may increase in order to ensure that personnel acquire the skills necessary to operate new equipment properly.

About 22 percent of plants that handle only surface water have an operator on site twenty-four hours per day. As the plants get larger and handle customer bases of more than fifty thousand, this percentage increases to 80 percent. Fully 95 percent of systems that serve more than 500,000 persons have operators on site at all times. All surface water plants that handle 100 million gallons per day or more have personnel on duty every day, around the clock. Groundwater plants are generally much less likely to have ersonnel available both day and night, as they generally are smaller systems and do not run at all hours of the night. These smaller systems generally pump their water into above-ground storage containers (water towers) at high elevations in their service areas so that the morning surge in water use can be handled properly.

Many plants that do not have twenty-four-hour coverage rely on supervisory control and data acquisition (SCADA) to handle either process monitoring or control. This technique allows a plant to monitor or control its systems when an operator is not present. Treatment plants that use groundwater and do not have personnel on site at all times rely on SCADA for process monitoring (19 percent) and process control (14 percent). These percentages approximately double for surface-water facilities.

Mergers and acquisitions of water purveyors that developed during the 1990's have continued and are expected to continue in the future. The drivers of this trend have been the economies of scale that can be achieved in larger systems, the expanded use and associated development of technical procedures that would not be feasible in smaller plants, and the increasing need to meet new and more stringent environmental regulations. These are some of the very strong pressures that encourage the growth of larger plants and make the operations of smaller plants that much less viable.

The trend of private investor firms acquiring smaller public water systems is expected to continue. Larger systems are more capable of obtaining capital than smaller systems, and this capital can be used to make the necessary changes to the infrastructure of smaller plants once they are acquired. Larger utilities, either public or private, have the benefit of spreading their overhead expenses over a much larger customer base, allowing them to reduce the per-customer costs of providing service.

Employment Advantages

Water is necessary to life, so employees in the water supply industry need not worry about changes in consumer preferences. They may also gain fulfillment from helping provide consumers with such a fundamental requirement. Jobs in the industry are expected to be relatively plentiful for those with the specific training required to obtain them. Those with interests in chemistry, microbiology, and other experimental sciences who wish their research to have obvious practical effects in the world may find the water supply industry particularly fulfilling. Management positions at large plants may also be good fits for those with a skill for contingency planning and responding quickly to sudden crises.

Annual Earnings

In 2000, publicly owned U.S. water systems earned revenues of $34.5 billion, and privately owned systems earned revenues of $4.3 billion, for a combined total of $39.8 billion. By 2009, this combined total had reached $55.01 billion.

RELATED RESOURCES FOR FURTHER RESEARCH

AMERICAN WATER RESOURCES ASSOCIATION
   4 W. Federal St.
   Middleburg, VA 20118
   Tel: (540) 687-8390
   Fax: (540) 687-8395
   http://www.awra.org

AMERICAN WATER WORKS ASSOCIATION
   6666 W. Quincy Ave.
   Denver, CO 80235
   Tel: (303) 794-7711

   Fax: (303) 347-0804
   http://www.awwa.org

NATIONAL ASSOCIATION OF WATER COMPANIES
   2001 L St. NW, Suite 850
   Washington, DC 20036
   Tel: (202) 833-8383
   Fax: (202) 331-7442
   http://www.nawc.org

WATER ENVIRONMENT FEDERATION
   601 Wythe St.
   Alexandria, VA 22314-1994
   Tel: (800) 666-0206
   Fax: (703) 684-2492
   http://www.wef.org

WATER QUALITY ASSOCIATION
   4151 Naperville Rd.
   Lisle, IL 60532
   Tel: (630) 505-0160
   Fax: (630) 505-9637
   http://www.wqa.org

ABOUT THE AUTHOR

Robert M. Hordon has taught for several decades at Rutgers University in New Jersey. His fields of speciality include hydrology, water resources, and physical geography. He has a B.A. from Brooklyn College and an M.A. and Ph.D. from Columbia University. Professor Hordon has served for several terms of office on the Executive Committee of the American Institute of Hydrology (AIH), a nonprofit scientific and educational organization that offers certification to professionals in all of the varied fields of hydrology (groundwater, surface water, and water quality). In 2009, he was appointed chair of the Examination Committee of the AIH for professional certification.

FURTHER READING

Brooks, Kenneth N., et al. *Hydrology and the Management of Watersheds.* 3d ed. Ames: Iowa State Press, 2003.

Career Information Center. *Agribusiness, Environment, and Natural Resources.* 9th ed. Vol. 1. Detroit: Thomas/Gale, 2007.

Cech, Thomas V. *Principles of Water Resources: History, Development, Management, and Policy.* 3d ed. Hoboken, N.J.: John Wiley, 2010.

Chin, David A. *Water-Resources Engineering.* 2d ed. Upper Saddle River, N.J.: Pearson Prentice Hall, 2006.

Dzurik, Andrew A. *Water Resources Planning.* 3d ed. Lanham, Md.: Rowman and Littlefield, 2003.

Fair, Gordon M., John C. Geyer, and Daniel A. Okun. *Water Supply and Wastewater Removal.* Vol. 1 in *Water and Wastewater Engineering.* New York: John Wiley, 1966.

Gleick, Peter H., et al. *The World's Water, 2008-2009: The Biennial Report on Freshwater Resources.* Washington, D.C.: Island Press, 2009.

Gray, N. F. *Drinking Water Quality: Problems and Solutions.* 2d ed. New York: Cambridge University Press, 2008.

Grigg, Neil S. "Water and Wastewater Workforce Stats: The Case for Improving Job Data." *Journal of the American Water Works Association* 101, no. 8 (August, 2009): 67-78.

Hammer, Mark J., and Mark J. Hammer, Jr. *Water and Wastewater Technology.* 5th ed. Upper Saddle River, N.J.: Pearson Prentice Hall, 2004.

IBISWorld. *Water Supply and Irrigation Systems in the U.S.: Industry Report 22131.* May 4, 2010. http://www.ibisworld.com/industry/outlook.aspx?indid=161.

Linsley, Ray K., and Joseph B. Franzini. *Water-Resources Engineering.* New York: McGraw-Hill, 1972.

Patrick, Roger, and Edward G. Means III. "Meeting Customer Expectations in a Fluid Utility Environment." *Journal of the American Water Works Association* 97, no. 9 (September, 2005): 56-61.

Pojasek, Robert B., ed. *Drinking Water Quality Enhancement Through Source Protection.* Ann Arbor, Mich.: Ann Arbor Science, 1977.

Speidel, David H., Lon C. Ruedisili, and Allen F. Agnew, eds. *Perspectives on Water: Uses and Abuses.* New York: Oxford University Press, 1988.

Spellman, Frank R. *The Science of Water: Concepts and Applications.* 2d ed. Boca Raton, Fla.: CRC Press, 2008.

Symons, James M. *Plain Talk: Questions and Answers About the Water You Drink.* 4th ed. Denver: American Water Works Association, 2001.

U.S. Bureau of Labor Statistics. *Career Guide to Industries,* 2010-2011 ed. http://www.bls.gov/oco/cg.

_____. "Water and Liquid Waste Treatment Plant and System Operators." In *Occupational Outlook Handbook,* 2010-2011 ed. http://www.bls.gov/oco/ocos229.htm.

U.S. Census Bureau. North American Industry Classification System (NAICS), 2007. http://www.census.gov/cgi-bin/sssd/naics/naicsrch?chart=2007.

U.S. Department of Commerce. International Trade Administration. Office of Trade and Industry Information. Industry Trade Data and Analysis. http://ita.doc.gov/td/industry/otea/OTII/OTII-index.html.

U.S. Environmental Protection Agency. Office of Water. *Community Water System Survey, 2000.* Washington, D.C.: Author, 2002.

Wurbs, Ralph A., and James P. Wesley. *Water Resources Engineering.* Upper Saddle River, N.J.: Prentice Hall, 2002.

Appendixes

Employment by Industry, 2008 and Projected 2018

Industry	2007 NAICS Number	Employment (thousands of jobs)	
		2008	Projected 2018
Total [1,2]		150,931.7	166,205.6
Nonagriculture wage and salary	NA	137,814.8	152,443.5
Mining	21	717.0	613.2
Oil and gas extraction	211	161.6	135.8
Mining, except oil and gas	212	227.7	225.7
Coal mining	2121	80.6	83.9
Metal ore mining	2122	39.9	35.9
Nonmetallic mineral mining and quarrying	2123	107.2	105.9
Support activities for mining	213	327.7	251.7
Utilities	22	559.5	500.5
Electric power generation, transmission, and distribution	2211	404.7	345.7
Natural gas distribution	2212	106.8	100.8
Water, sewage, and other systems	2213	48.0	54.0
Construction	23	7,214.9	8,552.0
Manufacturing	31-33	13,431.2	12,225.2
Food manufacturing	311	1,484.8	1,483.2
Animal food manufacturing	3111	50.9	49.0
Grain and oilseed milling	3112	62.6	61.4
Sugar and confectionery product manufacturing	3113	70.8	63.7
Fruit and vegetable preserving and specialty food manufacturing	3114	173.7	154.8
Dairy product manufacturing	3115	129.1	126.3
Animal slaughtering and processing	3116	512.1	538.7
Seafood product preparation and packaging	3117	40.6	44.7
Bakeries and tortilla manufacturing	3118	280.9	275.4
Other food manufacturing	3119	164.1	169.2
Beverage and tobacco product	312	199.0	180.9
Beverage manufacturing	3121	177.0	164.1
Tobacco manufacturing	3122	22.0	16.8
Textile mills	313	151.1	79.2
Fiber, yarn, and thread mills	3131	37.4	20.7
Fabric mills	3132	65.4	35.0
Textile and fabric finishing and fabric coating mills	3133	48.3	23.5
Textile product mills	314	147.6	91.3
Textile furnishings mills	3141	75.4	41.9
Other textile product mills	3149	72.2	49.4
Apparel manufacturing	315	198.4	88.4
Apparel knitting mills	3151	26.2	12.5
Cut and sew apparel manufacturing	3152	155.2	66.7

Industry	2007 NAICS Number	Employment (thousands of jobs)	
		2008	Projected 2018
Apparel accessories and other apparel manufacturing	3159	17.0	9.2
Leather and allied products	316	33.6	23.0
Leather and hide tanning and finishing, and other leather and allied product manufacturing	3161, 3169	17.8	13.0
Footwear manufacturing	3162	15.8	10.0
Wood product manufacturing	321	459.6	424.4
Sawmills and wood preservation	3211	103.6	84.9
Veneer, plywood, and engineered wood product manufacturing	3212	90.8	99.8
Other wood product manufacturing	3219	265.2	239.7
Paper manufacturing	322	445.8	337.5
Pulp, paper, and paperboard mills	3221	126.1	81.9
Converted paper product manufacturing	3222	319.7	255.6
Printing and related support activities	323	594.1	499.3
Petroleum and coal products manufacturing	324	117.1	90.8
Chemical manufacturing	325	849.8	793.2
Basic chemical manufacturing	3251	152.1	99.9
Resin, synthetic rubber, and artificial synthetic fibers and filaments manufacturing	3252	105.4	95.2
Pesticide, fertilizer, and other agricultural chemical manufacturing	3253	36.1	35.0
Pharmaceutical and medicine manufacturing	3254	289.8	307.4
Paint, coating, and adhesive manufacturing	3255	62.8	65.4
Soap, cleaning compound, and toilet preparation manufacturing	3256	108.2	101.1
Other chemical product and preparation manufacturing	3259	95.4	89.2
Plastics and rubber products manufacturing	326	734.3	678.0
Plastics product manufacturing	3261	589.0	555.2
Rubber product manufacturing	3262	145.3	122.8
Nonmetallic mineral product manufacturing	327	468.1	480.1
Clay product and refractory manufacturing	3271	52.4	53.9
Glass and glass product manufacturing	3272	96.5	83.8
Cement and concrete product manufacturing	3273	223.3	247.5
Lime, gypsum, and other nonmetallic mineral product manufacturing	3274, 3279	95.9	94.9
Primary metal manufacturing	331	443.2	399.5
Iron and steel mills and ferroalloy manufacturing	3311	98.9	79.9
Steel product manufacturing from purchased steel	3312	60.1	58.9
Alumina and aluminum production and processing	3313	67.9	64.9
Nonferrous metal (except aluminum) production and processing	3314	67.4	62.9
Foundries	3315	148.9	132.9
Fabricated metal product manufacturing	332	1,528.3	1,399.1
Forging and stamping	3321	107.9	84.9
Cutlery and handtool manufacturing	3322	49.1	35.9

Industry	2007 NAICS Number	Employment (thousands of jobs)	
		2008	Projected 2018
Architectural and structural metals manufacturing	3323	409.4	429.4
Boiler, tank, and shipping container manufacturing	3324	95.8	89.1
Hardware manufacturing	3325	29.3	24.0
Spring and wire product manufacturing	3326	51.5	41.9
Machine shops; turned product; and screw, nut, and bolt manufacturing	3327	360.1	319.5
Coating, engraving, heat treating, and allied activities	3328	143.7	124.8
Other fabricated metal product manufacturing	3329	281.5	249.6
Machinery manufacturing	333	1,185.5	1,095.2
Agriculture, construction, and mining machinery manufacturing	3331	242.1	249.6
Industrial machinery manufacturing	3332	120.8	92.9
Commercial and service industry machinery manufacturing	3333	105.3	104.8
Ventilation, heating, air-conditioning, and commercial refrigeration equipment manufacturing	3334	149.5	112.8
Metalworking machinery manufacturing	3335	191.7	189.7
Engine, turbine, and power transmission equipment manufacturing	3336	103.5	96.8
Other general purpose machinery manufacturing	3339	272.6	248.6
Computer and electronic product manufacturing	334	1,247.7	1,006.5
Computer and peripheral equipment manufacturing	3341	182.8	124.7
Communications equipment manufacturing	3342	129.0	120.1
Audio and video equipment manufacturing	3343	27.0	14.6
Semiconductor and other electronic component manufacturing	3344	432.4	286.8
Navigational, measuring, electromedical, and control instruments manufacturing	3345	441.6	434.3
Manufacturing and reproducing magnetic and optical media	3346	34.9	26.0
Electrical equipment, appliance, and component manufacturing	335	424.9	367.8
Electric lighting equipment manufacturing	3351	57.1	45.9
Household appliance manufacturing	3352	72.0	54.9
Electrical equipment manufacturing	3353	158.5	129.2
Other electrical equipment and component manufacturing	3359	137.3	137.8
Transportation equipment manufacturing	336	1,606.6	1,437.4
Motor vehicle manufacturing	3361	190.7	159.7
Motor vehicle body and trailer manufacturing	3362	141.9	130.8
Motor vehicle parts manufacturing	3363	544.4	443.3
Aerospace product and parts manufacturing	3364	503.9	502.4
Railroad rolling stock manufacturing	3365	28.4	17.5
Ship and boat building	3366	156.7	139.8
Other transportation equipment manufacturing	3369	40.6	43.9

Industry	2007 NAICS Number	Employment (thousands of jobs)	
		2008	Projected 2018
Furniture and related product manufacturing	337	481.0	511.5
Household and institutional furniture and kitchen cabinet manufacturing	3371	306.0	339.4
Office furniture (including fixtures) manufacturing	3372	131.2	129.8
Other furniture-related product manufacturing	3379	43.8	42.3
Miscellaneous manufacturing	339	630.7	758.9
Medical equipment and supplies manufacturing	3391	309.7	359.5
Other miscellaneous manufacturing	3399	321.0	399.4
Wholesale trade	42	5,963.9	6,219.8
Retail trade	44, 45	15,356.4	16,010.4
Transportation and warehousing	48, 492, 493	4,504.9	4,950.4
Air transportation	481	492.6	529.4
Rail transportation	482	229.5	240.4
Water transportation	483	65.2	66.9
Truck transportation	484	1,391.0	1,534.2
Transit and ground passenger transportation	485	418.0	471.4
Pipeline transportation	486	42.0	38.2
Scenic and sightseeing transportation and support activities for transportation	487, 488	617.9	726.1
Postal Service	491	747.5	650.0
Couriers and messengers	492	575.9	588.1
Warehousing and storage	493	672.8	755.7
Information	51	2,996.9	3,115.0
Publishing industries	511	882.6	842.0
Newspaper, periodical, book, and directory publishers	5111	618.9	499.2
Software publishers	5112	263.7	342.8
Motion picture, video, and sound recording industries	512	381.6	427.5
Broadcasting (except Internet)	515	316.0	339.5
Telecommunications	517	1,021.5	931.9
Data processing, hosting, related services, and other information services	518, 519	395.2	574.1
Finance and insurance	52	6,015.3	6,336.9
Monetary authorities, credit intermediation, and related activities	521, 522	2,758.1	2,895.5
Securities, commodity contracts, and other financial investments and related activities	523	858.1	959.1
Insurance carriers and related activities	524	2,308.8	2,376.4
Insurance carriers	5241	1,401.8	1,338.2
Agencies, brokerages, and other insurance-related activities	5242	907.0	1,038.2
Funds, trusts, and other financial vehicles	525	90.3	105.9
Real estate, rental, and leasing	53	2,130.2	2,365.8
Real estate	531	1,481.1	1,677.2
Rental and leasing services and lessors of intangible assets	532, 533	649.1	688.6
Automotive equipment rental and leasing	5321	194.6	214.6
Consumer goods rental and general rental centers	5322, 5323	298.1	308.3

Industry	2007 NAICS Number	Employment (thousands of jobs)	
		2008	Projected 2018
Commercial and industrial machinery and equipment rental and leasing	5324	128.2	127.8
Lessors of nonfinancial intangible assets (except copyrighted works)	533	28.2	37.9
Professional, scientific, and technical services	54	7,829.6	10,486.1
Legal services	5411	1,163.7	1,416.8
Accounting, tax preparation, bookkeeping, and payroll services	5412	950.1	1,149.2
Architectural, engineering, and related services	5413	1,444.7	1,769.5
Specialized design services	5414	143.1	208.7
Computer systems design and related services	5415	1,450.3	2,106.7
Management, scientific, and technical consulting services	5416	1,008.9	1,844.1
Scientific research and development services	5417	621.7	778.9
Advertising and related services	5418	462.3	499.3
Other professional, scientific, and technical services	5419	584.8	712.9
Management of companies and enterprises	55	1,894.6	1,997.0
Administrative and support and waste management and remediation services	56	8,053.8	9,484.8
Administrative and support services	561	7,693.6	9,033.8
Office administrative services	5611	403.3	483.3
Facilities support services	5612	132.7	173.6
Employment services	5613	3,144.4	3,744.1
Business support services	5614	823.2	948.3
Travel arrangement and reservation services	5615	227.7	224.7
Investigation and security services	5616	806.8	960.0
Services to buildings and dwellings	5617	1,847.1	2,182.6
Other support services	5619	308.4	317.2
Waste management and remediation services	562	360.2	451.0
Education services	61	3,036.5	3,842.0
Elementary and secondary schools	6111	854.9	1,089.7
Junior colleges, colleges, universities, and professional schools	6112, 6113	1,602.7	1,857.4
Other educational services	6114-7	578.9	894.9
Health care and social assistance	62	15,818.7	19,815.6
Ambulatory health care services	621	5,660.8	7,675.9
Offices of health practitioners	6211, 6212, 6213	3,713.3	4,978.6
Outpatient, laboratory, and other ambulatory care services	6214, 6215, 6219	989.5	1,297.9
Home health care services	6216	958.0	1,399.4
Hospitals, private	622	4,641.2	5,191.9
Nursing and residential care facilities	623	3,008.0	3,644.8
Social assistance	624	2,508.7	3,303.0
Individual and family services	6241	1,108.6	1,638.8
Community, and vocational rehabilitation services	6242, 6243	540.9	672.0
Child day care services	6244	859.2	992.2

Industry	2007 NAICS Number	Employment (thousands of jobs)	
		2008	Projected 2018
Arts, entertainment, and recreation	71	1,969.5	2,273.7
Performing arts, spectator sports, and related industries	711	406.4	468.1
Performing arts companies	7111	117.8	126.7
Spectator sports	7112	128.8	145.9
Promoters of events, and agents and managers	7113, 7114	109.4	130.7
Independent artists, writers, and performers	7115	50.4	64.8
Museums, historical sites, and similar institutions	712	131.8	160.7
Amusement, gambling, and recreation industries	713	1,431.3	1,644.9
Accommodation and food services	72	11,489.2	12,327.4
Accommodation	721	1,857.3	1,956.7
Food services and drinking places	722	9,631.9	10,370.7
Other services	81	6,333.2	7,141.9
Repair and maintenance	811	1,228.2	1,290.7
Automotive repair and maintenance	8111	858.3	911.9
Electronic and precision equipment repair and maintenance	8112	104.4	110.7
Commercial and industrial machinery and equipment (except automotive and electronic) repair and maintenance	8113	191.5	199.7
Personal and household goods repair and maintenance	8114	74.0	68.4
Personal and laundry services	812	1,326.7	1,588.7
Personal care services	8121	621.6	819.1
Death care services	8122	136.2	145.3
Drycleaning and laundry services	8123	334.8	347.9
Other personal services	8129	234.1	276.4
Religious, grantmaking, civic, professional, and similar organizatons	NA	2,973.3	3,352.5
Religious organizations	8131	1,684.2	1,881.8
Grantmaking and giving services and social advocacy organizations	8132, 8133	351.1	387.4
Civic, social, professional, and similar organizations	8134, 8139	938.0	1,083.3
Private households	814	805.0	910.0
Federal government	NA	2764.3	2859.1
Postal Service	491	747.5	650.0
Federal electric utilities	NA	24.0	19.0
Federal enterprises except the Postal Service and electric utilities	NA	63.5	44.9
Federal defense government	NA	496.3	547.1
Federal non-defense government except enterprises	NA	1433.0	1598.1
Federal government except enterprises	NA	1,929.3	2,145.2
State and local government	NA	19,735.2	21,326.7
Local government passenger transit	NA	268.6	342.6
Local government enterprises except passenger transit	NA	1,326.4	1,499.1
Local government hospitals—compensation	NA	662.6	669.0
Local government educational services—compensation	NA	8,075.6	8,728.3

Industry	2007 NAICS Number	Employment (thousands of jobs)	
		2008	Projected 2018
Local government excluding enterprises, educational services, and hospitals—compensation	NA	4,224.1	4,464.0
State government enterprises	NA	533.8	578.3
State government hospitals—compensation	NA	363.4	377.3
State government educational services—compensation	NA	2,359.0	2,584.0
State government, other compensation	NA	1,921.7	2,084.1
State and local government capital services	NA	—	—
General state and local government except compensation and capital services	NA	—	—
Owner-occupied dwellings	NA	—	—
Agriculture, forestry, fishing, and hunting [3]	11	2,098.3	2,020.1
Crop production	111	950.6	880.7
Animal production	112	860.6	823.9
Forestry	1131, 1132	16.8	18.0
Logging	1133	82.0	100.2
Fishing, hunting, and trapping	114	47.0	47.1
Support activities for agriculture and forestry	115	141.3	150.1
Nonagriculture self-employed and unpaid family worker [4]		9,312.6	9,943.1
Secondary wage and salary jobs in agriculture and private household industries [5]		181.7	191.6
Secondary jobs as a self-employed or unpaid family worker [6]		1,524.3	1,607.3

Source: Employment Projections Program, U.S. Department of Labor, U.S. Bureau of Labor Statistics. Accessed February, 2011. Available at http://www.bls.gov/emp/ep_table_207.htm.

— Dash indicates data not available.

NA = not applicable

n.e.c. = not elsewhere classified.

1. Employment data for wage and salary workers are from the U.S. Bureau of Labor Statistics' *Current Employment Statistics* survey, which counts jobs, whereas self-employed, unpaid family workers, and agriculture, forestry, fishing, and hunting are from the *Current Population Survey* (household survey), which counts workers.

2. Output subcategories do not necessarily add to higher categories as a by-product of chain-weighting.

3. Includes agriculture, forestry, fishing, and hunting wage and salary, self-employed, and unpaid family workers. Data from the *Current Population Survey*, except logging, which is from *Current Employment Statistics* survey. Government wage and salary workers are excluded.

4. Comparable estimate of output growth is not available.

5. Workers who hold a secondary wage and salary job in agricultural production, forestry, fishing, and private household industries.

6. Wage and salary workers who hold a secondary job as a self-employed or unpaid family worker.

Fortune 500 Companies by Industry, 2009

The following data are aggregated from CNN.Money.com, Fortune 500, http://money.cnn.com/magazines/fortune/fortune500/2010/industries/140/index.html. Revenues are rendered in millions of dollars. Employees are in real numbers, for the year 2009.

Advertising, Marketing

Rank	Company	F500 Rank	Revenues	Employees
1	Omnicom Group	198	11,720.7	63,000
2	Interpublic Group	358	6,027.6	40,000

Aerospace and Defense

Rank	Company	F500 Rank	Revenues	Employees
1	Boeing	28	68,281.0	157,100
2	United Technologies	37	52,920.0	206,700
3	Lockheed Martin	44	45,189.0	140,000
4	Northrop Grumman	61	35,291.0	120,700
5	General Dynamics	69	31,981.0	91,700
6	Honeywell International	74	30,908.0	122,000
7	Raytheon	95	24,881.0	75,000
8	L-3 Communications	148	15,615.0	67,000
9	ITT	214	10,904.5	40,200
10	Textron	220	10,548.0	32,000
11	Precision Castparts	325	6,913.8	20,600
12	Goodrich	334	6,685.6	24,000
13	Alliant Techsystems	454	4,583.2	19,000
14	Rockwell Collins	462	4,470.0	19,300

Airlines

Rank	Company	F500 Rank	Revenues	Employees
1	Delta Air Lines	84	28,063.0	81,106
2	AMR	120	19,917.0	78,900
3	UAL	140	16,335.0	47,000
4	Continental Airlines	183	12,586.0	39,640
5	US Airways Group	222	10,458.0	31,300
6	Southwest Airlines	229	10,350.0	34,726

Apparel

Rank	Company	F500 Rank	Revenues	Employees
1	Nike	124	19,176.1	34,300
2	VF	310	7,220.3	45,700
3	Polo Ralph Lauren	417	5,018.9	17,000

Automotive Retailing, Services

Rank	Company	F500 Rank	Revenues	Employees
1	AutoNation	212	11,015.6	18,000
2	Penske Automotive Group	245	9,558.1	13,950
3	Hertz Global Holdings	318	7,101.5	23,050
4	CarMax	323	7,028.3	13,035
5	Sonic Automotive	345	6,349.7	9,200
6	Avis Budget Group	409	5,131.0	18,700
7	Group 1 Automotive	457	4,525.7	6,990

Beverages

Rank	Company	F500 Rank	Revenues	Employees
1	Coca-Cola	72	30,990.0	92,800
2	Coca-Cola Enterprises	113	21,645.0	70,000
3	Pepsi Bottling	174	13,219.0	64,900
4	Dr Pepper Snapple Group	378	5,531.0	19,000
5	PepsiAmericas	464	4,421.3	18,700

Chemicals

Rank	Company	F500 Rank	Revenues	Employees
1	Dow Chemical	46	44,945.0	52,195
2	DuPont	86	27,328.0	58,000
3	PPG Industries	190	12,239.0	38,500
4	Monsanto	197	11,740.0	24,950
5	Mosaic	231	10,298.0	7,500
6	Praxair	262	8,956.0	26,164
7	Air Products & Chemicals	273	8,381.4	18,650
8	Ashland	280	8,106.0	14,700
9	Huntsman	293	7,763.0	11,000
10	Sherwin-Williams	319	7,094.2	29,220
11	Avery Dennison	362	5,952.7	31,300
12	Ecolab	365	5,900.6	25,930
13	Celanese	414	5,082.0	7,400
14	Eastman Chemical	415	5,047.0	10,000
15	Lubrizol	453	4,586.3	6,700

Commercial Banks

Rank	Company	F500 Rank	Revenues	Employees
1	Bank of America Corp.	5	150,450.0	283,717
2	JPMorgan Chase & Co.	9	115,632.0	222,316
3	Citigroup	12	108,785.0	267,150
4	Wells Fargo	19	98,636.0	267,300
5	Goldman Sachs Group	39	51,673.0	36,200
6	Morgan Stanley	70	31,515.0	61,388
7	American Express	88	26,730.0	58,300
8	U.S. Bancorp	121	19,490.0	58,229

Rank	Company	F500 Rank	Revenues	Employees
9	GMAC	122	19,403.0	18,800
10	PNC Financial Services Group	123	19,231.0	52,791
11	Capital One Financial	144	15,980.1	28,000
12	BB&T Corp.	217	10,818.0	32,394
13	SunTrust Banks	224	10,420.0	28,001
14	Fifth Third Bancorp	248	9,450.0	20,998
15	State Street Corp.	249	9,362.0	27,310
16	Regions Financial	254	9,087.1	28,509
17	Bank of New York Mellon Corp.	274	8,345.0	42,200
18	Discover Financial Services	286	7,985.7	10,500
19	KeyCorp	356	6,068.0	16,698
20	Northern Trust Corp.	497	4,193.1	12,400

Computer Peripherals

Rank	Company	F500 Rank	Revenues	Employees
1	EMC	166	14,025.9	43,200
2	Western Digital	304	7,453.0	45,991

Computer Software

Rank	Company	F500 Rank	Revenues	Employees
1	Microsoft	36	58,437.0	93,000
2	Oracle	105	23,252.0	86,000
3	Symantec	353	6,149.9	17,400
4	CA	482	4,271.0	13,200
5	Electronic Arts	494	4,212.0	9,100

Computers, Office Equipment

Rank	Company	F500 Rank	Revenues	Employees
1	Hewlett-Packard	10	114,552.0	304,000
2	Dell	38	52,902.0	95,150
3	Apple	56	36,537.0	36,800
4	Xerox	152	15,179.0	53,600
5	Sun Microsystems	204	11,449.0	29,000
6	Pitney Bowes	375	5,569.2	33,004
7	NCR	451	4,612.0	21,500

Construction and Farm Machinery

Rank	Company	F500 Rank	Revenues	Employees
1	Caterpillar	66	32,396.0	93,813
2	Deere	107	23,112.4	51,262
3	Cummins	218	10,800.0	34,900
4	AGCO	337	6,630.4	14,500
5	Terex	402	5,205.0	15,900

Diversified Financials

Rank	Company	F500 Rank	Revenues	Employees
1	General Electric	4	156,779.0	304,000
2	International Assets Holding	49	43,604.4	625
3	Freddie Mac	54	37,614.0	5,366
4	Fannie Mae	81	29,065.0	6,000
5	Marsh & McLennan	221	10,493.0	52,000
6	Ameriprise Financial	288	7,946.0	9,793
7	Aon	298	7,595.0	36,200
8	SLM	354	6,144.7	8,000
9	H&R Block	493	4,213.4	71,000

Diversified Outsourcing Services

Rank	Company	F500 Rank	Revenues	Employees
1	Aramark	189	12,297.9	210,000
2	Automatic Data Processing	265	8,867.1	45,000

Electronics, Electrical Equipment

Rank	Company	F500 Rank	Revenues	Employees
1	Emerson Electric	117	20,915.0	129,000
2	Whirlpool	136	17,099.0	66,884
3	General Cable	469	4,385.2	11,300
4	Rockwell Automation	476	4,332.5	19,000

Energy

Rank	Company	F500 Rank	Revenues	Employees
1	Constellation Energy	149	15,598.8	7,200
2	AES	156	14,690.0	27,000
3	American Electric Power	172	13,489.0	21,673
4	Energy Future Holdings	246	9,546.0	9,030
5	NRG Energy	263	8,952.0	4,607
6	Williams	276	8,255.0	4,801
7	Integrys Energy Group	302	7,499.8	5,025
8	Calpine	338	6,564.0	2,046
9	Global Partners	368	5,818.4	250
10	UGI	369	5,737.8	9,700

Engineering, Construction

Rank	Company	F500 Rank	Revenues	Employees
1	Fluor	111	21,990.3	36,152
2	KBR	193	12,105.0	51,000
3	Jacobs Engineering Group	203	11,467.4	46,050
4	Peter Kiewit Sons'	238	9,985.0	25,900
5	URS	252	9,249.1	41,700
6	Shaw Group	309	7,279.7	28,000

Rank	Company	F500 Rank	Revenues	Employees
7	AECOM Technology	352	6,192.4	43,200
8	Emcor Group	377	5,547.9	25,000
9	CH2M Hill	381	5,499.3	23,500
10	Tutor Perini	407	5,152.0	4,072

Entertainment

Rank	Company	F500 Rank	Revenues	Employees
1	Walt Disney	57	36,149.0	144,000
2	News Corp.	76	30,423.0	55,000
3	Time Warner	82	28,842.0	31,000
4	Viacom	170	13,619.0	11,200
5	CBS	177	13,014.6	25,580
6	CC Media Holdings	376	5,551.9	19,295
7	Live Nation Entertainment	490	4,232.0	4,300

Financial Data Services

Rank	Company	F500 Rank	Revenues	Employees
1	First Data	250	9,313.8	24,402
2	Visa	326	6,911.0	5,700
3	SunGard Data Systems	380	5,508.0	20,700
4	MasterCard	411	5,098.7	5,100
5	Western Union	413	5,083.6	6,800
6	Fiserv	491	4,224.0	20,000

Food and Drug Stores

Rank	Company	F500 Rank	Revenues	Employees
1	CVS Caremark	18	98,729.0	169,000
2	Kroger	23	76,733.2	334,000
3	Walgreen	32	63,335.0	202,000
4	Supervalu	47	44,564.0	178,000
5	Safeway	52	40,850.7	186,000
6	Rite Aid	89	26,289.5	80,340
7	Publix Super Markets	99	24,515.0	105,500
8	Great Atlantic & Pacific Tea	247	9,516.2	31,680
9	Whole Foods Market	284	8,031.6	47,750
10	Winn-Dixie Stores	306	7,367.0	36,500

Food Consumer Products

Rank	Company	F500 Rank	Revenues	Employees
1	PepsiCo	50	43,232.0	203,000
2	Kraft Foods	53	40,386.0	97,000
3	General Mills	155	14,691.3	30,000
4	ConAgra Foods	178	12,980.8	25,600
5	Sara Lee	180	12,881.0	41,000

Rank	Company	F500 Rank	Revenues	Employees
6	Kellogg	184	12,575.0	30,949
7	Dean Foods	208	11,158.4	27,157
8	Land O'Lakes	226	10,408.5	9,000
9	H. J. Heinz	233	10,148.1	32,400
10	Campbell Soup	299	7,586.0	18,700
11	Dole Food	331	6,782.7	57,350
12	Hormel Foods	340	6,533.7	18,600
13	Hershey	395	5,298.7	12,900

Food Production

Rank	Company	F500 Rank	Revenues	Employees
1	Archer Daniels Midland	27	69,207.0	28,200
2	Tyson Foods	87	27,165.0	117,000
3	Smithfield Foods	163	14,190.5	52,400
4	Pilgrim's Pride	317	7,113.8	41,240

Food Services

Rank	Company	F500 Rank	Revenues	Employees
1	McDonald's	108	22,744.7	385,000
2	Yum Brands	216	10,836.0	199,500
3	Starbucks	241	9,774.6	142,000
4	Darden Restaurants	311	7,217.5	179,000

Forest and Paper Products

Rank	Company	F500 Rank	Revenues	Employees
1	International Paper	104	23,366.0	56,100
2	Weyerhaeuser	379	5,528.0	14,900
3	Domtar	383	5,465.0	10,000
4	AbitibiBowater	472	4,366.0	12,100

General Merchandisers

Rank	Company	F500 Rank	Revenues	Employees
1	Wal-Mart Stores	1	408,214.0	2,100,000
2	Target	30	65,357.0	351,000
3	Sears Holdings	48	44,043.0	322,000
4	Macy's	103	23,489.0	161,300
5	JCPenney	133	17,556.0	154,000
6	Kohl's	135	17,178.0	81,000
7	Dollar General	195	11,796.4	79,800
8	Nordstrom	270	8,627.0	48,000
9	Family Dollar Stores	305	7,400.6	37,000
10	Dillard's	348	6,226.6	35,312

Health Care: Insurance and Managed Care

Rank	Company	F500 Rank	Revenues	Employees
1	UnitedHealth Group	21	87,138.0	80,000
2	WellPoint	31	65,028.1	40,500
3	Aetna	63	34,764.1	35,000
4	Humana	73	30,960.4	28,100
5	Cigna	129	18,414.0	29,300
6	Health Net	146	15,713.2	8,821
7	Coventry Health Care	168	13,993.3	14,400
8	WellCare Health Plans	328	6,878.2	3,419
9	Amerigroup	404	5,188.1	4,000
10	Universal American	425	4,963.5	2,200
11	Centene	486	4,248.0	3,900

Health Care: Medical Facilities

Rank	Company	F500 Rank	Revenues	Employees
1	Community Health Systems	191	12,149.7	68,885
2	Tenet Healthcare	253	9,215.0	50,411
3	DaVita	355	6,108.8	34,000
4	Universal Health Services	403	5,202.4	34,000
5	Health Management Associates	443	4,687.3	30,100
6	Kindred Healthcare	477	4,326.3	46,800

Health Care: Pharmacy and Other Services

Rank	Company	F500 Rank	Revenues	Employees
1	Medco Health Solutions	35	59,804.2	22,375
2	HCA	77	30,052.0	165,500
3	Express Scripts	96	24,748.9	14,270
4	Quest Diagnostics	303	7,455.2	43,000
5	Omnicare	347	6,242.7	14,450
6	Laboratory Corp. of America	442	4,694.7	28,000

Home Equipment, Furnishings

Rank	Company	F500 Rank	Revenues	Employees
1	Masco	291	7,858.0	35,400
2	Fortune Brands	351	6,205.4	24,248
3	Newell Rubbermaid	373	5,577.6	19,500
4	Jarden	406	5,152.6	20,000
5	Black & Decker	435	4,775.1	19,900

Hotels, Casinos, Resorts

Rank	Company	F500 Rank	Revenues	Employees
1	Marriott International	213	10,908.0	137,000
2	Harrah's Entertainment	264	8,907.4	69,000
3	MGM Mirage	360	5,978.6	54,000

Rank	Company	F500 Rank	Revenues	Employees
4	Starwood Hotels & Resorts	438	4,712.0	145,000
5	Las Vegas Sands	456	4,563.1	27,000
6	Host Hotels & Resorts	492	4,216.0	186

Household and Personal Products

Rank	Company	F500 Rank	Revenues	Employees
1	Procter & Gamble	22	79,697.0	135,000
2	Kimberly-Clark	126	19,115.0	56,000
3	Colgate-Palmolive	151	15,327.0	38,100
4	Avon Products	228	10,382.8	41,000
5	Estée Lauder	308	7,323.8	31,300
6	Clorox	384	5,450.0	8,300

Industrial Machinery

Rank	Company	F500 Rank	Revenues	Employees
1	Illinois Tool Works	169	13,903.6	59,000
2	Eaton	194	11,873.0	70,000
3	Parker Hannifin	230	10,309.0	51,639
4	Dover	367	5,831.0	29,300
5	SPX	427	4,935.9	15,000
6	Flowserve	473	4,365.3	15,000

Information Technology Services

Rank	Company	F500 Rank	Revenues	Employees
1	International Business Machines	20	95,758.0	399,409
2	Computer Sciences	138	16,739.9	92,000
3	SAIC	215	10,847.0	46,200
4	Affiliated Computer Services	341	6,523.2	74,000
5	Unisys	452	4,597.7	25,600

Insurance: Life, Health (mutual)

Rank	Company	F500 Rank	Revenues	Employees
1	New York Life Insurance	64	34,014.3	16,835
2	TIAA-CREF	90	26,278.0	6,890
3	Massachusetts Mutual Life Insurance	93	25,423.6	11,000
4	Northwestern Mutual	115	21,602.6	4,783
5	Guardian Life Ins. Co. of America	237	10,040.9	4,870
6	Thrivent Financial for Lutherans	342	6,514.8	3,010
7	Mutual of Omaha Insurance	408	5,149.6	5,067
8	Western & Southern Financial Group	420	5,014.4	2,275

Insurance: Life, Health (stock)

Rank	Company	F500 Rank	Revenues	Employees
1	MetLife	51	41,098.0	54,000
2	Prudential Financial	65	32,688.0	41,943
3	AFLAC	130	18,254.4	8,057
4	Unum Group	235	10,091.0	9,700
5	Lincoln National	256	9,071.8	9,539
6	Genworth Financial	257	9,069.0	6,000
7	Principal Financial	266	8,849.1	14,487
8	Reinsurance Group of America	321	7,066.8	1,367
9	Pacific Life	401	5,211.0	2,715
10	Conseco	475	4,341.4	3,500

Insurance: Property and Casualty (mutual)

Rank	Company	F500 Rank	Revenues	Employees
1	State Farm Insurance Cos.	34	61,479.6	67,500
2	Auto-Owners Insurance	418	5,017.1	3,627

Insurance: Property and Casualty (stock)

Rank	Company	F500 Rank	Revenues	Employees
1	Berkshire Hathaway	11	112,493.0	222,000
2	American International Group	16	103,189.0	96,000
3	Allstate	68	32,013.0	36,400
4	Liberty Mutual Insurance Group	71	31,094.0	45,000
5	Hartford Financial Services	97	24,701.0	28,000
6	Travelers Cos.	98	24,680.0	32,000
7	Nationwide	118	20,751.0	32,881
8	United Services Automobile Association	132	17,557.6	21,695
9	Progressive	161	14,563.6	24,661
10	Loews	165	14,123.0	18,500
11	Chubb	176	13,016.0	10,200
12	Assurant	268	8,700.5	14,709
13	American Family Insurance Group	344	6,453.4	7,745
14	First American Corp.	361	5,972.8	30,922
15	Fidelity National Financial	366	5,857.7	17,200
16	W.R. Berkley	463	4,431.2	6,072
17	American Financial Group	478	4,320.6	7,100
18	Erie Insurance Group	484	4,255.4	4,200

Internet Services and Retailing

Rank	Company	F500 Rank	Revenues	Employees
1	Amazon.com	100	24,509.0	24,300
2	Google	102	23,650.6	19,835
3	Liberty Media	227	10,398.0	23,073
4	eBay	267	8,727.4	16,400
5	Yahoo!	343	6,460.3	13,900

Mail, Package, and Freight Delivery

Rank	Company	F500 Rank	Revenues	Employees
1	United Parcel Service	43	45,297.0	408,000
2	FedEx	60	35,497.0	247,908

Medical Products and Equipment

Rank	Company	F500 Rank	Revenues	Employees
1	Medtronic	160	14,599.0	41,000
2	Baxter International	185	12,562.0	49,700
3	Boston Scientific	279	8,188.0	26,000
4	Becton Dickinson	312	7,216.7	29,116
5	Stryker	333	6,723.1	18,582
6	St. Jude Medical	445	4,681.3	14,000

Metals

Rank	Company	F500 Rank	Revenues	Employees
1	Alcoa	127	18,745.0	59,000
2	Nucor	206	11,190.3	20,400
3	United States Steel	211	11,048.0	43,000
4	Commercial Metals	327	6,883.4	13,586

Mining, Crude-Oil Production

Rank	Company	F500 Rank	Revenues	Employees
1	Occidental Petroleum	150	15,531.0	10,100
2	Freeport-McMoRan Copper & Gold	154	15,040.0	28,400
3	XTO Energy	258	9,064.0	3,335
4	Anadarko Petroleum	260	9,000.0	4,300
5	Devon Energy	261	8,960.0	5,500
6	Apache	271	8,614.8	3,452
7	Newmont Mining	295	7,737.0	14,500
8	Chesapeake Energy	296	7,701.9	8,300
9	Peabody Energy	346	6,313.9	7,300
10	EOG Resources	434	4,787.0	2,100
11	Consol Energy	449	4,621.9	8,012
12	MDU Resources Group	498	4,176.5	8,081

Motor Vehicles and Parts

Rank	Company	F500 Rank	Revenues	Employees
1	Ford Motor	8	118,308.0	198,000
2	General Motors	15	104,589.0	217,000
3	Johnson Controls	83	28,497.0	130,000
4	Goodyear Tire & Rubber	141	16,301.0	69,000
5	TRW Automotive Holdings	201	11,614.0	60,550
6	Navistar International	202	11,569.0	15,100
7	Lear	242	9,739.6	74,870

Rank	Company	F500 Rank	Revenues	Employees
8	Paccar	282	8,086.5	15,200
9	Icahn Enterprises	290	7,865.0	42,368
10	Visteon	335	6,685.0	29,500
11	Oshkosh	386	5,433.3	12,300
12	Dana Holding	398	5,228.0	24,000
13	Autoliv	410	5,120.7	34,053
14	Tenneco	446	4,649.0	21,000
15	ArvinMeritor	450	4,617.0	13,200

Network and Other Communications Equipment

Rank	Company	F500 Rank	Revenues	Employees
1	Cisco Systems	58	36,117.0	65,550
2	Motorola	110	22,063.0	53,000
3	Qualcomm	225	10,416.0	16,100
4	Harris	371	5,599.6	15,400
5	Corning	391	5,395.0	23,500

Oil and Gas Equipment, Services

Rank	Company	F500 Rank	Revenues	Employees
1	Halliburton	158	14,675.0	51,000
2	National Oilwell Varco	182	12,712.0	34,613
3	Baker Hughes	243	9,664.0	34,400
4	Smith International	277	8,218.6	21,931
5	Cameron International	399	5,223.2	18,100
6	FMC Technologies	467	4,405.4	10,400

Packaging, Containers

Rank	Company	F500 Rank	Revenues	Employees
1	Crown Holdings	289	7,938.0	20,510
2	Ball	307	7,345.3	14,500
3	Owens-Illinois	322	7,066.5	22,000
4	MeadWestvaco	357	6,049.0	20,000
5	Smurfit-Stone Container	374	5,574.0	19,000
6	Sealed Air	487	4,242.8	16,200

Petroleum Refining

Rank	Company	F500 Rank	Revenues	Employees
1	Exxon Mobil	2	284,650.0	102,700
2	Chevron	3	163,527.0	64,132
3	ConocoPhillips	6	139,515.0	30,000
4	Valero Energy	26	70,035.0	20,920
5	Marathon Oil	41	49,403.0	28,855
6	Sunoco	78	29,630.0	11,200
7	Hess	79	29,569.0	13,300

Rank	Company	F500 Rank	Revenues	Employees
8	Murphy Oil	125	19,138.0	5,815
9	Tesoro	139	16,589.0	5,500
10	Western Refining	330	6,807.4	3,300
11	Holly	431	4,834.3	1,632
12	Frontier Oil	488	4,237.2	843

Pharmaceuticals

Rank	Company	F500 Rank	Revenues	Employees
1	Johnson & Johnson	33	61,897.0	115,500
2	Pfizer	40	50,009.0	116,500
3	Abbott Laboratories	75	30,764.7	72,868
4	Merck	85	27,428.3	100,000
5	Eli Lilly	112	21,836.0	40,360
6	Bristol-Myers Squibb	114	21,634.0	28,000
7	Amgen	159	14,642.0	17,100
8	Gilead Sciences	324	7,011.4	3,874
9	Mylan	412	5,092.8	14,000
10	Genzyme	458	4,515.5	12,000
11	Allergan	459	4,503.6	8,300
12	Biogen Idec	471	4,377.3	4,750

Pipelines

Rank	Company	F500 Rank	Revenues	Employees
1	Enterprise GP Holdings	92	25,510.9	4,800
2	Plains All American Pipeline	128	18,520.0	3,400
3	Oneok	209	11,111.7	4,758
4	Kinder Morgan	315	7,185.2	7,931
5	Enbridge Energy Partners	364	5,905.4	2,000
6	Energy Transfer Equity	388	5,417.3	5,581
7	Spectra Energy	437	4,725.0	5,400
8	El Paso	447	4,631.0	4,991

Publishing, Printing

Rank	Company	F500 Rank	Revenues	Employees
1	R. R. Donnelley & Sons	240	9,857.4	56,800
2	McGraw-Hill	363	5,951.8	21,077
3	Gannett	370	5,613.0	35,000

Railroads

Rank	Company	F500 Rank	Revenues	Employees
1	Union Pacific	164	14,143.0	43,531
2	Burlington Northern Santa Fe	167	14,016.0	37,363
3	CSX	259	9,041.0	30,088
4	Norfolk Southern	287	7,969.0	28,593

Scientific, Photographic, and Control Equipment

Rank	Company	F500 Rank	Revenues	Employees
1	Danaher	207	11,184.9	46,600
2	Thermo Fisher Scientific	234	10,109.7	35,400
3	Eastman Kodak	297	7,606.0	20,250
4	Agilent Technologies	461	4,481.0	16,800

Securities

Rank	Company	F500 Rank	Revenues	Employees
1	BlackRock	441	4,699.3	8,629
2	NYSE Euronext	444	4,687.0	3,367
3	Charles Schwab	465	4,414.0	12,400
4	Franklin Resources	495	4,194.1	7,700

Semiconductors and Other Electronic Components

Rank	Company	F500 Rank	Revenues	Employees
1	Intel	62	35,127.0	79,800
2	Jabil Circuit	199	11,684.5	61,000
3	Texas Instruments	223	10,427.0	26,584
4	Advanced Micro Devices	390	5,403.0	13,395
5	Sanmina-SCI	405	5,177.5	35,150
6	Applied Materials	421	5,013.6	12,826
7	Micron Technology	432	4,803.0	18,200
8	Broadcom	460	4,490.3	7,407

Specialty Retailers

Rank	Company	F500 Rank	Revenues	Employees
1	Costco Wholesale	25	71,422.0	110,500
2	Home Depot	29	66,176.0	255,185
3	Lowe's	42	47,220.0	202,500
4	Best Buy	45	45,015.0	155,000
5	Staples	101	24,275.5	72,622
6	TJX	119	20,288.4	154,000
7	Gap	162	14,197.0	135,000
8	Toys "R" Us	171	13,568.0	67,425
9	Office Depot	192	12,144.5	41,000
10	BJ's Wholesale Club	232	10,187.0	23,500
11	GameStop	255	9,078.0	32,081
12	Limited Brands	269	8,632.5	54,600
13	OfficeMax	313	7,212.1	25,500
14	Bed Bath & Beyond	314	7,208.3	37,000
15	Ross Stores	316	7,184.2	29,450
16	AutoZone	329	6,816.8	47,100
17	Barnes & Noble	372	5,596.3	37,000
18	Pantry	382	5,472.0	11,052
19	Advance Auto Parts	389	5,412.6	39,000

Rank	Company	F500 Rank	Revenues	Employees
20	PetSmart	393	5,336.4	33,500
21	Dollar Tree	397	5,231.2	33,480
22	Foot Locker	428	4,854.0	26,018
23	O'Reilly Automotive	429	4,847.1	37,601
24	Big Lots	436	4,726.8	24,350
25	TravelCenters of America	440	4,699.8	14,680
26	Dick's Sporting Goods	466	4,412.8	17,700
27	RadioShack	481	4,276.0	35,750
28	Casey's General Stores	485	4,251.5	13,260
29	Blockbuster	500	4,161.8	36,500

Telecommunications

Rank	Company	F500 Rank	Revenues	Employees
1	AT&T	7	123,018.0	282,720
2	Verizon Communications	13	107,808.0	222,927
3	Comcast	59	35,756.0	107,000
4	Sprint Nextel	67	32,260.0	40,000
5	DirecTV Group	116	21,565.0	22,550
6	Time Warner Cable	131	17,868.0	46,300
7	Qwest Communications	188	12,311.0	30,138
8	DISH Network	200	11,664.2	24,500
9	Liberty Global	210	11,110.4	23,000
10	Cablevision Systems	292	7,773.3	22,368
11	Charter Communications	332	6,755.0	16,700
12	Virgin Media	359	6,013.6	12,201
13	Telephone & Data Systems	416	5,020.7	12,400
14	CenturyTel	423	4,974.2	20,200
15	NII Holdings	468	4,397.6	13,673

Temporary Help

Rank	Company	F500 Rank	Revenues	Employees
1	Manpower	143	16,038.7	28,000
2	Kelly Services	479	4,314.8	7,900

Tobacco

Rank	Company	F500 Rank	Revenues	Employees
1	Philip Morris International	94	25,035.0	77,300
2	Altria Group	137	16,824.0	10,000
3	Reynolds American	272	8,419.0	6,475

Transportation and Logistics

Rank	Company	F500 Rank	Revenues	Employees
1	C. H. Robinson Worldwide	301	7,577.2	7,347
2	Con-way	483	4,269.2	27,454

Trucking, Truck Leasing

Rank	Company	F500 Rank	Revenues	Employees
1	YRC Worldwide	396	5,282.8	36,000
2	Ryder System	426	4,957.6	22,900

Utilities: Gas and Electric

Rank	Company	F500 Rank	Revenues	Employees
1	Exelon	134	17,318.0	19,329
2	Southern	145	15,743.0	26,112
3	FPL Group	147	15,643.0	15,400
4	Dominion Resources	153	15,131.0	17,900
5	PG&E Corp.	173	13,399.0	19,425
6	Consolidated Edison	175	13,031.6	15,534
7	FirstEnergy	179	12,967.0	13,379
8	Duke Energy	181	12,731.0	18,680
9	Public Service Enterprise Group	186	12,406.0	10,352
10	Edison International	187	12,361.0	19,244
11	Entergy	219	10,745.7	15,181
12	Progress Energy	239	9,885.0	11,000
13	Xcel Energy	244	9,644.3	11,351
14	Pepco Holdings	251	9,259.0	5,110
15	CenterPoint Energy	275	8,281.0	8,810
16	Sempra Energy	280	8,106.0	13,839
17	DTE Energy	285	8,014.0	10,244
18	PPL	300	7,585.0	10,489
19	Ameren	320	7,090.0	9,780
20	NiSource	336	6,652.9	7,616
21	CMS Energy	350	6,212.0	8,039
22	Northeast Utilities	385	5,439.4	6,078
23	Atmos Energy	424	4,969.1	4,691
24	Scana	489	4,237.0	5,828
25	Wisconsin Energy	496	4,193.2	4,692

Waste Management

Rank	Company	F500 Rank	Revenues	Employees
1	Waste Management	196	11,791.0	43,400
2	Republic Services	278	8,199.1	31,000

Wholesalers: Diversified

Rank	Company	F500 Rank	Revenues	Employees
1	World Fuel Services	205	11,295.2	1,249
2	Genuine Parts	236	10,057.5	29,000
3	W. W. Grainger	349	6,222.0	17,250
4	Reliance Steel & Aluminum	394	5,318.1	8,870
5	Anixter International	422	4,982.4	7,811
6	Wesco International	448	4,624.0	6,100

Rank	Company	F500 Rank	Revenues	Employees
7	Graybar Electric	470	4,377.9	6,900
8	Airgas	474	4,349.5	14,000

Wholesalers: Electronics and Office Equipment

Rank	Company	F500 Rank	Revenues	Employees
1	Ingram Micro	80	29,515.4	13,750
2	Tech Data	109	22,099.9	7,628
3	Avnet	142	16,229.9	12,900
4	Arrow Electronics	157	14,684.1	11,300
5	Synnex	294	7,756.3	7,320
6	United Stationers	439	4,710.3	5,700

Wholesalers: Food and Grocery

Rank	Company	F500 Rank	Revenues	Employees
1	Sysco	55	36,853.3	47,000
2	CHS	91	25,729.9	8,211
3	Nash-Finch	400	5,212.7	6,297
4	Core-Mark Holding	419	5,015.6	4,267

Wholesalers: Health Care

Rank	Company	F500 Rank	Revenues	Employees
1	McKesson	14	106,632.0	32,500
2	Cardinal Health	17	99,612.9	46,500
3	AmerisourceBergen	24	71,789.0	9,700
4	Owens & Minor	283	8,037.6	4,800
5	Henry Schein	339	6,546.3	12,500

Miscellaneous

Rank	Company	F500 Rank	Revenues	Employees
1	3M	106	23,123.0	74,835
2	Mattel	387	5,430.8	27,000
3	Mohawk Industries	392	5,344.0	27,400
4	Harley-Davidson	430	4,838.6	7,900
5	Owens Corning	432	4,803.0	16,000
6	Washington Post	455	4,569.7	21,500
7	Spectrum Group International	480	4,293.3	142
8	CB Richard Ellis Group	499	4,165.8	29,000

Bibliography

The following electronic resources—both general and targeted by industry—will assist students and other career seekers in assessing the industry as a focal point of a career or job hunt.

GENERAL REFERENCE

Brock, James, ed. *The Structure of American Industry.* 12th ed. Upper Saddle River, N.J.: Pearson/Prentice Hall, 2009.

Career Information Center. 9th ed. New York: Macmillan Reference USA, 2006.

Duetsch, Larry L., ed. *Industry Studies.* 3d ed. Armonk, N.Y.: M. E. Sharpe, 2002.

Encyclopedia of American Industries. 5th ed. 2 vols. Millerton, N.Y.: Grey House, 2008.

Encyclopedia of Careers and Vocational Guidance. 15th ed. 5 vols. New York: Ferguson, 2010.

Encyclopedia of Emerging Industries. Armenia, N.Y.: Grey House, 2007.

Executive Office of the President. Office of Management and Budget. *North American Industry Classification System: United States, 2007.* Springfield, Va.: National Technical Information Service, U.S. Department of Commerce. 2007.

_____. *Standard Occupational Classification Manual.* 2010 ed. Alexandria, Va.: National Technical Information Service, U.S. Department of Commerce, 2010.

Farr, Michael. *One Hundred Fastest-Growing Careers: Your Complete Guidebook to Major Jobs with the Most Growth and Openings.* 11th ed. St. Paul, Minn.: JIST, 2010.

O*NET Dictionary of Occupational Titles. 4th ed. St. Paul, Minn.: JIST, 2007.

Salary Facts Handbook: The Definitive Source of Pay Information on Eight Hundred Jobs. St. Paul, Minn.: JIST, 2008.

2011 U.S. Industry and Market Outlook. Woolwich, Maine: Barnes Reports, 2010.

U.S. Department of Labor. Bureau of Labor Statistics. *The Big Book of Jobs.* 2009-2010 ed. New York: McGraw-Hill, 2010.

_____. *Occupational Outlook Handbook, 2010-2011: With Bonus Content.* St. Paul, Minn.: JIST, 2010.

Van Horn, Carl E., and Herbert A. Schaffner, eds. *Work in America: An Encyclopedia of History, Policy, and Society.* 2 vols. Santa Barbara, Calif.: ABC-CLIO, 2003.

Wilson, Richard L., ed. *Historical Encyclopedia of American Business.* 3 vols. Pasadena, Calif.: Salem Press, 2009.

Zielinski, Jennifer, ed. *Dun & Bradstreet/Gale Group Industry Handbook.* 5 vols. Detroit: Gale Group, 2000.

ACCOUNTING SERVICES

Albrecht, W. Steve, and Chad O. Albrecht. *Fraud Examination.* Cincinnati: Thomson South-Western, 2003.

Flesher, Dale L. *The IIA: Fifty Years of Progress Through Sharing.* Altamonte Springs, Calif.: Institute of Internal Auditors, 1991.

_____. *One Hundred Years of NASBA: Serving the Public Interest.* Nashville, Tenn.: National Association of State Boards of Accountancy, 2007.

Flesher, Dale L., and Tonya K. Flesher. *Accounting for the Middle Manager.* Albany, N.Y.: Van Nostrand Reinhold, 1979.

Gleim, Irvin N. *CPA Review.* 4 vols. Gainesville, Fla.: Gleim, 2010.

Gleim, Irvin N., and Dale L. Flesher. *CMA Review Part 1: Financial Planning, Performance, and Control.* 15th ed. Gainesville, Fla.: Gleim, 2010.

King, Thomas A. *More than a Numbers Game: A Brief History of Accounting.* New York: John Wiley & Sons, 2006.

Melancon, Barry. "Trends for CPAs in 2010." *New Accountant* 736 (March/April, 2010): 5ff.

Miranti, Paul J., Jr. *Accountancy Comes of Age: The Development of an American Profession, 1886-1940.* Chapel Hill: University of North Carolina Press, 1990.

Olson, Wallace E. *The Accounting Profession: Years of Trial, 1969-1980.* New York: American Institute of Certified Public Accountants, 1982.

Previts, Gary John, and Barbara Dubis Merino. *A History of Accountancy in the United States: The Cultural Significance of Accounting.* Columbus: Ohio State University Press, 1998.

Roehl-Anderson, Janice M., and Steven M. Bragg. *The Controller's Function: The Work of the Managerial Accountant.* 2d ed. New York: John Wiley & Sons, 2000.

U.S. Bureau of Labor Statistics. *Career Guide to Industries,* 2010-2011 ed. http://www.bls.gov/oco/cg.

U.S. Census Bureau. North American Industry Classification System (NAICS), 2007. http://www.census.gov/cgi-bin/sssd/naics/naicsrch?chart=2007.

U.S. Department of Commerce. International Trade Administration. Office of Trade and Industry Information. Industry Trade Data and Analysis. http://ita.doc.gov/td/industry/otea/OTII/OTII-index.html.

ADVERTISING AND MARKETING INDUSTRY

Berners-Lee, Tim, James Hendler, and Ora Lassila. "The Semantic Web." *Scientific American,* May, 2001.

Cappo, Joe. *The Future of Advertising: New Media, New Clients, New Consumers in the Post-television Age.* New York: Crain Communications, 2003.

Holme, Bryan. *Advertising: Reflections of a Century.* New York: Viking Press, 1982.

Lears, Jackson. *Fables of Abundance: A Cultural History of Advertising in America.* New York: Basic Books, 1994.

Luft, Oliver. "Advertising Boss: Print Will Struggle to Recover After Recession." *The Guardian,* May 5, 2009. http://www.guardian.co.uk/media/2009/may/05/maurice-levy-publicis-groupe.

Mackay, Adrian, ed. *The Practice of Advertising.* 5th ed. Oxford, England: Elsevier Butterworth-Heinemann, 2005.

Norris, James D. *Advertising and the Transformation of American Society, 1865-1920.* Westport, Conn.: Greenwood Press, 1990.

Pattis, S. William. *Careers in Advertising.* 3d ed. Chicago: VGM Career Books, 2004.

Scott, David Meerman. *The New Rules of Marketing and PR: How to Use Social Media, Blogs, News Releases, Online Video, and Viral Marketing to Reach Buyers Directly.* 2d ed. Hoboken, N.J.: John Wiley & Sons, 2010.

Strickland, Martha. "What the Semantic Web—or Web 3.0—Can Do for Marketers." *Advertising Age,* November 24, 2008. http://adage.com/digitalnext/post?article_id=132815.

Twitchell, James B. *Adcult USA: The Triumph of Advertising in American Culture.* New York: Columbia University Press, 1996.

U.S. Bureau of Labor Statistics. *Career Guide to Industries,* 2010-2011 ed. http://www.bls.gov/oco/cg.

U.S. Census Bureau. North American Industry Classification System (NAICS), 2007. http://www.census.gov/cgi-bin/sssd/naics/naicsrch?chart=2007.

U.S. Department of Commerce. International Trade Administration. Office of Trade and Industry Information. Industry Trade Data and Analysis. http://ita.doc.gov/td/industry/otea/OTII/OTII-index.html.

Wilkerson, David B. "U.S. Advertising Seen Plunging 13 Percent in 2009." Marketwatch, March 12, 2009. http://www.marketwatch.com/story/us-advertising-revenue-plunge-13-2009.

Wilmshurst, John, and Adrian Mackay. *The Fundamentals of Advertising.* 2d ed. Oxford, England: Elsevier Butterworth-Heinemann, 1999.

AIRLINE INDUSTRY

AVJobs.com. "Aviation Career Salary, Wages and Pay." http://www.avjobs.com/salaries-wages-pay/index.asp.

Belobaba, Peter, Amedeo Odoni, and Cynthia Barnhart, eds. *The Global Airline Industry.* Chichester, West Sussex, England: John Wiley & Sons, 2009.

Dillon, Tamara. "Sky-High Careers: Jobs Related to Airlines." *Occupational Outlook Quarterly*, Summer, 2007. http://stats.bls.gov/opub/ooq/2007/summer/art01.pdf.

Doganis, Rigas. *The Airline Business*. 2d ed. New York: Routledge, 2006.

Finnegan, Joy. "Special Report: Aviation Maintenance 2007 Salary Survey." *Aviation Maintenance*, September 1, 2007. http://www.aviationtoday.com/am/categories/commercial/15370.html.

Massachusetts Institute of Technology, Global Airline Industry Program. "Airline Industry Overview." 2010. http://web.mit.edu/airlines/analysis/analysis_airline_industry.html.

Morrison, Steven A., and Clifford Winston. *The Evolution of the Airline Industry*. Washington, D.C.: Brookings Institution, 1995.

Orenic, Liesl Miller. *On the Ground: Labor Struggle in the American Airline Industry*. Urbana: University of Illinois Press, 2009.

Shaw, Stephen. *Airline Marketing and Management*. 6th ed. Burlington, Vt.: Ashgate, 2007.

U.S. Bureau of Labor Statistics. *Career Guide to Industries*, 2010-2011 ed. http://www.bls.gov/oco/cg.

U.S. Census Bureau. North American Industry Classification System (NAICS), 2007. http://www.census.gov/cgi-bin/sssd/naics/naicsrch?chart=2007.

U.S. Department of Commerce. International Trade Administration. Office of Trade and Industry Information. Industry Trade Data and Analysis. http://ita.doc.gov/td/industry/otea/OTII/OTII-index.html.

Vasigh, Bijan, Ken Fleming, and Tom Tacker. *Introduction to Air Transport Economics: From Theory to Applications*. Burlington, Vt.: Ashgate, 2008.

Wensveen, John G. *Air Transportation: A Management Perspective*. Burlington, Vt.: Ashgate, 2007.

Alternative Energy Systems. Washington, D.C.: National Academies Press, 1980.

Brown, Amy Kathryn. *Powering the Future: The Problems and Possibilities of Green Energy*. New York: International Debate Education Association, 2010.

Carazo, Dan. *Green Electrical Sells: Profit from the Booming Markets for Green Building and Energy Efficiency*. Syosset, N.Y.: Carazo Communications, 2010.

Doyle, Kevin Lee, et al. *The Complete Guide to Environmental Careers in the Twenty-first Century*. Washington, D.C.: Island Press, 1999.

Fasulo, Michael, and Paul Walker. *Careers in the Environment*. 3d ed. New York: McGraw-Hill, 2007.

Heintzman, Andrew. *The New Entrepreneurs: Building a Green Economy for the Future*. Toronto: House of Anansi Press, 2010.

McNamee, Gregory. *Careers in Renewable Energy: Get a Green Job*. Masonville, Colo.: PixyJack Press, 2008.

Schlager, N., and J. Weisblatt, eds. *Alternative Energy*. 3 vols. Detroit: UXL, 2007.

U.S. Bureau of Labor Statistics. *Career Guide to Industries*, 2010-2011 ed. http://www.bls.gov/oco/cg.

U.S. Census Bureau. North American Industry Classification System (NAICS), 2007. http://www.census.gov/cgi-bin/sssd/naics/naicsrch?chart=2007.

U.S. Department of Commerce. International Trade Administration. Office of Trade and Industry Information. Industry Trade Data and Analysis. http://ita.doc.gov/td/industry/otea/OTII/OTII-index.html.

U.S. Department of Energy. *Geothermal Technologies Market Report*. Washington, D.C.: Author, 2009.

_____. *Solar Technologies Market Report*. Washington, D.C.: Author, 2010.

_____. *Wind Technologies Market Report*. Washington, D.C.: Author, 2009.

ALTERNATIVE POWER INDUSTRY

Brooks, H., et al. *Energy in Transition, 1985-2010: Final Report of the Committee on Nuclear and*

ANIMAL CARE SERVICES

Bennett, Laura. "Pet Industry Trends for 2009." *Small Business Trends*, January 15, 2009.

http://smallbiztrends.com/2009/01/pet
-industry-trends-2009.html.

CareerBuilder.com. Salary Calculator and Wage
Finder. http://www.cbsalary.com/salary
-calculator.

Hollow, Michele C., and William P. Rives. *The
Everything Guide to Working with Animals: From
Dog Groomer to Wildlife Rescuer—Tons of Great
Jobs for Animal Lovers*. Avon, Mass.: Adams
Media, 2009.

Lee, Mary Price, and Richard S. Lee. *Opportunities
in Animal and Pet Care Careers*. 2d ed. New York:
McGraw-Hill, 2009.

Miller, Louise. *Careers for Animal Lovers and Other
Zoological Types*. 3d ed. New York: McGraw-Hill,
2007.

Sandlin, Eileen Figure. *Pet Businesses*. Irvine,
Calif.: Entrepreneur Media, 2006.

Shenk, Ellen. *Careers with Animals: Exploring
Occupations Involving Dogs, Horses, Cats, Birds,
Wildlife, and Exotics*. Mechanicsburg, Pa.:
Stackpole Books, 2005.

Simpkins, Jason. "Despite the Recession, the U.S.
Pet Care Industry Is Staying Out of the Dog
House." *Money Morning*, May 29, 2009.
http://moneymorning.com/2009/05/29/pet
-care-industry.

U.S. Bureau of Labor Statistics. "Animal Care and
Service Workers." In *Occupational Outlook
Handbook*, 2010-2011 ed. http://www.bls.gov/
oco/ocos168.htm.

_____. *Career Guide to Industries*, 2010-2011 ed.
http://www.bls.gov/oco/cg.

U.S. Census Bureau. North American Industry
Classification System (NAICS), 2007.
http://www.census.gov/cgi-bin/sssd/naics/na
icsrch?chart=2007.

U.S. Department of Commerce. International
Trade Administration. Office of Trade and
Industry Information. Industry Trade Data
and Analysis. http://ita.doc.gov/td/
industry/otea/OTII/OTII-index.html.

APPAREL AND FASHION INDUSTRY

Baudot, Francois. *Fashion: The Twentieth Century*.
New York: Universe, 1999.

Blasczyk, Regina Lee. *Producing Fashion: Commerce,
Culture, and Consumers*. Philadelphia:
University of Pennsylvania Press, 2008.

Brown, Carol. *Fashion and Textiles: The Essential
Careers Guide*. London: Laurence King, 2010.

DePaola, Helena de, and Carol Stewart Mueller.
Marketing Today's Fashions. Englewood Cliffs,
N.J.: Prentice-Hall, 1980.

Easey, Mike, ed. *Fashion Marketing*. 2d ed. Oxford,
England: Blackwell Science, 2002.

Gross, Michael. *Model: The Ugly Business of
Beautiful Women*. New York: Perennial, 2003.

Karr, Rick. "Fashion Industry Copes with
Designer Knockoffs: With Copyright
Protection Elusive, Copies Are Common."
http://www.npr.org/templates/story/stotu.ph
p?storyId=1434815. September 18, 2003.

Manlow, Veronica. *Designing Clothes: The Culture
and Organization of the Fashion Industry*. New
Brunswick, N.J.: Transaction, 2007.

Martin, Richard, ed. *Contemporary Fashion*. New
York: St. James Press, 1995.

Rath, Jan. *Unraveling the Rag Trade: Immigrant
Entrepreneurship in Seven World Cities*. New York:
Berg, 2000.

Roscho, Bernard. *The Rag Trade: How New York
and Paris Run the Breakneck Business of Dressing
American Women*. New York: Funk & Wagnalls,
1963.

Sherrill, Marcia, and Carey Adina Karmel. *Style
Makers: Inside Fashion*. New York: Monacelli
Press, 2002.

Sluiter, Liesbeth. *Clean Clothes: A Global Movement
to End Sweatshops*. New York: Palgrave
Macmillan, 2009.

Snyder, Rachel Louise. *Fugitive Denim: A Moving
Story of People and Pants in the Borderless World of
Global Trade*. New York: W. W. Norton, 2008.

Timmerman, Kelsey. *Where Am I Wearing? A Global
Tour to the Countries, Factories, and People That
Make Our Clothes*. Hoboken, N.J.: Wiley, 2009.

UNITE HERE! "UNITE HERE! Textiles,
Manufacturing, and Retail." http://www
.unitehere.org/about/apparel.php.

U.S. Bureau of Labor Statistics. *Career Guide to
Industries*, 2010-2011 ed. http://www.bls.gov/
oco/cg.

_____. "Textile, Apparel, and Furnishings
Occupations." In *Occupational Outlook

Handbook, 2010-2011 ed. http://www.bls.gov/oco/ocos233.htm.

U.S. Census Bureau. North American Industry Classification System (NAICS), 2007. http://www.census.gov/cgi-bin/sssd/naics/naicsrch?chart=2007.

U.S. Department of Commerce. International Trade Administration. Office of Trade and Industry Information. Industry Trade Data and Analysis. http://ita.doc.gov/td/industry/otea/OTII/OTII-index.html.

U.S. Department of Defense. "Berry Amendment FAQ." http://www.acq.usd.mil/dpap/cpic/berry_amendment_faq.html.

U.S. Department of Labor. Bureau of International Labor Affairs. *The Apparel Industry and Codes of Conduct: A Solution to the International Child Labor Problem*. Washington, D.C: Author, 1996.

White, Nicola, and Ian Griffiths, eds. *The Fashion Business: Theory, Practice, Image*. New York: Berg, 2000.

AUTOMOBILES AND PERSONAL VEHICLES INDUSTRY

Carson, Iain, and Vijay V. Vaitheeswaran. *Zoom: The Global Race to Fuel the Car of the Future*. New York: Twelve, 2008.

Fuhs, Allen. *Hybrid Vehicles and the Future of Personal Transportation*. Boca Raton, Fla.: CRC Press, 2009.

Goodman, J. David. "An Electric Boost for Bicyclists." *The New York Times*, February 1, 2010.

Hachman, Mark. "Segway Quietly Sold; Dealers Remain Optimistic." *PC*, January 18, 2010. http://www.pcmag.com/article2/0,2817,2358173,00.asp.

Herlihy, David. *Bicycle: The History*. New Haven, Conn.: Yale University Press, 2004.

Ingrassia, Paul. *Crash Course: The American Automobile Industry's Road from Glory to Disaster*. New York: Random House, 2010.

Kraft, Thomas. "From High-Wheelers to High-Tech: Bicycle Manufacturing Past and Present." *Techdirections*, November, 2006.

Levy, Efraim. *Industry Survey: Autos and Auto Parts*. New York: Standard & Poor's, 2009.

Nieuwenhuis, Paul, and P. E. Wells. *Car Futures: Rethinking the Automotive Industry Beyond the American Model*. Cardiff, Wales: Trend Tracker, 2009.

Rossi, Renzo. *A History of Water Travel*. Detroit: Blackbirch Press, 2005.

Russ, Jonathan S. *Global Motivations: Honda, Toyota, and the Drive Toward American Manufacturing*. Lanham, Md.: University Press of America, 2009.

Smedman, Lisa. *From Boneshakers to Choppers: The Rip-Roaring History of Motorcycles*. Buffalo, N.Y.: Annick Press, 2007.

U.S. Bureau of Economic Analysis. "Gross Domestic Product by Industry Accounts." March 30, 2010. http://www.bea.gov/industry/gpotables/gpo_action.cfm?anon=501149&table_id=24759&format_type=0.

U.S. Bureau of Labor Statistics. *Career Guide to Industries*, 2010-2011 ed. http://www.bls.gov/oco/cg.

_____. *Occupational Outlook Handbook*, 2010-2011 ed. http://www.bls.gov/oco.

U.S. Census Bureau. North American Industry Classification System (NAICS), 2007. http://www.census.gov/cgi-bin/sssd/naics/naicsrch?chart=2007.

U.S. Department of Commerce. International Trade Administration. Office of Trade and Industry Information. Industry Trade Data and Analysis. http://ita.doc.gov/td/industry/otea/OTII/OTII-index.html.

_____. Office of Transportation and Machinery. "The Road Ahead: An Assessment of the U.S. Motor Vehicle Industry." April, 2009. http://trade.gov/wcm/groups/public/@trade/@mas/@man/@aai/documents/web_content/auto_report_roadahead09.pdf.

U.S. Library of Congress. "Who Invented the Automobile?" February 12, 2009. http://www.loc.gov/rr/scitech/mysteries/auto.html.

Woodsen, Mary. "Going for Green." *Popular Science* 276, no. 1 (2010): 50.

BANKING INDUSTRY

Careers-in-Finance.com. "Commercial Banking." http://careers-in-finance.com/cbsal.htm.

Dietz, Miklos, Robert Reibestein, and Cornelius Walter. "What's in Store for Global Banking." *The McKinsey Quarterly,* January, 2008.

Dilley, Deborah. *Essentials of Banking.* New York: Wiley, 2008.

Foster, John Bellamy, and Fred Magdoff. *The Great Financial Crisis: Causes and Consequences.* New York: Monthly Review Press, 2009.

Hanc, George. "The Future of Banking in America: Summary and Conclusions." *FDIC Banking Review* 16, no. 2 (2004): 1-28.

Heffernan, Shelagh. *Modern Banking.* New York: Wiley, 2005.

King, Brett. *Bank 2.0: How Customer Behavior and Technology Will Change the Future of Financial Services.* New York: Marshall Cavendish Reference, 2010.

Paradis, Adrian. *Opportunities in Banking Careers.* Rev. ed. New York: Contemporary, 2000.

Ring, Trudy. *Careers in Finance.* New York: McGraw-Hill, 2004.

Sumichrast, Michael, and Martin Sumichrast. *Opportunities in Financial Careers.* New York: McGraw-Hill, 2004.

U.S. Bureau of Labor Statistics. *Career Guide to Industries,* 2010-2011 ed. http://www.bls.gov/oco/cg.

U.S. Census Bureau. North American Industry Classification System (NAICS), 2007. http://www.census.gov/cgi-bin/sssd/naics/naicsrch?chart=2007.

BATTERIES AND FUEL CELLS INDUSTRY

Appleby, A. J., and F. R. Foulkes. *Fuel Cell Handbook.* New York: Van Nostrand Reinhold, 1989.

Avadikyan, Arman, Patrick Cohender, and Jean-Alain Héraud, eds. *The Economic Dynamics of Fuel Cell Technologies.* New York: Springer Verlag, 2003.

Basu, Suddhasatwa, ed. *Recent Trends in Fuel Cell Science and Technology.* New York: Springer, 2007.

Bode, Hans. *Lead-Acid Batteries.* New York: John Wiley & Sons, 1977.

Bossel, Ulf. *The Birth of the Fuel Cell, 1835-1845.* Oberrohrdorf, Switzerland: European Fuel Cell Forum, 2000.

Brandon, Nigel P., and Dave Thompsett. *Fuel Cells Compendium.* San Diego, Calif.: Elsevier, 2005.

Crompton, T. R. *Battery Reference Book.* 3d ed. Woburn, Mass.: Newnes, 2000.

Kordesch, Karl, and Günter Simader. *Fuel Cells and Their Applications.* New York: VCH, 1996.

Linden, David. *Handbook of Batteries and Fuel Cells.* New York: McGraw-Hill, 1983.

Long, Kenneth, and Joseph Iorillo. *World Batteries.* Cleveland, Ohio: Freedonia Group, 2004.

Norbeck, Joseph. *Hydrogen Fuel for Surface Transportation.* Warrendale, Pa.: Society of Automotive Engineers, 1996.

Parker, Philip M. *The 2009-2014 World Outlook for Lithium-Ion Batteries for Plug-In Hybrid and Pure Electric Vehicles.* San Diego, Calif.: Icon Group, 2008.

Spiegel, Colleen S. *Designing and Building Fuel Cells.* New York: McGraw-Hill, 2007.

Srinivasan, Supramanian. *Fuel Cells: From Fundamentals to Applications.* New York: Springer, 2006.

U.S. Bureau of Labor Statistics. *Career Guide to Industries,* 2010-2011 ed. http://www.bls.gov/oco/cg.

U.S. Census Bureau. North American Industry Classification System (NAICS), 2007. http://www.census.gov/cgi-bin/sssd/naics/naicsrch?chart=2007.

U.S. Department of Commerce. International Trade Administration. Office of Trade and Industry Information. Industry Trade Data and Analysis. http://ita.doc.gov/td/industry/otea/OTII/OTII-index.html.

Vincent, Colin A., et al. *Modern Batteries: An Introduction to Electrochemical Power Sources.* Baltimore: Edward Arnold, 1984.

Viswanathan, B., and M. Aulice Scigioh. *Fuel Cells: Principles and Applications.* Boca Raton, Fla.: CRC Press, 2007.

Yoshio, Masaki, Ralph J. Brodd, and Akiya Kozawa, eds. *Lithium-Ion Batteries: Science and Technologies.* New York: Springer, 2009.

BEVERAGE AND TOBACCO INDUSTRY

Allen, Gary, and Ken Albala. *The Business of Food: Encyclopedia of the Food and Drink Industries.* Westport, Conn.: Greenwood Press, 2007.

ClearWay Minnesota. *Unfiltered: A Revealing Look at Today's Tobacco Industry.* Minneapolis: Author, 2010.

Jones, Raymond. *Strategic Management in a Hostile Environment: Lessons from the Tobacco Industry.* Westport, Conn.: Quorum Books, 1997.

Mahon, John F., and Richard A. McGowan. "The Cigarette Industry." Chapter 4 in *Industry as a Player in the Political and Social Arena: Defining the Competitive Environment.* Westport, Conn.: Quorum Books, 1996.

Parker, Philip M. *The World Market for Beverages and Tobacco: A 2005 Global Trade Perspective.* San Diego, Calif.: ICON Group, 2004.

Plunkett, Jack W. *Plunkett's Food Industry Almanac, 2009.* Houston, Tex.: Plunkett Research, 2009.

U.S. Bureau of Labor Statistics. *Career Guide to Industries,* 2010-2011 ed. http://www.bls.gov/oco/cg.

U.S. Census Bureau. North American Industry Classification System (NAICS), 2007. http://www.census.gov/cgi-bin/sssd/naics/naicsrch?chart=2007.

U.S. Department of Commerce. International Trade Administration. Office of Trade and Industry Information. Industry Trade Data and Analysis. http://ita.doc.gov/td/industry/otea/OTII/OTII-index.html.

Van Liemt, Gijsbert. *The World Tobacco Industry: Trends and Prospects.* Geneva, Switzerland: International Labour Office, 2002.

BIOFUELS INDUSTRY

Bart, Jan C. J., and Natale Palmeri. *Biodiesel Science and Technology: From Soil to Oil.* Cambridge, England: Woodhead, 2010.

Bourne, Joel K. "Green Dreams." *National Geographic,* October, 2007, 38-59.

Briggs, Michael, and Palligarnai T. Vasudevan. "Biodiesel Production: Current State of the Art and Challenges." *Journal of Industrial Microbiology and Biotechnology* 35 (2008): 421-430.

Bryan, Tom. "2006 U.S. Ethanol Industry Salary Survey Report." *Ethanol Producer Magazine,* December, 2006. http://ethanolproducer.com/article.jsp?article_id=2539.

Clean Edge. *Clean Energy Trends, 2010.* Alameda, Calif.: Author, 2010. Available at http://www.cleanedge.com/reports/reports-trends2010.php.

Curtis, Brian. *U.S. Ethanol Industry: The Next Inflection Point.* Washington, D.C.: U.S. Department of Energy, 2008. Available at http://bcurtisenergies.com/pdf/Biomass2008.pdf.

Emerging Markets Online. *Algae, 2020: Advanced Biofuels Markets and Commercialization Outlook.* Houston, Tex.: Author, 2009.

Erbaum, Jason B. *Bioethanol: Production, Benefits, and Economics.* New York: Nova Science, 2009.

Hall, David O., and Joanna I. House. "Biomass: A Modern and Environmentally Acceptable Fuel." *Solar Energy Materials and Solar Cells* 38 (1995): 521-542.

Hokhman, Gal, et al. *The Effect of Biofuel on the International Oil Market.* Berkeley: University of California, Berkeley, Department of Agricultural and Resource Economics, 2010.

Korosec, Kristen. "Big Ethanol's Lobbying Investment of 2010: Tax Credits and Tariffs." BNET.com, February 17, 2010. http://industry.bnet.com/energy/10003067/big-ethanols-lobbying-investment-of-2010-tax-credits-and-tariffs.

Langeveld, Hans, Marieke Meeusen, and Johan Sanders. *The Biobased Economy: Biofuels, Materials, and Chemicals in the Post-oil Era.* Washington, D.C.: Earthscan, 2010.

Markov, S. A. "Potential of Using Microalgae for Biofuel Production and CO_2 Removal from Atmosphere." *International Scientific Journal of Alternative Energy and Ecology* 70 (2009): 83-91.

Mikityuk, Andrey. "Mr. Ethanol Fights Back." *Forbes,* November 24, 2008, 52-57.

National Renewable Energy Laboratory. *Department of Energy's Aquatic Species Program: Biodiesel from Algae.* Golden, Colo.: Author, 1998. http://www.nrel.gov/docs/legosti/fy98/24190.pdf.

Pahl, Greg. *Biodiesel: Growing a New Energy Economy*. White River Junction, Vt.: Chelsea Green, 2008.

Renewable Fuels Association. *Ethanol Industry Outlook, 2010: Climate of Opportunity*. Washington, D.C.: Author, 2010.

United Nations Environment Programme. *Towards Sustainable Production and Use of Resources: Assessing Biofuels*. Paris: Author, 2009. http://www.unep.fr/scp/rpanel/pdf/Assessing _Biofuels_Full_Report.pdf.

U.S. Bureau of Labor Statistics. *Career Guide to Industries*, 2010-2011 ed. http://www.bls.gov/ oco/cg.

U.S. Census Bureau. North American Industry Classification System (NAICS), 2007. http://www.census.gov/cgi-bin/sssd/naics/na icsrch?chart=2007.

U.S. Department of Commerce. International Trade Administration. Office of Trade and Industry Information. Industry Trade Data and Analysis. http://ita.doc.gov/td/industry/ otea/OTII/OTII-index.html.

U.S. Department of Energy. *Breaking the Biological Barriers to Cellulosic Ethanol: A Joint Research Agenda*. Report from the December 2005 Workshop, DOE/SC-0095. Washington, D.C.: U.S. Department of Energy Office of Science, 2006.

Westhoff, Patrick C. *The Economics of Food: How Feeding and Fueling the Planet Affects Food Prices*. Upper Saddle River, N.J.: FT Press, 2010.

Zarrilli, Simonetta. *The Emerging Biofuels Market: Regulatory, Trade, and Development Implications*. New York: United Nations, 2006.

BROADCAST INDUSTRY

Albarran, Alan B., and Gregory G. Pitts. *The Radio Broadcasting Industry*. Boston: Allyn & Bacon, 2001.

Anderson, Christopher. "National Broadcasting Company." In *The Encyclopedia of Television*. 2d ed. Chicago: The Museum of Broadcast Communications, 2004. Available at http://www.museum.tv/archives/etv/N/html N/nationalbroa/nationalbroa.htm.

Bensman, Marvin R. "The History of Broadcasting, 1920-1960." Bensman Radio Program Archive, University of Memphis. https://umdrive.memphis.edu/mbensman/ public/history1.html.

Curtin, Michael, and Jane Shattuc. *The American Television Industry*. New York: Palgrave Macmillan, 2009.

Duffy, Brooke Erin, and Joseph Turow, eds. *Key Readings in Media Today: Mass Communication in Contexts*. New York: Routledge, 2009.

Global Industry Analysts. "Global Radio Industry to Reach $62.08 Billion by 2015." June 29, 2009. http://www.cascademedia.net/a633203 -global-radio-industry-to-reach-.cfm.

Hanlon, Mike. "Internet Video Revenues to Exceed US$7 Billion in 2010." *Gizmag*, November 7, 2006. http://www.gizmag.com/ go/6577.

Hein, Gary, and Rota Jakuska. *Podcast Industry*. Dearborn: University of Michigan, School of Management, 2007. http://www.umdilabs.com/ casestudies/documents/Podcast%20Industry %20White%20Paper.pdf.

Kackman, Michael, ed. *Flow TV: Television in the Age of Media Convergence*. New York: Routledge, 2010.

M.C.: Marketing Charts. "SNL Kagan U.S. Cable TV Summary Data, 2006." http://www.marketing charts.com/television/snl-kagan-cable -subscription-data-contradicts-fcc-chairman -kevin-martin-2634/snl-kagan-cable-summary -data-2006 jpg/.

Mogel, Leonard. *This Business of Broadcasting: A Practical Guide to Jobs and Job Opportunities in the Broadcasting Industry*. New York: Billboard Books, 2004.

National Cable and Telecommunications Association. "History of Cable Television." 2009. http://www.ncta.com/About/ About/HistoryofCableTelevision.aspx.

PayScale.com. "Salary Survey for Country: United States." 2009. http://www.payscale.com/ research/US/Country=United_States/Salary.

Radio Business Report. "Radio Pros Look to the Near Future." September 23, 2009. http:// www.rbr.com/features/ideas-working-now/ 17234.html.

Rodman, George. *Mass Media in a Changing World: History, Industry, Controversy*. Boston: McGraw-Hill, 2010.

Schneider, Chris. *Starting Your Career in Broadcasting: Working On and Off the Air in Radio and Television.* New York: Allworth Press, 2007.

Soundararajan, Mani. "Penetration of Digital Technology Sustains Growth in the Broadcasting Industry." TMCnet.com. September 9, 2008. http://www.tmcnet.com/voip/ip-communications/articles/39170-report-penetration-digital-technology-sustains-growth-the-broadcasting.htm.

Teitelbaum, Michael. *Radio and Television.* Milwaukee: World Almanac Library, 2005.

U.S. Bureau of Labor Statistics. *Career Guide to Industries,* 2010-2011 ed. http://www.bls.gov/oco/cg.

U.S. Census Bureau. North American Industry Classification System (NAICS), 2007. http://www.census.gov/cgi-bin/sssd/naics/naicsrch?chart=2007.

U.S. Department of Commerce. International Trade Administration. Office of Trade and Industry Information. Industry Trade Data and Analysis. http://ita.doc.gov/td/industry/otea/OTII/OTII-index.html.

BUILDING ARCHITECTURE INDUSTRY

American Institute of Architects. *AIA Compensation Report: A Survey of U.S. Architecture Firms.* New York: Author, 2008.

_____. *Architect's Essentials of Starting, Assessing, and Transitioning a Design Firm.* Hoboken, N.J.: John Wiley & Sons, 2008.

_____. *The Business of Architecture: An AIA Report on Firm Characteristics.* New York: Author, 2009.

Clear, Nic. *Architectures of the Near Future.* Hoboken, N.J.: Wiley, 2009.

Franck, Karen A., and Teresa von Sommaruga Howard. *Design Through Dialogue: A Guide for Clients and Architects.* Chichester, West Sussex, England: Wiley, 2010.

Guthrie, Pat. *The Architect's Portable Handbook.* 4th ed. New York: McGraw-Hill, 2010.

Klingmann, Anna. *Brandscapes: Architecture in the Experience Economy.* Cambridge, Mass.: MIT Press, 2007.

Roaf, Susan. *Transforming Markets in the Built Environment: Adapting to Climate Change.* London: Earthscan, 2010.

U.S. Bureau of Labor Statistics. *Career Guide to Industries,* 2010-2011 ed. http://www.bls.gov/oco/cg.

_____. "Construction Trades and Related Workers." In *Occupational Outlook Handbook,* 2010-2011 ed. http://www.bls.gov/oco/oco1009.htm.

U.S. Census Bureau. North American Industry Classification System (NAICS), 2007. http://www.census.gov/cgi-bin/sssd/naics/naicsrch?chart=2007.

BUILDING CONSTRUCTION INDUSTRY

Allen, Edward, and Joseph Iano. *Fundamentals of Building Construction Materials and Methods.* 5th ed. Hoboken, N.J.: Wiley, 2009.

Associated General Contractors of America. *Project Delivery Systems for Construction.* Arlington, Va.: Author, 2004.

Careers in Focus: Construction. 5th ed. New York: Ferguson, 2010.

Chudley, R., and Roger Greeno. *Building Construction Handbook.* 8th ed. Burlington, Mass.: Butterworth-Heinemann, 2010.

Fisk, Edward. *Construction Project Administration.* 6th ed. Upper Saddle River, N.J.: Prentice Hall, 2000.

Kubal, Michael T. *Building Profits in the Construction Industry.* New York: McGraw-Hill, 2000.

Ryan, Mary Meghan, ed. *Handbook of U.S. Labor Statistics: Employment, Earnings, Prices, Productivity, and Other Labor Data.* 13th ed. Lanham, Md.: Bernam Press, 2010.

Schaufelberger, John. *Construction Business Management.* Upper Saddle River, N.J.: Prentice Hall, 2009.

Simmons, H. Leslie. *Construction: Principles, Materials, and Methods.* 7th ed. New York: John Wiley & Sons, 2001.

U.S. Bureau of Labor Statistics. *Career Guide to Industries,* 2010-2011 ed. http://www.bls.gov/oco/cg.

_____. "Construction Trades and Related Workers." In *Occupational Outlook Handbook*, 2010-2011 ed. http://www.bls.gov/oco/oco1009.htm.

U.S. Census Bureau. North American Industry Classification System (NAICS), 2007. http://www.census.gov/cgi-bin/sssd/naics/naicsrch?chart=2007.

BUSINESS SERVICES

Alexander, James A., and Mark W. Hordes. *S-Business: Reinventing the Services Organization.* New York: SelectBooks, 2003.

Burkholder, Nicholas C. *Outsourcing: The Definitive View, Applications, and Implications.* Hoboken, N.J.: John Wiley & Sons, 2006.

Business History. "Industries: Business History of Business Services." December, 2008. http://businesshistory.com/ind._bus._services.php.

Cohen, Linda, and Allie Young. *Multisourcing: Moving Beyond Outsourcing to Achieve Growth and Agility.* Boston: Harvard Business School Press, 2006.

Goolsby, Kathleen. "New Impacts on Outsourcing in 2009." *Outsourcing Journal*, November, 2008. http://www.outsourcing-journal.com/nov2008-outsourcing.html.

Hoover's. "Business Services Industry Overview." http://industries.hoovers.com/business-services.

International Association of Outsourcing Professionals. "Top Five Outsourcing Trends for 2009 Predicted by International Association of Outsourcing Professionals." Press release, December 29, 2008. http://www.outsourcingprofessional.org/content/23/196/1782.

Kaka, Noshir. "Strengthening India's Offshoring Industry." *McKinsey Quarterly*, August, 2009.

PayScale.com. "Salary Survey for Country: United States." 2009. http://www.payscale.com/research/US/Country=United_States/Salary.

Reuvid, Jonathan, ed. *Managing Business Support Services: Collaborating to Compete.* Sterling, Va.: Kogan Page, 2005.

Small Business Notes. "Professional and Business Services Industry." http://www.smallbusinessnotes.com/businesses/professional.html.

U.S. Bureau of Labor Statistics. *Career Guide to Industries*, 2010-2011 ed. http://www.bls.gov/oco/cg.

U.S. Census Bureau. North American Industry Classification System (NAICS), 2007. http://www.census.gov/cgi-bin/sssd/naics/naicsrch?chart=2007.

U.S. Department of Commerce. International Trade Administration. Office of Trade and Industry Information. Industry Trade Data and Analysis. http://ita.doc.gov/td/industry/otea/OTII/OTII-index.html.

CASINO INDUSTRY

Cornell Hospitality Quarterly. "Focusing on Gaming." May, 2008.

Durham, Steve, and Kathryn Hashimoto. *The History of Gambling in America.* Upper Saddle River, N.J.: Prentice Hall, 2007.

Eade, Vincent H., and Raymond H. Eade. *Introduction to the Casino Entertainment Industry.* Upper Saddle River, N.J.: Prentice Hall, 1997.

Institute for Career Research. *Careers in the Gaming Industry: Casino Resort Employment—Dealers to Managers, State Regulators.* Chicago: Author, 2007.

Roberts, Chris, and Kathryn Hashimoto. *Casinos: Organization and Culture.* Boston: Prentice Hall, 2010.

Rudd, Denis P., and Lincoln H. Marshall. *Introduction to Casino and Gaming Operations.* 2d ed. Upper Saddle River, N.J.: Prentice Hall, 2000.

U.S. Bureau of Labor Statistics. *Career Guide to Industries*, 2010-2011 ed. http://www.bls.gov/oco/cg.

U.S. Census Bureau. North American Industry Classification System (NAICS), 2007. http://www.census.gov/cgi-bin/sssd/naics/naicsrch?chart=2007.

U.S. Department of Commerce. International Trade Administration. Office of Trade and Industry Information. Industry Trade Data and Analysis. http://ita.doc.gov/td/industry/otea/OTII/OTII-index.html.

University of Nevada, Las Vegas, International Gaming Institute. *The Gaming Industry:*

Introduction and Perspectives. New York: John Wiley & Sons, 1996.

Vosk, Stephanie. "Indian Casinos' Revenue Growth Surges." *Cape Cod Times*, August 24, 2008.

CHEMICALS INDUSTRY

Aftalion, Fred. *History of the International Chemical Industry*. Philadelphia: University of Pennsylvania Press, 1991.

Arora, Ashish, Ralph Landau, and Nathan Rosenberg. *Chemicals and Long-Term Economic Growth: Insights from the Chemical Industry*. New York: John Wiley & Sons, 1998.

Blair, Margaret M. *Corporate Restructuring in the Chemical Industry in the Deal Decade: What Takeovers and Leveraged Buyouts Mean for Corporate Governance*. Washington, D.C.: Brookings Institution, 1993.

Boswell, Clay. "SMEs Continue to Hold a Sizeable Portion of the Market Place, Showing That It Still Pays to Be Nimble and Focused." *ICIS Chemical Business*, July 25, 2008. http://www.icis.com/Articles/2008/07/28/9142582/global-chemical-small-and-medium-sized-enterprises-profiled.html.

Chapman, K. *The International Petrochemical Industry*. Oxford, England: Basil Blackwell, 1991.

"Facts and Figures of the Chemical Industry." *Chemical and Engineering News*, July 10, 2006. http://pubs.acs.org/cen/coverstory/84/8428factsandfigures.html.

Landau, Ralph. "The Chemical Industry: From the 1850's Until Today." *Business Economics*, March 22, 2010. http://findarticles.com/p/articles/mi_m1094/is_4_34/ai_56973853/.

Landau, Ralph, and Ashish Arora. *The Dynamics of Long-Term Growth: Gaining and Losing Advantage in the Chemical Industry in U.S. Industry in 2000: Studies in Competitive Performance*. Washington, D.C.: National Research Council, 1999.

Milmo, Sean. "Employee Numbers in the Chemical Industry Are in Decline: And an Aging Population Will Pose Challenges." *ICIS Chemical Business*, February 28, 2008. http://www.icis.com/Articles/2008/03/03/9104613/chemical-industry-employment-levels-continue-to-decline-in-the-us-and-europe.html.

U.S. Bureau of Labor Statistics. *Career Guide to Industries*, 2010-2011 ed. http://www.bls.gov/oco/cg.

U.S. Census Bureau. North American Industry Classification System (NAICS), 2007. http://www.census.gov/cgi-bin/sssd/naics/naicsrch?chart=2007.

U.S. Department of Commerce. International Trade Administration. Office of Trade and Industry Information. Industry Trade Data and Analysis. http://ita.doc.gov/td/industry/otea/OTII/OTII-index.html.

CIVIL SERVICES: PLANNING

Bruegmann, Robert. *Sprawl: A Compact History*. Chicago: University of Chicago Press, 2005.

Federal Highway Administration. *Planning for Transportation in Rural Areas*. http://www.fhwa.dot.gov/planning/rural/planningfortrans/3resprurpln.html.

Houghton, Gillian. *Careers in Urban Planning*. New York: Rosen, 2003.

Howell-Moroney, Michael, and Donna Milam Handley. *Restoring the Intergovernmental Partnership: What Needs to Change*. Washington, D.C.: International City/County Management Association, 2009.

Kaliski, John. "Democracy Takes Command: The New Community Planning and Challenge to Urban Design." In *Urban Planning Today: A Harvard Design Magazine Reader*. Minneapolis: University of Minnesota Press, 2006.

PayScale.com "Salary Survey for Job: Urban Planner (United States)." http://www.payscale.com/research/US/Job=Urban_Planner/Salary/by_Employer_Type.

Staley, Samuel R., and Adrian T. Moore. *Mobility First: A New Vision for Transportation in a Globally Competitive Twenty-first Century*. Lanham, Md.: Rowman and Littlefield, 2009.

U.S. Bureau of Labor Statistics. *Career Guide to Industries*, 2010-2011 ed. http://wwwbls.gov/oco/cg.

_____. "Urban and Regional Planners." In *Occupational Outlook Handbook*, 2010-2011 ed. http://www.bls.gov/oco/ocos057.htm.

U.S. Census Bureau. North American Industry Classification System (NAICS), 2007. http://www.census.gov/cgi-bin/sssd/naics/naicsrch?chart=2007.

U.S. Department of Commerce. International Trade Administration. Office of Trade and Industry Information. Industry Trade Data and Analysis. http://ita.doc.gov/td/industry/otea/OTII/OTII-index.html.

Whitehouse.gov. "Urban Policy." http://www.whitehouse.gov/issues/urban- policy.

CIVIL SERVICES: PUBLIC SAFETY

Cole, George F., and Christopher E. Smith. *The American System of Criminal Justice.* 11th ed. Belmont, Calif.: Thomson Wadsworth, 2007.

Cordner, Gary, and Kathryn Scarborough. *Police Administration.* 7th ed. New Providence, N.J.: LexisNexis/Anderson, 2010.

Dempsey, John S., and Linda S. Forst. *An Introduction to Policing.* 5th ed. Belmont, Calif.: Cengage Learning, 2010.

Hess, Karen. *Introduction to Law Enforcement and Criminal Justice.* 9th ed. Belmont, Calif.: Cengage Learning, 2009.

O*NET OnLine. Summary Report for: 3303021.05—Immigration and Customs Inspectors. http://online.onetcenter.org/link/summary/33-3021.05.

Reaves, Brian A. *Census of State and Local Law Enforcement Agencies, 2004.* Washington, D.C.: U.S. Department of Justice, Bureau of Justice Statistics, 2007. http://bjs.ojp.usdoj.gov/index.cfm?ty=pbdetail&iid=539.

_____. *Federal Law Enforcement Officers, 2004.* Washington, D.C.: U.S. Department of Justice, Bureau of Justice Statistics, 2006. http://bjs.ojp.usdoj.gov/index.cfm?ty=pbdetail&iid=867.

Schmalleger, Frank. *Criminal Justice Today.* 9th ed. Upper Saddle River, N.J.: Prentice Hall, 2007.

Stojkovic, Stan, David Kalinich, and John Klofas. *Criminal Justice Organizations: Administration and Management.* 4th ed. Belmont, Calif.: Thomson Higher Education, 2008.

U.S. Bureau of Labor Statistics. *Career Guide to Industries,* 2010-2011 ed. http://www.bls.gov/oco/cg.

U.S. Census Bureau. North American Industry Classification System (NAICS), 2007. http://www.census.gov/cgi-bin/sssd/naics/naicsrch?chart=2007.

U.S. Department of Commerce. International Trade Administration. Office of Trade and Industry Information. Industry Trade Data and Analysis. http://ita.doc.gov/td/industry/otea/OTII/OTII-index.html.

Walker, Samuel, and Charles M. Katz. *Police in America.* 6th ed. Boston: McGraw-Hill, 2008.

COAL MINING INDUSTRY

Brister, Brian S., and L. Greer Price. *New Mexico's Energy, Present and Future.* Socorro: New Mexico Bureau of Geology and Mineral Resources, 2002.

Burke, D. Barlow, and Robert E. Beck. *The Law and Regulation of Mining: Minerals to Energy.* Durham, N.C.: Carolina Academic Press, 2010.

Craig, James R, David J. Vaughn, and Brian J. Skinner. *Resources of the Earth: Origin, Use, and Environmental Impact.* Upper Saddle River, N.J.: Prentice Hall, 2001.

Godell, Jeff. *Big Coal: The Dirty Secret Behind America's Energy Future.* New York: Houghton Mifflin, 2006.

Gore, Tony, et al. *Coalfields and Neighbouring Cities: Economic Regeneration, Labour Markets, and Governance.* York, North Yorkshire, England: Joseph Rowntree Foundation, 2007.

Kolker, Allan, et al. *Emissions from Coal Fires and Their Impact on the Environment.* Reston, Va.: U.S. Geological Survey, 2009.

Parker, Philip M. *The 2009-2014 World Outlook for Coal Mining.* San Diego, Calif.: ICON Group, 2008.

Rouse, Michael J., and Usher Fleising. "Miners and Managers: Workplace Cultures in a British Columbia Coal Mine." *Human Organization* 54 (1995): 238-248.

Schmidt, Richard A. *Coal in America: An Encyclopedia of Reserves, Production, and Use.* New York: McGraw-Hill, 1979.

Simpson, David. *Productivity in Natural Resource Industries: Improvement Through Innovation.* Washington, D.C.: Resources for the Future, 1999.

Thomas, Larry. *Coal Geology.* Hoboken, N.J.: John Wiley & Sons, 2002.

U.S. Bureau of Labor Statistics. *Career Guide to Industries,* 2010-2011 ed. http://www.bls.gov/oco/cg.

U.S. Census Bureau. North American Industry Classification System (NAICS), 2007. http://www.census.gov/cgi-bin/sssd/naics/naicsrch?chart=2007.

U.S. Department of Commerce. International Trade Administration. Office of Trade and Industry Information. Industry Trade Data and Analysis. http://ita.doc.gov/td/industry/otea/OTII/OTII-index.html.

COMPLEMENTARY AND ALTERNATIVE HEALTH CARE INDUSTRY

American Association of Professional Hypnotists. "How Profitable a Career Is Hypnotherapy?" http://www.aaph.org/node/166.

Anath, Sita. "CAM: An Increasing Presence in U.S. Hospitals." *Hospitals and Health Networks,* January 20, 2009. http://www.hhnmag.com/hhnmag_app/jsp/articledisplay.jsp?dcrpath=HHNMAG/Article/data/01JAN2009/090120HHN_Online_Ananth&domain=HHNMAG.

_____. "A Steady Growth in CAM Services." *Hospitals and Health Networks,* March 31, 2009. http://www.hhnmag.com/hhnmag_app/jsp/articledisplay.jsp?dcrpath=HHNMAG/Article/data/03MAR2009/090331HHN_Online_Anan th&domain=HHNMAG.

Brody, Jane E., et al. *The New York Times Guide to Alternative Health.* New York: Henry Holt and Company, 2001.

Cohen, Michael H. *Complementary and Alternative Medicine: Legal Boundaries and Regulatory Perspectives.* Baltimore: The Johns Hopkins University Press, 1998.

Ernst, Edzard, ed. *Healing, Hype, or Harm? A Critical Analysis of Complementary or Alternative Medicine.* Charlottesville, Va.: Societas Imprint Academic, 2008.

FeldHusen, Adrian E. "The History of Midwifery and Childbirth in America: A Time Line." http://www.midwiferytoday.com/articles/timeline.asp.

French, Nancy. *Complementary and Alternative Medicine.* Colleyville, Tex.: CAM, 2002.

Hartford Hospital. *Building Bridges Between Conventional and Complementary Medicine: A Manual.* Hartford, Conn.: Hartford Hospital, 2003.

Nahin, Richard L., et al. *National Health Statistics Report: Cost of Complementary and Alternative Medicine (CAM) and Frequency of Visits to CAM Practitioners—U.S., 2007.* Washington, D.C.: U.S. Department of Health and Human Services, 2009.

Santa, Colleen F. "The Adoption of Complementary and Alternative Medicine by Hospitals: A Framework for Decision Making." *The Journal of Health Care Management* 46 (July, 2001): 250-260. http://www.allbusiness.com/management/3604702-1.html.

Tierney, Gillian. *Opportunities in Holistic Medical Careers.* Rev. ed. New York: McGraw Hill, 2007.

U.S. Bureau of Labor Statistics. *Career Guide to Industries,* 2010-2011 ed. http://www.bls.gov/oco/cg.

_____. "Chiropractors." In *Occupational Outlook Handbook,* 2010-2011 ed. http://www.bls.gov/oco/ocos071.htm.

U.S. Census Bureau. North American Industry Classification System (NAICS), 2007. http://www.census.gov/cgi-bin/sssd/naics/naicsrch?chart=2007.

U.S. Department of Commerce. International Trade Administration. Office of Trade and Industry Information. Industry Trade Data and Analysis. http://ita.doc.gov/td/industry/otea/OTII/OTII-index.html.

Weil, Andrew. *Health and Healing.* Rev. ed. New York: Houghton Mifflin, 2004.

White House Commission on Complementary and Alternative Medicine Policy. *Final Report.* Washington, D.C.: Government Printing Office, 2002. http://www.whccamp .hhs .gov/final report.html.

World Health Organization. *National Policy on Traditional Medicine and Complementary/Alternative Medicine.* Geneva, Switzerland: Author, 2005.

_____. *National Policy on Traditional Medicine and Regulation of Herbal Medicines: Report of a WHO Global Survey.* Geneva, Switzerland: Author, 2005.

COMPUTER HARDWARE AND PERIPHERALS INDUSTRY

Allan, Roy A. *A History of the Personal Computer: The People and the Technology.* 2d ed. London, Ont.: Allan Publishing, 2001.

Burns, Julie Kling. *Opportunities in Computer Careers.* Chicago: VGM Career Books, 2002.

Campbell-Kelly, Martin, and William Aspray. *Computer: A History of the Information Machine.* 2d ed. Boulder, Colo.: Westview Press, 2004.

Computer History Museum. "Timeline." http://www.computerhistory.org/semiconductor/timeline.html.

Cortada, James W. *The Digital Hand: How Computers Changed the Work of American Manufacturing, Transportation, and Retail Industries.* New York: Oxford University Press, 2004.

Eberts, Marjorie, and Margaret Gisler. *Careers for Computer Buffs and Other Technological Types.* 3d ed. New York: McGraw-Hill, 2006.

Morley, Deborah. *Understanding Computers in a Changing Society.* Boston: Cengage Learning, 2009.

Swade, Doron. "The Babbage Engine." Computer History Museum, 2008. http://www.computerhistory.org/babbage.

U.S. Bureau of Labor Statistics. *Career Guide to Industries,* 2010-2011 ed. http://www.bls.gov/oco/cg.

_____. "Computer and Information Systems Managers." In *Occupational Outlook Handbook,* 2010-2011 ed. http://www.bls.gov/oco/ocos258.htm.

U.S. Census Bureau. North American Industry Classification System (NAICS), 2007. http://www.census.gov/cgi-bin/sssd/naics/naicsrch?chart=2007.

U.S. Department of Commerce. International Trade Administration. Office of Trade and Industry Information. Industry Trade Data and Analysis. http://ita.doc.gov/td/industry/otea/OTII/OTII-index.html.

Yost, Jeffrey R. *The Computer Industry.* Westport, Conn.: Greenwood Press, 2005.

COMPUTER SOFTWARE INDUSTRY

Arora, Ashish, and Alfonso Gambardella, eds. *From Underdogs to Tigers: The Rise and Growth of the Software Industry in Brazil, China, India, Ireland, and Israel.* New York: Oxford University Press, 2005.

Convergence Plus Journal. "InfoSecurity: F-Secure, VSNL Offer Internet Security Solutions for SMEs." January 22, 2007. http://www.convergenceplus.com/jan07%20infosec%2002.html.

Dale, Nell, and John Lewis. *Computer Science Illuminated.* 3d ed. Sudbury, Mass.: Jones and Bartlett, 2007.

D'Costa, Anthony P., and E. Sridharan, eds. *India in the Global Software Industry: Innovation, Firm Strategies, and Development.* New York: Palgrave Macmillan, 2004.

Hall, Pat, and Juan Fernández-Ramil. *Managing the Software Enterprise: Software Engineering and Information Systems in Context.* London: Thomson Learning, 2007.

Hoch, Detlev J., et al. *Secrets of Software Success: Management Insights from One Hundred Software Firms Around the World.* Boston: Harvard Business School Press, 2000.

Johnston, Jessica. *Technological Turf Wars: A Case Study of the Antivirus Industry.* Philadelphia: Temple University Press, 2009.

Lightstone, Sam. *Making It Big in Software: Get the Job—Work the Org—Become Great.* Upper Saddle River, N.J.: Prentice Hall, 2010.

Lopp, Michael. *Being Geek: The Software Developer's Career Handbook.* Sebastopol, Calif.: O'Reilly Media, 2010.

Mozilla.org. "About Mozilla." http://www.mozilla.org/about.

Qing, Liau Yun. "APAC to See Fastest Software Revenue Growth." ZDNet Asia, November 9, 2009. http://www.zdnetasia.com/news/business/0,39044229,62059188,00.htm.

Robat, Cornelis, ed. *The History of Computing Project.* http://www.thocp.net/index.html.

U.S. Bureau of Labor Statistics. *Career Guide to Industries,* 2010-2011 ed. http://www.bls.gov/oco/cg.

_____. "Computer and Information Systems Managers." In *Occupational Outlook Handbook*, 2010-2011 ed. http://www.bls.gov/oco/ocos258.htm.

_____. "Computer Support Specialists and Systems Administrators." In *Occupational Outlook Handbook*, 2010-2011 ed. http://www.bls.gov/oco/ocos268.htm.

U.S. Census Bureau. North American Industry Classification System (NAICS), 2007. http://www.census.gov/cgi-bin/sssd/naics/naicsrch?chart=2007.

U.S. Department of Commerce. International Trade Administration. Office of Trade and Industry Information. Industry Trade Data and Analysis. http://ita.doc.gov/td/industry/otea/OTII/OTII-index.html.

Yu, Eileen. "Global Security Software Revenue to Hit US$10.5 billion." ZDNet Asia, April 24, 2008. http://www.zdnetasia.com/news/security/0,39044215,62040592,00.htm.

COMPUTER SYSTEMS INDUSTRY

Bayles, D. L. *E-Commerce Logistics and Fulfillment.* Upper Saddle River, N.J.: Prentice Hall, 2001.

Chesbrough, H. W. *Open Business Models.* Boston: Harvard Business School Press, 2006.

Conference Board of Canada. *Canada's Computer Systems Design Industry: Industrial Outlook, Spring, 2010.* Ottawa, Ont.: Author, 2010.

Cowhey, Peter F., Jonathan David Aronson, and Donald Abelson. *Transforming Global Information and Communication Markets: The Political Economy of Innovation.* Cambridge, Mass.: MIT Press, 2009.

Fisher, Eran. *Media and New Capitalism in the Digital Age: The Spirit of Networks.* New York: Palgrave Macmillan, 2010.

Forrester Business Data Services. *Enterprise Network and Telecommunications Survey.* Boston: Author, 2007.

Gronstedt, A. *Training in Virtual Worlds.* New York: ASTD Press, 2008.

Hunter, R. *World Without Secrets: Business, Crime, and Privacy in the Age of Ubiquitous Computing.* New York: Wiley, 2002.

Kalakota, R., and M. Robinson. *E-Business 2.2 Roadmap for Success.* Boston: Addison Wesley, 2001.

Khosrow-Pour, M., ed. *Encyclopedia of E-Commerce, E-Government, and Mobile Commerce.* Hershey, Pa.: Idea Group Reference, 2006.

Prahalad, C. K., and M. S. Krishnan. *The New Age of Innovation.* New York: McGraw-Hill, 2008.

Sadeh, N. *M-Commerce.* New York: Wiley, 2002.

SalaryList.com. "Manager of Information Technology Jobs Salary, Ranked by Salary." http://xxx.salarylist.com/all-manager-of-information-technology-real-jobs-salary.htm.

Turban, E., et al. *Decision Support Systems and Intelligent Systems.* 8th ed. Upper Saddle River, N.J.: Prentice Hall, 2007.

U.S. Bureau of Labor Statistics. *Career Guide to Industries*, 2010-2011 ed. http://www.bls.gov/oco/cg.

U.S. Census Bureau. North American Industry Classification System (NAICS), 2007. http://www.census.gov/cgi-bin/sssd/naics/naicsrch?chart=2007.

U.S. Department of Commerce. International Trade Administration. Office of Trade and Industry Information. Industry Trade Data and Analysis. http://ita.doc.gov/td/industry/otea/OTII/OTII-index.html.

CONSTRUCTION EQUIPMENT INDUSTRY

Harris, Frank. *Modern Construction and Ground Engineering Equipment and Methods.* 2d ed. New York: Longman, 1994.

Huzij, Robert, Angelo Spano, and Sean Bennett. *Modern Diesel Technology: Heavy Equipment Systems.* Detroit: Delmar Cengage Learning, 2008.

Levy, Sidney M. *Construction Databook: Construction Materials and Equipment.* 2d ed. New York: McGraw-Hill, 2010.

Stearns, Peter. *The Industrial Revolution in World History.* 3d ed. Boulder, Colo.: Westview Press, 2007.

Stonehouse, Tom, and Eldon Brumbaugh. *J. I. Case: Agricultural and Construction Equipment, 1956-1994.* St. Joseph, Mich.: American Society of Agricultural Engineers, 1996.

U.S. Bureau of Labor Statistics. *Career Guide to Industries*, 2010-2011 ed. http://www.bls.gov/oco/cg.

———. "Construction Trades and Related Workers." In *Occupational Outlook Handbook*, 2010-2011 ed. http://www.bls.gov/oco/oco1009.htm.

Vorster, Michael C. *Construction Equipment Economics*. Christiansburg, Va.: Pen, 2009.

CORPORATE EDUCATION SERVICES

Analoui, Farhad. *The Changing Patterns of Human Resource Management*. Burlington, Vt.: Ashgate, 2002.

Brakeley, Harry H., and Jeanne C. Meister. "Greater Expectations: How Corporate Education Can Boost Company Performance." *Outlook*, February, 2005. http://www.accenture.com/Global/Research_and_Insights/Outlook/By_Issue/Y2005/ToAdvantage.htm.

Craig, Robert L., ed. *The ASTD Training and Development Handbook: A Guide to Human Resource Development*. 4th ed. New York: McGraw-Hill, 1996.

Greeno, Nathan J. *Corporate Learning Strategies*. Alexandria, Va.: American Society for Training and Development, 2006.

Haskell, Robert E. *Reengineering Corporate Training: Intellectual Capital and Transfer of Learning*. Westport, Conn.: Quorum Books, 1998.

Noe, Raymond A. *Employee Training and Development*. 4th ed. New York: McGraw-Hill/Irwin, 2008.

Paradise, Andrew. "Learning Remains Steady During the Downturn." American Society for Training and Development, State of the Industry Report, November, 2009. http://www.astd.org/TD/Archives/2009/Nov/Free/0911_SOIR.htm.

Rothwell, William J., John E. Lindholm, and William G. Wallick. *What CEOs Expect from Corporate Training: Building Workplace Learning and Performance Initiatives That Advance Organizational Goals*. New York: AMACOM, 2003.

Tyler, Kathryn. "Carve Out Training? Outsourcing the Entire Training Function Is a Huge Change That—When Handled Properly—Can Yield Improved Services and Decreased Costs." *HR Magazine*, February, 2004.

U.S. Bureau of Labor Statistics. *Career Guide to Industries*, 2010-2011 ed. http://www.bls.gov/oco/cg.

———. "Human Resources, Training, and Labor Relations Managers and Specialists." In *Occupational Outlook Handbook*, 2010-2011 ed. http://www.bls.gov/oco/ocos021.htm.

U.S. Census Bureau. North American Industry Classification System (NAICS), 2007. http://www.census.gov/cgi-bin/sssd/naics/naicsrch?chart=2007.

U.S. Department of Commerce. International Trade Administration. Office of Trade and Industry Information. Industry Trade Data and Analysis. http://ita.doc.gov/td/industry/otea/OTII/OTII-index.html.

COUNSELING SERVICES

Broskowski, Anthony, and Shelagh Smith. *Estimating the Cost of Preventive Services in Mental Health and Substance Abuse Under Managed Care*. Rockville, Md.: U.S. Department of Health and Human Services, Substance Abuse and Mental Health Services Administration, Center for Mental Health Services, Office of Managed Care, 2001.

Cummings, Nicholas A., William T. O'Donohue, and Michael A. Cucciare. *Universal Healthcare: Readings for Mental Health Professionals*. Reno, Nev.: Context Press, 2005.

Levin, Bruce Lubotsky, Kevin D. Hennessy, and John Petrila. *Mental Health Services: A Public Health Perspective*. New York: Oxford University Press, 2010.

Mark, Tami, et al. *National Expenditures for Mental Health Services and Substance Abuse Treatment, 1993-2003*. Rockville, Md.: U.S. Department of Health and Human Services, Substance Abuse and Mental Health Services Administration, 2007.

Munley, Patrick H., et al. "Counseling Psychology in the United States of America." *Wes*

Counselling Psychology Quarterly 17, no. 3 (2004): 247-271.

Pedrini, Laura, et al. "Burnout in Nonhospital Psychiatric Residential Facilities." *Psychiatric Services* 60 (November, 2009): 1547-1551.

Pistole, M. Carole. "Mental Health Counseling: Identity and Distinctiveness." ERIC Digest. http://www.ericdigests.org/2002-4/mental-health.html.

Reinhardt, Uwe E., et al. "U.S. Health Care Spending in an International Context." *Health Affairs: The Policy Journal of the Health Sphere* 23, no. 3 (2004): 10-25.

U.S. Bureau of Labor Statistics. *Career Guide to Industries*, 2010-2011 ed. http://www.bls.gov/oco/cg.

U.S. Census Bureau. North American Industry Classification System (NAICS), 2007. http://www.census.gov/cgi-bin/sssd/naics/naicsrch?chart=2007.

U.S. Department of Commerce. International Trade Administration. Office of Trade and Industry Information. Industry Trade Data and Analysis. http://ita.doc.gov/td/industry/otea/OTII/OTII-index.html.

Walfish, Steven, and Jeffrey E. Barnett. *Financial Success in Mental Health Practice: Essential Tools and Strategies for Practitioners.* Washington, D.C.: American Psychological Association, 2009.

Williams, Ruth F. G., and D. P. Doessel. *The Economics of Mental Health Care: Industry, Government, and Community Issues.* Burlington, Vt.: Ashgate, 2001.

CRIMINAL JUSTICE AND PRISON INDUSTRY

ASIS International. *Career Opportunities in Security.* Alexandria, Va.: Author, 2005. Available at http://www.asisonline.org/careercenter/careers2005.pdf.

Barlow, Hugh D., and Scott H. Decker. *Criminology and Public Policy: Putting Theory to Work.* Philadelphia: Temple University Press, 2010.

Culp, Richard F. "The Rise and Stall of Prison Privatization: An Integration of Policy Analysis Perspectives." *Criminal Justice Policy Review* 16, no. 4 (December, 2005): 412-442.

Federal Bureau of Prisons. *Employment Information Handbook.* Washington, D.C.: Author, 2010.

Kerle, Ken E. *Exploring Jail Operations.* Hagerstown, Md.: American Jail Association, 2003.

Lamont, Christopher K. *International Criminal Justice and the Politics of Compliance.* Burlington, Vt.: Ashgate, 2010.

Maguire, Mary, and Dan Okada. *Critical Issues in Crime and Justice: Thought, Policy, and Practice.* Los Angeles: Sage, 2011.

Pelaez, Vicky. *The Prison Industry in the United States: Big Business or a New Form of Slavery.* New York: El Diario-La Prensa, 2005.

Pew Charitable Trusts. *Public Safety, Public Spending: Forecasting America's Prison Population, 2007-2011.* Philadelphia: Author, 2007.

Shoham, S. Giora, Paul Knepper, and Martin Kett. *International Handbook of Criminology.* Boca Raton, Fla.: CRC Press, 2010.

Spivak, Andrew L., and Susan F. Sharp. "Inmate Recidivism as a Measure of Private Prison Performance." *Crime and Delinquency* 54, no. 3 (July, 2008): 482-508.

Sumpter, Melvina. "Faith-Based Prison Programs." *Criminology and Public Policy* 5, no. 3 (August, 2006): 523-528.

Tewksbury, Richard, and Elizabeth Ehrhardt Mustaine. "Insiders' View of Prison Amenities: Beliefs and Perceptions of Correctional Staff Members." *Criminal Justice Review* 30, no. 2 (September, 2005): 174-188.

U.S. Bureau of Justice Statistics. *Jail Inmates at Midyear.* Washington, D.C.: Author, 2009.

_____. *Prison Inmates at Midyear.* Washington, D.C.: Author, 2009.

U.S. Bureau of Labor Statistics. *Career Guide to Industries*, 2010-2011 ed. http://www.bls.gov/oco/cg.

U.S. Census Bureau. North American Industry Classification System (NAICS), 2007. http://www.census.gov/cgi-bin/sssd/naics/naicsrch?chart=2007.

U.S. Department of Commerce. International Trade Administration. Office of Trade and Industry Information. Industry Trade Data and Analysis. http://ita.doc.gov/td/industry/otea/OTII/OTII-index.html.

Walmsley, Roy. *World Prison Population List.* London: International Center for Prison Studies, 2009.

DAY-CARE SERVICES

Gestwicki, Carol, and Jane Bertrand. *Essentials of Early Childhood Education.* Toronto: Thomson Nelson, 2008.

Goldsmith, Seth M. *Long-Term Care Administration Handbook.* New York: Aspen, 1994.

Hearron, Patricia F., and Verna Hildebrand. *Management of Child Development Centers.* 7th ed. Boston: Pearson, 2011.

Institute for Career Research. *A Career as a Teacher: Early Childhood Education, Nursery Schools—Daycare.* Chicago: Author, 2004.

Leach, P. *Day Care Today: Getting It Right for Everyone.* New York: Random House, 2010.

Lynn, Jacquelyn, and Charlene Davis. *Start Your Own Senior Services Business.* 2d ed. Irvine, Calif.: Entrepreneur Press, 2010.

Moore, Keith Diaz, Lyn Dally Geboy, and Gerald D. Weisman. *Designing a Better Day: Guidelines for Adult and Dementia Day Services Centers.* Baltimore: The Johns Hopkins University Press, 2006.

Pruissen, Catherine A. *Start and Run a Home Daycare.* 3d ed. North Vancouver, B.C.: Self Counsel Press, 2002.

Schmitt, E. M., et al. "Adult Day Health Center Participation and Health-Related Quality of Life." *Gerontologist,* February 10, 2010.

U.S. Bureau of Labor Statistics. *Career Guide to Industries,* 2010-2011 ed. http://www .bls.gov/oco/cg.

————. "Child Care Workers." In *Occupational Outlook Handbook,* 2010-2011 ed. http://www .bls.gov/oco/ocos170.htm.

U.S. Census Bureau. North American Industry Classification System (NAICS), 2007. http:// www.census.gov/cgi-bin/sssd/naics/ naicsrch?chart=2007.

U.S. Department of Commerce. International Trade Administration. Office of Trade and Industry Information. Industry Trade Data and Analysis. http://ita.doc.gov/td/industry/ otea/OTII/OTII-index.html.

DEFENSE INDUSTRY

Anderson, Guy, and Keri Wagstaff-Smith. "Analysis: Can the Defence Industry Re-ignite the Economy?" Jane's Information Group, November 26, 2008. http://www.janes.com/ news/defence/business/jdi/jdi081126_1_n .shtml.

Ben-Ari, Guy, and Pierre A. Chao. *Organizing for a Complex World: Developing Tomorrow's Defense and Net-Centric Systems.* Washington, D.C.: Center for Strategic and International Studies, 2009.

Bialos, Jeffrey P., et al. *Fortresses and Icebergs: The Evolution of the Transatlantic Defense Market and the Implications for U.S. National Security Policy.* Washington, D.C.: Center for Transatlantic Relations, 2009.

Bitzinger, Richard. *The Modern Defense Industry: Political, Economic, and Technological Issues.* Santa Barbara, Calif.: Praeger Security International/ABC-CLIO, 2009.

"Boeing Wins $84 Million Contract from U.S. Air Force for B-1 Bomber's Avionics Software Upgradation." *Defense World,* October 30, 2009. http://www.defenseworld.net/go/defensenews .jsp?gcatid=2&id=3767&h=Boeing%20wins % 20$84%20million%20contract%20from % 20US%20Force%20B-1%20Bomber % 20avionics%20'software%20upgradation.

Finnegan, Philip. "U.S. Defense and Aerospace Industry Weakens During Worldwide Recession." Teal Group Corporation, October 14, 2009. http://www.tealgroup.com/index .php?option=com_content&view=article&id= 59:us-aerospace-and-defense-industry-weakens -in-face-of-worldwide-recession-&catid= 8:blogmain&Itemid=100004.

Lasou, Damien. "Five Key Trends Impacting the Aerospace and Defense Industry Amid Challenging Economic Times." *Aviation Spectator,* June 9, 2009. http://www.aviation spectator.com/blogs/admin/guest-post-five -key-trends-impacting-the-aerospace-and -defense-industry-amid-challenging.

Markowski, Stefan, Peter Hall, and Robert Wylie. *Defence Procurement and Industry Policy: A Small Country Perspective.* London: Routledge, 2010.

PayScale.com. "Salary Survey for Industry: Aerospace and Defense." http://www.payscale.com/research/US/Industry%3DAerospace_and_Defense/Salary.

Simply Hired. "Average Defense Industry Salaries." http://www.simplyhired.com/a/salary/search/q-Defense+Industry.

Smith, Ron. *Military Economics: The Interaction of Power and Money*. New York: Palgrave Macmillan, 2009.

Sorenson, David S. *The Process and Politics of Defense Acquisition: A Reference Handbook*. Westport, Conn.: Praeger Security International, 2009.

U.S. Bureau of Labor Statistics. *Career Guide to Industries*, 2010-2011 ed. http://www.bls.gov/oco/cg.

U.S. Census Bureau. North American Industry Classification System (NAICS), 2007. http://www.census.gov/cgi-bin/sssd/naics/naicsrch?chart=2007.

U.S. Department of Commerce. International Trade Administration. Office of Trade and Industry Information. Industry Trade Data and Analysis. http://ita.doc.gov/td/industry/otea/OTII/OTII-index.html.

DENTAL AND ORTHODONTICS INDUSTRY

American Dental Association. *2007 Survey of Dental Practices: Characteristics of Dentists in Private Practice and Their Patients*. Chicago: Author, 2007.

American Dental Education Association. *Trends in Dentistry and Dental Education*. Washington, D.C.: Author, 2008.

Bremner, M. D. K. *The Story of Dentistry*. 3d ed. Brooklyn, N.Y.: Dental Items of Interest, 1954.

Gelbier, S. "125 Years of Developments in Dentistry, 1880-2005." *British Dental Journal* 199 (2005): 470-473.

Hoffmann-Axthelm, Walter. *The History of Dentistry*. Berlin: Quintessential Books, 1990.

Levin, Roger P. "The Boutique Dental Practice." *Dental Angle*, July, 1996. http://www.dentalangle.com/07.96/levin-archived.html.

National Institute of Dental and Craniofacial Research. "Oral Health: Past, Present, and Future." http://www.nidcr.nih.gov/Research/ResearchPriorities/StrategicPlan/pastPresentFuture.htm.

Ring, Malvin E., and Neal Hurley. "James Beall Morrison: The Visionary Who Revolutionized the Practice of Dentistry." *Journal of the American Dental Association* 131, no. 8 (2000): 1161-1167.

Spielman, Andrew I., et al. "Dentistry, Nursing, and Medicine: A Comparison on Core Competencies." *Journal of Dental Education* 69, no. 11 (2005): 1257-1271.

U.S. Bureau of Labor Statistics. *Career Guide to Industries*, 2010-2011 ed. http://www.bls.gov/oco/cg.

_____. "Dentists." In *Occupational Outlook Handbook*, 2010-2011 ed. http://www.bls.gov/oco/ocos 072.htm.

U.S. Census Bureau. North American Industry Classification System (NAICS), 2007. http://www.census.gov/cgi-bin/sssd/naics/naicsrch?chart=2007.

U.S. Department of Commerce. International Trade Administration. Office of Trade and Industry Information. Industry Trade Data and Analysis. http://ita.doc.gov/td/industry/otea/OTII/OTII-index.html.

U.S. Department of Health and Human Services. Bureau of Health Professions. National Center for Health Workforce Analysis. *U.S. Health Workforce Personnel Factbook, 2002*. http://bhpr.hrsa.gov/healthworkforce/reports/factbook.htm.

World Salaries. "Dentist Salaries: International Comparison." http://www.worldsalaries.org/dentist.shtml.

ELECTRICAL AND GAS APPLIANCES INDUSTRY

Barnes Reports. *U.S. Major Appliance Manufacturing Industry Report*. Woolwich, Maine: Author, 2008.

_____. *Worldwide Household Appliance Stores Industry Report*. Woolwich, Maine: Author, 2009.

_____. *Worldwide Small Electrical Appliances Manufacturing Industry Report*. Woolwich, Maine: Author, 2009.

Bell, Sandra. *International Brand Management of Chinese Companies: Case Studies on the Chinese Household Appliances and Consumer Electronics Industry Entering US and Western European Markets.* Heidelberg, Germany: Physica-Verlag, 2008.

Castaneda, Christopher James. *Invisible Fuel: Manufactured and Natural Gas in America, 1800-2000.* New York: Twayne, 1999.

Harris InfoSource. *Consumer Appliances Industry Report.* Twinsburg, Ohio: Author, 2002.

Reis, Ronald A. *Becoming an Electronics Technician: Securing Your High-Tech Future.* 4th ed. Upper Saddle River, N.J.: Prentice Hall, 2000.

Snyder, Nancy T., and Deborah Duarte. *Unleashing Innovation: How Whirlpool Transformed an Industry.* San Francisco, Calif.: Jossey-Bass, 2008.

U.S. Bureau of Labor Statistics. *Career Guide to Industries,* 2010-2011 ed. http://www.bls.gov/oco/cg.

U.S. Census Bureau. North American Industry Classification System (NAICS), 2007. http://www.census.gov/cgi-bin/sssd/naics/naicsrch?chart=2007.

U.S. Department of Commerce. International Trade Administration. Office of Trade and Industry Information. Industry Trade Data and Analysis. http://ita.doc.gov/td/industry/otea/OTII/OTII-index.html.

ELECTRICAL POWER INDUSTRY

Baigrie, Brian S. *Electricity and Magnetism: A Historical Perspective.* Westport, Conn.: Greenwood Press, 2007.

Bodanis, David. *Electric Universe: How Electricity Switched on the Modern World.* New York: Three Rivers Press, 2005.

CareerBuilder.com. Salary Calculator and Wage Finder. http://www.cbsalary.com/salary-calculator.

Careers.org. Occupation Profiles: Descriptions, Earnings, Outlook. http://occupations.careers.org.

Friedel, Robert, Paul Israel, and Bernard S. Finn. *Edison's Electric Light.* Rev. ed. Baltimore: The Johns Hopkins University Press, 2010.

Galvin, Robert W., Kurt E. Yeager, and Jay Stuller. *Perfect Power: How the Microgrid Revolution Will Unleash Cleaner, Greener, and More Abundant Energy.* New York: McGraw-Hill, 2009.

Heppenheimer, T. A. "Nuclear Power: What Went Wrong?" *American Heritage of Invention and Technology* 18, no. 2 (2002): 46-56.

Jonnes, Jill. *Empires of Light: Edison, Tesla, Westinghouse, and the Race to Electrify the World.* New York: Random House, 2003.

Kaplan, Stan. *Power Plant Characteristics and Costs.* New York: Nova Science Publishers, 2010.

Levy, Salomon. *Fifty Years in Nuclear Power: A Retrospective.* La Grange Park, Ill.: American Nuclear Society, 2007.

Newton, David E. *Nuclear Power.* New York: Infobase, 2005.

PayScale.com. "Salary Snapshot for Nuclear Power Reactor Operator Jobs." January 29, 2010. http://www.payscale.com/research/US/Job=Nuclear_Power_Reactor_Operator/Salary.

Taylor, Allan, and James Robert Parish. *Career Opportunities in the Energy Industry.* New York: Ferguson, 2008.

U.S. Bureau of Labor Statistics. *Career Guide to Industries,* 2010-2011 ed. http://www.bls.gov/oco/cg.

U.S. Census Bureau. North American Industry Classification System (NAICS), 2007. http://www.census.gov/cgi-bin/sssd/naics/naicsrch?chart=2007.

U.S. Department of Commerce. International Trade Administration. Office of Trade and Industry Information. Industry Trade Data and Analysis. http://ita.doc.gov/td/industry/otea/OTII/OTII-index.html.

ENVIRONMENTAL ENGINEERING AND CONSULTATION SERVICES

Ausubel, J. H., and H. E. Sladovich. *Technology and Environment.* Washington, D.C.: National Academy of Engineering, 1989.

Committee on Industrial Competitiveness and Environmental Protection. *Fostering Industry-Initiated Environmental Protection Efforts.*

Washington, D.C.: National Academies Press, 1997.

Davis, M., and S. Masten. *Principles of Environmental Engineering and Science.* 2d ed. New York: McGraw-Hill, 2008.

Hoovers. "Environmental Consulting." http://www.hoovers.com/environmental-consulting/—ID__385—/free-ind-fr-profile-basic.xhtml.

IBS Year-End Report, December, 2009. http://www.cisionwire.com/ibs/ibs-year-end-report-january—december-2009.

Jackson, S. A., et al. *Envisioning a Twenty-first Century Science and Engineering Workforce for the United States: Tasks for University, Industry, and Government.* Washington, D.C.: National Academies Press, 2003.

Masters, G. M., and W. P. Ela. *Introduction to Environmental Engineering and Science.* 3d ed. London: Prentice Hall, 2007.

National Academy of Engineering. *Frontiers of Engineering: Reports on Leading-Edge Engineering from the 2006 Symposium.* Washington, D.C.: National Academies Press, 2007.

PayScale.com. "Salary Survey for Industry: Environmental Consulting (United States)." April, 2010. http://www.payscale.com/research/US/Industry=Environmental_Consulting/Salary.

Plunkett, Jack W. *Plunkett's Consulting Industry.* Houston, Tex.: Plunkett Research, 2010.

Richards, D. J., ed. *The Industrial Green Game: Implications for Environmental Design and Management.* Washington, D.C.: National Academies Press, 1997.

Richards, D. J., and G. Pearson, eds. *The Ecology of Industry: Sectors and Linkages.* Washington, D.C.: National Academies Press, 1998.

Sam, P. A. *International Environmental Consulting Practice: How and Where to Take Advantage of Global Opportunities.* New York: Wiley, 1998.

Schulze, P. C. *Measures of Environmental Performance and Ecosystem Condition.* Washington, D.C.: National Academies Press, 1999.

Smith, D. W., and D. S. Mavinic, eds. *Journal of Environmental Engineering and Science* 7, no. 6 (November, 2008).

U.S. Bureau of Labor Statistics. *Career Guide to Industries,* 2010-2011 ed. http://www.bls.gov/oco/cg.

U.S. Census Bureau. North American Industry Classification System (NAICS), 2007. http://www.census.gov/cgi-bin/sssd/naics/naicsrch?chart=2007.

_____. The 2009 Statistical Abstract. "Geography and Environment." http://www.census.gov/compendia/statab/2009/cats/geography_environment.html.

U.S. Department of Commerce. International Trade Administration. Office of Trade and Industry Information. Industry Trade Data and Analysis. http://ita.doc.gov/td/industry/otea/OTII/OTII-index.html.

FARMING INDUSTRY

Crowell, Susan. "2007 Census of Agriculture: Agriculture's 'Middle' Slipping Away." *Farm and Dairy,* February 9, 2009. http://www.farmanddairy.com/uncategorized/2007-census-of-agriculture-agricultures-middle-slipping-away/11165.html.

Hoag, Dana L. *Applied Risk Management in Agriculture.* Boca Raton, Fla.: CRC Press, 2010.

Hoppe, Robert A., and Penni Korb. "Large and Small Farms: Trends and Characteristics." Chapter 1 in *Structural and Financial Characteristics of U.S. Farms.* Washington, D.C.: USDA Economic Research Service, 2004. http://www.ers.usda.gov/publications/aib797/aib797c.pdf.

"Hungry Planet." *Commonweal* 135, no. 10 (May 23, 2008): 5. http://commonwealmagazine.org/hungry-planet-0.

Jurena, Remy. *Agriculture in the U.S. Free Trade Agreements: Trade with Current and Prospective Partners, Impact and Issues.* New York: Nova Science, 2008.

Leval, Kim, et al. *The Impact and Benefits of USDA Research and Grant Programs to Enhance Midsize Farm Profitability and Rural Community Success.* Lyons, Nebr.: Center for Rural Affairs, 2006.

Mapes, Kathleen. *Sweet Tyranny: Migrant Labor, Industrial Agriculture, and Imperial Politics.* Urbana: University of Illinois Press, 2009.

Ricketts, Cliff, and Kristina Ricketts. *Agribusiness: Fundamentals and Applications.* 2d ed. Clifton Park, N.Y.: Delmar Cengage Learning, 2009.

U.S. Bureau of Labor Statistics. *Career Guide to Industries*, 2010-2011 ed. http://www.bls.gov/oco/cg.

U.S. Census Bureau. North American Industry Classification System (NAICS), 2007. http://www.census.gov/cgi-bin/sssd/naics/naicsrch?chart=2007.

U.S. Department of Agriculture. Economic Research Service. "Special Feature: The Shift to Large Farms." In *Structure and Finances of U.S. Farms: Family Farm Report*, 2007 ed. Washington, D.C.: Author, 2007. http://www.ers.usda.gov/publications/eib24/eib24g.pdf.

U.S. Department of Agriculture. World Agricultural Outlook Board and U.S. Interagency Agricultural Projections Committee. *USDA Agricultural Projections to 2019*. Washington, D.C.: Author, 2010.

U.S. Department of Commerce. International Trade Administration. Office of Trade and Industry Information. Industry Trade Data and Analysis. http://ita.doc.gov/td/industry/otea/OTII/OTII-index.html.

FEDERAL PUBLIC ADMINISTRATION

Frederickson, H. George, and Kevin B. Smith. *The Public Administration Theory Primer.* Boulder, Colo.: Westview Press, 2003.

Goldsmith, Stephen, and William D. Eggers. *Governing by Network: The New Shape of the Public Sector.* Washington, D.C.: Brookings Institution Press, 2004.

Lane, Jan-Erik. *Public Administration and Public Management: The Principal-Agent Perspective.* New York: Routledge, 2005.

Morgan, Douglas F., et al. *Foundations of Public Service.* Armonk, N.Y.: M. E. Sharpe, 2008.

Office of Policy and Management. "Key Events: Ninety-six Premerit Years, 1789-1883." http://www.opm.gov/BiographyofAnIdeal/PUevents1789p01.htm.

O'Leary, Rosemary, and Lisa Bingham, eds. *The Collaborative Public Manager: New Ideas for the Twenty-first Century.* Washington, D.C.: Georgetown University Press, 2009.

U.S. Bureau of Labor Statistics. *Career Guide to Industries*, 2010-2011 ed. http://www.bls.gov/oco/cg.

_____. "Federal Government." In *Career Guide to Industries*, 2010-2011 ed. http://www.bls.gov/oco/cg/cgs041.htm.

U.S. Census Bureau. North American Industry Classification System (NAICS), 2007. http://www.census.gov/cgi-bin/sssd/naics/naicsrch?chart=2007.

U.S. Department of Commerce. International Trade Administration. Office of Trade and Industry Information. Industry Trade Data and Analysis. http://ita.doc.gov/td/industry/otea/OTII/OTII-index.html.

U.S. Department of State. "Department Organizational Chart: May, 2009." http://www.state.gov/r/pa/ei/rls/dos/99494.htm?

Wiarda, Howard J., ed. *Policy Passages: Career Choices for Policy Wonks.* Westport, Conn.: Praeger, 2002.

FINANCIAL SERVICES INDUSTRY

Addison, John A., et al. *Financial Services Leadership Strategies: Industry Leaders on Service Culture and the Impact of Technology.* New York: Aspatore Books, 2005.

Brighouse, David, and Janet Hontour. *Financial Services: The Commercial Environment.* Sterling, Va.: Global Professional Publishing, 2008.

Fitch, Thomas. *Career Opportunities in Banking, Finance, and Insurance.* New York: Checkmark Books, 2007.

Harvard Business School. *Guide to Careers in Finance.* Boston: Harvard Business School Press, 2002.

Mullen, David J. *The Million-Dollar Financial Services Practice: A Proven System for Becoming a Top Producer.* New York: AMACOM, 2007.

U.S. Bureau of Labor Statistics. *Career Guide to Industries*, 2010-2011 ed. http://www.bls.gov/oco/cg.

_____. "Management and Business and Financial Occupations." In *Occupational Outlook Handbook*, 2010-2011 ed. http://www.bls.gov/oco/oco1001.htm.

U.S. Census Bureau. North American Industry Classification System (NAICS), 2007. http://www.census.gov/cgi-bin/sssd/naics/naicsrch?chart=2007.

FISHING AND FISHERIES INDUSTRY

Banse, Tom. "First Microbreweries, Now Micro-Canneries Flourish." *OPB News* (Bellingham, Washington), November 9, 2009. http://news.opb.org/article/6177-first-microbreweries-now-micro-canneries-flourish.

Barrett, James, Alison Locker, and Callum Roberts. "The Origins of Intensive Marine Fishing in Medieval Europe: The English Evidence." *Proceedings: Biological Sciences* 271, no. 1556 (2004): 2417-2421.

Eilperin, Juliet. "World's Fish Supply Running Out, Researchers Warn." *The Washington Post*, November 3, 2006. http://www.washingtonpost.com/wp-dyn/content/article/2006/11/02/AR2006110200913.html.

Food and Agrigulture Organization of the United Nations. *Aquaculture Development*. Rome: Author, 2001.

———. *Report of the Expert Consultation on the Development of a Comprehensive Global Record of Fishing Vessels*. Rome: Author, 2008.

———. *The State of World Fisheries and Aquaculture*. Rome: Author, 2008.

Haggan, Nigel, Barbara Neis, and Ian G. Baird, eds. *Fishers' Knowledge in Fisheries Science and Management*. Paris: UNESCO, 2007.

Morris, Steven, and Severin Carrell. "Enforcement and Voluntary Deals Prompt a Renaissance." *The Guardian*, March 25, 2008. http://www.guardian.co.uk/environment/2008/mar/25/fishing.food1.

Myers, Ransom, and Boris Worm. "Rapid Worldwide Depletion of Predatory Fish Communities." *Nature* 423 (2003): 280-283.

National Oceanic and Atmospheric Administration Workforce Management Office. "Vessel Employment: Career Opportunities in the Pacific Fleet." http://www.wfm.noaa.gov/about_us.html.

Pillay, T. V. R., and M. N. Kutty. *Aquaculture: Principles and Practices*. Ames, Iowa: Blackwell, 2005.

Stickney, Robert R., ed. *Encyclopedia of Aquaculture*. New York: Wiley, 2000.

U.S. Bureau of Labor Statistics. *Career Guide to Industries*, 2010-2011 ed. http://www.bls.gov/oco/cg.

U.S. Census Bureau. North American Industry Classification System (NAICS), 2007. http://www.census.gov/cgi-bin/sssd/naics/naicsrch?chart=2007.

U.S. Department of Commerce. International Trade Administration. Office of Trade and Industry Information. Industry Trade Data and Analysis. http://ita.doc.gov/td/industry/otea/OTII/OTII-index.html.

Wright, Sarah Anne. "Gone Fishing: Rugged Job Can Pay." *The Seattle Times*, February 8, 2004. http://community.seattletimes.nwsource.com/archive/?date=20040208&slug=fisherman080.

Zugarramurdi, Aurora, Maria A. Parin, and Hector M. Lupin. *Economic Engineering Applied to the Fishery Industry*. Rome: Food and Agriculture Organization of the United Nations, 1995.

FOOD MANUFACTURING AND WHOLESALING INDUSTRY

Basu, Saikat K., James E. Thomas, and Surya N. Acharya. "Prospects for Growth in Global Nutraceutical and Functional Food Markets: A Canadian Perspective." *Australian Journal of Basic and Applied Sciences* 1, no. 4 (2007): 637-649.

Belasco, Warren, and Roger Horowitz, eds. *Food Chains: From Farmyard to Shopping Cart*. Philadelphia: University of Pennsylvania Press, 2009.

Bowden, Rob. *The Food Industry*. London: Wayland, 2009.

Cubbitt, Ben. "Food Distribution: The Supply Chain Optimization Challenge." *Food Manufacturing* 19, no. 3 (March, 2006): 12.

Fraser, Jill Andresky. "A Return to Basics at Kellogg: How a Focus on Profitability, Cash Management, and Realistic Forecasting Spurred Innovation and Revival at One of

America's Venerable Food Companies." *MIT Sloan Management Review* 45, no. 4 (Summer, 2004): 27-30.

Galvez, Farah R., and Sonia Yuson De Leon. *Food Technology and Globalization*. Manila, Philippines: Merriam Webster Bookstore, 2006.

Institute of Food Technologists. "Traceability (Product Tracing) in Food Systems: An IFT Report Submitted to the FDA." *Comprehensive Reviews in Food Science and Food Safety* 9, no. 1 (January, 2010): 92-175. http://www.ift.org/ Knowledge%20Center/Read%20IFT %20Publications/Science%20Reports/ Contract%20Reports/Traceability%20in %20Food%20Systems.aspx.

Kutz, Myer, ed. *Handbook of Farm, Dairy, and Food Machinery*. Norwich, N.Y.: William Andrew, 2007.

Maroulis, Zacharias B., and George D. Saravacos. *Food Plant Economics*. Boca Raton, Fla.: CRC Press, 2008.

Mattsson, Berit, and Ulf Sonesson, eds. *Environmentally Friendly Food Processing*. Boca Raton, Fla.: CRC Press, 2003.

Millstone, Erik, and Tim Lang. *The Atlas of Food: Who Eats What, Where, and Why*. Foreword by Marion Nestle. Rev. ed. Berkeley: University of California Press, 2008.

Morris, Charles E. "Seventy-five Years of Food Frontiers." *Food Engineering* 75, no. 9 (September, 2003): 54-63.

Murray, Sarah. "Food: The World's Biggest Industry." *Forbes*, November 15, 2007. http:// www.forbes.com/2007/11/11/growth -agriculture-business-forbeslife-food07-cx_sm _1113big food.html.

Nestle, Marion. *Food Politics: How the Food Industry Influences Nutrition and Health*. Berkeley: University of California Press, 2002.

Nützenadel, Alexander, and Frank Trentmann. *Food and Globalization: Consumption, Markets, and Politics in the Modern World*. New York: Berg, 2008.

Pehanich, Mike, and Dave Fusaro. "The Changing Fortunes of Food Manufacturing." FoodProcessing.com, September 7, 2007. http://www.foodprocessing.com/articles/ 2007/221.html.

Plunkett, Jack W., ed. *Plunkett's Food Industry Almanac, 2010: The Only Comprehensive Guide to Food Companies and Trends*. 7th ed. Houston, Tex.: Plunkett Research, 2010.

Trager, James. *The Food Chronology: A Food Lover's Compendium of Events and Anecdotes, from Prehistory to the Present*. New York: Henry Holt, 1995.

U.S. Bureau of Labor Statistics. "Animal and Food Scientists." In *Occupational Outlook Handbook*, 2010-2011 ed. http://www.bls.gov/ oco/ocos046.htm.

_____. *Career Guide to Industries*, 2010-2011 ed. http://www.bls.gov/oco/cg.

_____. "Food Processing Occupations." In *Occupational Outlook Handbook*, 2010-2011 ed. http://www.bls.gov/oco/ocos219.htm.

U.S. Census Bureau. North American Industry Classification System (NAICS), 2007. http://www.census.gov/cgi-bin/sssd/naics/ naicsrch?chart=2007.

U.S. Department of Commerce. International Trade Administration. Office of Trade and Industry Information. Industry Trade Data and Analysis. http://ita.doc.gov/td/industry/ otea/OTII/OTII-index.html.

U.S. Food and Drug Administration. *Investigations Operations Manual*. Falls Church, Va.: FDAnews, 2004.

FOOD RETAIL INDUSTRY

Brownstone, Douglass L. *How to Run a Successful Food Specialty Store*. New York: Wiley, 1978.

Groceteria.com. "A Quick History of the Supermarket." Available at http://www .groceteria.com/about/a-quick-history-of-the -supermarket.

Lewis, Jerre G., and Leslie D. Renn. *How to Start and Manage a Retail Grocery Store Business: A Practical Way to Start Your Own Business*. Interlochen, Mich.: Lewis & Renn Associates, 1999.

Lewis, Len. *The Trader Joe's Adventure: Turning a Unique Approach to Business into a Retail and Cultural Phenomenon*. Chicago: Dearborn Trade, 2005.

Lichtenstein, Nelson. *The Retail Revolution: How Wal-Mart Created a Brave New World of Business*.

New York: Metropolitan Books/Henry Holt, 2009.

Marion, Bruce W., et al. *The Food Retailing Industry: Market Structure, Profits, and Prices.* New York: Praeger, 1979.

Mueller, Willard F., and Leon Garoian. *Changes in the Market Structure of Grocery Retailing.* Madison: University of Wisconsin Press, 1961.

Pegler, Martin. *Food Retail Design and Display.* New York: Retail Reporting, 1994.

Regmi, Anita, and Mark J. Gelhar. *New Directions in Global Food Markets.* Washington, D.C.: U.S. Department of Agriculture, 2005. Available at http://www.ers/usda.gov/publications/alb794.

"A Short History of the Convenience Store Industry." Available at http://www.nacsonline.com/NACS/Resources/Research/History/Pages/default.aspx.

Speak, Hugh S. *Supermarket Merchandising and Management.* Englewood Cliffs, N.J.: Prentice-Hall, 1977.

U.S. Bureau of Labor Statistics. *Career Guide to Industries,* 2010-2011 ed. Available at http://www.bls.gov/oco/cg.

_____. *Occupational Outlook Handbook,* 2010-2011 ed. http://www.bls.gov/oco.

U.S. Census Bureau. North American Industry Classification System (NAICS), 2007. http://www.census.gov/cgi-bin/sssd/naics/naicsrch?chart=2007.

U.S. Congress. House Committee on the Judiciary. *Competitive Issues in Agriculture and the Food Marketing Industry.* 106th Congress, 1st session. Washington, D.C.: U.S. Government Printing Office, 2000.

Walsh, William. *The Rise and Decline of the Great Atlantic and Pacific Tea Company.* Secaucus, N.J.: Lyle Stuart, 1986.

FOOD SERVICES

Birchfield, John C. *Design and Layout of Foodservice Facilities.* 3d ed. Hoboken, N.J.: John Wiley & Sons, 2008.

Borges, Manuel P., ed. *National School Lunch Program Assessment.* Hauppauge, N.Y.: Nova Science, 2009.

Bright, Saunya N., et al. "Institutional Foodservice Benchmarking: Survey of Administrators' Attitudes and Practices in the USA." *Journal of Foodservice* 20, no. 3 (June, 2009): 123-132.

Buzalka, Mike. "*FM*'s Top Fifty Foodservice Management Companies—2009." *Food Management.* September 1, 2009. http://food-management.com/business_feature/fms-top-management-0909.

Chmelynski, Carol Caprione. *Opportunities in Food Service Careers.* Foreword by William P. Fisher. Rev. ed. New York: McGraw-Hill, 2006.

Engelund, Eva Høy, Gitte Breum, and Alan Friis. "Optimisation of Large-Scale Food Production Using Lean Manufacturing Principles." *Journal of Foodservice* 20, no. 1 (February, 2009): 4-14.

Farkas, David. "Finding Tomorrow's Foodservice Leaders Today." *Foodservice Equipment and Supplies* 62, no. 3 (March 1, 2010): 18.

Fenich, George G. *Meetings, Expositions, Events, and Conventions: An Introduction to the Industry.* 2d ed. Upper Saddle River, N.J.: Pearson/Prentice Hall, 2008.

Katsigris, Costas, and Chris Thomas. *Design and Equipment for Restaurants and Foodservice: A Management View.* 3d ed. Hoboken, N.J.: John Wiley & Sons, 2009.

Manask, Arthur M., with Mitchell Schechter. *The Complete Guide to Foodservice in Cultural Institutions: Keys to Success in Restaurants, Catering, and Special Events.* New York: John Wiley & Sons, 2002.

Mattel, Bruce, and the Culinary Institute of America. *Catering: A Guide to Managing a Successful Business Operation.* Hoboken, N.J.: John Wiley & Sons, 2008.

Millstone, Erik, and Tim Lang. *The Atlas of Food: Who Eats What, Where, and Why.* Foreword by Marion Nestle. Rev. ed. Berkeley: University of California Press, 2008.

Payne-Palacio, June, and Monica Theis. *Introduction to Foodservice.* 11th ed. Upper Saddle River, N.J.: Pearson/Prentice Hall, 2009.

Plunkett, Jack W., ed. *Plunkett's Food Industry Almanac, 2010: The Only Comprehensive Guide to Food Companies and Trends.* 7th ed. Houston, Tex.: Plunkett Research, 2010.

Strianese, Anthony J., and Pamela P. Strianese. *Dining Room and Banquet Management.* 4th ed.

Clifton Park, N.Y.: Thomson/Delmar Learning, 2008.

U.S. Bureau of Labor Statistics. *Career Guide to Industries*, 2010-2011 ed. http://www.bls.gov/oco/cg.

_____. "Food Service Managers." In *Occupational Outlook Handbook*, 2010-2011 ed. http://www.bls.gov/oco/ocos024.htm.

U.S. Census Bureau. North American Industry Classification System (NAICS), 2007. http://www.census.gov/cgi-bin/sssd/naics/naicsrch?chart=2007.

U.S. Department of Commerce. International Trade Administration. Office of Trade and Industry Information. Industry Trade Data and Analysis. http://ita.doc.gov/td/industry/otea/OTII/OTII-index.html.

FREIGHT TRANSPORT INDUSTRY

Donovan, Arthur and Joseph Bonney. *The Box That Changed the World: Fifty Years of Container Shipping—An Illustrated History*. East Windsor, N.J.: Commonwealth Business Media, 2006.

Global Insight. *The U.S. Truck Driver Shortage: Analysis and Forecasts*. Study prepared for the American Trucking Associations, May, 2005. http://www.cdlschool.com/_pdf/ATADriverShortageStudy05.pdf

Heitzman, William Ray. *Opportunities in Marine Science and Maritime Careers*. New York: McGraw-Hill, 2006.

Plunkett, Jack W. *Plunkett's Transportation and Logistics Industry Almanac, 2008*. Houston, Tex.: Plunkett Research, 2008.

Research and Innovative Technologies Administration, Bureau of Transportation Statistics. *National Transportation Statistics* 2010. http://www.bts.gov/publications/national_transportation_statistics/.

U.S. Bureau of Labor Statistics. *Career Guide to Industries*, 2010-2011 ed. http://www.bls.gov/oco/cg.

_____. "Transportation and Material Moving Occupations." In *Occupational Outlook Handbook*, 2010-2011 ed. http://www.bls.gov/oco/oco1011.htm.

U.S. Census Bureau. *U.S. International Trade in Goods and Services*. July, 2010. http://www.census.gov/foreign-trade/data/index.html.

_____. North American Industry Classification System (NAICS), 2007. http://www.census.gov/cgi-bin/sssd/naics/naicsrch?chart=2007.

U.S. Department of Commerce. International Trade Administration. Office of Trade and Industry Information. Industry Trade Data and Analysis. http://ita.doc.gov/td/industry/otea/OTII/OTII-index.html.

U.S. Department of Labor. "High Growth Industry Profile: Transportation." http://www.doleta.gov/BRG/Indprof/Transportation_profile.cfm.

FUNERARY INDUSTRY

Bowman, Leroy. *The American Funeral*. New York: Paperback Library, 1964.

Bryce, Robert. "The Dying Giant." *Salon*, September 29, 1999. http://www.salon.com/news/feature/1999/09/29/sci/index.html.

Hafenbrack Marketing. *Report: Analysis of Funeral Home Industry*. Dayton, Ohio: Author, 2007. Available at http://www.independentadvantage.com/assets/ReportHMC-FuneralServicesIndustryAnalysis-100207.pdf.

Hoovers. "Industrial Overview: Funeral Operations, 2010." http://www.hoovers.com/funeral-operations/—ID__55—/free-ind-fr-profile-basic.xhtml.

Laderman, Gary. *Rest in Peace: A Cultural History of Death and the Funeral Home in Twentieth-Century America*. New York: Oxford University Press, 2005.

Michaelson, Jo. *Step into Our Lives at the Funeral Home*. Amityville, N.Y.: Baywood, 2010.

Morton, Brian. "Vancouver Funeral Workers Strike: Average Workers' Income Is About $40,000 a Year." *The Vancouver Sun*, June 11, 2009, p. A3.

Papagno, Noella C. *The Hairdresser at the Funeral Home: Desairology Handbook Questions and Answers*. Hollywood, Fla.: J. J., 1981.

U.S. Bureau of Labor Statistics. *Career Guide to Industries*, 2010-2011 ed. http://www.bls.gov/oco/cg.

U.S. Census Bureau. North American Industry Classification System (NAICS), 2007. http://www.census.gov/cgi-bin/sssd/naics/naicsrch?chart=2007.

U.S. Department of Commerce. International Trade Administration. Office of Trade and Industry Information. Industry Trade Data and Analysis. http://ita.doc.gov/td/industry/otea/OTII/OTII-index.html.

U.S. Funerals On-Line. "U.S. Funeral Market." http://www.us-funerals.com/funeral-articles/usa-funeral-market.html.

Wolfelt, Alan. *Funeral Home Customer Service from A to Z.* Shippensburg, Pa.: Companion Press, 2001.

FURNITURE AND HOME FURNISHINGS INDUSTRY

Bennington, Richard R. *Furniture Marketing: From Product Development to Distribution.* New York: Fairchild Books, 2003.

Dugan, Michael K. *The Furniture Wars: How America Lost a Fifty Billion Dollar Industry.* Conover, N.C.: Goosepen Studio & Press, 2009.

International Trade Centre UNCTAD/WTO and International Tropical Timber Organization. *International Wooden Furniture Markets: A Review.* Geneva, Switzerland: Author, 2005.

Purdy, Warren G. *The Guide to Retail Business Planning.* Boston: Inc. Magazine Business Resources, 1997.

Schroeder, Carol L. *Specialty Shop Retailing.* Hoboken, N.J.: John D. Wiley and Sons, 2007.

Segel, Dick. *Retail Business Kit for Dummies.* Indianapolis: Wiley, 2008.

Taylor, Don, and Jeanne Smalling Archer. *Up Against the Wal-Marts.* 2d ed. New York: American Management Association, 2005.

U.S. Bureau of Labor Statistics. *Career Guide to Industries*, 2010-2011 ed. http://www.bls.gov/oco/cg.

U.S. Census Bureau. North American Industry Classification System (NAICS), 2007. http://www.census.gov/cgi-bin/sssd/naics/naicsrch?chart=2007.

U.S. Department of Commerce. International Trade Administration. Office of Trade and Industry Information. Industry Trade Data and Analysis. http://ita.doc.gov/td/industry/otea/OTII/OTII-index.html.

Wille, Stefan, ed. *Employment Conditions in the U.S. Furniture Sector.* Atlanta, Ga.: ATKRIN Furniture, 2004.

HAND TOOLS AND INSTRUMENTS INDUSTRY

Chuang, Steve. "Digital Tools to Drive Growth of Taiwan's Hand Tool Industry." China Economic News Service, November, 2009. http://cens.net/cens/html/en/news/news_inner_30792.html.

Chylinski, Manya. *Career Launcher: Manufacturing.* New York: Ferguson, 2010.

Korn, Peter. *The Woodworker's Guide to Hand Tools.* Newtown, Conn.: Taunton Press, 1997.

Leseure, Michel J. "Manufacturing Strategies in the Hand Tool Industry." *International Journal of Operations and Production Management* 20, no. 12 (2000): 1475-1487.

Mintel International Group. *DIY Review.* London: Author, 2008.

Trotman Real Life Guides. *Manufacturing and Product Design.* Richmond, England: Author, 2009.

U.S. Bureau of Labor Statistics. *Career Guide to Industries*, 2010-2011 ed. http://www.bls.gov/oco/cg.

U.S. Census Bureau. North American Industry Classification System (NAICS), 2007. http://www.census.gov/cgi-bin/sssd/naics/naicsrch?chart=2007.

U.S. Department of Commerce. International Trade Administration. Office of Trade and Industry Information. Industry Trade Data and Analysis. http://ita.doc.gov/td/industry/otea/OTII/OTII-index.html.

Vereen, Bob. *Surviving in Spite of Everything: A Postwar History of the Hardware Industry.* Indianapolis: Dog Ear, 2010.

Watson, Aldren A. *Hand Tools: Their Ways and Workings.* New York: W. W. Norton, 1982.

HEALTH AND FITNESS INDUSTRY

American College of Sports Medicine. *ACSM's Health/Fitness Facility Standards and Guidelines.* 3d ed. Champaign, Ill.: Human Kinetics, 2007.

Bates, Mike, ed. *Health Fitness Management.* 2d ed. Champaign, Ill.: Human Kinetics, 2008.

Maguire, Jennifer Smith. *Fit for Consumption: Sociology and the Business of Fitness.* New York: Routledge, 2008.

Oakley, Ben, and Martin Rhys, eds. *The Sport and Fitness Sector: An Introduction.* New York: Routledge, 2008.

Tharrett, Stephen J., and James A. Peterson. *Fitness Management.* 2d ed. Monterey, Calif.: Healthy Learning, 2008.

Thatcher, Ron, and Andy Li. *Fitness Memberships and Money.* Victoria, B.C.: Trafford, 2004.

Thompson, Walter R. "Worldwide Survey Reveals Fitness Trends for 2010." *ACSM's Health and Fitness Journal* 13, no. 6 (November/ December, 2009): 9-16.

U.S. Bureau of Labor Statistics. *Career Guide to Industries,* 2010-2011 ed. http://www.bls .gov/oco/cg.

U.S. Census Bureau. North American Industry Classification System (NAICS), 2007. http://www.census.gov/cgi-bin/sssd/naics/ naicsrch?chart=2007.

U.S. Department of Commerce. International Trade Administration. Office of Trade and Industry Information. Industry Trade Data and Analysis. http://ita.doc.gov/td/ industry/otea/OTII/OTII-index.html.

HEAVY MACHINES INDUSTRY

Dennis, Neil. "Economic Outlook: Measure of Manufacturing." *The Financial Times,* September 26, 2010.

Mitchel, Doug. *Anatomy of the John Deere.* Iola, Wis.: Krause, 2007.

Orlemann, Eric C. *Caterpillar Chronicle: The History of the World's Greatest Earthmovers.* St. Paul, Minn.: Motorbooks International, 2009.

Rosen, William. *The Most Powerful Idea in the World: A Story of Steam, Industry, and Invention.* New York: Random House, 2010.

Stearns, Peter N. *The Industrial Revolution in World History.* 3d ed. Boulder, Colo.: Westview Press, 2007.

Supplier Relations U.S. *Farm Machinery and Equipment Manufacturing Industry in the U.S. and Its International Trade.* 2010 ed. http:// www.marketresearch.com/product/display. asp?productid=2802962.

U.S. Bureau of Labor Statistics. *Career Guide to Industries,* 2010-2011 ed. http://www.bls.gov/ oco/cg.

_____. *Occupational Outlook Handbook,* 2010-2011 ed. http://www.bls.gov/oco.

U.S. Census Bureau. North American Industry Classification System (NAICS), 2007. http://www.census.gov/cgi-bin/sssd/naics/ naicsrch?chart=2007.

U.S. Department of Commerce. International Trade Administration. Office of Trade and Industry Information. Industry Trade Data and Analysis. http://ita.doc.gov/td/industry/ otea/OTII/OTII-index.html.

HIGHER EDUCATION INDUSTRY

Belson, Ken. "Universities Cutting Teams as They Trim Their Budgets." *The New York Times,* May 3, 2009.

Bridges, David, et al., eds. *Higher Education and National Development: Universities and Societies in Transition.* New York: Routledge, 2007.

Buller, Jeffrey. *The Essential College Professor: A Practical Guide to an Academic Career.* New York: John Wiley & Sons, 2010.

Chen, Sheying, ed. *Academic Administration: A Quest for Better Management and Leadership in Higher Education.* Hauppauge, N.Y.: Nova Science, 2009

Cohen, Arthur M., and Carrie B. Kisker. *The Shaping of American Higher Education: Emergence and Growth of the Contemporary System.* 2d ed. New York: John Wiley & Sons, 2010.

Duderstadt, James J. *A University for the Twenty-first Century.* Ann Arbor: University of Michigan Press, 2000.

Duesterhaus, Alan P. "College Board of Trustees and University—Structure and Composition, Governance, Authority, Responsibilities, Board Committees." Education Encyclopedia-State University.com. http://education.state university.com/pages/1793/ Board-Trustees -College-University.html.

Farrell, Maureen. "Universities That Turn Research into Revenue." Forbes.com, September 12, 2008. http://www.forbes.com/ 2008/09/12/google-general-electric-ent-tech -cx_mf_0912universitypatent.html.

Goldin, Claudia, and Lawrence F. Katz. *The Shaping of Higher Education: The Formative Years in the United States, 1890 to 1940*. Working Paper No. W6537. Cambridge, Mass.: National Bureau of Economic Research, 1988.

Musselin, Christine. *The Market for Academics*. New York: Routledge, 2010.

National Center for Education Statistics. "Contexts of Postsecondary Education." In *The Condition of Education*. http://nces.ed.gov/ programs/coe/2009/section5/index.asp.

Ruiz, Joaquin. "Research Universities Enrich State." *Arizona Daily Star*, August 12, 2009.

U.S. Bureau of Labor Statistics. *Career Guide to Industries*, 2010-2011 ed. http://www.bls.gov/ oco/cg.

_____. "Education Administrators." In *Occupational Outlook Handbook*, 2010-2011 ed. http://www.bls.gov/oco/ocos007.htm.

U.S. Census Bureau. North American Industry Classification System (NAICS), 2007. http://www.census.gov/cgi-bin/sssd/naics/ naicsrch?chart=2007.

U.S. Department of Commerce. International Trade Administration. Office of Trade and Industry Information. Industry Trade Data and Analysis. http://ita.doc.gov/td/industry/ otea/OTII/OTII-index.html.

HIGHWAY, ROAD, AND BRIDGE CONSTRUCTION INDUSTRY

Associated General Contractors of America. "Construction Industry Adds Jobs (but with a Caveat)." *Industry Today*, May 17, 2010. http:// www.industrytoday.com/article_view.asp ?ArticleID=we250.

"Highway and Street Construction." In *Encyclopedia of American Industries*. Farmington Hills, Mich.: Gale Group, 2010.

Institute for Career Research. *Careers in Infrastructure Building—Engineers, Contractors, Skilled Heavy Construction Workers: Building Our Nation's Highways, Bridges, Runnels, and Airports*. Chicago: Author, 2008.

_____. *Highway Building Careers: Working to Keep America Connected—Excellent Earnings Operating Heavy Machinery and Managing Huge Construction Projects*. Chicago: Author, 2005.

JobBank USA. "Jobs Outlook: Construction Laborers." http://www.jobbankusa.com/ career_employment/construction_laborers/ jobs_outlook.html.

Jones, Heather. "Industry Forecast II: Highways and Streets." *Construction Today*, September 25, 2007. http://www.construction-today .com/cms1/content/view/676/82.

Jones, Samantha R. *Highways: Construction, Management, and Maintenance*. Hauppauge, N.Y.: Nova Science, 2010.

Kelly, Anthony, and Kathleen Ripley. "IBISWorld Industry Report 23411a: Road, Street, and Highway Construction in the U.S." Santa Monica, Calif.: IBISWorld, 2010.

Khan, Mohiuddin A. *Bridge and Highway Structure Rehabilitation and Repair*. New York: McGraw-Hill, 2010.

LePatner, Barry B. *Too Big to Fall: America's Failing Infrastructure and the Way Forward*. New York: Foster, 2010.

Transportation for America et al. *Stranded at the Station: The Impact of the Financial Crisis in Public Transportation*. Washington, D.C.: Author, 2009. http://www.t4america .org/docs/081809_stranded_at_thestation .PDF.

United Nations Centre for Human Settlements. *Policies and Measures for Small-Contractor Development in the Construction Industry*. Nairobi, Kenya: Author, 1996.

U.S. Bureau of Labor Statistics. *Career Guide to Industries*, 2010-2011 ed. http://www.bls .gov/oco/cg.

_____. *Occupational Outlook Handbook*, 2010-2011 ed. http://www.bls.gov/oco.

U.S. Census Bureau. North American Industry Classification System (NAICS), 2007. http://www.census.gov/cgi-bin/sssd/naics/naicsrch?chart=2007.

U.S. Department of Commerce. International Trade Administration. Office of Trade and Industry Information. Industry Trade Data and Analysis. http://ita.doc.gov/td/industry/otea/OTII/OTII-index.html.

U.S. Department of Transportation. Federal Highway Administration. "Productivity and the Highway Network: A Look at the Economic Benefits to Industry from Investment in the Highway Network." Washington, D.C.: Author, 2006. http://www.fhwa.dot.gov/policy/otps/060320b/060320b.pdf.

World Bank. *Indian Road Construction Industry: Capacity Issues, Constraints, and Recommendations.* Washington, D.C.: Author, 2008.

HOME MAINTENANCE SERVICES

Barnes Reports. *U.S. Home and Garden Equipment Repair and Maintenance Industry Report.* Woolwich, Maine: Author, 2009.

Bewsey, Susan. *Start and Run a Profitable Home Cleaning Business.* North Vancouver, B.C.: International Self-Counsel Press, 1999.

Commercial and Residential Cleaning Services to 2013. Cleveland, Ohio: Freedonia Group, 2010.

Meany, Terry. *How to Start a Home-Based Handyman Business.* Guilford, Conn.: Globe Pequot Press, 2009.

Morrow, Beth. *How to Open and Operate a Financially Successful Cleaning Service.* Ocala, Fla.: Atlantic, 2008.

Price, Laurence. *How to Start Your Own Horticulture Business: Landscape Maintenance, Lawn Renovation, Landscaping Services, Home Nursery.* Bremerton, Wash.: Botany Books, 1983.

U.S. Bureau of Labor Statistics. *Career Guide to Industries,* 2010-2011 ed. http://www .bls .gov/oco/cg.

U.S. Census Bureau. North American Industry Classification System (NAICS), 2007. http://www.census.gov/cgi-bin/sssd/naics/naicsrch?chart=2007.

U.S. Department of Commerce. International Trade Administration. Office of Trade and Industry Information. Industry Trade Data and Analysis. http://ita.doc.gov/td/industry/otea/OTII/ OTII-index.html.

HOSPITAL CARE AND SERVICES

Cutler, David M., ed. *The Changing Hospital Industry: Comparing Not-for-Profit and For-Profit Institutions.* Chicago: University of Chicago Press, 2000.

Geisler, Eliezer, Koos Krabbendam, and Roel Schuring, eds. *Technology, Health Care, and Management in the Hospital of the Future.* Westport, Conn.: Praeger, 2003.

Gordon, Suzanne, John Buchanan, and Tanya Bretherton. *Safety in Numbers: Nurse-to-Patient Ratios and the Future of Health Care.* Ithaca, N.Y.: ILR Press/Cornell University Press, 2008.

Institute for Career Research. *Careers in Hospital and Health Services Administration: Healthcare Executives.* Chicago: Author, 2004.

Ohsfeldt, Robert L., and John E. Schneider. *The Business of Health: The Role of Competition, Markets, and Regulation.* Washington, D.C.: AEI Press, 2006.

Snook, I. Donald. *Opportunities in Hospital Administration Careers.* New York: McGraw-Hill, 2007.

U.S. Bureau of Labor Statistics. *Career Guide to Industries,* 2010-2011 ed. http://www.bls.gov/oco/cg.

U.S. Census Bureau. North American Industry Classification System (NAICS), 2007. http://www.census.gov/cgi-bin/sssd/naics/naicsrch?chart=2007.

U.S. Department of Commerce. International Trade Administration. Office of Trade and Industry Information. Industry Trade Data and Analysis. http://ita.doc.gov/td/industry/otea/OTII/OTII-index.html.

HOTELS AND MOTELS INDUSTRY

ASIS International. *Career Opportunities in Security.* Alexandria, Va.: Author, 2005. Available at http://www.asisonline.org/careercenter/careers2005.pdf.

Barrows, Clayton W., and Tom Powers. *Introduction to Management in the Hospitality Industry.* 9th ed. New York: John Wiley & Sons, 2009.

_____. *Introduction to the Hospitality Industry.* 7th ed. New York: John Wiley & Sons, 2009.

Brymer, Robert A. *Hospitality and Tourism.* 11th ed. Dubuque, Iowa: Kendall/Hunt, 2004.

Business Travel News. "STR Downgrades 2009 Hotel Forecast, but Sees Some Recovery." April 28, 2009. http://www.btnonline.com/businesstravelnews/search/article_display.jsp?vnu_content_id=1003967053.

CareerBuilder.com. Salary Calculator and Wage Finder. http://www.cbsalary.com/salary-calculator.

Careers.org. Occupation Profiles: Descriptions, Earnings, Outlook. http://occupations.careers.org.

Dopson, Lea R., and David K. Hayes. *Managerial Accounting for the Hospitality Industry.* Hoboken, N.J.: John Wiley & Sons, 2009.

Internal Revenue Service. "Hotel Industry Overview: August 2007—History of Industry." http://www.irs.gov/businesses/article/0,,id=174494,00.html.

Larkin, Enda. *How to Run a Great Hotel: Everything You Need to Achieve Excellence in the Hotel Industry.* Oxford, England: How to Books, 2009.

Lee-Ross, Darren, and Conrad Lashley. *Entrepreneurship and Small Business Management in the Hospitality Industry.* Boston: Butterworth-Heinemann, 2009.

Medlik, S., and H. Ingram. *The Business of Hotels.* 4th ed. Oxford, England: Butterworth-Heinemann, 2000.

PayScale.com. "Salary Survey for Job: Catering Sales Manager (United States)." January 28, 2010. http://www.payscale.com/ research/US/Job=Catering_Sales_Manager/ Salary.

PKF Hospitality Research. "PKF Revises 2009 U.S. Forecast." *Hotels,* October 28, 2008. http://www.hotelsmag.com/article/CA6609097.html.

Rogers, Tony. *Conferences and Conventions: A Global Industry.* 2d ed. London: Butterworth-Heinemann, 2008.

Rutherford, Denney G., and Michael J. O'Fallon. *Hotel Management and Operations.* 4th ed. New York: John Wiley and Sons, 2007.

SalaryList.com. "Manager of Information Technology Jobs Salary, Ranked by Salary." http://www.salarylist.com/all-manager-of-information-technology-real-jobs-salary.htm.

Smith Travel Research. "Hotel Industry Posts Record Revenue in 2008, Other Metrics Slide." Hotel News Resource, June 23, 2009. http://www.hotelnewsresource.com/HNR-detail-sid-39541.html.

Stoessel, Eric. "Marriott Posts Steep Declines." *Lodging Hospitality,* July 16, 2009. http://lhonline.com/news/marriott_second_quarter_0716.

United Nations World Tourism Organization. "Testing Times for International Tourism." *UNWTO World Tourism Barometer* 7, no. 2 (June 2009). http://www.unwto.org/facts/eng/pdf/barometer/UNWTO_Barom09_2_en_excerpt.pdf.

U.S. Bureau of Labor Statistics. *Career Guide to Industries,* 2010-2011 ed. http://www.bls.gov/oco/cg.

_____. "Hotel, Motel, and Resort Desk Clerks." In *Occupational Outlook Handbook,* 2010-2011 ed. http://www.bls.gov/oco/ocos132.htm.

U.S. Census Bureau. North American Industry Classification System (NAICS), 2007. http://www.census.gov/cgi-bin/sssd/naics/naicsrch?chart=2007.

U.S. Department of Commerce. International Trade Administration. Office of Trade and Industry Information. Industry Trade Data and Analysis. http://ita.doc.gov/td/industry/otea/OTII/OTII-index.html.

Venison, Peter. *One Hundred Tips for Hoteliers: What Every Successful Hotel Professional Needs to Know and Do.* New York: iUniverse, 2005.

Walker, John R., and Jack E. Miller. *Supervision in the Hospitality Industry: Leading Human Resources.* 6th ed. Hoboken, N.J.: Wiley, 2010.

HOUSEHOLD AND PERSONAL PRODUCTS INDUSTRY

Betton, C. I. *Global Regulatory Issues for the Cosmetics Industry.* Vol. 1. Norwich, N.Y.: William Andrew, 2007.

Boyd, Lydia. "Brief History of Beauty and Hygiene Products." Duke University Libraries Digital Collections. http://library.duke.edu/digitalcollections/adaccess/cosmetics.html.

Dowd, Timothy John. *The U.S. Market for Natural and Organic Personal Care Products.* New York: Packaged Facts, 2005.

Household and Personal Products Industry. "The International Top Thirty." http://www.happi.com/articles/2006/08/the-international-top-30.

Jones, Geoffrey. *Beauty Imagined: A History of the Global Beauty Industry.* Oxford, England: Oxford University Press, 2010.

Key Note Publications. *The Toiletries and Cosmetics Industry.* Teddington, Richmond Upon Thames, England: Author, 2010.

Packaged Facts and Netscribes. *The U.S. Market for Home Fragrance Products.* New York: Packaged Facts, 2004.

Purifoy, Jennifer. "History of Twentieth Century Fashion: Understanding the History of Cosmetics." http://www.digitalhistory.uh.edu/do_history/fashion/Cosmetics/cosmetics.html.

Richardson, Arna. "IBISWorld Industry Report 32562: Cosmetic and Beauty Products Manufacturing in the U.S." Santa Monica, Calif.: IBISWorld, 2010.

———. "IBISWorld Industry Report 44612: Beauty, Cosmetics, and Fragrance Stores in the U.S." Santa Monica, Calif.: IBISWorld, 2010.

Snyder, Sophia. "IBISWorld Industry Report 32561: Soap and Cleaning Compound Manufacturing in the U.S." Santa Monica, Calif.: IBISWorld, 2010.

———. "IBISWorld Industry Report 44611: Pharmacies & Drug Stores in the U.S." Santa Monica, Calif.: IBISWorld, 2010.

U.S. Bureau of Labor Statistics. *Career Guide to Industries,* 2010-2011 ed. http://www .bls.gov/oco/cg.

———. *Occupational Outlook Handbook,* 2010-2011 ed. http://www.bls.gov/oco.

U.S. Census Bureau. North American Industry Classification System (NAICS), 2007. http://www.census.gov/cgi-bin/sssd/naics/naicsrch?chart=2007.

U.S. Department of Commerce. International Trade Administration. Office of Trade and Industry Information. Industry Trade Data and Analysis. http://ita.doc.gov/td/industry/otea/OTII/OTII-index.html.

Willett, Julie A. *The American Beauty Industry Encyclopedia.* Santa Barbara, Calif.: Greenwood Press, 2010.

INDUSTRIAL DESIGN INDUSTRY

Esslinger, Hartmut. *A Fine Line: How Design Strategies Are Shaping the Future of Business.* San Francisco: Jossey-Bass, 2009.

Hiesinger, Kathryn B., and George H. Marcus. *Landmarks of Twentieth-Century Design: An Illustrated Handbook.* New York: Abbeville Press, 1993.

Kawasaki, Guy. *The Art of the Start: The Time-Tested, Battle-Hardened Guide for Anyone Starting Anything.* New York: Portfolio, 2004.

Meikle, Jeffrey L. *Twentieth Century Limited: Industrial Design in America, 1925-1939.* 2d ed. Philadelphia: Temple University Press, 2001.

Ōmae, Ken'ichi. *The Mind of the Strategist: The Art of Japanese Business.* 1983. Reprint. New York: McGraw-Hill, 1992.

Qu, Min, and Ran Li. "Industrial Design: Impetus from 'Made-in-China' to 'Created-in-China.'" In *Proceedings: 2009 International Symposium on Computational Intelligence and Design—Changsha, China, 12-14 December 2009,* edited by IEEE Computer Society, et al. Los Alamitos, Calif.: IEEE Computer Society, 2009.

Read, Herbert. *Art and Industry: The Principles of Industrial Design.* 1954. Reprint. London: Faber, 1964.

Reina, Peter, and Gary J. Tulacz. "The Top Two Hundred International Design Firms." *Engineering News-Record* 257, no. 4 (2006): 32-35.

U.S. Bureau of Labor Statistics. *Career Guide to Industries*, 2010-2011 ed. http://www.bls.gov/oco/cg.

U.S. Census Bureau. North American Industry Classification System (NAICS), 2007. http://www.census.gov/cgi-bin/sssd/naics/naicsrch?chart=2007.

U.S. Department of Commerce. International Trade Administration. Office of Trade and Industry Information. Industry Trade Data and Analysis. http://ita.doc.gov/td/industry/otea/OTII/OTII-index.html.

Welsbacher, Anne. *Earth-Friendly Design*. Minneapolis: Lerner, 2009.

INSURANCE INDUSTRY

Grossman, Michael, Björn Lindgren, and Avi Dor. *Pharmaceutical Markets and Insurance Worldwide*. Bingley, West Yorkshire, England: Emerald, 2010.

Parker, Philip M. *The 2009-2014 World Outlook for Automobile Insurance*. San Diego, Calif.: ICON Group, 2008.

Preker, Alexander S., et al. *Global Marketplace for Private Health Insurance: Strength in Numbers*. Washington, D.C.: World Bank, 2010.

Swiss Re. "Sigma: World Insurance in 2008." http://media.swissre.com/documents/sigma3_2009_en.pdf.

Thomsett M. *Insurance Dictionary*. Jefferson, N.C.: McFarland, 1989.

U.S. Bureau of Labor Statistics. *Career Guide to Industries*, 2010-2011 ed. http://www.bls.gov/oco/cg.

U.S. Census Bureau. North American Industry Classification System (NAICS), 2007. http://www.census.gov/cgi-bin/sssd/naics/naicsrch?chart=2007.

U.S. Department of Commerce. International Trade Administration. Office of Trade and Industry Information. Industry Trade Data and Analysis. http://ita.doc.gov/td/industry/otea/OTII/OTII-index.html.

U.S. Department of Labor. *The Big Book of Jobs*. 2009-2010 ed. New York: McGraw-Hill, 2010.

Ward Group and Jacobson Group. "Insurance Labor Market Study." February, 2010. http://www.wardinc.com/research-center/strategic-studies-detail.php?id=50.

Zevnik, R. W. *The Complete Book of Insurance*. Naperville, Ill.: Sphinx, 2004.

INTERNET AND CYBER COMMUNICATIONS INDUSTRY

Amazon.com. "About Amazon." http://www.amazon.com/Careers-Homepage/b?ie=UTF8&node=239364011.

Aspray, William, and Paul E. Ceruzzi, eds. *The Internet and American Business*. Cambridge, Mass.: MIT Press, 2008.

Campbell-Kelly, Martin, and William Aspray. *Computer: A History of the Information Machine*. 2d ed. Boulder, Colo.: Westview Press, 2004.

Computer History Museum. "Internet History." http://www.computerhistory.org/internet_history.

Discovery Institute. "U.S. Internet Traffic Projected to Grow Fifty-fold over Next Five Years." January 29, 2008. http://www.discovery.org/a/4444.

Kador, John. *Internet Jobs! The Complete Guide to Finding the Hottest Internet Jobs*. New York: McGraw-Hill, 2000.

Lacy, Sarah. *Once You're Lucky, Twice You're Good: The Rebirth of Silicon Valley and the Rise of Web 2.0*. New York: Gotham Books, 2008.

Singel, Ryan. "Google Profits up 27 Percent in Q3." *Wired*, October 15, 2009. http://www.wired.com/epicenter/2009/10/google-profits-up-3q-200.

Sorid, Daniel. "Writing the Web's Future in Numerous Languages." *The New York Times*, December 30, 2009.

Stair, Lisa, and Stair, Leslie. *Careers in Computers*. 3d ed. Chicago: VGM Career Books, 2001.

Stibel, Jeffrey M. *Wired for Thought: How the Brain Is Shaping the Future of the Internet*. Boston: Harvard Business Press, 2009.

Twitter. "Working at Twitter." http://twitter.com/jobs.

U.S. Bureau of Labor Statistics. *Career Guide to Industries*, 2010-2011 ed. http://www.bls.gov/oco/cg.

_____. "Computer and Information Systems Managers." In *Occupational Outlook Handbook*,

2010-2011 ed. http://www.bls.gov/oco/ocos258.htm.

———. "Computer Support Specialists and Systems Administrators." In *Occupational Outlook Handbook*, 2010-2011 ed. http://www.bls.gov/oco/ocos268.htm.

U.S. Census Bureau. North American Industry Classification System (NAICS), 2007. http://www.census.gov/cgi-bin/sssd/naics/naicsrch?chart=2007.

U.S. Department of Commerce. International Trade Administration. Office of Trade and Industry Information. Industry Trade Data and Analysis. http://ita.doc.gov/td/industry/otea/OTII/OTII-index.html.

Warman, Matt. "Macworld 2009: Apple's Cloud Computing Plans Will Threaten Google and Microsoft." *The Telegraph*, January 7, 2009. http://www.telegraph.co.uk/technology/apple/4160043/Macworld-2009-Apples-cloudcomputing-plans-will-threaten-Google-and-Microsoft.html.

LANDSCAPING SERVICES

Camenson, Blythe. *Careers for Plant Lovers and Other Green Thumb Types*. 2d ed. New York: McGraw-Hill, 2004.

———. *Opportunities in Landscape Architecture, Botanical Gardens, and Arboreta Careers*. New York: McGraw-Hill, 2007.

Craul, Timothy A., and Phillip J. Craul. *Soil Design Protocols for Landscape Architects and Contractors*. New York: John Wiley & Sons, 2006.

Davidson, Harold, Roy Mecklenburg, and Curtis Peterson. *Nursery Management: Administration and Culture*. 4th ed. Upper Saddle River, N.J.: Prentice Hall, 1999.

Garner, Jerry. *Careers in Horticulture and Botany*. 2d ed. New York: McGraw-Hill, 2006.

Giles, Floyd. *Landscape Construction Procedures, Techniques, and Design*. 4th ed. Champaign, Ill.: Stipes, 1999.

Hall, Charles R., Alan W. Hodges, and John J. Haydu. *Economic Impacts of the Green Industry in the United States, Final Report to the National Urban and Community Forestry Advisory Committee*. Knoxville: University of Tennessee, Extension Service, 2005.

Hannebaum, Leroy G. *Landscape Operations: Management, Methods, and Materials*. 3d ed. Upper Saddle River, N.J.: Prentice Hall, 1998.

Hensley, David L. *Professional Landscape Management*. 2d ed. Champaign, Ill.: Stipes, 2004.

Hoovers. "Landscaping Services." http://www.hoovers.com/landscaping-services/—ID__194—/free-ind-fr-profile-basic.xhtml.

Ingels, Jack E. *Landscaping Principles and Practices*. 7th ed. Clifton Park, N.Y.: Delmar Cengage Learning, 2009.

———. *Ornamental Horticulture: Science, Operations, and Management*. 3d ed. Clifton Park, N.Y.: Delmar Cengage Learning, 2000.

LaRusic, Joel. *Start and Run a Landscaping Business*. North Vancouver, B.C.: Self-Counsel Press, 2005.

Pigeat, Jean-Paul. *Gardens of the World: Two Thousand Years of Garden Design*. Paris: Flammarion, 2010.

Simonds, John O., and Barry Starke. *Landscape Architecture: A Manual of Land Planning and Design*. 4th ed. New York: McGraw-Hill Professional, 2006.

U.S. Bureau of Labor Statistics. *Career Guide to Industries*, 2010-2011 ed. http://www.bls.gov/oco/cg.

———. *Occupational Outlook Handbook*, 2010-2011 ed. http://www.bls.gov/oco.

U.S. Census Bureau. North American Industry Classification System (NAICS), 2007. http://www.census.gov/cgi-bin/sssd/naics/naicsrch?chart=2007.

U.S. Department of Commerce. International Trade Administration. Office of Trade and Industry Information. Industry Trade Data and Analysis. http://ita.doc.gov/td/industry/otea/OTII/OTII-index.html.

Wasnak, Lynn. *How to Own and Operate a Financially Successful Landscaping, Nursery, or Lawn Service Business*. Ocala, Fla.: Atlantic, 2009.

Williams, George S. *Nursery Crops and Landscape Designs for Agribusiness Studies*. 2d ed. Vero Beach, Fla.: Vero Media, 1984.

LEGAL SERVICES AND LAW FIRMS

Anderson, Wayne, and Marilyn Headrick. *The Legal Profession: Is It for You?* Cincinnati: Thomson Executive Press, 1996.

Echaore-McDavid, Susan. *Career Opportunities in Law and the Legal Industry.* New York: Facts On File, 2002.

Feuer, Alan. "A Study in How Major Law Firms Are Shrinking." *The New York Times,* June 5, 2009.

Friedman, Lawrence M. *American Law in the Twentieth Century.* New Haven, Conn.: Yale University Press, 2002.

Furi-Perry, Ursula. *Fifty Unique Legal Paths: How to Find the Right Job.* Chicago: American Bar Association, 2008.

Harvard Law School Program on the Legal Profession. "Analysis of the Legal Profession and Law Firms." http://www.law.harvard.edu/programs/plp/pages/statistics.php.

Hazard, Geoffrey C., and Angelo Dondi. *Legal Ethics: A Comparative Study.* Stanford, Calif.: Stanford University Press, 2004.

Munneke, Gary. *Careers in Law.* 3d ed. New York: McGraw-Hill, 2003.

U.S. Bureau of Labor Statistics. *Career Guide to Industries,* 2010-2011 ed. http://www.bls.gov/oco/cg.

_____. "Lawyers." In *Occupational Outlook Handbook,* 2010-2011 ed. http://www.bls.gov/oco/ocos053.htm.

_____. "Paralegals and Legal Assistants." In *Occupational Outlook Handbook,* 2010-2011 ed. http://www.bls.gov/oco/ocos114.htm.

U.S. Census Bureau. North American Industry Classification System (NAICS), 2007. http://www.census.gov/cgi-bin/sssd/naics/naicsrch?chart=2007.

U.S. Department of Commerce. International Trade Administration. Office of Trade and Industry Information. Industry Trade Data and Analysis. http://ita.doc.gov/td/industry/otea/OTII/OTII-index.html.

Williams, Sean, and David Nersessian. *Overview of the Professional Services Industry and the Legal Profession.* Cambridge, Mass.: Harvard Law School Program on the Legal Profession, 2007. http://www.law.harvard.edu/programs/plp/pdf/Industry_Report_2007.pdf.

LIBRARIES AND ARCHIVES INDUSTRY

Battles, Matthew. *Library: An Unquiet History.* New York: W. W. Norton, 2003.

Bogart, Dave, ed. *Library and Book Trade Almanac, 2009.* 54th ed. Medford, N.J.: Information Today, 2009.

Camenson, Blythe. *Opportunities in Museum Careers.* New York: McGraw-Hill, 2007.

Cox, Richard J. *Archives and Archivists in the Information Age.* New York: Neal-Schuman, 2005.

Eberhart, George M. *The Whole Library Handbook 4.* Chicago: American Library Association, 2006.

Grady, Jenifer, and Denise M. Davis. *ALA-APA Salary Survey—Librarian-Public and Academic: A Survey of Library Positions Requiring an ALA-Accredited Master's Degree.* Chicago: American Library Association, 2009.

Information Today. *American Library Directory.* 62d ed. Medford, N.J.: Author, 2009.

International Federation of Library Associations and Institutions. "Global Library Statistics, 1990-2000." The Hague, Netherlands, 2003. http://archive.ifla.org/III/wsis/wsis-stats4pub_v.pdf.

Lynch, Mary Jo. "Reaching Sixty-five: Lots of Librarians Will Be There Soon." *American Libraries* 33, no. 2 (March, 2002).

Simkin, Joyce P. *American Salary and Wages Survey.* 10th ed. Farmington Hills, Mich.: Gale Cengage, 2009.

Society of American Archivists. "So You Want to Be an Archivist: An Overview of the Archival Profession." http://www2.archivists.org/profession.

Spear, Martha J. "The Top Ten Reasons to Be a Librarian." *American Libraries* 33, no. 9 (October, 2002).

U.S. Bureau of Labor Statistics. *Career Guide to Industries,* 2010-2011 ed. http://www.bls.gov/oco/cg.

_____. "Librarians." In *Occupational Outlook Handbook*, 2010-2011 ed. http://www.bls.gov/oco/ocos068.htm.

U.S. Census Bureau. North American Industry Classification System (NAICS), 2007. http://www.census.gov/cgi-bin/sssd/naics/naicsrch?chart=2007.

_____. *Statistical Abstract of the United States: 2010.* 129th ed. Washington, D.C.: Author, 2009.

U.S. Department of Commerce. International Trade Administration. Office of Trade and Industry Information. Industry Trade Data and Analysis. http://ita.doc.gov/td/industry/otea/OTII/OTII-index.html.

LIGHT MACHINERY INDUSTRY

Abraham, Edward. *Competitive Assessment of the United States Power Tool Industry.* Washington, D.C.: Industrial Trade Administration, 1992.

Institute for Career Research. *Careers in the Machine Trades: Precision Machinist, Tool and Die Maker.* Author, 2009.

Paz, Emilio Bautista, et al. *A Brief Illustrated History of Machines and Mechanisms.* New York: Sprinter, 2010.

Rosen, William. *The Most Powerful Idea in the World: A Story of Steam, Industry, and Invention.* New York: Random House, 2010.

Stearns, Peter N. *The Industrial Revolution in World History.* 3d ed. Boulder, Colo.: Westview Press, 2007.

U.S. Bureau of Labor Statistics. *Career Guide to Industries*, 2010-2011 ed. http://www.bls.gov/oco/cg.

_____. *Occupational Outlook Handbook*, 2010-2011 ed. http://www.bls.gov/oco.

U.S. Department of Commerce. International Trade Administration. Office of Trade and Industry Information. Industry Trade Data and Analysis. http://ita.doc.gov/td/industry/otea/OTII/OTII-index.html.

LIVESTOCK AND ANIMAL PRODUCTS INDUSTRY

Dunn, Barry. "Characteristics of Successful Ranch Management." *National Cattlemen: Producer Education* 22, no. 5 (Fall, 2007): 6. Available at http://www.beefusa.org/uDocs/NC_ProED_Fall_07.pdf.

Food and Agriculture Organization of the United Nations. *The State of Food and Agriculture.* Rome: Author, 2009. Available at http://www.fao.org/docrep/012/i0680e/i0680e00.htm.

Gegner, Lance. *Hog Production Alternatives.* Fayetteville, Ark.: ATTRA-National Sustainable Agriculture Information Service, 2004. Available at http://attra.ncat.org/attra-pub/PDF/hog.pdf.

Henkel, Keri, ed. *Occupational Guidance for Agriculture.* Minneapolis: Finney, 2002.

Key, Nigel, and William McBride. *The Changing Economics of U.S. Hog Production.* Economic Research Report Number 52. Washington, D.C.: U.S. Department of Agriculture, Economic Research Service, 2007. Available at http://www.ers.usda.gov/publications/err52/err52.pdf.

McBride, William D., and Catherine Greene. "Organic Dairy Sector Evolves to Meet Changing Demand." *Amber Waves* 8, no. 1 (March, 2010): 28-33. Available at http://www.ers.usda.gov/AmberWaves/march10/PDF/OrganicDairySector.pdf.

McBride, William D., and Nigel Key. *Economic and Structural Relationships in U.S. Hog Production.* Agricultural Economic Report AER818. Washington, D.C.: U.S. Department of Agriculture, Economic Research Service, 2003. Available at http://www.ers.usda.gov/publications/aer818.

MacDonald, James M., and William D. McBride. *The Transformation of U.S. Livestock Agriculture: Scale, Efficiency, and Risks.* Economic Information Bulletin EIB-43. Washington, D.C.: U.S. Department of Agriculture, Economic Research Service, 2009. Available at http://www.ers.usda.gov/Publications/EIB43.

National Academy of Sciences. *Changes in the Sheep Industry in the United States.* Washington, D.C.: Author, 2008.

Organization for Economic Cooperation and Development and Food and Agriculture Organization of the United Nations. *OECD-FAO Agricultural Outlook, 2009-2018.* Paris: Author, 2009.

Perry, Janet, David Banker, and Robert Green. *Broiler Farms' Organization, Management, and Performance.* Agriculture Information Bulletin AIB748. Washington, D.C.: U.S. Department of Agriculture, Economic Research Service, 1999. Available at http://www.ers.usda.gov/Publications/AIB748/.

U.S. Bureau of Labor Statistics. "Agriculture, Forestry, and Fishing." In *Occupational Outlook Handbook,* 2010-2011 ed. http://www.bls.gov/oco/cg/cgs001.htm.

_____. *Career Guide to Industries,* 2010-2011 ed. http://www.bls.gov/oco/cg.

U.S. Census Bureau. North American Industry Classification System (NAICS), 2007. http://www.census.gov/cgi-bin/sssd/naics/naicsrch?chart=2007.

U.S. Department of Agriculture. Economic Research Service. *USDA Agricultural Projections to 2019.* Report OCE-2010-1. Washington, D.C.: Author, 2010. http:www.ers.usda.gov/publications/oce101.

U.S. Department of Commerce. International Trade Administration. Office of Trade and Industry Information. Industry Trade Data and Analysis. http://ita.doc.gov/td/industry/otea/OTII/OTII-index.html.

University of California Cooperative Extension. *Structure of the Cattle Business.* Livestock and Natural Resources Publication 31-609. Berkeley: Author, 1996.

LOCAL PUBLIC ADMINISTRATION

American Federation of Teachers. *Compensation Survey: A Survey of Professional, Scientific, and Related Jobs in State Government Prepared by AFT Public Employees.* Washington, D.C.: Author, 2009. Available at http://archive.aft.org/salary/2009/PubEmpsCompSurvey09.pdf.

Baxter, Neale, and Mark Rowh. *Opportunities in Government Careers.* Rev. ed. Chicago: VGM Career Books, 2001.

Frederickson, H. George, and Kevin B. Smith. *The Public Administration Theory Primer.* Boulder, Colo.: Westview Press, 2003.

Goldsmith, Stephen, and William D. Eggers. *Governing by Network: The New Shape of the Public Sector.* Washington, D.C.: Brookings Institution Press, 2004.

Lane, Jan-Erik. *Public Administration and Public Management: The Principal-Agent Perspective.* New York: Routledge, 2005.

Morgan, Douglas F., et al. *Foundations of Public Service.* Armonk, N.Y.: M. E. Sharpe, 2008.

Morphet, Janice. *Modern Local Government.* Thousand Oaks, Calif.: Sage, 2008.

Office of Citizen Services and Communications. "Statistics at the State and Local Levels." February 25, 2010. http://www.usa.gov/Government/State_Local/Statistics.shtml.

PublicServiceCareers.org. "Building a Professional Career in Public Service." http://www.publicservicecareers.org/index.asp?pageid=515.

U.S. Bureau of Labor Statistics. *Career Guide to Industries,* 2010-2011 ed. http://www.bls.gov/oco/cg.

U.S. Census Bureau. North American Industry Classification System (NAICS), 2007. http://www.census.gov/cgi-bin/sssd/naics/naicsrch?chart=2007.

U.S. Department of Commerce. International Trade Administration. Office of Trade and Industry Information. Industry Trade Data and Analysis. http://ita.doc.gov/td/industry/otea/OTII/OTII-index.html.

LOGGING INDUSTRY

Adams, Darius M., and Richard W. Haynes, eds. *Resource and Market Projections for Forest Policy Development: Twenty-five Years of Experience with the U.S. RPA Timber Assessment.* New York: Springer, 2007.

American Forest and Paper Association. "Our Industry—Forestry." http://www.afandpa.org/forestry.aspx.

Baldwin, Richard F. *Maximizing Forest Product Resources for the Twenty-first Century: New Processes, Products, and Strategies for a Changing*

World. San Francisco: Miller Freeman Books, 2000.

Careers.org. Occupation Profiles: Descriptions, Earnings, Outlook. http://occupations .careers.org.

Huber, Tim. "Timber Trouble: Hard Times Are Hitting the Timber Industry." *Desert News* (Salt Lake City), April 9, 2008.

Iannone, Don. "Industry Profile: Timber Operations." *Economic Development Futures Journal,* January 23, 2006. http://www.liberty parkusafd.org/lp/Jefferson/timber %20companies%5CProfile%20Timber %20Operations .htm.

Kallen, Stuart A., ed. *Managing America's Forests.* Detroit: Greenhaven Press, 2005.

PayScale.com. "Logging Workers, All Other Job Description." http://www.payscale .com/ Job _Description/Logging_Workers,_All_Other.

Rae, Stephen. "North American Forestry Outlook." In *ForestBook,* 2006. http://www .forestindustry.com/static/ForestBook/ 09outlook.html.

Ruhong, Li, et al. "Long-Term Effects of Eliminating Illegal Logging on the World Forest Industries, Trade, and Inventory." *Forest Policy and Economics* 10 (October, 2008): 480-490.

Solomon, Barry D., and Valerie A. Luzadis, eds. *Renewable Energy from Forest Resources in the United States.* New York: Routledge, 2009.

Talwar, Himanshu. "Wood Industry." 2009. http://www.economywatch.com/world-indust ries/wood-industry-timber-industry.html.

U.S. Bureau of Labor Statistics. *Career Guide to Industries,* 2010-2011 ed. http://www.bls.gov/ oco/cg.

_____. "Forest, Conservation, and Logging Workers." In *Occupational Outlook Handbook,* 2010-2011 ed. http://www.bls.gov/oco/ ocos178.htm.

U.S. Census Bureau. North American Industry Classification System (NAICS), 2007. http:// www.census.gov/cgi-bin/sssd/naics/naicsrch ?chart=2007.

U.S. Department of Agriculture. *An Economic Overview of the United States Solid Wood Industry.* Washington, D.C.: Author, 2007. http://www .fas.usda.gov/ffpd/Economic-Overview/An

_Economic_Overview_of_the_U.S_Solid _Wood_Industry.pdf.

U.S. Department of Commerce. International Trade Administration. Office of Trade and Industry Information. Industry Trade Data and Analysis. http://ita.doc.gov/td/industry/ otea/OTII/OTII-index.html.

MASS TRANSPORTATION VEHICLES INDUSTRY

American Public Transportation Association. *2009 Public Transportation Fact Book.* Washington, D.C.: Author, 2009.

Brown, Betty J. *Transportation.* Vol. 2 in *Encyclopedia of Business and Finance,* edited by Burton S. Kaliski. 2d ed. Detroit: Macmillan Reference, 2006.

Cheape, Charles W. *Moving the Masses: Urban Public Transit in New York, Boston, and Philadelphia, 1880-1912.* Harvard Studies in Business History 31. Cambridge, Mass.: Harvard University Press, 1980.

Cudahy, Brian J. *Cash, Tokens, and Transfers: A History of Urban Mass Transit in North America.* New York: Fordham University Press, 1990.

Karr, Ronald Dale. *Railroads.* Vol. 2 in *Encyclopedia of American Urban History.* New York: Sage Reference, 2007.

Levinson, Herbert S. "Bus Transit in the Twenty-first Century: Some Perspectives and Prospects." *Transportation Research Record: Journal of the Transportation Research Board* 1760, no. 1 (2001): 42-46. http://trb.metapress .com/content/q073w13683w14255.

McHoes, Ann McIver. *Computer Sciences: Railroad Applications,* edited by Roger R. Flynn. Vol. 3. New York: Macmillan Reference, 2002.

Meier, Albert E. *Over the Road: A History of Intercity Bus Transportation in the United States.* Upper Montclair, N.J.: Motor Bus Society, 1975.

Middleton, William D. *Metropolitan Railways: Rapid Transit in America.* Bloomington: Indiana University Press, 2003.

Miller, John A. *Fares, Please! A Popular History of Trolleys, Horse-Cars, Street-Cars, Buses, Elevateds, and Subways.* New York: Dover, 1960.

Parker, Jeffrey A. "Private Financing of Mass Transit." In *Private Innovations in Public Transit,* edited by John C. Weicher. Lanham, Md: University Press of America, 1988.

U.S. Bureau of Labor Statistics. *Career Guide to Industries*, 2010-2011 ed. http://www.bls.gov/oco/cg.

U.S. Bureau of Transportation Statistics. *National Transportation Statistics*, 2009-2010 ed. http://www.bts.gov/publications/national_transportation_statistics.

U.S. Census Bureau. North American Industry Classification System (NAICS), 2007. http://www.census.gov/cgi-bin/sssd/naics/naicsrch?chart=2007.

U.S. Department of Commerce. International Trade Administration. Office of Trade and Industry Information. Industry Trade Data and Analysis. http://ita.doc.gov/td/industry/otea/OTII/OTII-index.html.

Wallace, Jonathan. *Railroads*. Vol. 3 in *Encyclopedia of Science, Technology, and Ethics*, edited by Carl Mitcham. Detroit: Macmillan Reference, 2005.

Walsh, Margaret. *Making Connections: The Long-Distance Bus Industry in the United States*. Burlington, Vt.: Ashgate, 2000.

Wang, J., and S. McOwan. "Fast Passenger Ferries and Their Future." *Maritime Policy and Management: The Flagship Journal of International Shipping and Port Research* 27, no. 3 (2000): 231.

MEDICINE AND HEALTH CARE INDUSTRY

Dill, Monda. "A Brief History of Health Care in America." *Associated Content*, August 13, 2007. http://www.associatedcontent.com/article/339640/a_brief_history_of_health_care_in_america.html.

Dillon, Tamara. "Health Care Jobs You Might Not Know About." *Occupational Outlook Quarterly*, Summer, 2008. Available at http://www.bls.gov/opub/ooq/2008/summer/art03.pdf.

Fried, Bruce, and James A. Johnson, eds. *Human Resources in Health Care: Managing for Success*. Washington, D.C.: AUPHA Press/Health Administration Press, 2002.

Jonas, Steven, Anthony R. Kovner, and James Knickman. *Jonas and Kovner's Health Care Delivery in the United States*. New York: Springer, 2008.

Koss, W., and T. Sodeman. "The Workload Recording Method: A Laboratory Management Tool." *Clinical Lab Management Review* 12, no. 2 (June, 1992): 337-350.

Kotlikoff, Laurence J. *The Health Care Fix: Universal Insurance for All Americans*. Cambridge: Massachusetts Institute of Technology, 2007.

Merrit-Hawkins. *Physician Salary, Compensation, and Practice Surveys*. http://www.merritthawkins.com/compensation-surveys.aspx.

Plunkett, Jack W. *Plunkett Health Care Industry Update*. Houston, Tex.: Plunkett Research, 2010.

Stevens, Rosemary, Charles E. Rosenberg, and Lawton R. Burns. *History and Health Policy in the United States: Putting the Past Back In*. New Brunswick, N.J.: Rutgers University Press, 2006.

Swanson, Barbara M. *Careers in Health Care*. 5th ed. New York: McGraw-Hill, 2005.

U.S. Bureau of Labor Statistics. *Career Guide to Industries*, 2010-2011 ed. http://www.bls.gov/oco/cg.

U.S. Census Bureau. North American Industry Classification System (NAICS), 2007. http://www.census.gov/cgi-bin/sssd/naics/naicsrch?chart=2007.

U.S. Department of Health and Human Services. Office of Disease Prevention and Health Promotion. *Healthy People*. http://www.healthypeople.gov/.

World Health Organization. "Health Financing Policy." http://www.who.int/health_financing/functions/functions/en.

METALS MANUFACTURING INDUSTRY

Beddoes, J., and M. J. Bibby. *Principles of Metal Manufacturing Processes*. New York: John Wiley & Sons, 1999.

Creese, Robert C., et al. *Estimating and Costing for the Metal Manufacturing Industry*. Boca Raton, Fla.: CRC Press, 1992.

_____. *Introduction to Manufacturing Processes and Materials.* Speen, Newbury, Berkshire, England: Marcel Dekker, 1999.

Hoerr, John P. *And the Wolf Finally Came: The Decline of the American Steel Industry.* Pittsburgh: University of Pittsburgh Press, 1988.

Khare, Mukesh, et al. *Aluminium Smelting: Health, Environment and Engineering Perspectives.* Miami: Ian Randle, 2008.

Lankford, William T., Jr., et al. *The Making, Shaping, and Treating of Steel.* 11th ed. Pittsburgh: AISE Steel Foundation, 1998.

McDavid, Richard A., and Susan Echaore-McDavid. *Career Opportunities in Engineering.* New York: Ferguson, 2007.

Madar, Daniel. *Big Steel: Technology, Trade, and Survival in a Global Market.* Vancouver: University of British Columbia Press, 2009.

Peck, Merton J. *The World Aluminum Industry in a Changing Energy Era.* Baltimore: The Johns Hopkins University Press, 1988.

Preston, Richard. *American Steel: Hot Metal Men and the Resurrection of the Rust Belt.* New York: Prentice Hall, 1991.

Reutter, Mark. *Sparrows Point: Making Steel—The Rise and Ruin of American Industrial Might.* New York: Summit Books, 1988.

Rogers, Robert P. *An Economic History of the American Steel Industry.* New York: Routledge, 2009.

Tiffany, Paul A. *The Decline of American Steel: How Management, Labor, and Government Went Wrong.* New York: Oxford University Press, 1988.

U.S. Bureau of Labor Statistics. *Career Guide to Industries,* 2010-2011 ed. http://www.bls.gov/oco/cg.

U.S. Census Bureau. North American Industry Classification System (NAICS), 2007. http://www.census.gov/cgi-bin/sssd/naics/naicsrch?chart=2007.

U.S. Department of Commerce. International Trade Administration. Office of Trade and Industry Information. Industry Trade Data and Analysis. http://ita.doc.gov/td/industry/otea/OTII/OTII-index.html.

World Steel Association. *Steel Statistical Yearbook, 2009.* Brussels, Belgium: Committee on Economic Studies, 2010.

MINING INDUSTRY

Ali, Saleem H. *Treasures of the Earth: Need, Greed, and a Sustainable Future.* New Haven, Conn.: Yale University Press, 2009.

Bateman, Alan M. *Economic Mineral Deposits.* 2d ed. New York: John Wiley & Sons, 1950.

Bishop, A. C., A. R. Woolley, and W. R. Hamilton. *Guide to Minerals, Rocks, and Fossils.* Buffalo, N.Y.: Firefly Books, 2005.

Bouquet, Tim, and Byron Ousey. *Cold Steel: The Multi-Billion-Dollar Battle for a Global Empire.* Toronto: Key Porter Books, 2008.

Burke, D. Barlow, and Robert E. Beck. *The Law and Regulation of Mining: Minerals to Energy.* Durham, N.C.: Carolina Academic Press, 2010.

Dietrich, R. V., and B. F. Skinner. *Gems, Granites, and Gravels: Knowing and Using Rocks and Minerals.* New York: Cambridge University Press, 1990.

Erlichman, Howard J. *Conquest, Tribute, and Trade: The Quest for Precious Metals and the Birth of Globalization.* Amherst, N.Y.: Prometheus Books, 2010.

Hill, Mary. *Gold: The California Story.* Berkeley: University of California Press, 1999.

Horberry, Tim, Robin Burgess-Limerick, and Lisa J. Steiner. *Human Factors for the Design, Operation, and Maintenance of Mining Equipment.* Boca Raton, Fla.: CRC Press, 2011.

Perlez, Jane, Raymond Bonner, and Evelyn Rusli. "Below a Mountain of Wealth, a River of Waste." *New York Times* late ed. (East Coast), December 27, 2005.

Thompson, Tamara. *Uranium Mining.* Detroit: Greenhaven Press, 2010.

Tilton, John E., ed. *World Metal Demand: Trends and Prospects.* Washington, D.C.: Resources for the Future, 1990.

United Nations Statistical Division. *Statistical Yearbook.* 51st ed. New York: United Nations, 2007.

U.S. Bureau of Labor Statistics. *Career Guide to Industries,* 2010-2011 ed. http://www.bls.gov/oco/cg.

U.S. Census Bureau. North American Industry Classification System (NAICS), 2007. http://www.census.gov/cgi-bin/sssd/naics/naicsrch?chart=2007.

U.S. Department of Commerce. International Trade Administration. Office of Trade and Industry Information. Industry Trade Data and Analysis. http://ita.doc.gov/td/industry/otea/OTII/OTII-index.html.

U.S. Geological Survey. *Mineral Commodity Summaries, 2006.* Washington, D.C.: U.S. Government Printing Office, 2006. Available at http://minerals.usgs.gov/minerals/pubs/mcs/2006/msc2006.pdf.

_____. *Minerals Yearbook, 2007.* Washington, D.C.: U.S. Government Printing Office, 2007. http://minerals.usgs.gov/minerals/pubs/myb.html.

MOTION PICTURE AND TELEVISION INDUSTRY

Appleton, Dina, and Daniel Yankelevits. *Hollywood Dealmaking: Negotiating Talent Agreements for Film, TV, and New Media.* New York: Allworth Press, 2010.

Balio, Tino. *The American Film Industry.* Madison: University of Wisconsin Press, 1976.

_____. *Grand Design: Hollywood as a Modern Business Enterprise, 1930-1939.* New York: Maxwell Macmillan International, 1993.

Bielby, Denise D., and C. Lee Harrington. *Global TV: Exporting Television and Culture in the World Market.* New York: New York University Press, 2008.

Finney, Angus. *The International Film Business: A Market Guide Beyond Hollywood.* New York: Routledge, 2010.

Hoovers. "British Broadcasting Corporation." http://www.hoovers.com/company/British_Broadcasting_Corporation/hrfyri-1.html.

International Television Expert Group. "TV Market Data/Global TV Funding, 2008-2013." http://www.international-television.org/tv_market_data/pay-tv-and-tv-funding-worldwide_2008-2013.html.

Koszarski, Richard. *Hollywood on the Hudson: Film and Television in New York from Griffith to Sarnoff.* New Brunswick, N.J.: Rutgers University Press, 2008.

Langford, Barry. *Post-classical Hollywood: Film Industry, Style, and Ideology Since 1945.* Edinburgh: Edinburgh University Press, 2010.

Mehta, Rini Bhattacharya, and Rajeshwari Pandharipande. *Bollywood and Globalization: Indian Popular Cinema, Nation, and Diaspora.* New York: Anthem Press, 2010.

Motion Picture Association of America. *The Economic Impact of the Motion Picture and Television Industry on the United States.* Washington, D.C.: Author, 2009.

Musser, Charles. *The Emergence of Cinema: The American Screen to 1907.* New York: Maxwell Macmillan International, 1990.

Udelson, Joseph H. *The Great Television Race: A History of the American Television Industry, 1925-1941.* University: University of Alabama Press, 1982.

U.S. Bureau of Labor Statistics. *Career Guide to Industries,* 2010-2011 ed. http://www.bls.gov/oco/cg.

U.S. Census Bureau. North American Industry Classification System (NAICS), 2007. http://www.census.gov/cgi-bin/sssd/naics/naicsrch?chart=2007.

U.S. Department of Commerce. International Trade Administration. Office of Trade and Industry Information. Industry Trade Data and Analysis. http://ita.doc.gov/td/industry/otea/OTII/OTII-index.html.

U.S. Library of Congress. "History of Edison Motion Pictures." http://memory.loc.gov/ammem/edhtml/edmvhist.html.

MUSEUMS AND CULTURAL INSTITUTIONS INDUSTRY

Alexander, Edward P. *Museums in Motion: An Introduction to the History and Functions of Museums.* Walnut Creek, Calif.: AltaMira Press, 1996.

Burdick, Jan E. *Creative Careers in Museums.* New York: Allworth Press, 2008.

Center for the Future of Museums. *Museums and Society, 2034: Trends and Potential Futures.* Washington, D.C.: American Association of Museums, 2008. Available at http://aam-us.org/upload/museumssociety2034.pdf.

Chew, Ron. "In Praise of the Small Museum." *Museum News,* March/April, 2002. http://www.aam-us.org/pubs/mn/MN_MA02_Small Museums.cfm.

Institute for Career Research. *Careers in Museums: Director, Curator, Conservator, Exhibit Designer, Archivist.* Chicago: Author, 2007.

Rentzhog, Sten. *Open Air Museums: The History and Future of a Visionary Idea.* Stockholm: Carlsson, 2007.

Schlatter, N. Elizabeth. *Museum Careers: A Practical Guide for Novices and Students.* Walnut Creek, Calif.: Left Coast Press, 2008.

Society of American Archivists. "So You Want to Be an Archivist: An Overview of the Archival Profession." http://www2.archivists.org/profession.

U.S. Bureau of Labor Statistics. "Archivists, Curators, and Museum Technicians." In *Occupational Outlook Handbook,* 2010-2011 ed. http://www.bls.gov/oco/ocos065.htm.

_____. *Career Guide to Industries,* 2010-2011 ed. http://www.bls.gov/oco/cg.

U.S. Census Bureau. North American Industry Classification System (NAICS), 2007. http://www.census.gov/cgi-bin/sssd/naics/naicsrch?chart=2007.

U.S. Department of Commerce. International Trade Administration. Office of Trade and Industry Information. Industry Trade Data and Analysis. http://ita.doc.gov/td/industry/otea/OTII/OTII-index.html.

MUSIC INDUSTRY

Allen, Katie. "Downloads Fail to Stem Fall in Global Music Sales." *The Guardian,* July 3, 2007.

Borg, Bobby. *The Musician's Handbook: A Practical Guide to Understanding the Music Business.* New York: Billboard Books, 2008.

Cosper, Alex. "History of Record Labels and the Music Industry." Playlist Research, 2009. http://www.playlistresearch.com/recordindustry.htm.

Deloitte. "2009 Industry Outlook: Media and Entertainment." January 28, 2009. http://www.deloitte.com/view/en_US/us/Industries/Media-Entertainment/article/a5391ec6f6001210VgnVCM100000ba42f00aRCRD.htm.

The Economist. "Digital Music Sales." May 28, 2009.

Espejo, Roman, ed. *What Is the Future of the Music Industry?* Detroit: Greenhaven Press, 2009.

Gordon, Steve. *The Future of the Music Business.* 2d ed. Milwaukee: Hal Leonard Books, 2008.

Hefflinger, Mark. "Sony BMG Revenue Down 27.8%; Digital Up 40%." Digital Media Wire, March 20, 2008. http://www.dmwmedia.com/news/2008/03/20/sony-bmg-revenue-down-27.8%25%3B-digital-40%25.

Krasilovsky, M. William, and Sydney Shemel. *This Business of Music: The Definitive Guide to the Music Industry.* 10th ed. New York: Billboard Books, 2007.

Miller, Warren. "Live Nation, Ticketmaster Announce Plan to Merge." Morningstar, February 12, 2009. http://quicktake.morningstar.com/Stocknet/san.aspx?id=279588.

Negus, Keith. *Music Genres and Corporate Cultures.* New York: Routledge, 1999.

Rapaport, Diane. *A Music Business Primer.* Upper Saddle River, N.J.: Prentice Hall, 2003.

Thall, Peter W. *What They'll Never Tell You About the Music Business: The Myths, the Secrets, the Lies (and a Few Truths).* New York: Billboard Books, 2006.

U.S. Bureau of Labor Statistics. *Career Guide to Industries,* 2010-2011 ed. http://www.bls.gov/oco/cg.

_____. "Musicians, Singers, and Related Workers." In *Occupational Outlook Handbook,* 2010-2011 ed. http://www.bls.gov/oco/ocos095.htm.

U.S. Census Bureau. North American Industry Classification System (NAICS), 2007. http://www.census.gov/cgi-bin/sssd/naics/naicsrch?chart=2007.

U.S. Department of Commerce. International Trade Administration. Office of Trade and Industry Information. Industry Trade Data and Analysis. http://ita.doc.gov/td/industry/otea/OTII/OTII-index.html.

NATIONAL AND INTERNATIONAL SECURITY INDUSTRY

Bullock, Jane A., et al. *Introduction to Homeland Security: Principles of All-Hazards Response.* 3d ed. Boston: Butterworth Heinemann, 2009.

CareerBuilder.com. Salary Calculator and Wage Finder. http://www.cbsalary.com/salary-calculator.

Defence.Professionals. "Saab Half-Yearly Result Shows Increased Sales." July 24, 2009. http://www.defpro.com/news/details/8775.

Federation of American Scientists. "Fast Facts." 2009. http://www.fas.org/asmp/fast_facts.htm.

Homeland Security Research Corporation. *Global Homeland Security, Homeland Defense, and Intelligence Markets Outlook, 2009-2018.* Washington, D.C.: Author, 2009.

Howard, Russell D., and Reid L. Sawyer, eds. *Terrorism and Counterterrorism: Understanding the New Security Environment.* New York: McGraw-Hill, 2009.

Jones, Elka. "Careers in Homeland Security." *Occupational Outlook Quarterly,* Summer, 2006. Available at http://www.bls.gov/opub/ooq/2006/summer/art01.pdf.

Method, Jason. "Fed Pay: Rank-and-File Tops Private Average, Managers Fall Below." *USA Today,* June 24, 2007.

Nemeth, Charles P. *Homeland Security: An Introduction to Principles and Practice.* Boca Raton, Fla.: Auerback, 2010.

PayScale.com. "Salary Survey for Industry: Aerospace and Defense." http://www.payscale.com/research/US/Industry=Aerospace_and_Defense/Salary.

Renshon, Stanley Allen. *National Security in the Obama Administration: Reassessing the Bush Doctrine.* New York: Routledge, 2010.

Rosenbach, Eric, and Aki J. Peritz. *Confrontation or Collaboration? Congress and the Intelligence Community.* Cambridge, Mass.: John F. Kennedy School of Government, Belfer Center for Science and International Affairs, 2009.

Simply Hired. "Average Central Intelligence Agency Salaries." http://www.simplyhired.com/a/salary/search/q-Central+Intelligence+Agency+cia.

Thomas, Douglas, and Brian D. Loader, eds. *Cybercrime: Law Enforcement, Security, and Surveillance in the Information Age.* New York: Routledge, 2000.

U.S. Bureau of Labor Statistics. *Career Guide to Industries,* 2010-2011 ed. http://www.bls.gov/oco/cg.

U.S. Census Bureau. North American Industry Classification System (NAICS), 2007. http://www.census.gov/cgi-bin/sssd/naics/naicsrch?chart=2007.

U.S. Department of Commerce. International Trade Administration. Office of Trade and Industry Information. Industry Trade Data and Analysis. http://ita.doc.gov/td/industry/otea/OTII/OTII-index.html.

White, Jonathan R. *Terrorism and Homeland Security.* 6th ed. Belmont, Calif.: Wadsworth Cengage Learning, 2009.

NATURAL RESOURCES MANAGEMENT

Cassio, Jim, and Alice Rush. *Green Careers: Choosing Work for a Sustainable Future.* Gabriola Island, B.C.: New Society, 2009.

DeGalan, Julie. *Great Jobs for Environmental Studies Majors.* New York: McGraw-Hill, 2008.

Education-Portal.com. Natural Resource Manager Career Summary. http://education-portal.com/articles/Natural_Resource_Manager_Career_Summary.html.

Fasulo, Michael, and Paul Walker. *Careers in the Environment.* 3d ed. New York: McGraw-Hill, 2007.

Fraidenburg, Michael E. *Intelligent Courage: Natural Resource Careers That Make a Difference.* Malabar, Fla.: Krieger, 2007.

Greenland, Paul R., and Annamarie L. Sheldon. *Career Opportunities in Conservation and the Environment.* New York: Checkmark Books, 2007.

Hoovers. "Environmental Consulting." http://www.hoovers.com/environmental-consulting/—ID__385—/free-ind-fr-profile-basic.xhtml.

Hunter, M. J., D. B. Lindenmayer, and A. J. K. Calhoun. *Saving the Earth as a Career: Advice on Becoming a Conservation Professional.* Oxford, England: Blackwell, 2007.

Kroger, Richard. *Choosing a Conservation Vocation or a Bureaucratic Career: Your Personal Choices and the Environmental Consequences.* Victoria, B.C.: Trafford, 2006.

Llewellyn, A. B. *Green Jobs: A Guide to Eco-Friendly Employment*. Cincinnati: Adams Media, 2008.

Sharp, Bill. *The New Complete Guide to Environmental Careers*. Washington, D.C.: Island Press, 2001.

U.S. Bureau of Labor Statistics. *Career Guide to Industries*, 2010-2011 ed. http://www.bls.gov/oco/cg.

_____. "Conservation Scientists and Foresters." In *Occupational Outlook Handbook*, 2010-2011 ed. http://www.bls.gov/oco/ocos048.htm.

U.S. Census Bureau. North American Industry Classification System (NAICS), 2007. http://www.census.gov/cgi-bin/sssd/naics/naicsrch?chart=2007.

U.S. Department of Commerce. International Trade Administration. Office of Trade and Industry Information. Industry Trade Data and Analysis. http://ita.doc.gov/td/industry/otea/OTII/OTII-index.html.

NUCLEAR POWER INDUSTRY

CareerBuilder.com. Salary Calculator and Wage Finder. http://www.cbsalary.com/salary-calculator.

Careers.org. Occupation Profiles: Descriptions, Earnings, Outlook. http://occupations.careers.org.

Elliott, David. *Nuclear or Not? Does Nuclear Power Have a Place in a Sustainable Energy Future?* New York: Palgrave Macmillan, 2007.

Franceschetti, Donald R., David Rulloch, and Lee A. Paradise. "Can Radiation Waste from Fission Reactors Be Safely Stored?" In *Science in Dispute*, edited by Neil Schlager. Farmington Hills, Mich.: Gale, 2002.

Heppenheimer, T. A. "Nuclear Power: What Went Wrong?" *American Heritage of Invention and Technology* 18, no. 2 (2002): 46-56.

Herbst, Alan M., and George W. Hopley. *Nuclear Energy Now: Why the Time Has Come for the World's Most Misunderstood Energy Source*. Hoboken, N.J.: John Wiley & Sons, 2007.

Lejzerovič, Aleksander. *Wet-Steam Turbines for Nuclear Power Plants*. Tulsa, Okla.: PennWell, 2005.

Levy, Salomon. *Fifty Years in Nuclear Power: A Retrospective*. La Grange Park, Ill.: American Nuclear Society, 2007.

Newton, David E. *Nuclear Power*. New York: Infobase, 2005.

Taylor, Allan, and James Robert Parish. *Career Opportunities in the Energy Industry*. New York: Ferguson, 2008.

U.S. Bureau of Labor Statistics. *Career Guide to Industries*, 2010-2011 ed. http://www.bls.gov/oco/cg.

U.S. Census Bureau. North American Industry Classification System (NAICS), 2007. http://www.census.gov/cgi-bin/sssd/naics/naicsrch?chart=2007.

U.S. Department of Commerce. International Trade Administration. Office of Trade and Industry Information. Industry Trade Data and Analysis. http://ita.doc.gov/td/industry/otea/OTII/OTII-index.html.

Wood, J. *Nuclear Power*. London: Institution of Engineering and Technology, 2007.

OUTDOOR RECREATION INDUSTRY

Beech, John G., and Simon Chadwick. *The Business of Tourism Management*. Upper Saddle River, N.J.: Prentice Hall, 2006.

Bell, Simon. *Design for Outdoor Recreation*. New York: Taylor and Francis, 1997.

Broadhurst, Rich. *Managing Environments for Leisure and Recreation*. New York: Routledge, 2001.

Fennell, David A. *Ecotourism: An Introduction*. New York: Routledge, 2003.

Forbes, M. S., F. S. Liljegren, J. T. Liljegren, and V. E. Lovejoy. *Outdoor Recreation Business Plan Guidebook*. Denver: U.S. Department of the Interior, Bureau of Reclamation, Policy and Program Services, Denver Federal Center, 2008. Available at http://www.usbr.gov/recreation/publications/BusPlanGuide.pdf.

Gartner, W. C., and D. W. Lime. *Trends in Outdoor Recreation, Leisure, and Tourism*. Oxfordshire, England: CABI Press, 2000.

Jenkins, John. *Outdoor Recreation Management*. New York: Routledge, 1999.

Jensen, Clayne R., and Steven Guthrie. *Outdoor Recreation in America*. Champaign, Ill.: Human Kinetics, 2006.

Pigram, J. J. J., and John Michael Jenkins. *Outdoor Recreation Management*. New York: Taylor and Francis, 2006.

U.S. Bureau of Labor Statistics. *Career Guide to Industries*, 2010-2011 ed. http://www.bls.gov/oco/cg.

_____. *Occupational Outlook Handbook*, 2010-2011 ed. http://www.bls.gov/oco.

U.S. Census Bureau. North American Industry Classification System (NAICS), 2007. http://www.census.gov/cgi-bin/sssd/naics/naicsrch?chart=2007.

U.S. Department of Commerce. International Trade Administration. Office of Trade and Industry Information. Industry Trade Data and Analysis. http://ita.doc.gov/td/industry/otea/OTII/OTII-index.html.

U.S. Global Change Research Program. "Regional Paper: Rocky Mountain/Great Basin Region." 2003. http://www.usgcrp.gov/usgcrp/nacc/education/rockies-greatbasin/default.htm.

Zueflie, Matt. "Leisure and Tourism Changing Through the Great Recession." *The Athens News* (Ohio), July 30, 2009.

PAPER MANUFACTURING AND PRODUCTS INDUSTRY

Bjorkman, A., D. Paun, and C. Jacobs-Young. "Financial Performance, Capital Expenditures, and International Activities of the North American Pulp and Paper Industry at Mid-Decade." *TAPPI Journal* 80, no. 10 (October, 1997): 71-84.

Carson, Thomas, and Mary Bonk. *Gale Encyclopedia of U.S. Economic History*. Detroit: Gale Group, 1999.

Converter. "New Technology Active in Sector." 46, no. 6 (October 28, 2008). Retrieved from Business Source Complete database.

Datamonitor. *Global Paper Products: Industry Profile*. March 8, 2010. Retrieved from MarketLine database.

_____. *Paper and Paperboard in the United States*. March 15, 2010. Retrieved from MarketLine database.

Encyclopedia of American Industries. Millerton, N.Y.: Grey House, 2008.

Holik, Herbert. *Handbook of Paper and Board*. Weinheim, Germany: Wiley-VCH, 2006.

Hunter, Dard. *Papermaking: The History and Technique of an Ancient Craft*. New York: Knopf, 1947.

IBISWorld. *Cardboard Box and Container Manufacturing in the U.S.: Industry Report 32221*. February, 2010. Retrieved from IBISWorld Industry Market Research database.

_____. *Cardboard Mills in the U.S.: Industry Report 32213*. June, 2009. Retrieved from IBISWorld Industry Market Research database.

_____. *Coated and Laminated Paper Manufacturing in the U.S.: Industry Report 32222*. February, 2010. Retrieved from IBISWorld Industry Market Research database.

_____. *Labels, Egg Cartons, and Other Paper Product Manufacturing the U.S.: Industry Report 32229b*. January, 2010. Retrieved from IBISWorld Industry Market Research database.

_____. *Office Stationery Manufacturing the U.S.: Industry Report 32223*. May, 2010. Retrieved from IBISWorld Industry Market Research database.

_____. *Paper Mills in the U.S.: Industry Report 32212*. February, 2009. Retrieved from IBISWorld Industry Market Research database.

_____. *Sanitary Paper Product Manufacturing in the U.S.: Industry Report 32229a*. February, 2010. Retrieved from IBISWorld Industry Market Research database.

_____. *Wood Pulp Mills in the U.S.: Industry Report 32211*. November, 2009. Retrieved from IBISWorld Industry Market Research database.

Nurmi, Ville. "Future Trends of HRD in the Finnish Pulp and Paper Industry." *Human Resource Development International* 10, no. 1 (2007): 107-113.

O'Hara, Frederick M., Jr., and F. M. O'Hara III. *Handbook of United States Economic and Financial Indicators*. Westport, Conn.: Greenwood Press, 2000.

Organization for Economic Cooperation and Development. *OECD Environmental Outlook to 2030*. Paris: Author, 2008.

Packaged Facts. *The U.S. Market for Household Paper Products.* December, 2005. Retrieved from MarketResearch.com Academic database.

Parker, Philip M. *The 2006-2011 World Outlook for Paper Mills.* San Diego, Calif.: ICON Group, 2005.

Parsons, Charles K. *Workplace Transformation and Human Resource Management Practices in the Pulp and Paper Industry.* Atlanta: Center for Paper Business and Industry Studies, Georgia Institute of Technology, 2004.

Patrick, Ken, and Glenn Ostle. "Outlook: North America 2010." *Paper 360* 5, no. 1 (January/February, 2010): 8-11.

PricewaterhouseCoopers. *CEO Perspectives: Viewpoints of CEOs in the Forest, Paper, and Packaging Industry Worldwide.* Available at http://www.Pwc.Com/en_gx/gx/forest-paper-packaging/ceo2009/index.Jhtml.

_____. *Global Forest, Paper, and Packaging Industry Survey.* Available at http://www.Pwc.Com/en_gx/gx/forest-paper-packaging/2009-fpp-survey/index.Jhtml.

Smith, Maureen. *The U.S. Paper Industry and Sustainable Production: An Argument for Restructuring.* Cambridge, Mass.: MIT Press, 1997.

Standard and Poor's Industry Surveys. *Paper and Forest Products.* Available at http://www.netadvantage.standardandpoors.com.

Thompson, Claudia G., and the American Institute of Graphic Arts, Boston Chapter. *Recycled Papers: The Essential Guide.* Cambridge, Mass.: MIT Press, 1992.

U.S. Bureau of Labor Statistics. *Career Guide to Industries,* 2010-2011 ed. http://www.bls.gov/oco/cg.

_____. *Occupational Outlook Handbook,* 2010-2011 ed. http://www.bls.gov/oco.

U.S. Census Bureau. North American Industry Classification System (NAICS), 2007. http://www.census.gov/cgi-bin/sssd/naics/naicsrch?chart=2007.

Wilkinson, Norman B. *Papermaking in America.* Greenville, Del.: Hagley Museum, 1975.

Young, Rod. "Rollercoaster Ride in Recovered Paper Continues." *PPI: Pulp and Paper International* 52, no. 5 (2010): 48-48.

PASSENGER TRANSPORTATION AND TRANSIT INDUSTRY

Cudahy, Brian. *Cash, Tokens, and Transfers: A History of Urban Mass Transit in North America.* New York: Fordham University Press, 1990.

Guess, George. *Public Policy and Transit System Management.* New York: Greenwood Press, 1990.

Landefeld, Steven, Brent R. Moulton, and Cindy M. Vojtech. "Chained-Dollar Indexes: Issues, Tips on Their Use, and Upcoming Changes." *Survey of Current Business* (November, 2003): 8-16.

McDavid, Richard, and Susan Echaore-McDavid. *Career Opportunities in Transportation.* New York: Ferguson, 2009.

Transit Cooperative Research Program. *2008 Annual Report.* Washington, D.C.: Transportation Research Board, 2008.

U.S. Bureau of Labor Statistics. *Career Guide to Industries,* 2010-2011 ed. http://www.bls.gov/oco/cg.

U.S. Census Bureau. North American Industry Classification System (NAICS), 2007. http://www.census.gov/cgi-bin/sssd/naics/naicsrch?chart=2007.

U.S. Department of Commerce. International Trade Administration. Office of Trade and Industry Information. Industry Trade Data and Analysis. http://ita.doc.gov/td/industry/otea/OTII/OTII-index.html.

PERSONAL SERVICES

Brown, Bobbi, and Sally Wadyka. *Bobbi Brown Beauty Evolution: A Guide to a Lifetime of Beauty.* New York: HarperCollins, 2002.

Careers in Focus: Personal Services. 2d ed. New York: Ferguson, 2007.

Clarke-Stewart, A., and V. D. Allhusen. *What We Know About Childcare.* Cambridge, Mass.: Harvard University Press, 2005.

Ferri, E., and M. E. Siegel. *Finger Tips: A Professional Manicurist's Techniques for Beautiful Hands and Feet.* New York: C. N. Potter, 1988.

Mendelson, C. *Home Comforts: The Art and Science of Keeping House.* New York: Scribner, 1999.

Riordan, T. *Inventing Beauty: A History of the Innovations That Have Made Us Beautiful.* New York: Broadway Books, 2004.

Smith, G., and T. V. Beeck. "Personal Services: A Fast Growing Sector with Unique Risks." *RMA Journal,* July/August, 2009, 60-64.

U.S. Bureau of Labor Statistics. *Career Guide to Industries,* 2010-2011 ed. http://www.bls.gov/oco/cg.

U.S. Census Bureau. North American Industry Classification System (NAICS), 2007. http://www.census.gov/cgi-bin/sssd/naics/naicsrch?chart=2007.

U.S. Department of Commerce. International Trade Administration. Office of Trade and Industry Information. Industry Trade Data and Analysis. http://ita.doc.gov/td/industry/otea/OTII/OTII-index.html.

Wittenberg, R. *Opportunities in Child Care Careers.* New York: McGraw-Hill, 2007.

PETROLEUM AND NATURAL GAS INDUSTRY

Anderson, Robert O. *Fundamentals of the Petroleum Industry.* Norman: University of Oklahoma Press, 1984.

Bader, Jeffrey, et al. *The Global Politics of Energy.* Washington, D.C.: Aspen Institute, 2008.

Boudreaux, Terry. *Ethanol and Biodiesel: What You Need to Know.* McLean, Va.: Hart Energy, 2007.

Deffeyes, Kenneth S. *Hubbert's Peak: The Impending World Oil Shortage.* Princeton, N.J.: Princeton University Press, 2001.

Drapes, Michaela. *Vault Guide to the Top Energy and Oil and Gas Employers, 2009.* New York: Vault Reports, 2008.

Engler, Robert. *The Brotherhood of Oil: Energy Policy and the Public Interest.* Chicago: University of Chicago Press, 1977.

Falola, Toyin, and Ann Genova. *The Politics of the Global Oil Industry: An Introduction.* Westport, Conn.: Praeger, 2005.

Grace, Robert. *Oil: An Overview of the Petroleum Industry.* Houston, Tex.: Gulf, 2007.

Johnson, Arthur M. *Pipelines: A Study in Private Enterprise and Public Policy.* Ithaca, N.Y.: Cornell University Press, 1956. Reprint. Westport, Conn.: Greenwood Press, 1982.

Miesner, Thomas O., and William L. Leffier. *Oil and Gas Pipelines in Nontechnical Language.* Tulsa, Okla.: Pennwell, 2006.

Odell, Peter R. *Global Issues.* Vol. 1 in *Oil and Gas: Crises and Controversies, 1961-2000.* Brentwood, Essex, England: Multi-Science, 2004.

Raymond, Martin S., and William L. Leffier. *Oil and Gas Production in Nontechnical Language.* Tulsa, Okla.: Pennwell, 2005.

Roberts, Paul. *The End of Oil: On the Edge of a Perilous New World.* New York: Mariner Books, 2005.

Sampson, Anthony. *The Seven Sisters: The Great Oil Companies and the World They Shaped.* New York: Viking Press, 1980.

Simmons, Matthew R. *Twilight in the Desert: The Coming Saudi Oil Shock and the World Economy.* New York: Wiley, 2006.

U.S. Bureau of Labor Statistics. *Career Guide to Industries,* 2010-2011 ed. http://www.bls.gov/oco/cg.

U.S. Census Bureau. North American Industry Classification System (NAICS), 2007. http://www.census.gov/cgi-bin/sssd/naics/naicsrch?chart=2007.

U.S. Department of Commerce. International Trade Administration. Office of Trade and Industry Information. Industry Trade Data and Analysis. http://ita.doc.gov/td/industry/otea/OTII/OTII-index.html.

PHARMACEUTICALS AND MEDICATIONS INDUSTRY

Alliance for Retired Americans Educational Fund. *Outrageous Fortune: How the Drug Industry Profits from Pills.* Washington, D.C.: Author, 2007.

Angell, Marcia. *The Truth About Drug Companies: How They Deceive Us and What to Do About It.* New York: Random House, 2004.

Bastianelli, Enrico, Jurg Eckhardt, and Olivier Teirlynck. "Pharma: Can the Middle Hold?" *The McKinsey Quarterly,* May 29, 2001, 118.

Campbell, John J. *Understanding Pharma: The Professional's Guide to How Pharmaceutical and Biotech Companies Really Work.* 2d ed. Raleigh, N.C.: Pharmaceutical Institute, 2008.

Cockburn, Iain M. "The Changing Structure of the Pharmaceutical Industry." *Health Affairs* 23, no. 1 (January/February, 2004): 10-22.

Davidson, Larry, and Gennadiy Greblov. "The Pharmaceutical Industry in the Global Economy." Bloomington: Indiana University Kelley School of Business, 2005.

Jacobsen, Thomas M., and Albert I. Wertheimer. *Modern Pharmaceutical Industry: A Primer.* Sudbury, Mass.: Jones and Bartlett, 2010.

McCarthy, Robert L., and Kenneth W. Schafermeyer. *Introduction to Health Care Delivery: A Primer for Pharmacists.* 2d ed. Gaithersburg, Md.: Aspen, 2001.

Niebyl, Jennifer R. "The Pharmaceutical Industry: Friend or Foe?" *American Journal of Obstetrics and Gynecology,* April, 2008, 435.

Organization for Economic Cooperation and Development. *Pharmaceutical Pricing Policies in a Global Market.* Paris: Author, 2008.

Paul, Steven M., et al. "How to Improve R&D Productivity: The Pharmaceutical Industry's Grand Challenge." *Nature Reviews: Drug Discovery* 9, no. 3 (March, 2010): 203-214.

U.S. Bureau of Labor Statistics. *Career Guide to Industries,* 2010-2011 ed. http://www.bls.gov/oco/cg.

U.S. Census Bureau. North American Industry Classification System (NAICS), 2007. http://www.census.gov/cgi-bin/sssd/naics/naicsrch?chart=2007.

U.S. Congressional Budget Office. *Research and Development in the Pharmaceutical Industry: A CBO Study.* Washington, D.C.: Author, 2006.

U.S. Department of Commerce. International Trade Administration. Office of Trade and Industry Information. Industry Trade Data and Analysis. http://ita.doc.gov/td/industry/otea/OTII/OTII-index.html.

U.S. Internal Revenue Service. "Pharmaceutical Industry Overview." http://www.irs.gov/businesses/article/0,,id=169579,00.html.

World Trade Organization. "TRIPS and Pharmaceutical Patents: Fact Sheet." Geneva, Switzerland: Author, 2006. http://www.wto.org/english/tratop_e/trips_e/factsheet_pharm00_e.htm.

PHILANTHROPIC, CHARITABLE, RELIGIOUS, CIVIC, AND GRANT-MAKING INDUSTRY

Boris, Elizabeth T., et al. *What Drives Foundation Expenses and Compensation: Results of a Three-Year Study.* New York: Urban Institute, Foundation Center, and Philanthropic Research, 2008. Available at http://foundationcenter.org/gainknowledge/research/pdf/fec_report.pdf.

Charities Aid Foundation. *International Comparison of Charitable Giving, November, 2006.* Kings Hill, West Malling, Kent, England: Author, 2006. Available at http://www.cafonline.org/pdf/International Giving highlights.pdf.

Elazar, Daniel J. *Community and Polity: The Organizational Dynamics of American Jewry.* Philadelphia: Jewish Publication Society of America, 1976.

Gassler, Robert Scott. *The Economics of Nonprofit Enterprise: A Study in Applied Economic Theory.* Lanham, Md.: University Presses of America, 1986.

Grobman, Gary M., and Gary B. Grant. *The Non-Profit Internet Handbook.* Harrisburg, Pa.: White Hat Communications, 1997.

Independent Sector. "The Sector's Economic Impact." http://www.independentsector.org/economic_role.

Keating, Barry P., and Maryann O. Keating. *Not-for-Profit.* Glen Ridge, N.J.: Thomas Horton and Daughters, 1980.

Knauft, E. B., Renee A. Berger, and Sandra T. Gray. *Profiles of Excellence: Achieving Success in the Nonprofit Sector.* San Francisco: Jossey-Bass, 1991.

Lowell, Stephanie. *Careers in the Nonprofit Sector.* Cambridge, Mass.: Harvard Business School, 2000.

Olasky, Marvin. *The Tragedy of American Compassion.* Preface by Charles Murray. Washington, D.C.: Regnery, 1992.

Organization for Economic Cooperation and Development. *The Non-profit Sector in a Changing Economy.* Paris: Author, 2003.

Pallotta, Dan. *Uncharitable: How Restraints on Nonprofits Undermine Their Potential.* Hanover, N.H.: University Press of New England, 2008.

Raymond, Susan U. *The Future of Philanthropy: Economics, Ethics, and Management.* Hoboken, N.J.: John Wiley & Sons, 2004.

Shaw, Sondra C., and Martha A. Taylor. *Reinventing Fundraising: Realizing the Potential of Women's Philanthropy.* San Francisco: Jossey-Bass, 1995.

U.S. Bureau of Labor Statistics. *Career Guide to Industries*, 2010-2011 ed. http://www.bls.gov/oco/cg.

————. *Occupational Outlook Handbook*, 2010-2011 ed. http://www.bls.gov/oco.

U.S. Census Bureau. North American Industry Classification System (NAICS), 2007. http://www.census.gov/cgi-bin/sssd/naics/naicsrch?chart=2007.

U.S. Department of Commerce. International Trade Administration. Office of Trade and Industry Information. Industry Trade Data and Analysis. http://ita.doc.gov/td/industry/otea/OTII/OTII-index.html.

Von Drehle, David. "The Other Financial Crisis." *Time*, June 28, 2010, 22-28.

White, Michelle J., ed. *Nonprofit Firms in a Three-Sector Economy.* Washington, D.C.: Urban Institute, 1991.

Wing, Kennard T., Katie L. Roediger, and Thomas H. Pollak. *The Nonprofit Sector in Brief: Public Charities, Giving, and Volunteering, 2009.* Washington, D.C.: Urban Institute, 2010. http://www.urban.org/uploadedpdf/412085-nonprofit-sector-brief.pdf.

Wolch, Jennifer L. *The Shadow State: Government and Voluntary Sector in Transition.* New York: Foundation Center, 1990.

PLASTICS AND RUBBER MANUFACTURING INDUSTRY

Aftalion, Fred. *A History of the International Chemical Industry.* Philadelphia: University of Pennsylvania Press, 1991.

Chamis, Alice Yanosoko. "The Literature of Synthetic Rubber." In *Literature of Chemical Technology*, edited by Julian F. Smith. Washington, D.C.: American Chemical Society, 1968.

Chandler, Alfred D. *Shaping the Industrial Century: The Remarkable Story of the Evolution of the Modern Chemical and Pharmaceutical Industries.* Cambridge, Mass.: Harvard University Press, 2005.

Ciesielski, Andrew. *An Introduction to Rubber Technology.* Shawsbury, Shrewsbury, Shropshire, England: RAPRA Technology, 1999.

International Institute of Synthetic Rubber Producers. *Synthetic Rubber: The Story of an Industry.* New York: Author, 1973.

Kaufman, M. *The First Century of Plastics: Celluoid and Its Sequel.* London: Plastics Institute, 1963.

Mossman, Susan, ed. *Early Plastics: Perspectives, 1850-1950.* London: Leicester University Press, 1997.

Schidrowitz, P., and T. R. Dawson. *History of the Rubber Industry.* London: Institution of the Rubber Industry, 1952.

Stevens, Eugene S. *Green Plastics: An Introduction to the New Science of Biodegradable Plastics.* Princeton, N.J.: Princeton University Press, 2001.

U.S. Bureau of Labor Statistics. *Career Guide to Industries*, 2010-2011 ed. http://www.bls.gov/oco/cg.

U.S. Census Bureau. North American Industry Classification System (NAICS), 2007. http://www.census.gov/cgi-bin/sssd/naics/naicsrch?chart=2007.

U.S. Department of Commerce. International Trade Administration. Office of Trade and Industry Information. Industry Trade Data and Analysis. http://ita.doc.gov/td/industry/otea/OTII/OTII-index.html.

U.S. Environmental Protection Agency. Office of Compliance. *Profile of the Rubber and Plastics Industry.* 2d ed. Washington, D.C.: Author, 2005.

POLITICAL ADVOCACY INDUSTRY

Bimbaum, Jeffrey H. "In a Harsh Climate for Lobbyists, the Forecast Calls for . . . More

Lobbyists." *The Washington Post*, August 12, 2008.

"Biography of Ulysses S. Grant." Incredible People. http://profiles.incredible-people .com/ulysses-s-grant.

Center for Responsive Politics. Communications. "Washington Lobbying Grew to $3.2 Billion Last Year, Despite Economy." *Capitol Eye Blog*, January 29, 2009. http://www.opensecrets .org/news/2009/01/washington-lobbying -grew-to-32.html.

Clarke, Conor. "The Dire State of the Lobbying Industry." *The Atlantic*, March 12, 2009. http://politics.theatlantic.com/2009/03/the _dire_state_of_the_lobbying_industry.php.

Cummings, Jeanne. "Inside the Lobbying Industry's Evolution." *Politico*, August 14, 2007. http://www.politico.com/news/stories/0807/ 5368.html.

Danzinger, Danny, and John Gillingham. *1215: The Year of Magna Carta*. New York: Simon and Schuster, 2004.

Hrebenar, Ronald J., and Bryson B. Morgan. *Lobbying in America: A Reference Handbook*. Santa Barbara, Calif.: ABC-CLIO, 2009.

Luneburg, William V., Thomas M. Susman, and Rebecca H. Gordon. *The Lobbying Manual: A Complete Guide to Federal Lobbying Law and Practice*. 4th ed. Chicago: American Bar Association, 2009.

McGrath, Conor. *Interest Groups and Lobbying in the United States and Comparative Perspectives: Essays in Ethics, Institutional Pluralism, Regulation, and Management*. Lewiston, N.Y.: Edwin Mellen Press, 2009.

Mahoney, Christine. *Brussels Versus the Beltway: Advocacy in the United States and the European Union*. Washington, D.C.: Georgetown University Press, 2008.

_____. "Why Lobbying in America Is Different." EuropeanVoice.com, April 6, 2009. http://www.europeanvoice.com/article/2009/ 06/why-lobbying-in-america-isdifferent/65078 .aspx.

Newton, Adam, and Ronald K. L. Collins. "Petition." First Amendment Center. http:// www.firstamendmentcenter.org/petition/ overview.aspx.

Public Affairs Links. http://www.publicaffairs links.co.uk.

Public Citizen. "History of the Lobbying Disclosure Act." July 23, 2005. http://www .lobbyinginfo.org/laws/page.cfm?pageid=15.

Salary Expert. "Political Analyst Compensation Data." http://www.salaryexpert.com/index .cfm?fuseaction=Browse.Political-Analyst -salary-data-details&PositionId=17475.

Salent, Jonathan D., and Kristin Jensen. "Lobbyist-Bashing by Obama Doesn't Dim Industry's Boom Forecast." Bloomberg.com, November 20, 2008. http://www.bloomberg .com/apps/news?pid=20601070&refer=home &sid=aEZoCjCjrYDE.

SimplyHired. "Average Business Development Salaries." http://www.simplyhired.com/a/ salary/search/q-business+development.

_____. "Average Political Consultant Salaries." http://www.simplyhired.com/a/salary/search/ q-Political+Consultant.

Taminiau, Yvette, and Arnold Wilts. "Corporate Lobbying in Europe: Managing Knowledge and Information Strategies." *Journal of Public Affairs* 6, no. 2 (May, 2006): 122-130.

U.S. Bureau of Labor Statistics. *Career Guide to Industries*, 2010-2011 ed. http://www.bls .gov/oco/cg.

_____. *Occupational Outlook Handbook*, 2010-2011 ed. http://www.bls.gov/oco.

U.S. Census Bureau. North American Industry Classification System (NAICS), 2007. http:// www.census.gov/cgi-bin/sssd/naics/naicsrch ?chart=2007.

U.S. Department of Commerce. International Trade Administration. Office of Trade and Industry Information. Industry Trade Data and Analysis. http://ita.doc.gov/td/industry/ otea/OTII/OTII-index.html.

Vance, Stephanie D. *The Advocacy Handbook: A Practitioner's Guide to Achieving Policy Goals Through Organization Networks*. Bethesda, Md.: Columbia Books, 2009.

Young, McGhee. *Developing Interests: Organizational Change and the Politics of Advocacy*. Lawrence: University Press of Kansas, 2010.

POSTAL AND PACKAGE DELIVERY SERVICES

Frock, Roger. *Changing How the World Does Business: FedEx's Incredible Journey to Success—The Inside Story.* San Francisco: Berrett-Koehler, 2006.

Hill, Rowland. *Post Office Reform: Its Importance and Practicability.* London: Charles Knight, 1837.

Kosar, Kevin. *The U.S. Postal Service's Financial Condition: Overview and Issues for Congress.* Washington, D.C.: Congressional Research Service, 2010.

Niemann, Greg. *Big Brown: The Untold Story of UPS.* San Francisco: Jossey-Bass, 2007.

Oxford Economics. *The Impact of the Express Delivery Industry on the Global Economy.* Oxford, England: Author, 2009.

Potter, John. "Five Myths About the U.S. Postal Service." *Washington Post,* February 28, 2010. http://www.washingtonpost.com/wp-dyn/content/article/2010/02/25/AR2010022504888.html.

Rubio, Philip F. *There's Always Work at the Post Office: African American Postal Workers and the Fight for Jobs, Justice, and Equality.* Chapel Hill: University of North Carolina Press, 2010.

U.S. Bureau of Labor Statistics. *Career Guide to Industries,* 2010-2011 ed. http://www.bls.gov/oco/cg.

U.S. Census Bureau. North American Industry Classification System (NAICS), 2007. http://www.census.gov/cgi-bin/sssd/naics/naicsrch?chart=2007.

U.S. Congress. House. Committee on the Judiciary. *Competition in the Package Delivery Industry.* Washington, D.C.: Government Printing Office, 2009.

U.S. Department of Commerce. International Trade Administration. Office of Trade and Industry Information. Industry Trade Data and Analysis. http://ita.doc.gov/td/industry/otea/OTII/OTII-index.html.

U.S. Postal Service. *Annual Report, 2009.* Washington, D.C.: Author, 2009.

_____. *Envisioning a Viable Postal Service for America: An Action Plan for the Future.* Washington, D.C.: Author, 2010.

_____. *2008 Sustainability Report: Delivering a Greener Tomorrow.* Washington, D.C.: Author, 2009. http://www.usps.com/green/report/2008/welcome.htm.

Workplace Economics. "The Relative Size of Labor Costs at UPS, FedEx, and the U.S. Postal Service." Washington, D.C.: American Postal Workers Union, 2002.

PRINTING INDUSTRY

Career Overview. "Prepress Technician Careers, Jobs, and Employment Information." http://www.careeroverview.com/prepress-technician-careers.html.

_____. "Printing Machine Operator Careers, Jobs, and Employment Information." http://www.careeroverview.com/printing-machine-operator-careers.html.

Casals, Ricard. *The Future of Printed Signage: Market Opportunities.* Leatherhead, Surrey, England: Pira International, 2008.

Clark, Richard P., and Pamela Fehl. *Career Opportunities in the Visual Arts.* New York: Checkmark, 2006.

Davis, Ronnie H. *Beyond the Horizon: Key Dynamics Shaping Print Markets and Printers over the Next Decade.* Sewickley, Pa.: Printing Industries of America, 2009.

_____. *Profiling the Economy and Print Markets, 2009-2010.* Sewickley, Pa.: Printing Industries of America, 2009.

Febvre, Lucien, and Henri-Jean Martin. *The Coming of the Book: The Impact of Printing, 1450-1800.* 3d ed. New York: Verso, 2010.

Flecker, Sally Ann, and Deanna M. Gentile. *Careers in Printing: The Original Information Media.* Sewickley, Pa.: Graphic Arts Technical Foundation, 2002.

MacDougall, Andy. *Screen Printing Today.* Cincinnati: ST Books, 2005.

Parker, Philip M. *The 2009-2014 World Outlook for Printing and Binding of General and Trade Books.* San Diego, Calif.: ICON Group, 2008.

Rose, David S. *Introduction to Letterpress Printing in the Twenty-first Century.* http://www.fiveroses.org/intro.htm.

U.S. Bureau of Labor Statistics. *Career Guide to Industries*, 2010-2011 ed. http://www.bls.gov/oco/cg.

———. *Occupational Outlook Handbook*, 2010-2011 ed. http://www.bls.gov/oco.

U.S. Census Bureau. North American Industry Classification System (NAICS), 2007. http://www.census.gov/cgi-bin/sssd/naics/naicsrch?chart=2007.

U.S. Department of Commerce. International Trade Administration. Office of Trade and Industry Information. Industry Trade Data and Analysis. http://ita.doc.gov/td/industry/otea/OTII/OTII-index.html.

Webb, Joe. "How Printing Industry Employment Has Changed Since 2000." WhatTheyThink?, February 10, 2010. http://blogs.whattheythink.com/economics/2010/02/how-printing-industry-employment-has-changed-since-2000.

PRIVATE EDUCATION INDUSTRY

Associated Press. "Career Education 4Q Profit Up, Revenue Down." Boston.com, February 19, 2009. http://www.boston.com/business/articles/2009/02/19/career_education_4q_profit_up_revenue_down.

Bailey, Thomas, Norena Badway, and Patricia J. Gumport. *For-Profit Higher Education and Community Colleges.* Stanford, Calif.: National Center for Postsecondary Improvement, 2001. Available at http://www.stanford.edu/group/ncpi/documents/pdfs/forprofitandcc.pdf.

Bensinger, Greg. "Washington Post Reports Profit on Education Revenue." Bloomberg.com, July 31, 2009. http://www.bloomberg.com/apps/news?pid=20601204&sid=a99eeXcdQ4Z4.

Burch, Patricia. *Hidden Markets: The New Education Privatization.* New York: Routledge, 2009.

Butler, Amy. *Wages in the Nonprofit Sector: Occupations Typically Found in Educational and Research Institutions.* Washington, D.C.: U.S. Bureau of Labor and Statistics, 2009. Available at http://www.bls.gov/opub/cwc/cm20081124ar01p1.htm.

Coleman, James, and Richard Vedder. *For Profit Education in the United States: A Primer.*

Washington, D.C.: Center for College Affordability and Productivity, 2008. Available at http://www.centerforcollegeaffordability.org/uploads/For-Profit_corr_2.pdf.

Hallinan, Maureen T. *Handbook of the Sociology of Education.* New York: Springer Press, 2006.

The Handbook of Private Schools: An Annual Descriptive Survey of Independent Education. Boston: Porter Sargent Handbooks, 2009.

Herrera, Debbi. *Resource Guide for Private School Administrators.* Danvers, Mass.: LRP Publications, 2007.

"Institutional Eligibility Under the Higher Education Act of 1965, as Amended, and the Secretary's Recognition of Accrediting Agencies; Proposed Rule." *Federal Register* 74, no. 150 (August 6, 2009). http://edocket.access.gpo.gov/2009/pdf/E9-18368.pdf.

Jones, Steven L. *Religious Schooling in America: Private Education and Public Life.* Westport, Conn.: Praeger, 2008.

Morphew, Christopher C., and Peter D. Eckel. *Privatizing the Public University: Perspectives from Across the Academy.* Baltimore: The Johns Hopkins University Press, 2009.

Sandler, Michael R. *Social Entrepreneurship in Education: Private Ventures for the Public Good.* Lanham, Md.: Rowman & Littlefield Education, 2010.

StateUniversity.com. "Private Schooling: What Is a Private School? History of Private Schools in the United States." http://education.stateuniversity.com/pages/2334/Private-Schooling.html.

U.S. Bureau of Labor Statistics. *Career Guide to Industries*, 2010-2011 ed. http://www.bls.gov/oco/cg.

———. *Occupational Outlook Handbook*, 2010-2011 ed. http://www.bls.gov/oco.

U.S. Census Bureau. North American Industry Classification System (NAICS), 2007. http://www.census.gov/cgi-bin/sssd/naics/naicsrch?chart=2007.

U.S. Department of Commerce. International Trade Administration. Office of Trade and Industry Information. Industry Trade Data and Analysis. http://ita.doc.gov/td/industry/otea/OTII/OTII-index.html.

U.S. Department of Education. Institute of Education Sciences. National Center for

Education Statistics. "The Condition of Education." 2007. http://nces.ed.gov/programs/coe/2007/section4/indicator32.asp.
_____. "Private School Universe Survey." 2007-2008 ed. http://nces.ed.gov/surveys/pss/index.asp.
_____. "Projections of Education Statistics to 2016." 2007. http://nces.ed.gov/programs/projections/projections2016/sec1a.asp.

PUBLIC ELEMENTARY AND SECONDARY EDUCATION INDUSTRY

Caillier, James. "Paying Teachers According to Student Achievement: Questions Regarding Pay-for-Performance Models in Public Education." *The Clearing House* 83, no. 2 (2010): 58-61.

Fry, Richard. *The High Schools Hispanics Attend: Size and Other Key Characteristics*. Washington, D.C.: Pew Hispanic Center, 2005.

Gardiner, Mary E., Kathy Canfield-Davis, and Keith LeMar Anderson. "Urban School Principals and the 'No Child Left Behind' Act." *The Urban Review* 41, no. 2 (September, 2008): 141-160.

Graves, Michael F., Bonnie B. Graves, and Connie Juel. *Teaching Reading in the 21st Century*. 4th ed. Boston: Pearson/Allyn & Bacon, 2007.

Herbst, Jürgen. *The Once and Future School: Three Hundred and Fifty Years of American Secondary Education*. New York: Routledge, 1996.

Hursh, David. "The Growth of High Stakes Testing in the USA: Accountability, Markets and the Decline in Educational Equality." *British Educational Research Journal* 31, no. 5 (October, 2005): 605-622.

Johnson, James Allen, et al. *Foundations of American Education: Perspectives on Education in a Changing World*. 15th ed. Boston: Pearson/Allyn & Bacon, 2010.

Lee, Valerie E., et al. "Inside Large and Small High Schools: Curriculum and Social Relations." *Educational Evaluation and Policy Analysis* 22, no. 2 (Summer, 2000): 147-171.

"No Child Left Behind Revisited: The New Debate on Education Reform." *Congressional Digest* 87, no. 5 (May, 2008).

Parkay, Forrest W., and Beverly Hardcastle Stanford. *Becoming a Teacher*. 3d ed. Boston: Allyn & Bacon, 1998.

Pulliam, John D., and James J. Van Patten. *The History of Education in America*. 9th ed. Upper Saddle River, N.J.: Merrill, 2007.

U.S. Bureau of Labor Statistics. *Career Guide to Industries*, 2010-2011 ed. http://www.bls.gov/oco/cg.

U.S. Census Bureau. North American Industry Classification System (NAICS), 2007. http://www.census.gov/cgi-bin/sssd/naics/naicsrch?chart=2007.

U.S. Department of Commerce. International Trade Administration. Office of Trade and Industry Information. Industry Trade Data and Analysis. http://ita.doc.gov/td/industry/otea/OTII/OTII-index.html.

PUBLIC HEALTH SERVICES

Allied Physicians.com. "Physician Salaries and Salary Surveys." June, 2006. http://www.allied-physicians.com/salary_surveys/physician-salaries.htm.

Bayer, Ronald, et al. *Public Health Ethics: Theory, Policy, and Practice*. Rev. ed. New York: Oxford University Press, 2007.

Billings, Molly. "The 1918 Influenza Pandemic." Palo Alto, Calif.: Human Virology at Stanford University, 1997. Available at http://virus.stanford.edu/uda/index.html.

Experience.com. "What Sectors Make Up the Nonprofit Industry?" http://www.experience.com/alumnus/article?channel_id=nonprofit&source_page=additional_articles&article_id=article_1159823736672.

First Research.com. "Hospitals Industry Profile Excerpt." June 22, 2009. http://www.firstresearch.com/Industry-Research/Hospitals.html.

Harvard School of Public Health. "About HSPH." http://www.hsph.harvard.edu/about.

Jenkins, Wiley D. *Public Health Laboratories: Analysis, Operations, and Management*. Sudbury, Mass.: Jones and Bartlett, 2011.

Loue, Sana. *Forensic Epidemiology: Integrating Public Health and Law Enforcement*. Sudbury, Mass.: Jones and Bartlett, 2010.

MedicineNet. "Definition of Public Health." October 2, 2001. http://www.medterms.com/script/main/art.asp?articlekey=5120.

PayScale.com. "Salary Snapshot for Medical and Public Health Social Worker Jobs." http://www.payscale.com/research/US/Job=Medical_and_Public_Health_Social_Worker/Salary.

Rosen, George. *A History of Public Health*. Baltimore: The Johns Hopkins University Press, 1993.

Rosner, David, and Gerald E. Markowitz. *Are We Ready? Public Health Since 9/11*. Berkeley: University of California Press, 2006.

Salary.com. http://swz.salary.com.

Schneider, Mary-Jane. *Introduction to Public Health*. 2d ed. Sudbury, Mass.: Jones and Bartlett, 2006.

Scutchfield, F. Douglas, and William Keck. *Principles of Public Health Practice*. 3d ed. Clifton Park, N.Y.: Delmar Cengage Learning, 2009.

"Statistics on Nonprofit Hospital Revenue, Expense, and Excess Revenue." *Becker's Hospital Review*, February 26, 2009. http://www.hospitalreviewmagazine.com/news-and-analysis/current-statistics-and-lists/statistics-on-nonprofit-hospital-revenue-expenses-and-excess-revenue.html.

Styles, Paula. "The Black Death, 1347-1351." http://medievalhistory.suite101.com/article.cfm/the_black_death_13471351.

Themedica.com. "Medical Industry Overview." http://www.themedica.com/industry-overview.html.

U.S. Bureau of Labor Statistics. *Career Guide to Industries*, 2010-2011 ed. http://www.bls.gov/oco/cg.

_____. *Occupational Outlook Handbook*, 2010-2011 ed. http://www.bls.gov/oco.

U.S. Census Bureau. North American Industry Classification System (NAICS), 2007. http://www.census.gov/cgi-bin/sssd/naics/naicsrch?chart=2007.

U.S. Department of Commerce. International Trade Administration. Office of Trade and Industry Information. Industry Trade Data and Analysis. http://ita.doc.gov/td/industry/otea/OTII/OTII-index.html.

U.S. Internal Revenue Service. Colleges and Universities Compliance Project. http://www.irs.gov/charities/article/0,,id=186865,00.html.

_____. Exemption Requirements. http://www.irs.gov/charities/charitable/article/0,,id=96099,00.html.

PUBLISHING AND INFORMATION INDUSTRY

Burns, A. *The Power of the Written Word*. New York: Peter Lang, 1989.

"*Chicago Sun-Times* Files for Bankruptcy." *Chicago Tribune*, March 31, 2009.

"Conde Nast to Close *Gourmet* Magazine." *The Guardian*, October 5, 2009.

Henderson, J. *The World of the Ancient Maya*. Ithaca, N.Y.: Cornell University Press, 1997.

"Indian Media Industry to Outshine Global Peers." *Financial Express*, July 31, 2009.

Madigan, C. *The Collapse of the Great American Newspaper*. Chicago: Ivan R. Dee, 2007.

Martin, S., and D. Copeland. *The Function of Newspapers in Society: A Global Perspective*. Westport, Conn.: Greenwood Press, 2003.

Meyer, P. *The Vanishing Newspaper*. Columbia: University of Missouri Press, 2004.

Moorehouse, A. C. *The Triumph of the Alphabet: A History of Writing*. New York: Henry Schuman, 1953.

Moscati, S. *The Face of the Orient: A Panorama of Near Eastern Civilizations in Pre-classical Times*. Chicago: Quadrangle Books, 1960.

"The New Austerity in Publishing." *The New York Times*, January 4, 2009.

Peddie, R. A. *Printing: A Short History of the Art*. London: Grafton, 1927.

"Seattle P-I to Publish Last Edition Tuesday." *Seattle Post-Intelligencer*, March 17, 2009.

"Tribune Co. Files for Bankruptcy." *Chicago Tribune*, December 9, 2008.

U.S. Bureau of Labor Statistics. *Career Guide to Industries*, 2010-2011 ed. http://www.bls.gov/oco/cg.

U.S. Census Bureau. North American Industry Classification System (NAICS), 2007. http://www.census.gov/cgi-bin/sssd/naics/naicsrch?chart=2007.

U.S. Department of Commerce. International Trade Administration. Office of Trade and Industry Information. Industry Trade Data and Analysis. http://ita.doc.gov/td/industry/otea/OTII/OTII-index.html.

REAL ESTATE INDUSTRY

CB Richard Ellis Group. "CB Richard Ellis's 2009 Review and 2010 Outlook for Commercial Real Estate in Europe." December, 2009/January, 2010. http://www.cbre.com/EN/AboutUs/MediaCentre/2010/Pages/011110.aspx.

Harkins, Phil. *Everybody Wins: The Story and Lessons Behind RE/MAX*. Hoboken, N.J.: John Wiley & Sons, 2004.

Keller, Gary, with Dave Jenks and Jay Papasan. *The Millionaire Real Estate Agent: It's Not About the Money . . . It's About Being the Best You Can Be!* New York: McGraw-Hill, 2004.

Lindahl, David. *Emerging Real Estate Markets: How to Find and Profit from Up-and-Coming Areas*. Hoboken, N.J.: John Wiley & Sons, 2008.

Malpass, Peter, and Robert Rowlands. *Housing, Markets, and Policy*. New York: Routledge, 2010.

National Association of REALTORS. *Field Guide to the History of the National Association of REALTORS*. July, 2008. http://www.realtor.org/library/library/fg002.

Plunkett, Jack W. *Plunkett's Real Estate and Construction Industry Almanac, 2010*. Houston, Tex.: Plunkett Research, 2010.

Riley, Rowan. *Real Estate: An All-in-One Guide to Navigating Toward a New Career*. New York: Ferguson, 2010.

Urban Land Institute and Pricewaterhouse Coopers. *Emerging Trends in Real Estate, 2009-2010*. Washington, D.C.: Author, 2009.

U.S. Bureau of Labor Statistics. *Career Guide to Industries*, 2010-2011 ed. http://www.bls.gov/oco/cg.

U.S. Census Bureau. North American Industry Classification System (NAICS), 2007. http://www.census.gov/cgi-bin/sssd/naics/naicsrch?chart=2007.

U.S. Department of Commerce. International Trade Administration. Office of Trade and Industry Information. Industry Trade Data and Analysis. http://ita.doc.gov/td/industry/otea/OTII/OTII-index.html.

RENTAL AND LEASING SERVICES

Auto Rental News. "U.S. Car Rental Revenues Rise in 2010." December 1, 2010. http://www.autorentalnews.com/News/Story/2010/12/Revenues-Rise-in-2010.aspx.

Barton, Robert. "American Car Rental Association Chief: I'm 'Adamantly Opposed' to á la Carte Pricing." Interview by Christopher Elliott. Elliott Blog, April 24, 2009. http://www.elliot.org/first-person/6333.

The Economist. "Wheels When You Need Them: Car-Sharing." 396, no. 8698 (September 4, 2010): 70.

Jahn, Tim. "Creating the Textbook Rental Industry—With Aayush Phumbhra, Founder of Chegg.com." *Beyond the Pedway*, November 9, 2010. http://www.beyond thepedway.com/chegg-interview-aayush-phumbhra.

Jakl, Thomas, and Petra Schwager, eds. *Chemical Leasing Goes Global: Selling Services Instead of Barrels: A Win-Win Business Model for Environment and Industry*. New York: SpringerWien, 2008.

Kazanjian, Kirk. *Exceeding Customer Expectations: What Enterprise, America's Number-One Car Rental Company, Can Teach You About Creating Lifetime Customers*. Foreword by Andrew C. Taylor. New York: Currency Doubleday/Random House, 2007.

Keegan, Paul. "Zipcar: The Best New Idea in Business." *Fortune* 160, no. 5 (September 14, 2009): 42-52.

Lacko, James M., Signe-Mary McKernan, and Manoj Hastak. *Survey of Rent-to-Own Customers*. Washington, D.C.: Federal Trade Commission, Bureau of Economics, 2000.

Menkin, Christopher. "The $650 Billion Leasing Industry Has Dramatically Changed." *Seeking Alpha: Financial Stocks*, March 27, 2009. http://seekingalpha.com/article/128189-the-650-billion-leasing-industry-has-dramatically-changed.

Monitor Daily. "Equipment Finance Industry Confidence Shows More Improvement."

November 19, 2010. http://www.monitordaily.com/story_page.asp?news_id=26889.

Paul, Lisa, ed. *World Leasing Yearbook 2010*. Colchester, Essex, England: Euromoney Institutional Investor, 2009.

Phelan, Kim. "Soaring Inflatables Industry Gets a Second Look from Insurance." *Rental Pulse*. http://www.rentalpulse.com/Article/tabid/95/smid/426/ArticleID/234/reftab/113/Default.aspx.

Roseman, Brett T. "Rental Car Industry Starts to Emerge from the 'Perfect Storm.'" *USA Today*, April 5, 2010. http://www.usatoday.com/travel/news/2010-04-06-rentalcars06_CV_N.htm.

Saunders, Harris, Sr. *Top Up or Down? The Origin and Development of the Automobile and Truck Renting and Leasing Industry—Since 1916*. Birmingham, Ala.: Harris Saunders, 1985.

Smith, Brandey. "Dreamgirls: Women Succeeding in the Rental Industry." *Rental Equipment Register*, April 1, 2007. http://rermag.com/features/equipment_dream_girls.

Stoller, Gary. "Hertz to Acquire Dollar Thrifty; Cash, Stock Rental Car Deal Valued at $1.2B." *USA Today*, April 27, 2010, p. 3B.

Transportation Security Administration. *Safeguarding America's Transportation System: Security Guide for Truck Rental Company Employees*. Washington, D.C.: U.S. Department of Homeland Security, 2005.

U.S. Bureau of Labor Statistics. *Career Guide to Industries*, 2010-2011 ed. http://www.bls.gov/oco/cg.

———. "Counter and Rental Clerks." In *Occupational Outlook Handbook*, 2010-2011 ed. http://www.bls.gov/oco/ocos117.htm.

U.S. Census Bureau. North American Industry Classification System (NAICS), 2007. http://www.census.gov/cgi-bin/sssd/naics/naicsrch?chart=2007.

Wortham, Jenna. "Haute Couture, Available Through the Netflix Model." *The New York Times*, November 9, 2009, p. B-1.

RESIDENTIAL MEDICAL CARE INDUSTRY

Giacolone, Joseph A. *The U.S. Nursing Home Industry*. Armonk, N.Y.: M. E. Sharpe, 2001.

New Strategist Publications. *American Health: Demographics and Spending of Health Care Consumers*. Ithaca, N.Y.: Author, 2005.

Parker, Philip M. *The 2007-2012 Outlook for Nursing Homes in the United States*. San Diego, Calif.: ICON Group, 2006.

Santerre, Rexford E., John A. Vernon, and the National Bureau of Economic Research. *Testing for Ownership Mix Efficiency: The Case of the Nursing Home Industry*. Cambridge, Mass.: National Bureau of Economic Research, 2005.

U.S. Bureau of Labor Statistics. *Career Guide to Industries*, 2010-2011 ed. http://www.bls.gov/oco/cg.

U.S. Census Bureau. North American Industry Classification System (NAICS), 2007. http://www.census.gov/cgi-bin/sssd/naics/naicsrch?chart=2007.

U.S. Congressional Budget Office. *The Impact of Medicare's Payment Rates on the Volume of Services Provided by Skilled Nursing Facilities*. Washington, D.C.: Author, 2007.

U.S. Department of Commerce. International Trade Administration. Office of Trade and Industry Information. Industry Trade Data and Analysis. http://ita.doc.gov/td/industry/otea/OTII/OTII-index.html.

Verity, Jane, and Daniel Kuhn. *The Art of Dementia Care*. Clifton Park, N.Y.: Thomson Delmar Learning, 2008.

RESTAURANT INDUSTRY

Beriss, David, and David Evan Sutton. *The Restaurants Book: Ethnographies of Where We Eat*. Oxford, England: Berg, 2007.

"Economics and Origin of the Restaurant." *Cornell Hotel and Restaurant Administration Quarterly*, August, 2002. http://www.arts.cornell.edu/econ/kiefer/Restaurant.PDF.

Fine, Gary Alan. *Kitchens: The Culture of Restaurant Work*. Berkeley: University of California Press, 2008.

Fullen, Sharon L. *Restaurant Design: Designing, Constructing, and Renovating a Food Service Establishment*. Ocala, Fla.: Atlantic, 2002.

Gabriel, Vincent A. *Success in the Food Business*. Singapore: Rank Books, 2008.

Lee, Ronald. *The Everything Guide to Starting and Running a Restaurant*. New York: Everything Books, 2005.

Miller, Richard K. *The 2009 Retail Business Market Research Handbook*. 11th ed. Loganville, Ga.: Richard K. Miller and Associates, 2009.

National Restaurant Association. "Restaurant Industry: Facts at a Glance." http://www .restaurant.org/research/ind_glance.cfm.

Pilzer, Paul Zane. *The New Wellness Revolution: How to Make a Fortune in the Next Trillion Dollar Industry*. New York: John Wiley & Sons, 2007.

Research and Markets. "Leisure: Global Industry Guide." http://www.researchandmarkets .com/reports/838291/leisure_global_industry _guide.

Simon, Michèle. *Appetite for Profit: How the Food Industry Undermines Our Health and How to Fight Back*. New York: Nation Books, 2006.

StarChefs.com "Salary Survey." http://www .starchefs.com/features/editors_dish/salary _survey/2008/html/index.shtml.

U.S. Bureau of Labor Statistics. *Career Guide to Industries*, 2010-2011 ed. http://www.bls .gov/oco/cg.

U.S. Census Bureau. North American Industry Classification System (NAICS), 2007. http:// www.census.gov/cgi-bin/sssd/naics/naicsrch ?chart=2007.

U.S. Department of Commerce. International Trade Administration. Office of Trade and Industry Information. Industry Trade Data and Analysis. http://ita.doc.gov/td/ industry/otea/OTII/OTII-index.html.

U.S. Internal Revenue Service. "Food Industry Overview." http://www.irs.gov/businesses/ article/0,,id=175715,00.html.

Walker, John R. *The Restaurant: From Concept to Operation*. New York: John Wiley & Sons, 2007.

Watson, James L., and Melissa L. Caldwell. *The Cultural Politics of Food and Eating: A Reader*. New York: Wiley-Blackwell, 2005.

RETAIL TRADE AND SERVICE INDUSTRY

Fisher, Marshall L., and Ananth Raman. *The New Science of Retailing: How Analytics Are Transforming the Supply Chain and Improving Performance*. Boston: Harvard Business Press, 2010.

JobBank USA. "Training, Certifications, Skills and Advancement: Purchasing Managers, Buyers, and Purchasing Agents." http://www .jobbankusa.com/career_employment/ purchasing_managers_buyers_purchasing _agents/training_certifications_skills _advancement.html.

Krafft, Manfred, and Murali K. Mantrala. *Retailing in the Twenty-first Century: Current and Future Trends*. New York: Springer, 2010.

Lichtenstein, Nelson. *The Retail Revolution: How Wal-Mart Created a Brave New World of Business*. New York: Metropolitan Books, 2009.

Miller, Michael. *Selling Online 2.0: Migrating from eBay to Amazon, Craigslist, and Your Own E-commerce Website*. Indianapolis, Ind.: Que, 2009.

Moody's Investor Services. "Annual Outlook: U.S. Retail Industry." Alacra Store. http://www .alacrastore.com/research/moodys-global -credit-research-Annual_Outlook_U_S_Retail _Industry_Sluggish_Economy_Will_Limit _Earnings_Growth_in_2011-PBC_128312.

PayScale.com. "Salary for Industry: Retail." January 11, 2011. http://www.payscale.com/ research/US/ Industry=Retail/Salary.

_____. "Salary Snapshot for Web Administrator Jobs." January 7, 2011. http://www.payscale .com/research/US/Job=Web_Administrator/ Salary.

Salary.com. "Salary Wizard: Storekeeper." http://www1.salary.com/Storekeeper-salary .html.

Simply Hired. "Average Building Maintenance Salaries." http://www.simplyhired .com/ a/salary/search/q-building+maintenance.

_____. "Average Online Retail Sales Salaries." http://www.simplyhired.com/a/salary/search/ q-online+retail+sales/l-logan,+ut.

StateUniversity.com. "Stock Clerk Job Description, Career as a Stock Clerk, Salary,

Employment." http://careers.stateuniversity
.com/pages/633/Stock-Clerk.html.

U.S. Bureau of Labor Statistics. "Clothing,
Accessory, and General Merchandise Stores."
In *Occupational Outlook Handbook*, 2010-2011
ed. http://www.bls.gov/oco/cg/cgs022.htm.

_____. "Retail Salespersons." In *Occupational
Outlook Handbook*, 2010-2011 ed.
http://www.bls.gov/oco/ocos121.htm.

_____. "Sales Worker Supervisors." In
Occupational Outlook Handbook, 2010-2011 ed.
http://www.bls.gov/oco/ocos025.htm
#earnings.

U.S. Census Bureau. North American Industry
Classification System (NAICS), 2007. http://
www.census.gov/cgi-bin/sssd/naics/naicsrch
?chart=2007.

_____. *Career Guide to Industries*, 2010-2011 ed.
http://www.bls.gov/oco/cg.

_____. "Engineers." In *Occupational Outlook
Handbook*, 2010-2011 ed. http://www.bls.gov/
oco/ocos027.htm.

U.S. Census Bureau. North American Industry
Classification System (NAICS), 2007. http://
www.census.gov/cgi-bin/sssd/naics/naicsrch
?chart=2007.

_____. Service Annual Survey. 2008 http://
www.census.gov/services/sas/historic_data
.html.

U.S. Department of Commerce. International
Trade Administration. Office of Trade and
Industry Information. Industry Trade Data
and Analysis. http://ita.doc.gov/td/industry/
otea/OTII/OTII-index.html.

Yates, J. K. *Global Engineering and Construction*.
Hoboken, N.J.: Wiley, 2007.

SCIENTIFIC AND TECHNICAL SERVICES

Adeola, Bayo. *Engineering Is Development: Towards
a New Role for Consultancy in Nation Building*.
Lagos, Nigeria: Comprehensive Project
Management Services, 2009.

Camenson, Blythe. *Opportunities in Forensic Science
Careers*. New York: McGraw-Hill, 2009.

Careers in Focus: Engineering. 2d ed. New York:
Ferguson, 2007.

Erickson, Aaron. *The Nomadic Developer: Surviving
and Thriving in the World of Technology
Consulting*. Upper Saddle River, N.J.:
Addison-Wesley, 2009.

Gartner, John. *Confessions of a Consultant: Survival
Business Skills for Scientists and Engineers*.
Belleville, Ont.: Epic Press, 2008.

Kenney, Martin. *Biotechnology: The
University-Industrial Complex*. New Haven,
Conn.: Yale University Press, 1986.

Simon, Françoise, and Philip Kotler. *Building
Global Biobrands: Taking Biotechnology to Market*.
New York: Free Press, 2003.

Skrzeszewski, Stan. *The Knowledge Entrepreneur*.
Lanham, Md.: Scarecrow Press, 2006.

U.S. Bureau of Labor Statistics. "Biological
Scientists." In *Occupational Outlook Handbook*,
2010-2011 ed. http://www.bls.gov/oco/
ocos047.htm.

SCIENTIFIC, MEDICAL, AND HEALTH EQUIPMENT AND SUPPLIES INDUSTRY

Babler, Scott D. *Pharmaceutical and Biomedical
Project Management in a Changing Global
Environment*. Oxford, England: Wiley-
Blackwell, 2010.

Baxter, Jenny. *Market Report, 2009: Medical
Equipment*. Hampton, England: Key Note,
2009.

Bronzino, Joseph D. *Medical Devices and Systems*.
Boca Raton, Fla.: CRC Press, 2006.

Espicom Business Intelligence. *The True State of
the Medical Device Industry*. Chichester, West
Sussex, England: Author, 2009.

Mehta, Shreefal S. *Commercializing Successful
Biomedical Technologies: Basic Principles for the
Development of Drugs, Diagnostics, and Devices*.
New York: Cambridge University Press, 2008.

Parker, Philip M. *The 2009-2014 World Outlook for
Health Care Equipment and Supplies*. San Diego,
Calif.: ICON Group, 2008.

_____. *The 2009-2014 World Outlook for Surgical
and Medical Instruments*. San Diego, Calif.:
ICON Group, 2008.

Teixeira, Marie B., and Richard Bradley. *Design
Controls for the Medical Device Industry*. New
York: Marcel Dekker, 2003.

U.S. Bureau of Labor Statistics. *Career Guide to Industries*, 2010-2011 ed. http://www.bls.gov/oco/cg.

U.S. Census Bureau. North American Industry Classification System (NAICS), 2007. http://www.census.gov/cgi-bin/sssd/naics/naicsrch?chart=2007.

U.S. Department of Commerce. International Trade Administration. Office of Trade and Industry Information. Industry Trade Data and Analysis. http://ita.doc.gov/td/industry/otea/OTII/OTII-index.html.

U.S. International Trade Commission. *Medical Devices and Equipment: Competitive Conditions Affecting U.S. Trade in Japan and Other Principal Foreign Markets.* Washington, D.C.: Author, 2007.

Wiklund, Michael E., Jonathan Kendler, and Allison S. Yale. *Usability Testing of Medical Devices.* Boca Raton, Fla.: Taylor & Francis, 2011.

Zenios, Stefanos, et al. *Biodesign: The Process of Innovating Medical Technologies.* New York: Cambridge University Press, 2009.

SHIPBUILDING, SUBMARINES, AND NAVAL TRANSPORT INDUSTRY

Benamara, Hassiba. *Shipping and Global Trade: A Review of Major Developments.* New York: United Nations Conference on Trade and Development, 2010.

Crowell, John Franklin. "Present Status and Future Prospects of American Shipbuilding." *Annals of the American Academy of Political and Social Science* 19 (January, 1902): 46-60.

De la Pedraja Tomán, René. *A Historical Dictionary of the U.S. Merchant Marine and Shipping Industry: Since the Introduction of Steam.* Westport, Conn.: Greenwood Press, 1994.

Dear, I. C. B., and Peter Kemp, eds. *The Oxford Companion to Ships and the Sea.* 2d ed. New York: Oxford University Press, 2005.

Finamore, Daniel. *America and the Sea: Treasures from the Collections of Mystic Seaport.* New Haven, Conn.: Yale University Press, 2005.

Fox, Nancy Ruth, and Lawrence J. White. "U.S. Shipping Policy: Going Against the Tide."

Annals of the American Academy of Political and Social Science 553 (September, 1997): 75-86.

Gardiner, Robert, and Arne Emil Christensen, eds. *The Earliest Ships: The Evolution of Boats into Ships.* Annapolis, Md.: Naval Institute Press, 1996.

Harley, C. K. "On the Persistence of Old Techniques: The Case of North American Wooden Shipbuilding." *The Journal of Economic History* 33, no. 2 (June, 1973): 372-398.

Harris, Brayton. *The Navy Times Book of Submarines: A Political, Social, and Military History.* New York: Berkley Books, 1997.

Havighurst, Walter. *The Long Ships Passing: The Story of the Great Lakes.* 1942. Reprint. Minneapolis: University of Minnesota Press, 2002.

Heitzmann, William Ray. *Opportunities in Marine Science and Maritime Careers.* New York: McGraw-Hill, 2006.

Keeny, Sandy. "The Foundations of Government Contracting." *Journal of Contract Management* (Summer, 2007): 7-19.

Kennedy, Greg. *The Merchant Marine in International Affairs, 1850-1950.* London: Frank Cass, 2000.

Kotar, S. L., and J. E. Gessler. *The Steamboat Era: A History of Fulton's Folly on American Rivers, 1807-1860.* Jefferson, N.C.: McFarland, 2009.

Labaree, Benjamin W., et al. *America and the Sea: A Maritime History.* Mystic, Conn.: Mystic Seaport Museum, 1998.

Landström, Björn. *The Ship: An Illustrated History.* Garden City, N.Y.: Doubleday, 1961.

Levinson, Marc. *The Box: How the Shipping Container Made the World Smaller and the World Economy Bigger.* Princeton, N.J.: Princeton University Press, 2006.

National Academy of Sciences. *Shipbuilding Technology and Education.* Washington, D.C.: Author, 1996.

Roland, Alex, W. Jeffrey Bolster, and Alexander Keyssar. *The Way of the Ship: America's Maritime History Reenvisioned, 1600-2000.* Hoboken, N.J.: John Wiley, 2008.

Stopford, Martin. *Maritime Economics.* 3d ed. New York: Routledge, 2009.

Talley, Wayne K. "Dockworker Earnings, Containerization, and Shipping Deregulation." *Journal of Transport Economics and Policy* 36, no. 3 (September, 2002): 447-467.

Thiesen, William H. *Industrializing American Shipbuilding: New Perspectives on Maritime History and Nautical Archaeology.* Gainesville: University Press of Florida, 2006.

U.S. Bureau of Labor Statistics. *Career Guide to Industries,* 2010-2011 ed. http://www.bls.gov/oco/cg.

U.S. Census Bureau. North American Industry Classification System (NAICS), 2007. http://www.census.gov/cgi-bin/sssd/naics/naicsrch?chart=2007.

Walters, William D. "American Naval Shipbuilding. 1890-1989." *Geographical Review* 90, no. 3 (July, 2000): 418-431.

SPACE EXPLORATION AND SPACE SCIENCE INDUSTRY

Aldridge, Edward C., et al. *A Journey to Inspire, Innovate, and Discover: Report of the President's Commission on Implementation of United States Space Exploration Policy.* Washington, D.C.: Government Printing Office, 2004.

Augustine, Norman R., et al. *Seeking a Human Spaceflight Program Worthy of a Great Nation.* Washington, D.C.: National Aeronautics and Space Administration, 2009.

Borrelli, Carmine, et al. *The Space Industry.* Ft. Belvoir, Va.: Defense Technical Information Center, 2007.

Collins, P., and A. Autino. "What the Growth of a Space Tourism Industry Could Contribute to Employment, Economic Growth, Environmental Protection, Education, Culture, and World Peace." *Acta Astronautica* 66, nos. 11/12 (June/July, 2010): 1553-1562.

Commercial Space Transportation Study Alliance. *Commercial Space Transportation Study.* Washington, D.C.: National Aeronautics and Space Administration, 1997. Available at http://www.hq.nasa.gov/webaccess/CommSpaceTrans.

Federal Aviation Administration. Office of the Associate Administrator for Commercial Space Transportation. *The Economic Impact of Commercial Space Transportation on the U.S. Economy: 2002 Results and Outlook for 2010.*

Springfield, Va.: National Technical Information Service, 2004.

Greenberg, Joel S., and Henry R. Hertzfeld, eds. *Space Economics.* Progress in Astronautics and Aeronautics 144. Washington, D.C.: American Institute of Aeronautics and Astronautics, 1992.

Gunther, Jocelyn S. *Commercial Space Transportation.* Hauppauge, N.Y.: Nova Science, 2010.

Jasentuliyana, Nandasiri, ed. *Space Law: Development and Scope.* Westport, Conn.: Praeger, 1992.

Komerath, N. M., J. Nally, and E. Taing. "Policy Model for Space Economy Infrastructure." *Acta Astronautica* 61, nos. 11/12 (December, 2007): 1066-1075.

Lamassoure, E., J. H. Saleh, and D. E. Hastings. "Space Systems Flexibility Provided by On-Orbit Servicing: Part 2." *Journal of Spacecraft and Rockets* 39, no. 4 (2002): 561-570.

Lewis, J. S., and R. A. Lewis. *Space Resources: Breaking the Bonds of Earth.* New York: Columbia University Press, 1987.

Longuski, Jim. *Advice to Rocket Scientists: A Career Survival Guide for Scientists and Engineers.* Reston, Va.: American Institute of Aeronautics and Astronautics, 2004.

National Research Council. *Defending Planet Earth: Near-Earth Object Surveys and Hazard Mitigation Strategies.* Washington, D.C.: National Academies Press, 2010.

_____. *An Enabling Foundation for NASA's Earth and Space Science Missions.* Washington, D.C.: National Academies Press, 2010.

Nicogaossian, Arnauld E., and Joseph H. Rothenburg. *Commercial Development Plan for the International Space Station: Final Draft.* Washington, D.C.: National Aeronautics and Space Administration, 1998.

U.S. Bureau of Labor Statistics. *Career Guide to Industries,* 2010-2011 ed. http://www.bls.gov/oco/cg.

U.S. Census Bureau. North American Industry Classification System (NAICS), 2007. http://www.census.gov/cgi-bin/sssd/naics/naicsrch?chart=2007.

U.S. Department of Commerce. International Trade Administration. Office of Trade and Industry Information. Industry Trade Data and Analysis. http://ita.doc.gov/td/industry/otea/OTII/OTII-index.html.

U.S. National Aeronautics and Space Administration. NASA History Office. "The Decision to Go to the Moon: President John F. Kennedy's May 25, 1961 Speech before a Joint Session of Congress." http://history.nasa.gov/moondec.html.

Walker, Robert Smith, et al. *Anyone, Anywhere, Anytime, Anything: Final Report of the Commission on the Future of the United States Aerospace Industry.* Arlington, Va.: Commission on the Future of the Aerospace Industry, 2002.

Zubrin, R. *Entering Space: Creating a Spacefaring Civilization.* New York: Tarcher, 1999.

SPECTATOR SPORTS INDUSTRY

Bowles, Tom. "As NASCAR Money Gap Widens, Start and Parkers Soldier On." *Sports Illustrated,* June 11, 2009. http://sportsillustrated.cnn.com/2009/writers/tom_bowles/06/11/Start-and-park/index.html.

Fowler, Elizabeth M. "Careers: Learning to Manage a Race Track." *The New York Times,* May 1, 1990. http://www.nytimes.com/1990/05/01/business/careers-learning-to-manage-a-race-track.html.

Funk, Daniel C. *Consumer Behaviour in Sport and Events: Marketing Action.* Boston: Butterworth-Heinemann/Elsevier, 2008.

Hart, Chris J., Corinne M. Daprano, and Peter J. Titlebaum. "Rules of the Game: Ethics in Sports Marketing." *Sports Media* 33 (March, 2005): http://www.sports-media.org/newpedimension7.htm.

Horrow, Richard B., and Karla Swatek. *Beyond the Box Score: An Insider's Guide to the $750 Billion Business of Sports.* New York: Morgan James, 2010.

Jozsa, Frank P. *Global Sports: Cultures, Markets, and Organizations.* Hackensack, N.J.: World Scientific, 2009.

López-Egea, Sandalio Gómez, Kimio Kase, and Ignacio Urrutia. *Value Creation and Sport Management.* New York: Cambridge University Press, 2010.

Mather, Victor. "Two Horse-Racing Syndicates Flourish on Line. *The New York Times,* June 4, 1998. http://www.nytimes.com/1998/06/04/technology/2-horse-racing-syndicates-flourish-on-line.html.

PayScale.com. "Salary Survey for Industry: Spectator Sports." http://www.payscale.com/research/US/Industry=Spectator_Sports/Salary.

_____. "Salary Survey for Industry: Sports Agency." http://www.payscale.com/research/US/Industry=Sports_Agency/Salary/by_Company_Size.

_____. "Salary Survey for Job: Referee, Umpire, or Other Sports Official." http://www.payscale.com/research/US/Job=Umpire%2c_Referee%2c_or_Other_Sports_Official/Salary.

Plunkett, Jack W. *Plunkett's Sports Industry Almanac, 2010.* Houston, Tex.: Plunkett Research, 2009.

Quinn, Kevin G. *Sports and Their Fans: The History, Economics, and Culture of the Relationship Between Spectator and Sport.* Jefferson, N.C.: McFarland, 2009.

Szymanski, Stefan. *The Comparative Economics of Sport.* New York: Palgrave Macmillan, 2010.

U.S. Bureau of Labor Statistics. *Career Guide to Industries,* 2010-2011 ed. http://www.bls.gov/oco/cg.

U.S. Census Bureau. North American Industry Classification System (NAICS), 2007. http://www.census.gov/cgi-bin/sssd/naics/naicsrch?chart=2007.

U.S. Department of Commerce. International Trade Administration. Office of Trade and Industry Information. Industry Trade Data and Analysis. http://ita.doc.gov/td/industry/otea/OTII/OTII-index.html.

Van Riper, Tom. "The Most Valuable Teams in Sports." *Forbes,* January 13, 2009. http://www.forbes.com/2009/01/13/nfl-cowboys-yankees-biz-media-cx_tvr_0113values.html.

Zimbalist, Andrew S. *The Bottom Line: Observations and Arguments on the Sports Business.* Philadelphia: Temple University Press, 2006.

_____. *Circling the Bases: Essays on the Challenges and Prospects of the Sports Industry.* Philadelphia: Temple University Press, 2011.

SPORTS EQUIPMENT INDUSTRY

Carbasho, Tracy. *Nike.* Santa Barbara, Calif.: Greenwood Press, 2010.

Fenn, Dominic. *Sports Clothing and Footwear.* Hampton, Middlesex, England: Key Note, 2009.

Fuss, F. K., A. J. Subic, and S. Ujihashi, eds. *The Impact of Technology on Sport II.* London: Taylor & Francis, 2008.

Lipsey, Richard A. *The Sporting Goods Industry: History, Practices, and Products.* Jefferson, N.C.: McFarland, 2006.

Museo Del Tessuto. *Superhuman Performance: The Evolution of Textiles for Sports/L'evoluzione del tessuto per lo sport.* Prato, Italy: Author, 2008.

Plunkett, Jack W. *Plunkett's Sports Industry Almanac, 2010: The Only Comprehensive Guide to the Sports Industry.* Houston, Tex.: Plunkett Research, 2009.

Ross, Stewart. *Higher, Further, Faster: Is Technology Improving Sport?* Hoboken, N.J.: Wiley, 2008.

Smit, Barbara. *Sneaker Wars: The Enemy Brothers Who Founded Adidas and Puma and the Family Feud That Forever Changed the Business of Sport.* New York: Ecco, 2008.

Sporting Goods Manufacturers Association. *The State of the Industry, 2009: SGMA's Annual Report on the U.S. Sporting Goods Market.* Washington, D.C.: Author, 2009.

"The Sports Industry." *BERA: Business and Economics Research Advisor* 3/4 (Summer, 2005): http://www.loc.gov/rr/business/BERA/issue3/issue3_main.html.

U.S. Bureau of Labor Statistics. *Career Guide to Industries,* 2010-2011 ed. http://www.bls.gov/oco/cg.

_____. "Sporting Goods Sales by Product Category, 1990 to 2003." In *Statistical Abstract of the United States, 2004-2005.* Washington, D.C.: Author, 2004.

U.S. Census Bureau. North American Industry Classification System (NAICS), 2007. http://www.census.gov/cgi-bin/sssd/naics/naicsrch?chart=2007.

U.S. Department of Commerce. Industry Trade Data and Analysis. http://ita.doc.gov/td/industry/otea/OTII/OTII-index.html.

TELECOMMUNICATIONS EQUIPMENT INDUSTRY

Buehler, Kevin S., Lee Scoggins, and Mark D. Shapiro. "Caveat Vendor." *McKinsey Quarterly,* August, 2001.

Business Communications Review. *New World Telecom: A Survival Guide for Global Equipment Suppliers,* September, 2005.

Columbia School of International and Public Affairs. *Career Opportunities in Telecommunications.* http://sipa.columbia.edu/resources_services/career_services/current _students/career _resources/opportunities/ CareerOpp _Telecommunications.pdf.

Courcoubetis, Costas. *Pricing Communication Networks: Economics, Technology. and Modelling.* Hoboken, N.J.: John Wiley & Sons, 2003.

Gruber, Harold. *The Economics of Mobile Telecommunications.* New York: Cambridge University Press, 2008.

Huurdeman, Anton A. *The Worldwide History of Telecommunications.* Hoboken, N.J.: John Wiley & Sons, 2003.

Laffont, Jean Jacques. *Competition in Telecommunications.* Cambridge, Mass.: MIT Press, 2001.

Plunkett, Jack W. *Plunkett's Telecommunications Industry Almanac Statistics, 2010.* Houston, Tex.: Plunkett Research, 2009.

Rosenberg, Robert. *The 2008 Telecommunications Industry Review: An Anthology of Market Facts and Forecasts.* Boonton, N.J.: Insight Research, 2007. http://www.insight-corp.com/ExecSummaries/review08ExecSum.pdf.

U.S. Bureau of Labor Statistics. *Career Guide to Industries,* 2010-2011 ed. http://www.bls.gov/oco/cg.

_____. *A New Approach to Classifying Industries in the Information Sector.* http://www.bls.gov/opub/ils/pdf/opbils75.pdf.

U.S. Census Bureau. North American Industry Classification System (NAICS), 2007. http://www.census.gov/cgi-bin/sssd/naics/naicsrch?chart=2007.

U.S. Department of Commerce. International Trade Administration. Office of Trade and Industry Information. Industry Trade Data and Analysis. http://ita.doc.gov/td/industry/otea/OTII/OTII-index.html.

TELECOMMUNICATIONS INFRASTRUCTURE INDUSTRY

Columbia School of International and Public Affairs. *Career Opportunities in Telecommunications.* http://sipa.columbia.edu/resources_services/career_services/current_students/career_resources/opportunities/CareerOpp_Telecommunications.pdf.

Harte, Lawrence. *Voice over Data Networks for Managers.* Fuquay Varina, N.C.: Althos, 2007.

Huurdeman, Anton A. *The Worldwide History of Telecommunications.* Hoboken, N.J.: John Wiley & Sons, 2003.

International Telecommunications Union. *ICT Statistics Database.* http://www.itu.int/ITU-D/ICTEYE/Indicators/Indicators.aspx.

Lee, Beong Gi. *Broadband Wireless Access and Local Networks: Mobile WiMax and WiFi.* Fitchburg, Mass.: Artech House, 2008.

Plunkett, Jack W. *Plunkett's Telecommunications Industry Almanac Statistics, 2010.* Houston, Tex.: Plunkett Research, 2009. http://www.plunkettresearch.com/Industries/Telecommunications/TelecommunicationsStatistics/tabid/96/Default.aspx.

Simpson, Wes. *Video Over IP: IPTV, Internet Video, H.264, P2P, Web TV, and Streaming.* 2d ed. Burlington, Mass.: Focal Press, 2008.

U.S. Bureau of Labor Statistics. *Career Guide to Industries,* 2010-2011 ed. http://www.bls.gov/oco/cg.

_____. *A New Approach to Classifying Industries in the Information Sector.* http://www.bls.gov/opub/ils/pdf/opbils75.pdf.

U.S. Census Bureau. North American Industry Classification System (NAICS), 2007. http://www.census.gov/cgi-bin/sssd/naics/naicsrch?chart=2007.

U.S. Department of Commerce. International Trade Administration. Office of Trade and Industry Information. Industry Trade Data and Analysis. http://ita.doc.gov/td/industry/otea/OTII/OTII-index.html.

TEXTILE AND FABRICS INDUSTRY

Aggarwal, Vinod K. *Liberal Protectionism: The International Politics of Organized Textile Trade.* Berkeley: University of California Press, 1985.

Blewett, Mary H. *Constant Turmoil: The Politics of Industrial Life in Nineteenth Century New England.* Amherst: University of Massachusetts Press, 2000.

Clairmonte, Frederick, and John Cavanagh. *The World in Their Web: The Dynamics of Textile Multinationals.* London: Zed Press, 1981.

Colchester, Chloe. *Textiles Today: A Global Survey of Trends and Traditions.* New York: Thames and Hudson, 2007.

Copeland, Melvin Thomas. *The Cotton Manufacturing Industry of the United States.* New York: Augustus M. Kelley, 1917.

Delfino, Susanna, and Michele Gillespie, eds. *Global Perspectives on Industrial Transformation in the American South.* Columbia: University of Missouri Press, 2005.

English, Beth. *A Common Thread: Labor, Politics and Capital Mobility in the Textile Industry.* Athens: University of Georgia Press, 2006.

Goldenburg, David. *The U.S. Man-Made Fiber Industry: Its Structure and Organization Since 1948.* Westport, Conn.: Praeger, 1992.

McCormack, Richard. "Good Luck Competing Against Chinese Labor Costs—Mfg. Job Growth in China Is Headed Up, Not Down; 109 Million Mfg. Workers in China Dwarfs Number in U.S." *Manufacturing & Technology News* 13, no. 9 (May 2, 2006). Available at http://www.manufacturingnews.com/news/06/0502/art1.html.

Mortimer, John. *Cotton Spinning: The Story of the Spindle.* Manchester, England: Palmer, Howe, 1895.

Munro, John H. *Textiles, Towns and Trade.* Brookfield, Vt.: Varorium, 1994.

Pack, Howard. *Productivity, Technology and Industrial Development: A Case Study in Textiles.* New York: Oxford University Press, 1987.

Rivard, Paul E. *A New Order of Things: How the Textile Industry Transformed New England.* Hanover, N.H.: University Press of New England, 2002.

Ruhm, Herman D. *Marketing Textiles*. New York: Fairchild, 1970.

Toyne, Brian, et al. *The Global Textile Industry*. London: George Allen and Unwin, 1984.

U.S. Bureau of Labor Statistics. *Career Guide to Industries*, 2010-2011 ed. http://www.bls .gov/oco/cg.

U.S. Census Bureau. North American Industry Classification System (NAICS), 2007. http:// www.census.gov/cgi-bin/sssd/naics/naicsrch ?chart=2007.

Vogel, J. Thomas, and Barbara W. Lowry. *The Textile Industry: An Information Sourcebook*. Phoenix, Ariz.: Oryx Press, 1989.

Yafa, Stephen. *Big Cotton: How a Humble Fiber Created Fortunes, Wrecked Civilzations, and Put America on the Map*. New York: Viking Penguin, 2005.

THEATER AND PERFORMING ARTS INDUSTRY

Alliance for the Arts. *The Recession and the Arts: The Impact of the Economic Downturn on Nonprofit Cultural Groups in New York City*. New York: Author, 2009. Available at http://www.alliance forarts.org/images/EcImpactSurvey_2009 report.pdf.

Carson, Nancy. *Raising a Star: The Parent's Guide to Helping Kids Break into Theater, Film, Television, or Music*. New York: St. Martin's Press, 2005.

Gaquin, Deirdre. *Artists in the Workforce: 1990-2005*. Washington, D.C.: National Endowment for the Arts, 2008.

McCarthy, Kevin, et al. *The Performing Arts in a New Era*. Santa Monica, Calif.: RAND, 2001.

O'Neil, Brian. *Acting as a Business: Strategies for Success*. New York: Vintage Books, 2009.

Stein, Tobie, and Jessica Bathurst. *Performing Arts Management: A Handbook of Professional Practices*. New York: Allworth Press, 2008.

U.S. Bureau of Labor Statistics. *Career Guide to Industries*, 2010-2011 ed. http://www.bls .gov/oco/cg.

U.S. Census Bureau. North American Industry Classification System (NAICS), 2007. http:// www.census.gov/cgi-bin/sssd/naics/naicsrch ?chart=2007.

Vogel, Harold L. *Entertainment Industry Economics: A Guide for Financial Analysis*. New York: Cambridge University Press, 2007.

Webb, Duncan. *Running Theaters: Best Practices for Leaders and Managers*. New York: Allworth Press, 2004.

THEMED ENTERTAINMENT INDUSTRY

Adams, Judith A. *The American Amusement Park Industry: A History of Technology and Thrills*. Boston: Twayne, 1991.

Clavé, Salvador Anton. *The Global Theme Park Industry*. Cambridge, Mass.: CABI, 2007.

Davis, Susan G. *Spectacular Nature: Corporate Culture and the Sea World Experience*. Berkeley: University of California Press, 1997.

Dickey, Robert. *Dynasty of Dimes: Eccentric Entrepreneur Engineers Empire*. St. Augustine, Fla.: St. Margaret, 2009.

Harris, Richard. *Early Amusement Parks of Orange County*. Charleston, S.C.: Arcadia, 2008.

Indeed.com. "Zookeeper Salaries." http://www .indeed.com/salary/Zoo-Keeper.html.

Kurtti, Jeff. *Walt Disney's Imagineering Legends: And the Genesis of the Disney Theme Park*. New York: Disney Editions, 2008.

Marketdata Enterprises. *The U.S. Amusement and Theme Parks Industry: A Marketing, Operational and Competitive Analysis*. Tampa, Fla.: Author, 1999.

Merryman, John Henry, and Albert Edward Elsen. *Law, Ethics, and the Visual Arts*. 4th ed. New York: Kluwer Law International, 2002.

Telotte, J. P. *The Mouse Machine: Disney and Technology*. Urbana: University of Illinois Press, 2008.

U.S. Bureau of Labor Statistics. *Career Guide to Industries*, 2010-2011 ed. http://www.bls.gov/ oco/cg.

U.S. Census Bureau. North American Industry Classification System (NAICS), 2007. http:// www.census.gov/cgi-bin/sssd/naics/naicsrch ?chart=2007.

U.S. Department of Commerce. International Trade Administration. Office of Trade and Industry Information. Industry Trade Data and Analysis. http://ita.doc.gov/td/industry/ otea/OTII/OTII-index.html.

TOYS AND GAMES INDUSTRY

British Library Business and IP Centre. "Toys and Games Industry Guide." June 3, 2009. http://www.bl.uk/reshelp/pdfs/Toy_and_Games_Industry_Guide.pdf.

Cross, Gary. *Kids' Stuff: Toys and the Changing World of American Childhood.* Cambridge, Mass.: Harvard University Press, 1997.

Datamonitor. *Global Toys and Games: Industry Profile.* New York: Author, 2009.

_____. *Toys and Games in the United States: Industry Profile.* New York: Author, 2009.

Giacobello, John. *Choosing a Career in the Toy Industry.* New York: Rosen, 2001.

Miller, Richard K. *The 2009 Retail Business Market Research Handbook.* 11th ed. Loganville, Ga.: Richard K. Miller and Associates, 2009.

Parker, Philip M. *The 2006-2011 World Outlook for Accessories, Clothes, Parts, and Playsets for Dolls, Toy Animals, and Action Figures.* San Diego, Calif.: ICON Group, 2005.

Phillips, Sam. "Toys to Fight Their Corner." *License,* January/February, 2010, 12.

Scott, Sharon. *Toys and American Culture.* Santa Barbara, Calif.: ABC-CLIO, 2010.

Torpey, Elka Maria. "Toy Jobs: Work in the Business of Play." *Occupational Outlook Quarterly,* Winter, 2008-2009. Available at http://www.bls.gov/opub/ooq/2008/winter/art01.pdf.

U.S. Bureau of Labor Statistics. *Career Guide to Industries,* 2010-2011 ed. http://www.bls.gov/oco/cg.

_____. *Occupational Outlook Handbook,* 2010-2011 ed. http://www.bls.gov/oco.

U.S. Census Bureau. North American Industry Classification System (NAICS), 2007. http://www.census.gov/cgi-bin/sssd/naics/naicsrch?chart=2007.

U.S. Department of Commerce. International Trade Administration. Office of Trade and Industry Information. Industry Trade Data and Analysis. http://ita.doc.gov/td/industry/otea/OTII/OTII-index.html.

The Wall Street Journal. "U.S. Tramples Small Toy Makers," September 19, 2009, p. A14.

TRAVEL AND TOURISM INDUSTRY

Beaverstock, Jonathan V., et al. *International Business Travel in the Global Economy.* Burlington, Vt.: Ashgate, 2010.

Chin, Christine B. N. *Cruising in the Global Economy: Profits, Pleasure, and Work at Sea.* Burlington, Vt.: Ashgate, 2008.

Goeldner, Charles R., and J. R. Brent Ritchie. *Tourism: Principles, Practices, Philosophies.* Hoboken, N.J.: John Wiley & Sons, 2008.

Mancini, Marc. *Cruising: A Guide to the Cruise Line Industry.* 2d ed. Florence, Ky.: Cengage Learning, 2003.

Medlik, S. *Dictionary of Travel, Tourism, and Hospitality.* 3d ed. Oxford: Butterworth-Heinemann, 2003.

Mintzer, Rich. *Start Your Own Travel Business.* New York: Entrepreneur Media, 2007.

Smith, Melanie K., and László Puczkó. *Health and Wellness Tourism.* Boston: Elsevier/ Butterworth-Heinemann, 2009.

United Nations World Tourism Organization. http://www.unwto.org/facts.

U.S. Bureau of Labor Statistics. *Career Guide to Industries,* 2010-2011 ed. http://www.bls.gov/oco/cg.

U.S. Census Bureau. North American Industry Classification System (NAICS), 2007. http://www.census.gov/cgi-bin/sssd/naics/naicsrch?chart=2007.

U.S. Department of Commerce. International Trade Administration. Office of Trade and Industry Information. Industry Trade Data and Analysis. http://ita.doc.gov/td/industry/otea/OTII/OTII-index.html.

Vogel, Harold L. *Travel Industry Economics: A Guide for Financial Analysis.* Cambridge, England: Cambridge University Press, 2001.

VETERINARY INDUSTRY

American Veterinary Medical Association. "Market Research Statistics." http://www.avma.org/reference/marketstats/1yremploy.asp.

Aspinall, Victoria. *The Complete Textbook of Veterinary Nursing.* St. Louis, Mo.: Elsevier Health Sciences, 2006.

Dobbs, Katherine. *101 Veterinary Technician Questions Answered.* Lakewood, Colo.: American Animal Hospital Association, 2009.

Fox, Michael W. *Laboratory Animal Husbandry: Ethology, Welfare, and Experimental Variables.* New York: SUNY Press, 1986.

Heinke, Marsha. *Practice Made Perfect: A Guide to Veterinary Practice Management.* Lakewood, Colo.: American Animal Hospital Association, 2009.

Hoover's. "Veterinary Services." http://www .hoovers.com/veterinary-services/—ID__110 —/free-ind-fr-profile-basic.xhtml.

Hunter, Pamela. *Veterinary Medicine: A Guide to Historical Sources.* Surrey, England: Ashgate, 2004.

Koshgarian, Lindsay, et al. *Veterinary Medicine in New England: State-by-State Industry Characteristics and Economic Impacts.* Boston: UMass Donahue Institute, Economics and Public Policy Research Unit, 2008.

Miller, Louise. *Careers for Animal Lovers and Other Zoological Types.* 3d ed. New York: McGraw-Hill, 2007.

Pratt, Paul W. *Medical, Surgical, and Anesthetic Nursing for Veterinary Technicians.* Goleta, Calif.: American Veterinary Publications, 1994.

Rose, Rebecca. *Career Choices for Veterinary Technicians: Opportunities for Animal Lovers.* Lakewood, Colo.: American Animal Hospital Association, 2009.

Shenk, Ellen. *Careers with Animals: Exploring Occupations Involving Dogs, Horses, Cats, Birds, Wildlife, and Exotics.* Mechanicsburg, Pa.: Stackpole Books, 2005.

Shilcock, Maggie, and Georgina Stutchfield. *Veterinary Practice Management: A Practical Guide.* St. Louis, Mo.: Elsevier Health Sciences, 2003.

Swope, Robert E., and Julie Rigby. *Opportunities in Veterinary Medicine Careers.* New York: McGraw-Hill Professional, 2001.

U.S. Bureau of Labor Statistics. *Career Guide to Industries,* 2010-2011 ed. http://www.bls .gov/oco/cg.

U.S. Census Bureau. North American Industry Classification System (NAICS), 2007. http:// www.census.gov/cgi-bin/sssd/naics/naicsrch ?chart=2007.

U.S. Department of Commerce. International Trade Administration. Office of Trade and Industry Information. Industry Trade Data and Analysis. http://ita.doc.gov/td/ industry/otea/OTII/OTII-index.html.

U.S. Department of Labor. *The Big Book of Jobs.* 2009-2010 ed. New York: McGraw-Hill, 2010.

U.S. National Commission on Veterinary Economic Issues. *Study of the Current and Future Market for Veterinarians and Veterinary Medical Services in the United States.* Schaumburg, Ill.: Author, 2000.

Warren, Dean Marvin. *Small Animal Care and Management.* Florence, Ky.: Cengage Learning, 2002.

VIDEO, COMPUTER, AND VIRTUAL REALITY GAMES INDUSTRY

Boyd, S. Gregory, and Brian Green. *Business and Legal Primer for Game Development.* Boston: Charles River Media, 2007.

Chaplin, Heather, and Aaron Ruby. *Smartbomb: The Quest for Art, Entertainment, and Big Bucks in the Videogame Revolution.* Chapel Hill, N.C.: Algonquin Books of Chapel Hill, 2005.

"Computer and Video Game Designers." *Encyclopedia of Careers and Vocational Guidance.* 13th ed. Vol. 2. New York: Ferguson, 2005.

Edery, David, and Ethan Mollick. *Changing the Game: How Video Games Are Transforming the Future of Business.* Upper Saddle River, N.J.: FT Press, 2009.

Ewing, Richard Daniel. "China's Online Video Game Wars." *China Business Review,* July, 2007, 45-49.

Glenn, Lawrence M., and F. Martin Nikirk. "How Career and Technical Education Can Jumpstart a New Industry." *Techniques,* October, 2009, 26-29.

Hodgson, David S. J., Bryan Stratton, and Alice Rush. *Video Game Careers.* Rev. ed. Roseville, Calif.: Prima Games, 2008.

McAllister, Ken. *Game Work: Language, Power, and Computer Game Culture.* Tuscaloosa: University of Alabama Press, 2004.

Novak, Jeannie. *Game Development Essentials: An Introduction*. Clifton Park, N.Y.: Thomson/Delmar Learning, 2005.

Rutter, Jason, and Jo Bryce. *Understanding Digital Games*. Thousand Oaks, Calif.: SAGE, 2006.

Sheffield, Brandon, and Jeffrey Fleming. "Ninth Annual Game Developer Salary Survey." *Game Developer*, April, 2010, 7-13.

Taylor, T. Allan, and James Robert Parrish. *Careers in the Internet, Video Games, and Multimedia*. New York: Ferguson, 2007.

U.S. Bureau of Labor Statistics. *Career Guide to Industries*, 2010-2011 ed. http://www.bls.gov/oco/cg.

_____. "Computer Software Engineers and Computer Programmers." In *Occupational Outlook Handbook*, 2010-2011 ed. http://www.bls.gov/oco/ocos303.htm.

U.S. Census Bureau. North American Industry Classification System (NAICS), 2007. http://www.census.gov/cgi-bin/sssd/naics/naicsrch?chart=2007.

U.S. Department of Commerce. International Trade Administration. Office of Trade and Industry Information. Industry Trade Data and Analysis. http://ita.doc.gov/td/industry/otea/OTII/OTII-index.html.

WAREHOUSING AND STORAGE INDUSTRY

Bourlakis, Paul W., and W. H. Weigtman, eds. *Food Supply Chain Management*. Hoboken, N.J.: John D. Wiley and Sons, 2004.

Center for Chemical Process Safety. *Guidelines for Safe Warehousing of Chemicals*. Hoboken, N.J.: John D. Wiley and Sons, 2008.

Martin, James William. *Lean Six Sigma for Supply Chain Management: The Ten-Step Solution Process*. New York: McGraw-Hill, 2006.

Morris, Peter, and Jeffrey K. Pinto, eds. *The Wiley Guide to Project Technology Management, Supply Chain, and Procurement*. Hoboken, N.J.: John D. Wiley and Sons, 2007.

Ryan, Mary Meghan, ed. *Handbook of U.S. Labor Statistics: Employment, Earnings, Prices, Productivity, and Other Labor Data*. 13th ed. Lanham, Md.: Bernam Press, 2010.

Toigo, Jon William. *The Holy Grail of Data Storage Management*. New York: Prentice Hall, 1999.

U.S. Bureau of Labor Statistics. *Career Guide to Industries*, 2010-2011 ed. http://www.bls.gov/oco/cg.

_____. *Occupational Outlook Handbook*, 2010-2011 ed. http://www.bls.gov/oco.

U.S. Census Bureau. North American Industry Classification System (NAICS), 2007. http://www.census.gov/cgi-bin/sssd/naics/naicsrch?chart=2007.

U.S. Department of Commerce. International Trade Administration. Office of Trade and Industry Information. Industry Trade Data and Analysis. http://ita.doc.gov/td/industry/otea/OTII/OTII-index.html.

WASTE MANAGEMENT INDUSTRY

BCC Research. "Global Markets for Hazardous Waste Remediation Technologies." MarketResearch.com, April 1, 2006. http://www.marketresearch.com/product/display.asp?productid=1300222&SID=31904368-463897374-440422766&partnerid=811788012&kw =global%09waste%09revenues.

Dijkgraaf, E., and R. H. J. M. Gradus. *The Waste Market: Institutional Developments in Europe*. Dordrecht: Springer, 2008.

Hoover's. "Industry Overview: Waste Management." http://www.hoovers.com/waste-management/—ID__99—/free-ind-fr-profile-basic.xhtml.

Institute for Career Research. *Careers in the Waste Management Industry*. Chicago: Author, 2007.

Key Note Publications. *Recycling and Waste Management*. Hampton, Middlesex, England: Author, 2009.

Miller, Debra A. *Garbage and Recycling*. Detroit: Lucent Books, 2010.

Renner, Michael, et al. *Green Jobs: Working for People and the Environment*. Washington, D.C.: Worldwatch Institute, 2008.

Stuart, Tristram. *Waste: Uncovering the Global Food Scandal*. New York: W. W. Norton, 2009.

U.S. Bureau of Labor Statistics. *Career Guide to Industries*, 2010-2011 ed. http://www.bls.gov/oco/cg.

U.S. Census Bureau. North American Industry Classification System (NAICS), 2007. http://www.census.gov/cgi-bin/sssd/naics/naicsrch?chart=2007.

U.S. Department of Commerce. International Trade Administration. Office of Trade and Industry Information. Industry Trade Data and Analysis. http://ita.doc.gov/td/industry/otea/OTII/OTII-index.html.

U.S. Government Accountability Office. "Nuclear Waste: DOE's Environmental Management Initiatives Report Is Incomplete." June 2, 2009. http://www.gao.gov/new.items/d09697r.pdf.

WATCHES AND JEWELRY INDUSTRY

Barnes Reports. *U.S. Jewelry and Silverware Manufacturing Industry Report.* Woolwich, Maine: Author, 2010.

Blakemore, Kenneth. *Management for the Retail Jeweler: A Companion Volume to the Retail Jeweler's Guide.* London: Iliffe Books, 1973.

Cipriani, Curzio, and Alessandro Borelli. *Simon and Schuster's Guide to Gems and Precious Stones.* New York: Simon and Schuster, 1986.

Glasmeier, Amy. *Manufacturing Time: Global Competition in the Watch Industry, 1795-2000.* New York: Guilford Press, 2000.

Griffiths, Jane. *Jewelry, Watches, and Fashion Accessories: 2000 Market Report.* Hampton, England: Key Note, 2000.

Harrold, Michael C. *American Watchmaking: A Technical History of the American Watch Industry, 1850-1930.* n.p.: Author, 1981.

IBISWorld. *U.S. Industry Report: Jewelry Stores, 2010.* http://www.ibisworld.com/industry/default.aspx?indid=1075.

Institute for Career Research. *Careers in the Jewelry Industry: Design, Manufacturing, Retailing.* Chicago: Institute for Career Research, 2003.

Jewelers of America. *Careers in the Jewelry Industry: Your Guide to a Bright and Shining Future.* New York: Jewelers of America, 200[?].

Morton Research Corporation. *The Jewelry Industry: An Economic, Marketing, and Business Manual of the U.S. Precious Metal Jewelry Industry.* Boca Raton, Fla.: Morton Research Company, 1997.

O'Donoghue, Michael. *Synthetic, Imitation, and Treated Gemstones.* London: Robert Hale, 2008.

Parker, Philip M. *The 2007-2012 Outlook for Jewelry Stores in the United States.* San Diego, Calif.: ICON Group, 2006.

Unity Marketing Group. *Jewelry and Watch Report, 2007.* http://www.unitymarketingonline.com/cms_jewelry/jewelry/jewelry_2007.php.

U.S. Bureau of Labor Statistics. *Career Guide to Industries,* 2010-2011 ed. http://www.bls.gov/oco/cg.

_____. "Jewelers and Precious Stone and Metal Workers" In *Occupational Outlook Handbook,* 2010-2011 ed. http://www.bls.gov/oco/ocos222.htm.

U.S. Census Bureau. North American Industry Classification System (NAICS), 2007. http://www.census.gov/cgi-bin/sssd/naics/naicsrch?chart=2007.

_____. *2002 Economic Census: Manufacturing Industry Series. Watch, Clock and Parts Manufacturing.* U.S. Department of Commerce, Economics and Statistics Administration, 2004.

U.S. Department of Commerce. International Trade Administration. Office of Trade and Industry Information. Industry Trade Data and Analysis. http://ita.doc.gov/td/industry/otea/OTII/OTII-index.html.

_____. *The U.S. Jewelry Industry: Federal Interagency Report on U.S. Jewelry Competitiveness Issues.* Washington, D.C.: Author, 1997.

U.S. International Trade Commission. *A Competitive Assessment of the U.S. Jewelry Industry, Phase I: Costume Jewelry: Report to the Commission.* Washington, D.C.: Author, 1986.

U.S. Small Business Administration. *Starting and Managing a Small Retail Jewelry Store.* Washington, D.C.: Author, 1971.

WATER SUPPLY INDUSTRY

Brooks, Kenneth N., et al. *Hydrology and the Management of Watersheds.* 3d ed. Ames: Iowa State Press, 2003.

Career Information Center. *Agribusiness, Environment, and Natural Resources.* 9th ed. Vol. 1. Detroit: Thomas/Gale, 2007.

Cech, Thomas V. *Principles of Water Resources: History, Development, Management, and Policy.* 3d ed. Hoboken, N.J.: John Wiley, 2010.

Chin, David A. *Water-Resources Engineering.* 2d ed. Upper Saddle River, N.J.: Pearson Prentice Hall, 2006.

Dzurik, Andrew A. *Water Resources Planning.* 3d ed. Lanham, Md.: Rowman and Littlefield, 2003.

Fair, Gordon M., John C. Geyer, and Daniel A. Okun. *Water Supply and Wastewater Removal.* Vol. 1 in *Water and Wastewater Engineering.* New York: John Wiley, 1966.

Gleick, Peter H., et al. *The World's Water, 2008-2009: The Biennial Report on Freshwater Resources.* Washington, D.C.: Island Press, 2009.

Gray, N.F. *Drinking Water Quality: Problems and Solutions.* 2d ed. New York: Cambridge University Press, 2008.

Grigg, Neil S. "Water and Wastewater Workforce Stats: The Case for Improving Job Data." *Journal of the American Water Works Association* 101, no. 8 (August, 2009): 67-78.

Hammer, Mark J., and Mark J. Hammer, Jr. *Water and Wastewater Technology.* 5th ed. Upper Saddle River, N.J.: Pearson Prentice Hall, 2004.

IBISWorld. *Water Supply and Irrigation Systems in the U.S.: Industry Report 22131.* May 4, 2010. http://www.ibisworld.com/industry/outlook.aspx?indid=161.

Linsley, Ray K., and Joseph B. Franzini. *Water-Resources Engineering.* New York: McGraw-Hill, 1972.

Patrick, Roger, and Edward G. Means III. "Meeting Customer Expectations in a Fluid Utility Environment." *Journal of the American Water Works Association* 97, no. 9 (September, 2005): 56-61.

Pojasek, Robert B., ed. *Drinking Water Quality Enhancement Through Source Protection.* Ann Arbor, Mich.: Ann Arbor Science, 1977.

Speidel, David H., Lon C. Ruedisili, and Allen F. Agnew, eds. *Perspectives on Water: Uses and Abuses.* New York: Oxford University Press, 1988.

Spellman, Frank R. *The Science of Water: Concepts and Applications.* 2d ed. Boca Raton, Fla.: CRC Press, 2008.

Symons, James M. *Plain Talk: Questions and Answers About the Water You Drink.* 4th ed. Denver: American Water Works Association, 2001.

U.S. Bureau of Labor Statistics. *Career Guide to Industries,* 2010-2011 ed. http://www.bls.gov/oco/cg.

_____. "Water and Liquid Waste Treatment Plant and System Operators." In *Occupational Outlook Handbook,* 2010-2011 ed. http://www.bls.gov/oco/ocos229.htm.

U.S. Census Bureau. North American Industry Classification System (NAICS), 2007. http://www.census.gov/cgi-bin/sssd/naics/naicsrch?chart=2007.

U.S. Department of Commerce. International Trade Administration. Office of Trade and Industry Information. Industry Trade Data and Analysis. http://ita.doc.gov/td/industry/otea/OTII/OTII-index.html.

U.S. Environmental Protection Agency. Office of Water. *Community Water System Survey, 2000.* Washington, D.C.: Author, 2002.

Wurbs, Ralph A., and James P. Wesley. *Water Resources Engineering.* Upper Saddle River, N.J.: Prentice Hall, 2002.

Electronic Resources

The following electronic resources—both general and targeted by industry—will assist both students and career seekers in learning about various industries and their potential for jobs and careers.

GENERAL RESOURCES

Web Sites

Career Overview. Careers and Occupations Guide: Complete List of Career Choices.
http://www.careeroverview.com/careers.html
Career Overview is designed to help students, job seekers, and career changers obtain information about employment. The site's Careers and Occupations Guide lists eighteen types of industry, such as education, engineering, law enforcement, sales, and transportation. After selecting a category, users can retrieve a list of specific occupations, and they can then access job descriptions and information about training, qualifications, employment opportunities, and salaries for these jobs.

Deloitte Development LLC. Industries.
http://www.deloitte.com/view/en_US/us/
    Industries/index.htm
Deloitte, an international accountancy and business consulting firm, provides information about selected industries on its Web site. The site's Industries page contains a list of about twenty industries, including aerospace and defense, automotive, oil and gas, state and federal government, and retail. The individual pages for each of these industries provides access to articles and analyses of current issues in these fields.

Global Edge. Industry Profiles.
http://globaledge.msu.edu/industries
The Global Edge site was created by the International Business Center at Michigan State University to provide information about global business activities. The Industries page enables users to access information about twenty industries, including discussions of an industry's composition, history, leading companies, trends, and future outlook. There are also trade and sales statistics and links to additional Web-based resources for each industry.

Hoover's, Inc. Hoovers.com.
hoovers.com
Hoover's, Inc., a veteran business publisher, provides some information about industries on its free Web site, although it offers more extensive data on its subscription database, First Research. The free site allows users to obtain brief overviews of many industries, with descriptions of these industries and data about top companies.

JobBank USA. Career Profile, Career Profiles, Career Statistics.
http://www.jobbankusa.com/career-profiles
JobBank USA, an online recruiting site, contains data about several industries, including business, education, social services, engineering, and health care, on its career profiles and statistics page. Users can retrieve general information about these industries, as well as statistics about specific occupations within them. For example, the business career page contains a list of job titles with statistics about the number of workers, expected growth, median salaries, and number of employees with college degrees for each job. Users can then click on the job titles to obtain additional information about specific jobs.

U.S. Census Bureau. 2007 Economic Census.
www.census.gov/econ/census07
The Economic Census is conducted every five years and provides a detailed portrait of the American economy. The 2007 census contains data about selected industries, including mining, utilities, construction, manufacturing, finance and insurance, and health care.

U.S. Census Bureau. North American Industry Classification System, 2007.
http://www.census.gov/cgi-bin/sssd/naics/
    naicsrch?chart=2007
The North American Industry Classification System (NAICS) is, according to its Web site, "the stan-

dard used by Federal statistical agencies in classifying business establishments for the purpose of collecting, analyzing, and publishing statistical data related to the U.S. business economy." The official NAICS Manual for 2007, which is also available in print and on CD-ROM, provides definitions for each industry, background information about industries, and tables outlining changes in each industry between 2002 and 2007.

U.S. Department of Commerce. International Trade Administration. Manufacturing and Services.

http://trade.gov/mas/index.asp

The Manufacturing and Services unit of the International Trade Administration aims to increase the global competitiveness of American industry. Its Web site provides statistical data about specific manufacturing and service industries, including aerospace, health, financial services, and travel and tourism.

U.S. Department of Commerce. International Trade Administration. Office of Industry Analysis.

http://www.trade.gov/mas/ian/index.asp

This section of the Department of Commerce Web site offers analysis and information about issues affecting U.S. industry, including the national employment outlook, an overview of U.S. trade, trade statistics, and analyses of the effects of international trade on the economies of each of the fifty states.

U.S. Department of Labor. Bureau of Labor Statistics. Career Guide to Industries, 2010-2011 ed.

http://www.bls.gov/oco/cg

The 2010-2011 edition of Career Guide to Industries (CGI) provides a wealth of information about American industries, including specific occupations within an industry, training and advancement, salaries, expected job prospects, and working conditions. This information can be accessed in several ways: Users can enter a term in a search box located on every page; they can browse through a list of industries featured on the home page; or they can use CGI's index, accessible from the home page, to retrieve an alphabetical listing of industries.

U.S. Department of Labor. Bureau of Labor Statistics. Occupational Outlook Handbook. 2010-2011 ed.

http://www.bls.gov/oco

Occupational Outlook Handbook offers information about hundreds of jobs, describing the required training and education, earnings, expected job prospects, what workers do on the job, and working conditions. Users can retrieve information in three ways: They can enter a term in a search box located on every page; they can browse through a list of occupations featured on the home page; or they can use the handbook's index, accessible from the home page, to retrieve an alphabetical listing of job titles. This Web site also provides information in Spanish about one hundred occupations.

U.S. Department of Labor. Bureau of Labor Statistics. Occupational Outlook Quarterly Online (OOQ Online).

http://www.bls.gov/opub/ooq

OOQ Online is an online version of the print periodical *Occupational Outlook Quarterly* and, according to the site, provides "practical information on jobs and careers," including "career- and work-related topics such as unusual occupations, tips for job seekers, salary trends, and results of new studies from the Bureau of Labor Statistics." The online version enables users to read a "nutshell" description or "snippet" from each article, as well as obtain a full-text version available in portable document format (PDF), which can be printed for easier reading. The Web site also features indexes of articles from previous issues.

U.S. Department of Labor. Employment and Training Administration. CareerOneStop.

http://www.careeronestop.org

CareerOneStop is designed for job seekers, career professionals, students, and other people who wish to learn more about occupations and industries. The "Explore Careers" page provides access to "Industries," where users can retrieve profiles about significant industries in specific metropolitan areas and counties of the fifty states. The "Industries" section also contains data about the fastest-growing and highest-paying industries and industries with both increasing and declining employment; users can also learn about employment trends in the metropolitan areas and counties of the fifty states.

U.S. Department of Labor. Employment and Training Administration. O*Net Online.

http://www.onetonline.org

The home page of O*Net Online explains that the site is a "tool for career exploration and job analysis" providing "detailed descriptions of the world of work." The site is divided into three sections: "Find Occupations" enables users to browse groups of similar occupations to obtain information about careers. "Advanced Search" retrieves information about occupations that require specified skills or the use of specific tools, machinery, and software. "Crosswalks" allows users to enter job titles or classification codes to obtain information.

Subscription Databases

The following Web-based databases are available only to paying subscribers. Public, college, and university libraries subscribe to these sources. Readers can consult library Web sites or ask reference librarians about availability.

EBSCO Publishing. Business Source Complete.

http://www.ebscohost.com/academic/business-source-complete

Business Source Complete features articles from more than thirteen hundred business-related journals, as well as financial data, major reference works, conference proceedings, case studies, investment research reports, industry reports, market research reports, country reports, and company profiles.

EBSCO Publishing. Career Guidance System.

http://www.ebscohost.com/government/career-guidance-system

Career Guidance System is designed to provide students with information about colleges and careers. Users can access information about twenty-five hundred occupations, apprenticeships, and military jobs, including job descriptions, salary data, employment prospects, and related college majors. Students also can assess their skills and interests to identify occupations in which they might be interested.

Gale Cengage Learning. Business and Company Resource Center.

http://www.gale.cengage.com/BusinessRC

The Business and Company Resource Center contains information about companies and industries, with separate search engines for each of these categories. Users can enter the name of an industry or a classification code to obtain market research reports about broad industry categories or specific industry sectors. The site also enables users to retrieve magazine and journal articles about business and industry.

Gale/Info Trac. Vocations and Careers Collection.

http://www.gale.cengage.com/pdf/facts/GML36309_VocCareCollection.pdf

This database contains content from almost four hundred journals, which include general career guides as well as specialized industry journals.

Hoover's, Inc. First Research

http://www.firstresearch.com

First Research is a division of Hoover's, Inc., a long-standing publisher of business-related information. The database offers profiles of more than nine hundred industry segments that contain analysis, statistics and forecasts and are updated every quarter.

Infogroup, Inc. Reference USA.

http://www.referenceusa.com

Reference USA contains a database of fourteen million U.S. businesses. Information can be accessed via the business's name; the first or last name of an executive; and the city, state, or telephone number of a business. There is specific information about each business's location; profiles of the business itself and the industry in which it operates; and demographic data about sales volume, number of employees, and credit rating. Additional information includes a management directory, company news reports, stock data for publicly traded firms, and lists of competing companies.

Standard and Poor's. NetAdvantage.

http:www.netadvantage.standardandpoors.com

Created by Standard and Poor's investors' service, NetAdvantage enables subscribers to access the company's industry surveys, as well as its research, data, and commentary on stocks, bonds, and mutual funds.

ACCOUNTING SERVICES

Academy of Accounting Historians, Weatherhead School of Management
https://www.netforumondemand.com/eweb/
StartPage.aspx?Site=AAH

American Accounting Association
http://www.aaahq.org

American Institute of Certified Public Accountants
http://www.aicpa.org

Association of Certified Fraud Examiners
http://www.acfe.com

Association of Government Accountants
http://www.agacgfm.org

Gleim Publications
http://www.gleim.com

Institute of Internal Auditors
http://www.theiia.org

Institute of Management Accountants
http://www.imanet.org

National Library of the Accounting Profession, University of Mississippi
http://www.olemiss.edu/depts/general_library/
aicpa

ADVERTISING AND MARKETING INDUSTRY

American Advertising Federation
http://www.aaf.org

American Association of Advertising Agencies
http://www2.aaaa.org

Asian American Advertising Federation
http://www.3af.org

Association of Hispanic Advertising Agencies
http://www.ahaa.org

International Advertising Association
http://www.iaaglobal.org

World Advertising Research Center
http://www.warc.com

AIRLINE INDUSTRY

Air Transport Association of America
http://www.airlines.org

Association of European Airlines
http://www.aea.be

European Regions Airline Association
http://www.eraa.org

International Air Transport Association
http://www.iata.org

Regional Airline Association
http://www.raa.org

ALTERNATIVE POWER INDUSTRY

American Solar Energy Society
http://www.ases.org

American Wind Energy Association
http://awea.org

Energy Information Administration
http://www.eia.doe.gov

National Biodiesel Board
http://www.biodiesel.org

National Renewable Energy Laboratory
http://www.nrel.gov

ANIMAL CARE SERVICES

American Kennel Club
http://www.akc.org

American Pet Products Association
http://www.americanpetproducts.org

American Society for the Prevention of Cruelty to Animals
http://www.aspca.org

Association of Pet Dog Trainers
http://www.apdt.com

Cat Fanciers' Association
http://www.cfainc.org

Certification Council for Professional Dog Trainers
http://www.ccpdt.org

National Dog Groomers Association of America
http://www.nationaldoggroomers.com

APPAREL AND FASHION INDUSTRY

American Apparel and Footwear Association
http://www.apparelandfootwear.org

American Apparel Producers' Network
http://www.aapnetwork.net

Fashion Group International
http://www.fgi.org

International Association of Clothing Designers and Executives
http://www.iacde.com

Professional Fashion Photography Organization
http://pfpo.net

AUTOMOBILES AND PERSONAL VEHICLES INDUSTRY

Alliance of Automobile Manufacturers
http://www.autoalliance.org

Automotive Service Association
http://www.asashop.org

Center for Automobile Research
http://www.cargroup.org

National Automobile Dealers Association
http://www.nada.org

National Bicycle Dealers Association
http://nbda.com

National Marine Manufacturers Association
http://www.nmma.org

National Motorcycle Dealers Association
http://www.nationalmda.com

BANKING INDUSTRY

American Bankers Association
http://www.aba.com

Credit Union National Association
http://www.cuna.org

Independent Community Bankers of America
http://www.icba.org

Mortgage Bankers Association
http://www.mortgagebankers.org

National Bankers Association
http://nationalbankers.org

BATTERIES AND FUEL CELLS INDUSTRY

American Chemical Society
http://www.acs.org

American Institute of Chemical Engineers
http://www.aice.org

Battery Council International
http://www.batterycouncil.org

Electrochemical Society
http://www.electrochem.org

National Hydrogen Association
http://www.hydrogenassociation.org

U.S. Fuel Cell Council
http://www.usfcc.com

BEVERAGE AND TOBACCO INDUSTRY

Alcohol and Tobacco Tax and Trade Bureau
http://www.ttb.gov

American Beverage Association
http://www.ameribev.org

International Council of Beverages Associations
http://www.icba-net.org

International Tobacco Growers Association
http://www.tobaccoleaf.org

National Alcohol Beverage Control Association
http://www.nabca.org

Tobacco Merchants Association
http://www.tma.org

BIOFUELS INDUSTRY

American Coalition for Ethanol
http://www.ethanol.org

Biomass Power Association
http://usabiomass.org

Biotechnology Industry Organization
http://www.bio.org

International Energy Agency
http://www.iea.org

National Biodiesel Board
http://www.biodiesel.org

Renewable Fuels Association
http://www.ethanolrfa.org

U.S. Department of Energy
http://www.energy.gov

BROADCAST INDUSTRY

Association of International Broadcasting
http://www.aib.org.uk

British Broadcasting Company
http://www.bbc.co.uk

International Association of Broadcasting Manufacturers
http://www.thiabm.org

National Association of Broadcasters
http://www.nab.org

North American Broadcasters Association
http://www.nabanet.com

BUILDING ARCHITECTURE INDUSTRY

American Institute of Architects
http://www.aia.org

American Institute of Architecture Students
http://www.aias.org

National Architectural Accrediting Board
http://www.naab.org

National Council of Architectural Registration Boards
http://www.ncarb.org

BUILDING CONSTRUCTION INDUSTRY

American Institute of Constructors and the Constructor Certification Commission
http://www.aicnet.org

Associated Builders and Contractors
http://www.abc.org

Associated General Contractors of America
http://www.agc.org

Building and Construction Trades Department, AFL-CIO
http//www.buildingtrades.org

BUSINESS SERVICES

Association of Executive and Administrative Professionals
http://www.theaeap.com

Association of Executive Search Consultants
http://www.aesc.org

Association of Management Consulting Firms
http://www.amcf.org

International Association of Outsourcing Professionals
http://www.outsourcingprofessional.org

Travel Industry Association
http://www.tia.org

CASINO INDUSTRY

American Gaming Association
http://www.americangaming.org

Casino Careers
http://www.casinocareers.com

National Indian Gaming Association
http://www.indiangaming.org

Navegante Group
http://www.navegantegroup.com

CHEMICALS INDUSTRY

American Chemical Society
http://www.acs.org

American Chemistry Council
http://www.americanchemistry.com

American Institute of Chemical Engineers
http://www.aiche.org

Chemical and Engineering News
http://pubs.acs.org/cen

CIVIL SERVICES: PLANNING

American Planning Association
http://www.planning.org

Community Development Society
http://wwwcomm-dev.org

National Association of Development Organizations
http://www.nado.org

National Association of Local Government Environmental Professionals
http://nalgep.org

Urban Land Institute
http://www.uli.org

CIVIL SERVICES: PUBLIC SAFETY

Administrative Office of the United States Courts
http://www.uscourts.gov

Government Accountability Office
http://www.gao.gov

Office of Personnel Management
http://www.opm.gov

U.S. Department of Homeland Security
http://www.dhs.gov

U.S. Department of Justice
http://www.justice.gov

COAL MINING INDUSTRY

Energy Information Administration
http://www.eia.doe.gov

Mine Safety and Health Association
http://www.nsga.gov

National Mining Association
http://www.nma.org

Society for Mining, Metallurgy, and Exploration
http://www.smenet.org

United Mine Workers of America
http://www.umwa.org

World Coal Association
http://www.worldcoal.org

COMPLEMENTARY AND ALTERNATIVE HEALTH CARE INDUSTRY

American Holistic Medicine Association
http://www.holisticmedicine.org

Global Institute for Alternative Medicine
http://www.gifam.org

National Association for Integrative Health Care Practitioners
http://aihcp-norfolkva.org

National Center for Complementary and Alternative Medicine, National Institutes of Health
http://nccam.nih.gov

COMPUTER HARDWARE AND PERIPHERALS INDUSTRY

Association for Computing Machinery
http://www.acm.org

CompTIA
http://www.comptia.org

Computer Society
http://www.computer.org

Information Technology Association of America
http://www.itaa.org

Institute for Certification of Computing Professionals
http://www.iccp.org

Society for Information Management
http://www.simnet.org

Society for Technical Communication
http://www.stc.org

USENIX, the Advanced Computing Systems Association
http://www.usenix.org

COMPUTER SOFTWARE INDUSTRY

Computer Society
http://www.computer.org

Institute for Certification of Computing Professionals
http://www.iccp.org

National Workforce Center for Emerging Technologies
http://www.nwcet.org

Software and Information Industry Association
http://www.siia.net

COMPUTER SYSTEMS INDUSTRY

Association for Computing Machinery
http://www.acm.org

Computer Society
http://www.computer.org

National Center for Women and Information Technology, University of Colorado
http://www.ncwit.org

National Workforce Center for Emerging Technologies
http://www.nwcet.org

University of Washington Computer Science and Engineering Department
http://www.cs.washington.edu/WhyCSE

CONSTRUCTION EQUIPMENT INDUSTRY

Caterpillar
http://www.cat.com

Deere & Company
http://www.deere.com

Equipment World
http://www.equipmentworld.com

Freedonia
http://www.freedoniagroup.com

Institute for Supply Management
http://www.ism.ws

Komatsu
http://www.komatsu.com

MarketResearch.com
http://www.marketresearch.com

Mitsubishi Heavy Industries
http://www.mhi.co.jp/en

Technik Manufacturing
http://www.technikmfg.com

CORPORATE EDUCATION SERVICES

American Society of Training and Development
http://www.astd.org

Conference Board
http://www.conference-board.org

Human Capital Institute
http://www.humancapitalinstitute.org

International Society for Performance Improvement
http://www.ispi.org

Society for Human Resource Management
http://www.shrm.org

World at Work
http://www.worldatwork.org

COUNSELING SERVICES

American College of Medical Practice Management
http://www.epracticemanagement.org

American Counseling Association
http://www.counseling.org

Healthcare Financial Management Association
http://www.hfma.org

Medical Group Management Association
http://www.mgma.com

CRIMINAL JUSTICE AND PRISON INDUSTRY

American Correctional Association
http://www.aca.org

American Jail Association
http://www.corrections.com/aja

Federal Bureau of Prisons
http://www.bop.gov

U.S. Bureau of Justice Statistics
http://bjs.ojp.usdoj.gov

U.S. Department of Justice
http://www.justice.gov

DAY-CARE SERVICES

Center for the Study of Child Care Employment, Institute for Research on Labor and Employment
http://www.irle.berkeley.edu/cscce/index.html

National Adult Day Services Association
http://www.nadsa.org

National Association for the Education of Young Children
http://www.naeyc.org

National Association of Child Care Resource and Referral Agencies
http://www.naccrra.org

National Child Care Association
http://www.nccanet.org

National Resource Center for Health and Safety in Child Care and Early Education, University of Colorado Health and Sciences Center at Fitzsimons
http://nrckids.org

DEFENSE INDUSTRY

AeroSpace and Defence Industries Association of Europe
http://www.asd-europe.org

Aerospace Industries Association
http://www.aia-aerospace.org

American Institute of Aeronautics and Astronautics
http://www.aiaa.org

BAE Systems
http://www.baesystems.com

Defence Manufacturers Association
http://www.the-dma.org.uk

Lockheed Martin
http://www.lockheedmartin.com

National Defense Industry Association
http://www.ndia.org

DENTAL AND ORTHODONTICS INDUSTRY

Academy of General Dentistry
http://www.agd.org

American Association of Orthodontists
http://www.braces.org

American Dental Association
http://www.ada.org
http://jada.ada.org

American Dental Hygienists' Association
http://www.adha.org

National Institute of Dental and Craniofacial Research
http://www.nidcr.nih.gov

ELECTRICAL AND GAS APPLIANCES INDUSTRY

Air-Conditioning, Heating and Refrigeration Institute
http://www.ahrinet.org

Appliance Design
http://www.appliancedesign.com

Appliance Magazine
http://www.appliancemagazine.com

Appliance Service News
http://www.asnews.com

Association of Home Appliance Manufacturers
http://www.aham.org

Broom, Brush, and Mop
http://www.rankinpublishing.com

Energy Star, U.S. Environmental Protection Agency
http://www.energystar.gov

Kitchenware News & Housewares Review
http://www.kitchenwarenews.com

National Electrical Manufacturers Association
http://www.nema.org

ELECTRICAL POWER INDUSTRY

American Public Power Association
http://www.publicpower.org

International Brotherhood of Electrical Workers
http://www.ibew.org

Nuclear Energy Institute
http://www.nei.org

Power and Energy Society
http://www.ieee.org

U.S. Energy Information Administration
http://www.eia.gov

Utility Workers Union of America
http://uwua.net

ENVIRONMENTAL ENGINEERING AND CONSULTATION SERVICES

Air and Waste Management Association
http://www.awma.org

American Academy of Environmental Engineers
http://www.aaee.net

Entec UK
http://www.entecuk.com

Keystone Environmental
http://www.keystoneenviro.com

Water Environment Federation
http://www.wef.org

FARMING INDUSTRY

National Plant Data Center
http://npdc.usda.gov

National Soil Survey Center
http://soils.usda.gov

North Dakota State University Extension Service
http://www.ag.ndsu.edu/extension

U.S. Department of Agriculture
http://www.usda.gov

FEDERAL PUBLIC ADMINISTRATION

Office of Citizen Services and Communications
http://www.usa.gov

Office of Personnel Management
http://www.opm.gov

U.S. Department of Homeland Security
http://www.dhs.gov

U.S. Equal Opportunity Employment Commission
http://www.eeoc.gov

FINANCIAL SERVICES INDUSTRY

AdvisorOne
http://www.advisorone.com

Advisor's Edge
http://www.advisor.ca

Association for Financial Professionals
http://www.afponline.org

Bond Market Association
http://www.bondmarkets.com

Broker World Magazine
http://www.brokerworldmag.com

Industry Trade Data and Analysis
http://ita.doc.gov

New York Stock Exchange
http://www.nyse.com

On Wall Street
http://www.onwallstreet.com

FISHING AND FISHERIES INDUSTRY

American Fisheries Society
http://www.fisheries.org

Food and Agriculture Organization of the United Nations
http://www.fao.org

Food Institute Online
http://www.foodinstitute.com

Intergovernmental Oceanographic Commission
http://ioc-unesco.org

National Marine Fisheries Service
http://www.nmfs.noaa.gov/fishwatch

Northwest Atlantic Fisheries Organization
http://www.nafo.int

WorldFish Center
http://www.worldfishcenter.org

FOOD MANUFACTURING AND WHOLESALING INDUSTRY

Food Engineering Magazine
http://www.foodengineeringmag.com

Food Marketing Institute
http://www.fmi.org

Grocery Manufacturers Association
http://www.gmabrands.com

Institute of Food Technologists
http://www.ift.org

National Frozen and Refrigerated Foods Association
http://www.nfraweb.org

FOOD RETAIL INDUSTRY

American Wholesale Marketers Association
http://www.awmanet.org

Careers in Food
http://www.careersinfood.com

Food Industry Suppliers Association
http://www.fisanet.org

Food Marketing Institute
http://www.fmi.org

Grocery Manufacturers Association
http://www.gmaonline.org

Mexican-American Grocers Association
http://www.buscapique.com/latinusa/buscafile/oeste/maga.htm

National Association of Convenience Stores
http://www.nacsonline.com

National Grocers Association
http://www.nationalgrocers.org/

United Food and Commercial Workers International Union
http://www.ufcw.org

FOOD SERVICES

Association for Healthcare Foodservice
http://www.healthcarefoodservice.org

Catersource
http://www.catersource.com

International Foodservice Distributors Association
http://www.ifdaonline.org

National Association of College and University Food Services
http://www.nacufs.org

Society for Foodservice Management
http://www.sfm-online.org

FREIGHT TRANSPORT INDUSTRY

American Trucking Associations
http://www.truckline.com

American Waterways Operators
http://www.americanwaterways.org

Association of American Railroads
http://www.aar.org

International Freight Association
http://www.ifa-online.com

National Motor Freight Traffic Association
http://www.nmfta.org

U.S. Department of Transportation
http://www.dot.gov

U.S. Merchant Marine Academy
http://www.usmma.edu

FUNERARY INDUSTRY

Family Funeral Home Association
http://www.familyfuneral.org

National Funeral Directors and Morticians Association
http://www.nfdma.com

New York State Funeral Directors Association
http://www.nysfda.org

Selected Independent Funeral Homes
http://www.selectedfuneralhomes.org

Service Corporation International
http://www.sci-corp.com

FURNITURE AND HOME FURNISHINGS INDUSTRY

Furniture Today **Magazine**
http://www.furnituretoday.com

National Home Furnishings Association
http://www.nhfa.org

Upholstered Furniture Council
http://www.ufac.org

HAND TOOLS AND INSTRUMENTS INDUSTRY

Antique Tools and Trades in Connecticut
http://www.attic-us.org

Hand Tools Institute
http://www.hti.org

Missouri Valley Wrench Club
http://www.mvwc.org

Potomac Antique Tools and Industries Association
http://www.patinatools.org

Tools of the Trade **Magazine**
http://www.toolsofthetrade.net

HEALTH AND FITNESS INDUSTRY

American College of Sports Medicine
http://www.acsm.org

American Council on Exercise
http://www.acefitness.org

International Health, Racquet, and Sportsclub Association
http://cms.ihrsa.org

National Strength and Conditioning Association
http://www.nsca-lift.org

HEAVY MACHINES INDUSTRY

Caterpillar
http://www.cat.com

Deere & Company
http://www.deere.com

Equipment World
http://www.equipmentworld.com

Institute for Supply Management
http://www.ism.ws

Komatsu
http://www.komatsu.com

MarketResearch.com
http://www.marketresearch.com

Mitsubishi Heavy Industries
http://www.mhi.co.jp/en

Technik Manufacturing
http://www.technikmfg.com

HIGHER EDUCATION INDUSTRY

American Association of Collegiate Registrars and Admissions Officers
http://www.aacrao.org

American Association of University Professors
http://www.aaup.org

APPA: Leadership in Educational Facilities
http://www.appa.org

College Board
http://www.collegeboard.com

National Association of Student Personnel Administrators
http://www.naspa.org

HIGHWAY, ROAD, AND BRIDGE CONSTRUCTION INDUSTRY

American Association of State Highway and Transportation Officials
http://www.transportation.org

American Road and Transportation Builders Association
http://www.artba.org

Associated General Contractors of America
http://www.agc.org

Association Mondiale de la Route/World Road Association
http://www.piarc.org/en

Engineering News-Record
http://enr.construction.com

Reed Construction Data
http://www.reedconstructiondata.com

World Highways
http://www.worldhighways.com

HOME MAINTENANCE SERVICES

Association of Residential Cleaning Services International
http://www.arcsi.org

Building Services Contractors Association International
http://www.bscai.org

Cleaning Management Institute
http://www.cminstitute.net

Professional Landcare Network (PLANET)
http://www.landcarenetwork.org

HOSPITAL CARE AND SERVICES

American College of Healthcare Executives
http://www.ache.org

American College of Medical Practice Management
http://www.epracticemanagement.org

American Counseling Association
http://www.counseling.org

American Hospital Association
http://www.aha.org

Healthcare Financial Management Association
http://www.hfma.org

Medical Group Management Association
http://www.mgma.com

National Association of Public Hospitals and Health Systems
http://www.naph.org

HOTELS AND MOTELS INDUSTRY

American Hotel and Lodging Association
http://www.ahla.com

American Resort Development Association
http://www.arda.org

Hospitality Net BV
http://www.hospitalitynet.org

Hospitality Sales and Marketing Association
http://www.hsmai.org

International Hotel and Restaurant Association
http://www.ih-ra.com

HOUSEHOLD AND PERSONAL PRODUCTS INDUSTRY

American Cleaning Institute
http://www.cleaninginstitute.org

Cosmetic News, **Communications International Group**
http://www.cosmeticnews.com

CosmeticsDesign.com, Decision News Media
http://www.cosmeticsdesign.com

Happi
http://www.happi.com

INDUSTRIAL DESIGN INDUSTRY

American Institute of Graphic Arts
http://www.aiga.org

The Design Society
http://www.designsociety.org

Industrial Designers Society of America
http://www.idsa.org

International Council of Societies for Industrial Design
http://www.icsid.org

INSURANCE INDUSTRY

American Council of Life Insurance
http://www.acli.com

American Insurance Association
http://www.aiadc.org

American Risk and Insurance Association
http://www.aria.org

Independent Insurance Agents and Brokers of America
http://www.iiaba.net

Insurance Information Institute
http://www.iii.org

National Association of Insurance and Financial Advisors
http://www.naifa.org

National Association of Insurance Commissioners
http://www.naic.org

National Association of Professional Insurance Agents
http://www.pianet.com

Society of Actuaries
http://www.soa.org

INTERNET AND CYBER COMMUNICATIONS INDUSTRY

Association for Computing Machinery
http://www.acm.org

Institute of Electrical and Electronics Engineers
http://www.ieee.org

Internet Corporation for Assigned Names and Numbers
http://www.icann.org

Internet Engineering Task Force
http://www.ietf.org

Internet Society
http://www.isoc.org

Software and Information Industry Association
http://www.siia.net

LANDSCAPING SERVICES

American Nursery and Landscape Association
http://www.anla.org

American Society of Landscape Architects
http://www.asla.org

Lawn and Landscape Magazine, GIE Media
http://www.baumpub.com

Professional Landcare Network (PLANET)
http://www.lawnandlandscape.com

Tree Care Industry Association
http://www.treecareindustry.org

LEGAL SERVICES AND LAW FIRMS

American Association for Justice
http://www.justice.org

American Bar Association
http://www.abanet.org

American Civil Liberties Union
http://www.aclu.org

Amnesty International USA
http://www.amnestyusa.org

Legal Aid Society
http://www.legal-aid.org

National Association for Law Placement
http://www.nalp.org

National Association of Criminal Defense Lawyers
http://www.criminaljustice.org

National Legal Aid and Defender Organization
http://www.nlada.org

LIBRARIES AND ARCHIVES INDUSTRY

American Archivist
http://www.archivists.org

American Association of School Librarians
http://www.ala.org/aasl

American Library Association
http://www.ala.org

Library Journal
http://www.libraryjournal.com

Society of American Archivists
http://www.archivists.org

LIGHT MACHINERY INDUSTRY

Deere & Company
http://www.deere.com

Equipment World
http://www.equipmentworld.com

Institute for Supply Management
http://www.ism.ws

Komatsu
http://www.komatsu.com

Makita USA
http://www.makita.com

Robert Bosch LLC
http://www.boschtools.com

Techtronic Industries North America
http://www.ttigroupna.com

LIVESTOCK AND ANIMAL PRODUCTS INDUSTRY

Food and Agriculture Organization of the United Nations
http://www.fao.org

National Institute for Animal Agriculture
http://www.animalagriculture.org

U.S. Department of Agriculture, Economic Research Service
http://www.ers.usda.gov

LOCAL PUBLIC ADMINISTRATION

American Society for Public Administration
http://www.aspanet.org

Association for Public Policy Analysis and Management
http://www.appam.org

California State Personnel Board
http://www.spb.ca.gov

City of Houston
http://www.houstontx.gov

National Association of Schools of Public Affairs and Administration
http://www.naspaa.org

National Conference of State Legislatures
http://www.ncsl.org

LOGGING INDUSTRY

American Forest and Paper Association
http://www.afandpa.org

European Biomass Industry Association
http://www.eubia.org

Forest Industry Network
http://www.forestindustry.com.

International Tropical Industry Association
http://www.itto.int

Truck Loggers Association
http://www.tla.ca

MASS TRANSPORTATION VEHICLES INDUSTRY

American Boat Builders and Repairers Association
http://www.abbra.org

American Bus Association
http://www.buses.org

American Public Transportation Association
http://www.apta.com

American Society for Engineering Education
http://www.asee.org

American Society of Mechanical Engineers
http://www.asme.org

Federal Transit Administration, U.S. Department of Transportation
http://www.fta.dot.gov

Institute of Electrical and Electronics Engineers
http://www.ieee.org

Institute of Industrial Engineers
http://www.iie2net.org

National Bus Rapid Transit Institute, Center for Urban Transportation Research
http://www.nbrti.org
http://www.rsiweb.org

National Council of Examiners for Engineering and Surveying
http://www.ncees.org

National Society of Professional Engineers
http://www.nspe.org

SAE International
http://www.sae.org

Society of Naval Architects and Marine Engineers
http://www.sname.org

Transportation Research Board, the National Academies
http://www.trb.org

MEDICINE AND HEALTH CARE INDUSTRY

American Medical Association
http://www.ama-assn.org

American Nurses Association
http://www.nursingworld.org

American Society for Clinical Laboratory Science
http://www.ascls.org

Center for Health Care Strategies
http://www.chcs.org

Centers for Medicare and Medicaid Services
http://www.cms.hhs.gov

National Association for Home Care and Hospice
http://www.nahc.org

METALS MANUFACTURING INDUSTRY

American Chemical Society
http://www.acs.org

American Institute for International Steel
http://www.aiis.org

American Institute of Chemical Engineers
http://www.aice.org

Minerals, Metals, and Materials Society
http://www.tms.org

MINING INDUSTRY

American Institute of Mining, Metallurgical, and Petroleum Engineers
http://www.aimehq.org

National Mining Association
http://www.nma.org

National Stone, Sand, and Gravel Association
http://www.nssga.org

MOTION PICTURE AND TELEVISION INDUSTRY

Academy of Motion Picture Arts and Sciences
http://www.oscars.org

Academy of Television Arts and Sciences
http://www.emmys.org

British Film Institute
http://www.bfi.org.uk

Canadian Film and Television Production Association
http://www.cftpa.ca

Centre International de Liaison des Ecoles de Cinema et de Television
http://www.cilect.org

Motion Picture Association of America
http://www.mpaa.org

Screen Actors Guild
http://www.sag.org

MUSEUMS AND CULTURAL INSTITUTIONS INDUSTRY

American Association for State and Local History
http://www.aaslh.org

American Association of Museums
http://www.aam-us.org

Association for Living History, Farms, and Agricultural Museums
http://www.alhfam.org

Association of Children's Museums
http://www.childrensmuseums.org

Association of College and University Museums and Galleries
http://www.acumg.org

Association of Zoos and Aquariums
http://www.aza.org

International Council of Museums
http://icom.museum/

Museum Studies and Reference Library
http://www.sil.si.edu

Society of American Archivists
http://www.archivists.org

MUSIC INDUSTRY

American Society of Composers, Authors, and Publishers
http://www.ascap.com

American Symphony Orchestra League
http://www.symphony.org

Billboard
http://www.billboard-online.com

International Federation of the Phonographic Industry
http://www.ifpi.org

Music Week
http://www.musicweek.com

Pollstar
http://www.pollstar.com

Recording Industry Association of America
http://www.riaa.com

NATIONAL AND INTERNATIONAL SECURITY INDUSTRY

ASIS International
http://www.asisonline.org

Lawrence Livermore National Laboratory
http://www.llnl.gov

North Atlantic Treaty Organization
http://www.nato.int

U.S. Department of Homeland Security
http://www.dhs.gov

NATURAL RESOURCES MANAGEMENT

Environmental Careers Center
http://environmentalcareer.com
http://www.ecojobs.com

Environmental Careers Organization
http://www.eco.org

National Association of Environmental Professionals
http://www.naep.org

NUCLEAR POWER INDUSTRY

American Nuclear Society
http://www.ans.org

Health Physics Society
http://www.hps.org

Nuclear Energy Institute
http://www.nei.org

U.S. Nuclear Regulatory Commission
http://www.nrc.gov

OUTDOOR RECREATION INDUSTRY

American Alliance for Health, Physical Education, Recreation, and Dance
http://www.aahperd.org

American Camp Association
http://www.ACAcamps.org

American Recreation Coalition
http://www.funoutdoors.com

National Park Service
http://www.nps.gov

National Parks and Conservation Association
http://www.npca.org

National Recreation and Park Association
http://www.nrpa.org

Outdoor Amusement Business Association
http://www.oaba.org

Outdoor Foundation
http://www.outdoorfoundation.org

PAPER MANUFACTURING AND PRODUCTS INDUSTRY

American Forest and Paper Association
http://www.afandpa.org

Center for Paper Business and Industry Studies
http://www.cpbis.gatech.edu

Paper Industry Technical Association
http://pita.co.uk

TAPPI (Technical Association of the Pulp and Paper Industry)
http://www.tappi.org

PASSENGER TRANSPORTATION AND TRANSIT INDUSTRY

American Public Transportation Association
http://www.apta.com

Federal Transit Administration, U.S. Department of Transportation
http://www.fta.dot.gov

Institute of Transportation Studies, University of California, Berkeley
http://its.berkeley.edu

International Association of Public Transport
http://www.uitp.org

Taxicab, Limousine, and Paratransit Association
http://www.tlpa.org

Transportation Research Board, the National Academies
http://www.trb.org

PERSONAL SERVICES

American Association of Family and Consumer Sciences
http://www.aafcs.org

National Association for Family Child Care
http://www.nafcc.org

National Association for the Education of Young Children
http://www.naeyc.org

National Association of Child Care Resource and Referral Agencies
http://www.naccrra.net

National Child Care Association
http://www.nccanet.org

National Child Care Information Center
http://www.nccic.org

National Extension Association of Family and Consumer Sciences
http://www.neafcs.org

PETROLEUM AND NATURAL GAS INDUSTRY

American Petroleum Institute
http://www.api.org

ExxonMobil
http://www.exxonmobil.com

Saudi Aramco
http://www.saudiaramco.com

Shell
http://www.shell.us

PHARMACEUTICALS AND MEDICATIONS INDUSTRY

Biotechnology Industry Organization
http://www.bio.org

Drug Information Association
http://www.diahome.org

International Federation of Pharmaceutical Manufacturers and Associations
http://www.ifpma.org

International Society for Pharmaceutical Engineering
http://www.ispe.org

Pharmaceutical Research and Manufacturers Association of America
http://www.phrma.org

PHILANTHROPIC, CHARITABLE, RELIGIOUS, CIVIC, AND GRANT-MAKING INDUSTRY

Alliance for Nonprofit Management
http://www.allianceonline.org

Association for Research on Nonprofit Organization and Voluntary Action
http://www.arnova.org

Council on Foundations
http://www.cof.org

Foundations Center
http://foundationcenter.org

National Council of Churches
http://www.nccsusa.org

PLASTICS AND RUBBER MANUFACTURING INDUSTRY

American Chemical Society
http://www.acs.org

American Institute of Chemical Engineers
http://www.aice.org

International Institute of Synthetic Rubber Producers
http://www.azom.com

Plastics Industry Trade Association
http://www.plasticsindustry.org

Society of Plastics Engineers
http://www.4spe.org

POLITICAL ADVOCACY INDUSTRY

American League of Lobbyists
http://www.alldc.org

Association of Accredited Lobbyists to the European Parliament
http://www.eulobby.net

Cassidy and Associates
http://www.cassidy.com

Center for Public Integrity
http://www.publicintegrity.org

Library of Congress
http://thomas.loc.gov

Public Affairs Council
http://www.pac.org

POSTAL AND PACKAGE DELIVERY SERVICES

Association of International Courier and Express Services
http://www.aices.org

Express Delivery and Logistics Association
http://www.expressassociation.org

Global Postal Strategy
http://www.postinsight.com

Universal Postal Union
http://www.upu.int

PRINTING INDUSTRY

Graphic Arts Education and Research Foundation
http://www.gaerf.org

National Association for Printing Leadership
http://www.napl.org

National Association of Printing Ink Manufacturers
http://www.napim.org

Printing Industries of America
http://www.printing.org

Seybold Report, Beard Group
http://www.seyboldreport.com

PRIVATE EDUCATION INDUSTRY

Association of Private Enterprise Education
http://www.apee.org

Center for Teaching Excellence, University of Medicine & Dentistry of New Jersey, School of Health Related Professions
http://cte.umdnj.edu

College Board
http://www.collegeboard.com

National Education Association
http://www.nea.org

National Independent Private Schools Association
http://www.nipsa.org

U.S. Department of Education
http://www.ed.gov

PUBLIC ELEMENTARY AND SECONDARY EDUCATION INDUSTRY

American Federation of Teachers
http://www.aft.org

Center for Public Education
http://www.centerforpubliceducation.org

National Center for Education Statistics
http://nces.ed.gov

National Education Association
http://www.nea.org

Public Education Network
http://www.publiceducation.org

U.S. Department of Education, Office of Elementary and Secondary Education
http://www2.ed.gov/oese

PUBLIC HEALTH SERVICES

American Diabetes Association
http://www.diabetes.org

American Public Health Association
http://www.apha.org

Centers for Disease Control and Prevention
http://www.cdc.gov

Harvard School of Public Health
http://www.hsph.harvard.edu

U.S. Department of Health and Human Services
http://www.hhs.gov

World Health Organization
http://www.who.int

PUBLISHING AND INFORMATION INDUSTRY

American Society of Newspaper Editors
http://www.asne.org

Association of American Publishers
http://www.publishers.org

International Publishers Association
http://www.internationalpublishers.org

Magazine Publishers of America
http://www.magazine.org

Newspaper Association of America
http://www.naa.org

Small Publishers Association of North America
http://www.spannet.org

REAL ESTATE INDUSTRY

Appraisal Institute
http://www.appraisalinstitute.org

CCIM Institute
http://www.ccim.com

Council of Residential Specialists
http://www.crs.com

Institute of Real Estate Management
http://www.irem.org

National Association of Realtors
http://www.realtor.org

U.S. Department of Housing and Urban Development
http://portal.hud.gov

RENTAL AND LEASING SERVICES

American Rental Association
http://www.ARArental.org

Association of Progressive Rental Organizations
http://www.rtohq.org

Canadian Rental Association
http://www.CRArental.org

Equipment Leasing and Finance Association
http://www.elfaonline.org

Truck Rental and Leasing Association
http://www.trala.org

RESIDENTIAL MEDICAL CARE INDUSTRY

AARP
http://www.aarp.org

American College of Healthcare Executives
http://www.ache.org

American Hospital Association
http://www.aha.org

Healthcare Financial Management Association
http://www.hfma.org

Medical Group Management Association
http://www.mgma.com

RESTAURANT INDUSTRY

American Culinary Federation
http://www.acfchefs.org

American Institute of Wine and Food
http://www.aiwf.org

International Association of Culinary Professionals
http://www.iacp.com

International Hotel and Restaurant Association
http://www.ih-ra.com

National Restaurant Association
http://www.restaurant.org

Technomic
http://www.technomic.com

RETAIL TRADE AND SERVICE INDUSTRY

Global Entertainment Retail Association-Europe
http://www.gera-europe.org

International Council of Shopping Centers
http://www.icsc.org

National Grocers Association
http://www.nationalgrocers.org

National Retail Federation
http://www.nrf.com

Retail Industry Leaders Association
http://www.rila.org/pages/default.aspx

SCIENTIFIC AND TECHNICAL SERVICES

American Institute of Chemical Engineers
http://www.aiche.org

American Society of Mechanical Engineers
http://www.asme.org

Biotechnology Industry Organization
http://www.bio.org

National Institutes of Health
http://www.nih.gov

National Science Foundation
http://www.nsf.gov

National Society of Professional Engineers
http://www.nspe.org

SCIENTIFIC, MEDICAL, AND HEALTH EQUIPMENT AND SUPPLIES INDUSTRY

Advanced Medical Technology Association
http://advamed.org

Association for the Advancement of Medical Instrumentation
http://www.aami.org

Eucomed—Medical Technologies Industry in Europe
http://eucomed.be

MEDEC (Medical Devices Canada)
http://medec.org

Medical Equipment Suppliers Association
http://www.mesanet.org

Medical Technology and Practice Patterns Institute
http://www.mtppi.org

SHIPBUILDING, SUBMARINES, AND NAVAL TRANSPORT INDUSTRY

American Association of Port Authorities Headquarters
http://www.aapa-ports.org

American Shipbuilding Association
http://www.americanshipbuilding.com

American Society of Naval Engineers
http://www.navalengineers.org

International Brotherhood of Boilermakers, Iron Shipbuilders, Blacksmiths, Forgers, and Helpers
http://www.boilermakers.org

International Maritime Organization
http://www.imo.org

International Trade Administration, U.S. Department of Commerce
http://www.ita.doc.gov

Maritime Administration, U.S. Department of Transportation
http://www.marad.dot.gov

Naval Vessel Register
http://www.nvr.navy.mil/class.htm

Public Affairs Office, Military Sealift Command
http://www.msc.navy.mil

Shipbuilders Council of America
http://www.shipbuilders.org

Society of Naval Architects and Marine Engineers
http://www.sname.org

U.S. Coast Guard National Maritime Center
http://www.uscg.mil/nmc

SPACE EXPLORATION AND SPACE SCIENCE INDUSTRY

Aerospace Industries Association
http://www.aia-aerospace.org

American Institute of Aeronautics and Astronautics
http://www.aiaa.org

Eighth Continent Project
http://www.8cproject.com

European Space Agency
http://www.esa.int

Institute of Electrical and Electronics Engineers
http://www.ieee.org

National Aeronautics and Space Administration
http://www.nasa.gov

Office of Space Commercialization, National Oceanic and Atmospheric Administration
http://www.space.commerce.gov

Satellite Industry Association
http://www.sia.org

Space Studies Board, the National Academies
http://sites.nationalacademies.org/SSB/
    index.htm

Space.com, Space Library
http://www.space.com/spacelibrary/

United Nations Office for Outer Space Affairs
http://www.oosa.unvienna.org

SPECTATOR SPORTS INDUSTRY

Amateur Athletic Union
http://www.aausports.org

International Olympic Committee
http://www.olympic.org

National Athletic Trainer's Association
http://www.nata.org

North American Society for Sport Management
http://www.nassm.com

Sports Turf Managers Association
http://www.stma.org

U.S. Olympic Committee
http://www.olympic-usa.org

SPORTS EQUIPMENT INDUSTRY

American Society for Testing and Materials
http://www.astm.org

National Operating Committee on Standards for Athletic Equipment
http://www.nocsae.org

National Sporting Goods Association
http://www.nsga.org

Sporting Goods Manufacturers Association
http://www.sgma.com

World Federation of Sporting Goods Industry/Maison du Sport International
http://www.wfsgi.org

TELECOMMUNICATIONS EQUIPMENT INDUSTRY

Broadband for America
http://www.broadbandforamerica.com

CTIA-The Wireless Association
http://files.ctia.org

Institute of Electrical and Electronics Engineers
http://www.ieee.org

International Telecommunication Union
http://www.itu.int

Journal of Telecommunications and Information Technology, **National Institute of Telecommunications**
http://www.nit.eu

Microwave Journal
http://www.mwjournal.com

Telecommunications Industry Association
http://www.tiaonline.org

TELECOMMUNICATIONS INFRASTRUCTURE INDUSTRY

Broadband for America
http://www.broadbandforamerica.com

CTIA-The Wireless Association
http://www.ctia.org

Institute of Electrical and Electronics Engineers
http://www.ieee.org

International Communication Association
http://www.icahdq.org

International Telecommunication Union
http://www.itu.int

Journal of Telecommunications and Information Technology, **National Institute of Telecommunications**
http://www.nit.eu

Microwave Journal
http://www.mwjournal.com

Telecommunications Industry Association
http://www.tiaonline.org

TEXTILE AND FABRICS INDUSTRY

American Association of Textile Chemists and Colorists
http://www.aatcc.org

Handweavers Guild of America
http://www.weavespindye.org

Industrial Fabrics Association International
http://www.ifai.com

International Textile Manufacturers Federation
http://www.itmf.org/cms

Textile Institute International
http://www.texi.org

THEATER AND PERFORMING ARTS INDUSTRY

Actors' Equity Association
http://www.actorsequity.org

American Federation of Musicians
http://www.afm.org

Americans for the Arts
http://www.artsusa.org

National Dances Education Association
http://www.ndeo.org

National Endowment for the Arts
http://www.nea.gov

THEMED ENTERTAINMENT INDUSTRY

American Association of Museums
http://www.aam-us.org

American Gaming Association
http://www.americangaming.org

International Association of Amusement Parks and Attractions
http://www.iaapa.org

International Hotel and Restaurant Association
http://www.ih-ra.com

Smithsonian Institution
http://www.si.edu

Themed Entertainment Association
http://Info@themeit.com

World Association of Zoos and Aquariums
http://www.waza.org

TOYS AND GAMES INDUSTRY

American Specialty Toy Retailing Association
http://www.astratoy.org

International Council of Toy Industries
http://www.toy-icti.org

Playthings **Magazine**
http://www.playthings.com

Toy Industry Association
http://www.toyassociation.org

TRAVEL AND TOURISM INDUSTRY

American Society of Travel Agents
http://www.asta.net.org

National Association of Cruise Oriented
   Agencies
http://www.nacoa.com

VETERINARY INDUSTRY

American Animal Hospital Association
http://www.aahanet.org

**American Association for Laboratory Animal
   Science**
http://www.aalas.org

**American Society for the Prevention of Cruelty
   to Animals**
http://www.aspca.org

American Veterinary Medical Association
http://www.avma.org

Animal Behavior Society
http://www.abs.org

**Association of American Veterinary Medical
   Colleges**
http://www.aavmc.org

Humane Society of the United States
http://www.hsus.org

International Veterinary Information Service
http://www.ivis.org

**National Association of Veterinary Technicians in
   America**
http://www.navta.net

United States Animal Health Association
http://www.usaha.org

VIDEO, COMPUTER, AND VIRTUAL REALITY GAMES INDUSTRY

Entertainment Software Association
http://www.theesa.com

International Game Developers Association
http://www.igda.org

Major League Gaming
http://www.mlgpro.com

Software and Information Industry Association
http://www.siia.net

WAREHOUSING AND STORAGE INDUSTRY

Dangerous Goods Advisory Council
http://www.dgac.org

**International Association of Refrigerated
   Warehouses**
http://www.iarw.org

Material Handling Industry of America
http://www.mhia.org

Modern Materials Handling
http://www.mmh.com

Supply Chain Management Review
http://www.scmr.com

Warehousing Education and Research Council
http://www.werc.org

WASTE MANAGEMENT INDUSTRY

Air and Waste Management Association
http://www.awma.org

American Council on Renewable Energy
http://www.acore.org

Association of Compost Producers
http://www.healthysoil.org

Energy Recovery Council
http://www.energyrecoverycouncil.org

International Solid Waste Association
http://www.iswa.org

National Recycling Coalition
http://www.nrc-recycle.org

National Solid Waste Management Association
http://www.environmentalistseveryday.org

Solid Waste Association of North America
http://www.swana.org

WATCHES AND JEWELRY INDUSTRY

Accredited Gemologists Association
http://www.accreditedgemologists.org

Accrediting Commission of Career Schools and Colleges
http://www.accsc.org

American Gem Society
http://www.americangemsociety.org

American Jewelry Design Council
http://www.ajdc.org

American Watch Association
http://www.americanwatchassociation.com

American Watchmakers-Clockmakers Institute
http://www.awci.com

Gemological Institute of America
http://www.gia.edu

Jewelers of America
http://www.jewelers.org

Jewelers' Security Alliance
http://www.jewelerssecurity.org

Jewelers Vigilance Committee
http://www.jvclegal.org

Jewelry Career Fair
http://www.careerfair.gia.org

Manufacturing Jewelers and Suppliers of America
http://www.mjsa.polygon.net

WATER SUPPLY INDUSTRY

American Water Resources Association
http://www.awra.org

American Water Works Association
http://www.awwa.org

National Association of Water Companies
http://www.nawc.org

Water Environment Federation
http://www.wef.org

Water Quality Association
http://www.wqa.org

Indexes

Industries by Career Cluster

The industries that appear in Survey of American Industry and Careers *have been categorized by the following sixteen career clusters to make it easier to understand which industries provide opportunities to pursue specific career paths. For those interested in a particular job or occupation, the next section of this index lists selected occupations. Some positions, such as chief executive officer, administrative assistant, and payroll manager, can be found in nearly every industry, so mentions of these positions were indexed only when they were discussed at length or played a significant role in a particular industry.*

Jobs and Careers

This index lists selected jobs and careers that are available in the industries in Survey of American Industry and Careers. *Some positions, such as chief executive officer, administrative assistant, and payroll manager, can be found in nearly every industry, so mentions of these positions were indexed only when they were discussed at length or played a significant role in a particular industry.*

Subject Index